Grace Aguilar

The Jewish Faith

Its Spiritual Consolation, Moral Guidance, and Immortal Hope...

Grace Aguilar

The Jewish Faith
Its Spiritual Consolation, Moral Guidance, and Immortal Hope...

ISBN/EAN: 9783744700504

Printed in Europe, USA, Canada, Australia, Japan

Cover: Foto ©Lupo / pixelio.de

More available books at **www.hansebooks.com**

THE
JEWISH FAITH:

ITS

SPIRITUAL CONSOLATION, MORAL GUIDANCE, AND IMMORTAL HOPE.

WITH

A BRIEF NOTICE OF THE REASONS FOR MANY OF ITS
ORDINANCES AND PROHIBITIONS.

A Series of Letters

ANSWERING THE INQUIRIES OF YOUTH.

BY

GRACE AGUILAR,

AUTHOR OF "THE WOMEN OF ISRAEL," "SPIRIT OF JUDAISM," ETC.

THE AMERICAN HEBREW PUBLISHING AND PRINTING HOUSE,
THE BLOCH PUBLISHING AND PRINTING COMPANY,
CINCINNATI.

PREFACE.

It is now about twenty-two years ago, when the editor had the gratification of presenting to the public the first work of any magnitude—"The Spirit of Judaism"—written by the gifted daughter of Israel, Grace Aguilar, who, since then, in the few years which elapsed before her untimely decease, obtained a high rank, excelled by few, among the female writers of Great Britain. The present publication may be regarded as her dying confession of faith; as she was summoned to her reward within a few months after its first appearance, which, having taken place in England, no doubt caused it to be less familiar to American Israelites than all her other works which were issued or reprinted here. Repeated demand for it having been made lately, without the possibility of gratifying it, induced the editor to issue this permanent edition (it being stereotyped), as much to serve as a literary monument to his departed friend, as to render it accessible to his fellow-Israelites, who, he trusts, may be both benefited and instructed by its perusal. In sending it out to the world on its renewed mission, the editor has made no changes except verbal ones, to remove some inaccuracies almost inseparable in printing from manuscript, especially, as in the case of the author, when bodily infirmity prevents a careful revision as the work passes through the press. No material alteration, however, has been made, even to gratify the editor's dissenting views; as this would not have been dealing fairly with the literary legacy of his friend, which he wished to preserve, not to disfigure by any additions or changes of his own.

It is needless to remark—for this has been done in the "Spirit," which will accompany this—that the editor had often occasion to regard his religion from a different point of view from Miss Aguilar: their education and social relations varied so greatly, that it would have been strange indeed if their minds had not received varying impressions; but, this fact once known, there was no need to call attention to it again and again; for every one can readily distinguish between what is derived from approved authority and what is advanced as the author's private opinion.

It is, however, deemed requisite to remark, that the editor by no means approves of the forced construction of Isaiah's predictions of the future Jerusalem, and applying them to personal immortality. To his view, there is nothing gained for the truth by piling needless proof on proof; especially since the undoubted references to the life of the soul are so clear throughout the Bible, that, as our author truly says, it would be without meaning, if the doctrine teaching eternal life had been unknown to the Israelites from the days of the Patriarchs. Still, there was every excuse for Miss A. to pursue this line of argument, in her endeavour to remove all misgivings from the minds of doubting Israelites, represented by her *fictitious* correspondent, in order to silence all objections derived from the absence of a direct revelation of the immortality of the soul in so many words, and to refute the assertion that life eternal was first preached by an offshoot of the Jewish religion.

It would, indeed, be a matter of sincere congratulation, if the present enterprise of issuing religious works for the people would meet that encouragement as to induce those who have the talent to follow in the footsteps of our sainted sister. But, whether this be so or not, the editor has discharged a simple duty to send forth a new edition of the least known, though the best, works of Miss Aguilar, and which she valued more than her tales and novels, so that they may be made instrumental in cementing in the minds of many believing Israelites an undying love for their Father in heaven, who selected in times of old their fathers to be His people for all times.   I. L.

PHILADELPHIA, { Nissan 6, 5624.
              { April 12, 1864.

THE JEWISH FAITH.

INTRODUCTION.

CHILDHOOD is the age of belief—youth, of inquiry. The former is satisfied to receive, and believe in the information imparted. It is very seldom (except in the case of the childhood of genius), that infant minds will either examine or doubt the lessons of parents and teachers, but will imbibe them almost unconsciously, and act upon them instinctively, satisfied, that to obey is the happiest course of acting, and that they cannot do wrong, if they imitate those about them. Even in badly regulated children, rebellion and defiance and disobedience proceed, not from an idea of superior intelligence and greater power, but simply from the supremacy, for the time being, of those strong passions and evil inclinations inherent in man's nature. We do not mean to assert that childhood has neither character nor sensibilities of its own, that heart and mind are both stagnant, and therefore that its training is of little consequence. Far from it. We believe most thoroughly, that childhood is the germ of after-being, and that much, *very* much, depends upon the guiding and cherishing of that germ, towards the full and beautiful development of the perfect flower. But the impressions, though last-

ing, are imbibed unconsciously. That which causes the
parent, especially the mother, so many wakeful nights
and anxious days, her child receives indeed, and rewards
in after-years; but at the time, it can give no answer,
either to herself or others, if questioned as to why it
thus acts and feels, except, "Because mamma tells me,
and she does it, or says it; and therefore it must be
right." If it do not say this in words, it still feels so;
and wisely and mercifully is it thus ordained. The
little human being, heir from the first moment he draws
breath, as ourselves, to the rich possession of being a
child of God, and destined for immortality, is, in the
period of childhood, too frail and weak a thing, for more
than the quick susceptibility to joy and sorrow, the
thoughtless fault and eager impulse, the lasting love and
momentary wrath, the necessity for and burden of ac-
quirements, peculiarly, and so touchingly its own. The
perplexing doubt, the desire to examine and to reason,
is entirely distinct from the ready observation, and aptitude to question natural to some children. They want
to know all they can, but do not stop to doubt and question the answers they receive. They go on from year
to year acquiring, some more, some less, according to
natural ability; but it is not till childhood has merged
into youth, that the bright light of conscious intellect
flashes up, and the mind, awakened to a knowledge
of itself, gazes with a curious eye on the seeds there
planted, and in the first plenitude of power desires to
examine, and to analyse, and reason, and so believes
unquestioningly no more.·

The period of this remarkable change varies from
fourteen to eighteen years, and often extends to five-
and-twenty, ere the mind once more finds rest on itself,
and can again calmly and thankfully believe. It is this

which so often occasions youth to be denominated forward and self-sufficient, and so conceited, as to imagine it knows more, and judges better, than the experience of years. But this is a mistaken judgment, and much of the heart-burning sometimes endured by parents and old and affectionate relatives, from the incomprehensible change and presumption of their youthful charge, might be averted, if they would only regard it as the restless consciousness of a new state of existence, and no longer treat as children those, who are feeling with quivering intensity in every nerve of mind and frame, that childhood must be passed; for they have entered a new, strange, and at first, even to themselves, incomprehensible state of being.

If we would but recall our own youthful experiences, this change would appear so natural, that we should be prepared to soothe and endeavor to satisfy, instead of regarding it as wilful presumption, which ought to be checked and reproved. It seems, indeed, at first disappointing, that all our own example and instructions during childhood have been of so little avail, that they are now subject to doubt and question; but, if instead of being disheartened, we calmly meet and discuss these doubts, invite, and reply to, instead of eluding enquiries, we shall find our early lessons, instead of being lost, sink at once, and for ever in the heart and mind, and influence the future, not from tacit acquiescence, but from firm unalterable conviction of their truth.

Nothing is more wounding to the vividly susceptible emotions of youth, and nothing more injurious to our own hope of influence, than the constantly repeated reproof, how they can be so presumptuous as to think and allege, what they can know nothing about; for such observations tend to lower self-esteem, and so really create its spurious likeness—self-conceit, and raise an insuperable barrier between our experience, and those whom we think it ought to guide.

Nothing will give us so much influence as that ready sympathy, which raises self-esteem, and so permits youth to feel, that its inward convictions *are* correct, and that it has attained another and higher state of being. We must, indeed, still guide;—but it can no longer be, as in the case of childhood, by *command.* We must meet reason with reason, permit the awakening mind to disclose itself fearlessly, and give its young fresh thoughts, and often original, it may be at first startling, hypotheses, encouragement and love. We must know, if we only look back on every half century, that human nature is always advancing, each generation is more forward, more mentally perfected than the last; and therefore, mortifying as to some it may be, we often actually *learn* from those, whom it is still our duty to teach and guide. If this have been the case, and fearlessly we grant it, and give the sweet meed of approval and encouragement to the new thought, instead of reproving its boldness: we have gained an influence, which no after-difference in opinion can remove; our experience will henceforth be appreciated and valued, and our councils sought with sentiments of respect and love, which a contrary course of acting never would have obtained.

Far more than any period of life, does youth need affection and forbearance. It is restless in itself, conscious of power, of yearning wishes, of a more intense susceptibility to pleasure and to pain, than it has ever experienced before; the joys of childhood no longer either sought or felt, it is seeking and longing for something higher, and deeper, and more lasting, yet unable to define of what nature; if to these inward trials, we add harshness of judgment, undue control, and an absence of all sympathy, we not only increase incalculably the restlessness already theirs, but by neglecting the influence for good, which we might so very easily obtain, have neither right, nor reason to be astonished, if they turn in disappointment and bitterness from their natural guardians, and seek the sympathy, and are guided by the influence of strangers, who, never having known them as *children*, are ready and willing to love and regard them with interest, in the new period of *youth*.

It is for this eventful, and most interesting era of life, that the following letters are intended. In the new and restless state of mind, which must follow the calm belief of childhood, religion is the one subject of intense inquiry. We do not, of course, allude to those weak and contentedly unformed characters, who are satisfied to vegetate through life, ask no more than they perceive, follow certain forms because others do, and never dream, that as individuals they are responsible and immortal beings, and will have to account for every hour wasted, every talent unused. We allude to those young aspiring minds, who, beginning to be conscious of thought and the powers of reason, turn restless and dissatisfied from the religion of tacit belief and customary form, and demand and *must have*, if indeed we would give them a ruling and consoling principle, a religion of the *understanding*. They must know what they believe, and why. Even those who have been tenderly and carefully brought up "in the way they should go," who have been guided by anxious and loving parents to the Fountain of living waters, who have had the blessing of example as well as precept,—yes, even these *must have* a period of doubt and inquiry, less painful indeed, and less lasting, than is the case with those who in youth must begin from the very beginning; but still it will be theirs also, and we must expect, and provide for it, instead of being saddened and dispirited, that so it is. Nay we should rather invite inquiry. We must not be indolently contented, if we see youth quietly satisfied, to continue doing as they have done in child-hood, and merely religious, because their parents and friends are. This will never satisfy the mind when trial comes, and their active faith is called for, instead of passive and almost unconscious obedience.

To assist in satisfying this craving in youth itself, and to aid parents and teachers in their precious, but re-sponsible task, there are aids innumerable in Christian England. Powerful and spiritual minds, of both sexes, are constantly sending forth eloquent and appealing and guiding works, both for heart and mind. The churches (open every Sunday, with not merely learned, but spiritual divines, ready and willing to answer every doubt and question of their youthful flock) would be in themselves sufficient to inculcate the religion of the un-derstanding, as well as of belief, and give to youth almost all they need. But for the Hebrews of England, we look for such auxiliaries almost in vain. True, there is (and we hail it with grateful rejoicing as the rising sun for another generation) one Synagogue in the metropolis, where every Sabbath there are sermons in the vernacu-lar idiom, tending to remove doubt, answer enquiry, satisfy feeling, and confirm belief. There are ministers in the Provinces and the Colonies (as also in the Me-tropolis, if freedom of speech and liberty of action would be allowed them), periodically to do the same, rendering their Synagogues, as they were ever intended, houses of instruction as well as of prayer. There is a new spirit breathing through the "dry bones" and scattered remnant of Israel, from North to South, and East to West, even to the remotest isles of the sea, a spirit that is of God, and will lead back to Him. There is hope, more hope for the regeneration of spiritual Israel, than there has been for many centuries. Men are thinking and enquiring, and separating in their holy religion the chaff from the wheat; and though the fearful evils of contention, and party spirit, and individual enmity, and general bitterness, alloy and darken the Present, and render it in appearance far more stormy than the Past, there is far, far more hope for the Future, than in the apathy and indifference of former years. Decided evil, nationally speaking, in some cases is better than negative good. Men rise and strive against the former, and work on and on, till it is trampled under foot, and the fair bright light of the distant horizon, which had been shrouded in the dense masses of mental darkness, gleams before them "shining more and more unto the perfect day." The Israelites were contented slaves to Pharaoh, while their burdens were not sufficiently heavy as to be considered actual evil, regarding their safety in all probability as a negative species of good, which might be lost if they sought greater privileges. But when the evil was felt as an evil, when so terrible became their position, so intolerable their burden, that it could no longer be endured, Israel rose up and subdued it, and, from a band of cowed and trembling slaves, became a great and holy nation. Let us not then despair and doubt, because, in the present state of the Hebrew nation, there are more storm and contention, and their grievous accompaniments, than in former years. It is the awakening into life, the bursting from the fearful grave of apathy and stagnation. The tempest-clouds

may alone be *visible;* but there is endless joy and love
and harmony beyond.

Such being the present condition of Israel, our youth
indeed need help and guidance, or they are likely to be
lost in the fearful vortex of contending opinions around
them.   To rest indifferent and unenquiring, always unnatural to youth, would actually be impossible now; and
more than ever, books are needed on which the mind and
heart may rest,—and more especially for our FEMALE
YOUTH.   For them, there is literally no help in the way
of vernacular religious literature.   For our young men,
there are the works of our ancient sages; there are
ministers and teachers to instruct them in their obsolete
and difficult languages, and explain their often puzzling
and metaphysical sense.   There is a vast fund of Hebrew
learning and theology open to them.   Their larger
intellect, deeper reasoning, greater intensity and power
of concentrating thought, will enable them to enter
into, and master them; but this to woman is utterly
impossible.   Destined for home and home duties,—to
enliven and rejoice all the members of that home, be
they parents, brothers and sisters, husband and children,
—to be ever ready to come out of self for others, and
willingly sacrifice her leisure whenever called upon to
do so, even for such apparently trifling duties as entering
into and sharing others' *pleasures* and *amusements*, as
well as smoothing their difficulties, and soothing their
sorrows,—how could she (granting she has the requisite
mental powers, which we do not deny, if circumstances
would allow her to concentrate them) find the time
requisite for such absorbing employment, without neglecting duties of infinitely more importance?

But that our huge tomes of Hebrew wisdom and
learning are inaccessible to woman, is no reason that she

is to have no aid in the acquirement of her religion—no guide as to spiritual aspirations, and no comfort in her need. Metaphysics and speculative theories, indeed, are not for her. All she requires, is to understand the unspeakable comfort of her Bible, and the religion she follows, so as to obey its dictates from the calm conviction of the mind, as well as the impulse of the heart. Many suppose that this comes intuitively, and requires neither instruction nor sympathy. It may be so with some; but the generality of our youth demand it, yearn for it with such an intensity of longing, that finding no books of their own, they are compelled to seek the works of Christian writers—and then we are astonished, if they are more Christian than Jewish in their thoughts. A charge, by the way, incomprehensible to us individually, as we know not, and never could discover, the distinction between Jewish and Christian *spirituality*, on which some good, but prejudiced persons, lay so great a stress. The distinction of creeds is, indeed, very clearly to be understood and defined, as also the difference in their respective ordinances and modes of thought; but spirituality is common to every creed and to every nation who earnestly seeks to know and love the Lord, according to the dictates of the Laws that each believes that He has given, and so observes. And if this be the case with every creed, how much more in common ought those to have, who acknowledge the same Book, and the same foundation?

But if the imbibing of Christian spirituality will do our young sisters no harm whatever, (for it is Jewish spirituality as well,) the imbibing of the peculiar creed of the Christian undoubtedly will, and this is the great evil to be counteracted in the indiscriminate perusal of Christian books. Liberal as their writers may be, they must infuse their works with the doctrine in which they believe, and, in fact, they would be little worth to their own if they did not. Religion is the only subject in which prejudice in favour of one's own is a positive virtue; for it is a widely distinct sentiment from prejudice against another, contradictory as the assertion may at first sight appear. All who have in the least studied human nature, will allow, that the heart most honest, most faithful, and most clearly comprehending its own, is endowed with the greatest charity and liberality towards the religion of another.

As an humble help in supplying the painful want of Anglo-Jewish literature, to elucidate for our female youth the tenets of their own, and so remove all danger from the perusal of abler and better works by spiritual Christians, not to attempt to vie with them, the present work is undertaken. The familiar and appealing form of letters is chosen, as more likely to touch the heart and to convince the understanding, than in the graver form of essays or chapters. No learned dissertation is attempted, the author merely wishing to reply as simply, affectionately and concisely, as is compatible with the weighty subject, to the doubts and questions which she has observed to rise in the minds of youth, and, especially, on the Jewish belief in Immortality. Youth, in its high aspirations and eager thoughts, will never be satisfied with the vague and fanciful belief in immortality, which it has imbibed in childhood. It must have something to rest on, something wherewith to guide its aspirings,— and oh! who would not aid in giving these, when we look on the youthful being standing in such beauty, and joy, and hope on the threshold of life, about to enter a world, which, without the belief in, and knowledge of another, must too soon seem so dark and woe-fraught, as to bewilder the mind with doubt and fear, and fling a dense cloud between the aspiring heart, and the consoling attributes of its God? Trials of sickness, or care, or sorrow, or bereavement, *must* sooner or later be the portion of our youthful charges, seeming, in their early freshness, as if neither sorrow nor care could ever approach to sadden them. And shall we fail to provide them with the strength and comfort which, for such alternations, a God of Love has provided, when we can? Should we not think that parent strangely unwise and cruel, who would send her child to a country of cold and snow, provided only with summer clothing? And is it not the same, if our experience teaches us that trials must assail our cherished ones, and yet we provide them with nothing which would soften their suffering, strengthen to endure, and infuse a hope and faith in that better life, which will last for ever, and so shine, as even in the darkest hours to invigorate and bless?

The trial, supposed to have been encountered by the young girl to whom the letters are addressed, is indeed an extreme case, but unhappily, far from being one without a parallel. Many of my young sisters may feel, and with perfect justice, that they are infinitely more spiritual, and must know a great deal more of their religion, than she does, for they already know and feel the truth of what she is doubting and questioning. But even to them, we hope sympathy will not be wholly unacceptable, though we acknowledge our letters are intended far more for those, whom circumstances have deprived of a decidedly religious education, who from the ages of sixteen to twenty-one are beginning to think for themselves, and whose peculiar disposition compels them to seek, and find the Rock of Refuge and Shield of Salvation, whose infinite love and exhaustless

2*

mercy is proffered unto *all* His creatures, without any distinctions of age or sex.

For those of my own faith the following pages are written, and to them they are addressed. Young Christian women have such advantages and privileges in following the religion of the Land, in having teachers and guides without number, male and female—that it would be indeed a presumptuous hope to interest them in the subject under discussion ; yet even to them it may not be entirely useless. Christianity in all, save its actual doctrine of belief, is the offspring of Judaism; and as one of our most enlightened and purest feeling divines very lately said, "The differences between Christianity and Judaism, however *great and weighty in their speculative doctrines*, disappear in the *moral truths and principles alike upheld by both*."* And the more we know of each other's faith and practice, the more clear and striking becomes this fact. Works then, tending to elucidate the religion of another, must ever be welcome to the candid and liberal mind ; and though to my young Christian sisters the following letters may proffer nothing in the way of religious instruction, they will at least prove that the Hebrew faith is not one of spiritless form, meaningless observances, and comfortless belief, which some suppose it, not from wilful illiberality, but from actual ignorance. They may perhaps discover, that the foundation of all spiritual religion is the same— that from Judaism and the Bible all *their* privileges spring—and that if they deny the divinity of the one, that of the other falls to the ground; and then what becomes of Christianity ? These are, or ought to be,

---

* Rev. M. J. Raphall. See Jewish Chronicle of 9th January, 1846.

important considerations to every Christian; and we trust, therefore, in this age of advanced enlightenment, and more especially in our own free, happy, sheltering England, that no work tending to explain and elevate the Jewish religion will be pronounced useless, or, if not regarded as controversial, merely considered as interesting only to the Jews. We have been charged as having exhibited in a former work an intolerant spirit—a charge to a heart filled with love for all its kind, be their creed what it may, more exquisitely painful than any other censure It may be, that in earnest defence of our own, we may not have been as careful or as charitable in words, as God knows we are in heart—that the warmth of defence may have merged into attack; but if so, it was as unintentional at the time, as deeply regretted when pointed out afterwards. We shrink from all controversy. We would give every man that liberty of conscience which we ask for ourselves. We would simply instil the beauty, the holiness, the comfort, and the eternal duration of the religion God gave to Moses, into the inmost hearts of our own; and if, in the earnestness of this attempt, we *appear* to judge harshly of others, it is wholly and utterly opposed to the sentiments of either heart or mind.

We beg our readers of either denomination to remember, ere we proceed, that, written expressly for *youth* just beginning to think and inquire for themselves, the various subjects are more minutely examined, and entered upon, than if we had been writing for adults; and this fact must therefore be our excuse, if we have treated too much at length subjects of religion generally, and the Jewish religion in particular, which are supposed, and may be, universally known.

LETTER I.

INEZ VILLENA TO ANNIE MONTAGUE.

Retrospective sympathy—Comfort of an assured religious hope—
Causes of trial; the best mode of regarding and enduring it—Heavy
sorrows do not deaden us to smaller ones—Apathy and indifference,
not resignation.

1845.

GRIEVED, indeed, am I, my dearest Annie, at the intelligence which greeted me on my return to England last week. I have been so long residing where it was difficult, almost impossible, for letters to reach me, that for the last six months I have been in utter ignorance of the health and welfare of my friends at home; and little did I anticipate the heavy trial, which ere we met again, was to befall the youngest, and almost the dearest, of all I had left behind. My own Annie, how can I comfort you, when circumstances prevent my even being with you, to supply in some measure the place of the beloved ones you have lost? and even if I were, not even the dearest and most affectionate sympathy could as yet bring balm. The sufferings you witnessed in your father's last illness three years ago, reconciled you in some measure to his loss; and you had then a mother, for whose beloved sake you could exert your energy, and in whose deep love you could find comfort. You had a sweet young sister, whose heavenly mind and peculiar beauty, while it called forth the deepest, and most yearning affection, always made me tremble for her long resting upon this uncongenial earth. And now both are gone ; how, then, can human affection attempt consolation ? Many would say, I am opening the wound afresh by thus referring to it when some months have past. By some I am told that you are becoming reconciled and happy ; and by others again, that you are sunk in such despondency and apathy, that neither remonstrance nor affection is of any avail. I do not quite believe either of these reports. You must be very much changed in three years, the term of my absence, as in a few months to become reconciled to such an awful bereavement, and be happy as before; or still more changed, to be careless of either remonstrance or affection. Write to me, Annie, love, and write freely. Your mother, as you have long known, was my dearest, best beloved friend. My first heavy grief was our compelled separation, when she accompanied her husband to ———— for an indefinite period, and left you to the care of those same aged and affectionate relatives, who had been the only parents she had ever known. It was her only hope of saving you; for not only had she to encounter the hardships of a long voyage in a stormy season, and the miseries of a strange land, but she was told you could not bear the voyage, and that her only chance of rearing you was to leave you to English air and English nursing. When struggling with care and illness, and all the privations of a half-savage life, her unselfish heart indeed rejoiced that you were spared it, and under affectionate training, growing up into healthy and beautiful maturity. And when after thirteen years she returned, and found the ailing and fractious infant a sweet, amiable, affectionate girl of fourteen, all her fond anticipations were indeed realised ! To weak human reasoning it does indeed seem hard and inscrutable, that only four years of parental

love and cherishing should be granted you, when so
many pass through life with all their beloved around
them. But, darling Annie, to those who have an assured
hope, as we have, in a world beyond the grave, that when
the young, and good, and lovely go, it is because their
God so loved them, that He called them to Himself,
sparing them all farther trial, there *must* be comfort
even in our deepest grief. The idea that their lot is all
joy; that neither change nor sorrow can ever cloud it;
that they are not only with their God, the infinite
Source of all love, but have rejoined those beloved ones
who have gone before them, must deprive the thinking of
them of all sting, however intensely, however agonisingly
we may and must feel our own bereavement.

Do not think, that I wish to prove to you that your
trial is less heavy than you must believe it. There
never yet was any sorrow soothed by an attempt to lessen
its magnitude. God does not send trial, to be unfelt, or
its pang to be conquered, even by the idea, nay the conviction, that because He sent it, it must have its source
in love. We may feel this conviction to our heart's
inmost core, and yet be susceptible of intense mental
suffering; and it is *because* His unerring wisdom sees this
suffering necessary to fit us for eternal joy, that it is
sent. We are sometimes called upon to endure the most
agonising bodily pain, not for present relief, because we
may not be suffering at all at the moment; but because
the skilful physician, in whom, from his superior wisdom
and learning, we place implicit trust, assures us it is
absolutely necessary for our health and strength. We
never dream of doubting his judgment, or of resisting
the remedy he proposes, even though we ourselves,
from the absence of all present inconvenience, cannot
imagine why he should thus decide. We endure the

pain as pain, and our friends would certainly not think of trying to persuade us, that we are not suffering much, and so urge us to exertion; but they rather do all they can to alleviate the suffering, and by sympathy to encourage us bravely to endure. Why then should we not treat the wounds it may please God to send in the same manner? Surely, we must feel Him to be wiser and more merciful than the most skilful and tenderest physician of earth, and that He would not so afflict us, if He did not perceive it absolutely necessary for our immortal health? It is, indeed, hard to think so; when we have tried so earnestly to do our duty to Him and to man, and we see so many much less earnest, and apparently without any religion, prosperous and happy. It is hard; and yet, dearest Annie, the brief but thrilling sentence, "THE LORD LOVETH WHOM HE CORRECTETH," and again, "BLESSED BE HE WHOM THOU CHASTENEST, O LORD," contrasted with verses like these, "When the wicked spring up like grass, and the workers of iniquity do flourish, it is that they shall be destroyed for ever," would seem a clear and convincing answer, and satisfy us, that it is no proof of our heavenly Father's love to let us pass through this life, without any event occurring, which would draw us nearer Him, and help us to think more seriously than we might otherwise have done.

Perhaps, even this consoling conviction, will read harsh and irrelevant to such grief as yours: forgive me if it does. I meant only to have expressed my deep earnest sympathy, and to entreat you as I do again, to write freely to me. It will not be the first time, by very many, that you have permitted me to read your inmost thoughts. In your childhood, we so often conversed of serious things, that though, for the last four years, I have communicated with you only through your mother,

I do not believe you are so changed, that the soothing voice of religious hope and consolation from one who so dearly loves you for your own sake, as well as for that of the departed, will be entirely unfelt. I fear, too, that your present situation is sufficiently uncongenial to add to your burden; for I am not one of those who think, that great trials deaden us to the sting of small ones. It *is* a trial to live with those who though, perhaps, intrinsically kind and good, are yet so incapable of understanding us, that we have no subject in common, save the most trifling and worldly topics, and to whom I fear that soothing and strengthening *spirit* of religion, which can be your only comfort now, is as unknown as unpractised. I trust, however, that this is only a temporary evil. I do not refer you to a brighter future, to bid you not grieve now; for when was present pain ever soothed by the thought of future relief? For your present feelings there is but one source of consolation, there can be but one healer. Seek Him, my beloved girl, trust in Him, even while your tears flow, and the pain you must endure will be sanctified and blessed. It is only the fruitless effort to break from its chain and wile away its pang by frivolous amusement, that can render it too hard to bear. I do not tell you to refrain from occupation; I would rather beseech you, to make some employment which would prevent the ascendency of apathy and indifference, so often supposed to be resignation. But I will not write more now, though my heart is so full of affection, that it is difficult to check its expression. My own darling Annie, seek, and may you find the only consolation, the only strength, which in such sorrow can be yours—the peace "which passeth all understanding;"—for it exists even in grief and pain, and is the blessing of your God.

LETTER II.

FROM THE SAME TO THE SAME.

Painful effect of circumstances on natural character—Erroneous sentiments refuted—Necessity of a religion of love—Religion does not
exempt us from suffering, and why?—Its importance in the petty
sorrows of daily life, as great, if not greater, than in heavy trial—
Youth, a new existence—Importance of an early spiritual life.

I WILL not say your letter has not pained me, my
dearest Annie, or that it was the answer I expected. I
should be a false friend, if, even at such a moment, when
you need all the indulgence affection can bestow, I should
refrain from telling you, where I think you are in error,
or allow you, by my silence, to suppose you are following
a right train of thought and feeling, when both judgment and experience convince me, that the relief, you
tell me, that they give you, is not only of but temporary
duration, but intrinsically false, and will betray you
into increased and more painful despondency, ere many
weeks are over. Do not throw my letter aside as a harsh
and uncalled-for reproof. Annie, dearest, if you are
inclined to do so, pause for a moment, and recall the
days of your childhood, when, even if I had the inclination or necessity to chide, far more than I have now,
you would fold your arms round my neck, and nestle
your head on my shoulder, and tell me you would listen
to all I had to say, and try and profit by it, however
severe it might be, if I would only call you my Annie,
and love you as before. Have four brief years of separation so estranged me from you, that these fond
associations are all forgotten? and is the girl so altered

3

from the child, that the pleadings of truth and affection will be unheeded? I do not believe it. Nor do I believe the letter which has so grieved me came from the depths of your own fresh, true, and warm feeling heart. You think it did; but you are under a delusion, brought about by circumstances, but which, if you do not nerve your every energy to break from, will make you very miserable.

You thanked me for my letter; you wrote, "It was very very kind, and very good of me to think of you, but that its subject was far too painful to dwell upon. You resolved to banish it so entirely from your mind, as never to recur to it even for a moment's thought. That you could not enter into the spirit in which I wrote: it might be very wicked of you, but you could not help it. That you were living with those who never spoke or thought of religion, more than the daily prayer and customary form, but who were always merry, and happier than any family you knew. That they had lost some near and very dear relations, but they found the very best remedy for such grief was not to think about it, but to plunge more and more in the vortex of pleasure and amusement. That they seemed to think it almost folly to allude to those they had lost, as, what could their memory be but sources of pain when they were separated for ever? That you must think the reasoning good from its effects upon them, and in the quiet, easy way in which life flows on."

Four months is but a short interval to pronounce judgment on the easy flow of a life, my dear Annie; but whether or not, this reasoning may appear to hold good with them, trust my affection, and believe that yours, is neither the character, nor disposition, to find either strength or comfort from it. Your peculiarly formed woman-heart must have something higher, and better, and purer than earth to rest on. Your high aspirations which, if properly directed, will tend to both your temporal and spiritual happiness, must become sources of wretchedness, if you seek satisfaction and fulness in this world alone; your craving after the good and beautiful must remain unsatisfied, if you wilfully turn away from Him, in whose light alone the true and exquisite beauty even of this world is fully displayed. Your inquiring mind will be tossed in a chaos of doubt and misery, from the dark and awful mystery which, without a firm belief in an ever-acting Providence of Love, seems to surround the daily routine of life. Your very affections, so warm, so clinging, will never be other than sources of pain, if you do not love God first, and his creatures in Him. Without faith in Him, all must seem evil, which is, in reality, creative of good; and how are you to bear it? Dearest Annie, you little knew yourself, when you wrote the words I have quoted. There may be some who continue to pass through life happily and contentedly without religion; though *how* they can, especially amongst our sex, is to me so incomprehensible a mystery, that even to believe it is almost impossible; but high characters, such as yours ever promised to be, *cannot*, try as they may, unless, indeed, they voluntarily and consciously sentence themselves to misery, which no after-effort may avert. I do not allude to great misfortunes. Religion will not exempt us from suffering; if it did, we should pursue it, not from love of God, but from a selfish feeling of security, which would at once degrade it from a high and pure aspiration, to the wages paid a harsh, exacting master. This is not the character of our Father in heaven, who has in His mercy revealed to us that His love is so inexhaustible, that neither heaven nor earth can contain it; that it never wearies, never changes, and, like the glorious light of His beautiful orb, shines on all alike, but is revealed in its depth and fulness only to those who seek and trust in it, and try to render loving service as the sole acknowledgment our Father asks. But if religion will not exempt us from suffering, you will ask me, why do I lay so much stress on it, and say that without it you must be miserable, when with it you will also be called on to endure? Because the sufferings borne with the filial spirit of devotedness and love, and with a firm and unchanging trust, that our Parent in heaven knows far better what is good for us, than our dearest, tenderest friends of earth can do, and the sufferings which have no such thought, are so utterly distinct, and the latter so much the more terrible, that they ought not to be classed under the same denomination. But even were this not the case, and the religious and the irreligious subject to exactly the same amount of pain, under the misfortunes of bereavement, sickness, change of fortune, privation, and care, which *may* befall us all : it is not so much to these great events of life I allude, as to its daily temper, and the thousand petty trials of home and heart,—trials to which *all* are subject, though some dispositions feel them in an infinitely greater degree than others. It is from these I would save you, or rather conjure you to save yourself; because I know that your disposition is such, as to expose you to them in all their unmitigated bitterness. You tell me, or rather, I read it through your letter, that you are now so perfectly indifferent, as to be insensible to either pain or pleasure. I am not surprised. It is the natural consequence of the intense mental suffering you have lately endured, and far more physical than mental; but it will not last. As elasticity of frame returns, so will your keen susceptibility of enjoyment, and as keen, if not keener, sense of pain.   You will not then be satisfied with the easy current of the existence of those around you, nor will the pleasures and amusements to which they may introduce you satisfy your earnest cravings after the holy and the good, intellectual enjoyment, and perfect sympathy and love.   Your quickness of feeling exposes you to the charge of quickness of temper, and I fear when you cease to be a novelty, the easy dispositions which you at present admire will not bear with it, as may be the case at present, and you will meet with harshness and reproof; and how can you endure this, accustomed, as you have been from your earliest infancy, to the tenderest and most indulgent love?   Annie, my own precious child, for such must I ever feel you—do not, I conjure you, turn wilfully from the only true changeless Source of strength and comfort; do not cast from you the infinite love which a Father proffers and reiterates in every variety of tenderness and mercy, through His most Holy Book.   Come to Him now that you are of an age to give Him, not only the first freshness of your young and guileless HEART, but the willing obedience, which springs from the conviction and acquiescence of the MIND.   He has indeed stricken you; but do seek Him, and He will not only heal present grief, but so strengthen, so spiritualize you, that though the memories of your beloved ones must ever be a source of tearful regret, you will become more quietly, but more intensely, happy than you have yet been; and such peace will become your own, that you need dread no trial, petty or great, that He may please to send.   You are standing on the threshold of a new period of existence.   In addition to acute sorrow, you have to contend

with the doubts, and questions, and indefinable sensations, ever busy in the mind and heart of youth. The
term of your present mourning over, you will be called
upon to enter that world, which you are looking on now
as far distant and unknown, and, from your present
natural depression, perhaps undesired; but when once
entered, you will have no wish to draw back. It will
be fraught with pleasures and with pains, trials and
temptations, petty ones perhaps, but not the less painful
to endure and to resist, or the less deteriorating to the
character, unless influenced by some higher principle,
than the mere *conveniences* of the world. You may, it
is very probable you will, marry; and when once a wife
and mother, the duties, anxieties, and responsibilities of
life will so throng around you, as to leave you little
leisure and less inclination to cultivate that ever-acting
and silently infusing piety which, at your present age,
and under your late affliction, may, with an earnest
wish and heartfelt prayer, so easily be attained. I cannot bear to think of one so dearly loved, so fondly
cherished, and with a disposition too likely to suffer,
even from causes which more obtuse natures would pass
unfelt, exposed to the great and petty trials of woman's
life, without the shield of spiritual faith and love, which
alone can strengthen her for earth, and purify for heaven.

Dearest Annie, choose the better and the happier
path: cast off the delusion concerning your own disposition which has so enchained you; trust to the love of
one who has watched over you from infancy, and believe
that, if *no* woman can be truly and purely happy without religion, *you* must be miserable; for your very nature
needs it, yearns for it, and must sink listlessly and sor-
rowfully to earth, unless it grasp the rock of refuge
which a Father proffers.

Do not throw my letter aside, as a grave sermon, fit only for Sabbath reading. For your mother's sake, if no longer for mine, read it in the spirit of your childhood, and, without fear of either grieving or surprising me, write me unhesitatingly your own sentiments, not those of the persons around you, in reply. Do not fear harsh censure, or even hinted reproof; the religion our Father desired Moses to teach, is a religion of love, and in love only should be taught, as in love received.

LETTER III.

FROM THE SAME TO THE SAME.

Painfulness of separation—Miserable doubts and unrest on the subject of religion—Natural to youth—Different impressions on the same subject—Hebrews and Christians; differences and agreement; difficult position of the Jewish youth—Necessity for being well grounded in our own faith—Advance of spirituality—Distinction between the spiritualist and the formalist greater than between opposing creeds.

WHAT will you say to me, dearest Annie, when I tell you, that your last, though it told me of physical suffering and consequent return of mental despondency, has grieved me much less than your former one, and that I trace, in the midst of this deep darkness, a brighter hope for your returning and lasting happiness, than in the sunless, starless twilight which preceded it? Would indeed, that I could have been with you in your illness, my poor child! Nay, would that I could be near you at all times, or have you with me, as my whole heart longs to do! I could almost murmur at the imperative

circumstances which so utterly prevent this; but it is
wrong to do so, and I must be grateful, not only that
time and space have no power on affection and sympathy, but that you are willing to believe in, and rest
on my affection, even as in former years. You tell me,
·that in your illness things have appeared in a different
light; that what seemed happiness and mirth, proved
indifference and coldness; that you thought, you were
really loved, but in the long hours of solitude, when
you were too weak to join the family, you seemed so
utterly forgotten, so little cared for, you could no longer
believe it; your sufferings had no power to ruffle the
easy flow of life you had once admired, and you would
rather suffer pain itself than be so utterly indifferent to
others ; that you had already felt the truth of my warning words in the little kindness and forbearance evinced
towards you, when from pure physical weakness you
gave way to the depression, the vain yearnings for your
beloved mother, which so overpowered you, that they
called it ill-temper and ingratitude, and reproved it accordingly. My poor girl, I did not think you would
have discovered this so soon; but, thank God, it has led
you to seek and pray for the only source of consolation.
You tell me, and you can perhaps hardly imagine the
happiness of such information, that my letters were your
greatest comfort; you do not know how you could
have written so coldly and ungratefully in answer to
my first, or how you can love me enough for forgiving
it, and writing again so fondly; that you would, O
how willingly! follow my advice, and try and find in
religion all the strength and comfort, I assure you it will
bestow, but that your whole mind feels so tempest-
tossed, so utterly unable to satisfy itself, that you are
almost afraid to write to me, when you recollect all our

conversations in your childhood, and how easy then it felt to believe all I said, and how delightful it was to think of, and try and love God; that try all you can, you cannot feel this now; that you must be grown very very wicked, for you cannot even think on religion, without such painful doubts and bewildering fancies arising, that, instead of finding repose, heart and mind are both so fevered and restless, you are glad to fly to other employments. And these doubts, these questions, seem so idle, if not so actually sinful, that you dare not confess them even to me.

My darling Annie, dismiss this fear at once. I am neither surprised, nor grieved, nor will I even accuse you of either forgetting or undervaluing the lessons of your childhood. Nay, I am actually glad that you are no longer satisfied tacitly to believe, and to go on from year to year the mere formalist, which is unhappily the case with many. All you have written only convinces me, that I am correct in my impressions, and that your mind is of that enlarged, enquiring nature, which I believed it to be, but which will never rest satisfied with the mere habit of education and general belief. Do not hesitate, and I entreat you do not *fear*, to write me every doubt and every question. I cannot judge them harshly; for I have not yet forgotten my own youth, when I experienced exactly the same feelings. Those who think deeply and feel strongly, *cannot* exchange childhood for youth unconsciously. That many may pass through life, without revealing or even thinking about the doubts and bewildering sensations you describe, does not prove their non-existence, but that in very many dispositions, they are not strong or loud enough, to over-balance the pleasures, amusements, and freedom, also natural to youth. Others, again, are of such naturally easy indolent characters, that they are quite satisfied to do as others do; if momentary doubts trouble them, they are immediately dismissed as requiring too much exertion to be solved, or they rest perfectly satisfied with being told, they cannot understand such things, and it is folly to attempt it. Others again, like yourself, *fear* to express what feels to them a sinful falling off from the religion of their childhood; or if they do venture to reveal it, are perhaps told it is wicked and blasphemous to doubt, or speak of such things; the eager enquiry is checked and chidden, and so returns to the mind to engender farther doubts, which become at last so engrossing and irksome, that unbelief is almost sure to follow, simply for the sake of repose—a false one indeed. Yet, how can we blame, when it is the experienced answerer who is at fault, not the enquiring youth?

Ask what you will: if I cannot answer you, I will endeavour to find wiser ones who are able. You have not only to contend with sorrow, which has, perhaps, advanced and increased the perplexing thoughts inherent to your age; but our very position, aliens in a land whose religion is not ours—and yours especially, in a small county town almost entirely surrounded by Christians, and where our Jewish brethren, I fear, are but little likely to elevate our holy faith in your mind—must increase the mental difficulties you are now enduring, and render me more and more desirous to help you in attaining rest and strength. As it was with myself in early youth, circumstances have thrown you almost entirely amongst Protestants; and from your peculiar disposition, longing unconsciously for the high and pure, you have always made those your intimate friends, who are serious thinkers, and have infused even the mere pleasures and amusements of their age with the spirit

which, though not of earth itself, makes all of earth so
lovely. The only Hebrews you have known are unhappily not of this class. Not thinking very deeply, they
imagine it quite impossible for any serious Christian to
take an interest in a young Jewess without desiring her
conversion, and that Hebrews and Christians may have
much, very much in common; that the very link between
them may be religion, entirely and wholly distinct from
doctrines of creed, is so utterly incomprehensible to
them, that they not only disbelieve in its possibility, but
are always looking for some ulterior motive. I have no
such feelings. No true and enlightened Protestant ever
yet descended to the petty and wicked meanness, of
tampering with the faith of a young and almost friend-
less girl as yourself. Mistaken zealots there are, indeed, who deem the attempt to convert the most meritorious act they can perform; but these are seldom
found among calm enlightened Protestants. Know your
own religion well, observe it from mental as well as loving conviction, and you will find yourself and your faith
too truly respected, ever to fear even an attempt at conversion. It is the mere formalists amongst us, who
have thrown such odium on the Jewish faith; but you
must not judge the whole nation by the few among
whom you are thrown. Could you visit London, which
I hope you will one day, or even Liverpool, or Birming-
ham, where there are large communities of Jews, you
would find very many to respond to all your ardent and
spiritual feelings. The advance towards regaining that
vital element of our religion, spirituality, has been indeed most cheering the last ten or twenty years, and
inspires the hope and belief of its spreading more and
more. If we once inculcate in the hearts of our youth
the spirituality and the comfort of our holy religion,

we shall have nothing whatever to fear in our closest intercourse with Christians. We shall find so much on which to agree, that there will be neither leisure nor inclination for allusion to those points on which we differ ; but then, of course, we must *know* our own, or we are more than likely to become mentally entangled and confused. The wider the dissimilitude, the less danger for either the ignorant or the unwary; but where there is so much alike, the points of difference must be very distinctly and clearly traced, or we may be liable to lose them altogether. I am quite aware, that the assertion of similitude between religions, whose doctrines of belief are so opposed, would meet with violent opposition, from many who term themselves orthodox Hebrews ; but opposition will not alter truth, and I am ready to agree with them, that between the *formalist* and the *spiritualist*, there is indeed a barrier which can never be passed ; but this holds as good between Jew and Jew, Christian and Christian, as between Hebrew and Protestant. It is not the *doctrines*, but the *feelings* which are so impassably opposed. I would not check your intimacy with any Christian friend. All I ask of you is to examine your own religion thoroughly, ere you pronounce that the Christian is the most spiritual, the most consoling. I am not at all astonished at your fancying so just now, and that this very fancy should be one of the many causes, creating such painful and bewildering doubts, of which you complain as removing all comfort from religion. Have I guessed right?

LETTER IV.

FROM THE SAME TO THE SAME.

Superior advantages and more visible consoling religion of the Christian—The Bible open to both faiths and bringing spirituality and peace—Causes of non-religious instruction amongst the Hebrews of former years—Wrong to judge of the whole nation by a few—Benefit and danger of Christian books—How to avert the danger—The Bible and its privileges given to us first—Its consequences on the nations—Causes of non-spirituality in the German Hebrews of former times—Appeal for our own.

YOU are astonished at my penetration, dearest Annie, astonished that I should so exactly have defined your feelings regarding Christianity and Judaism, though you did not write a word on the subject. I am truly happy that I have done so, and that my sympathy has given you courage to confess, what you are quite sure must otherwise have remained untold—that when I wrote to you in my first letter of the necessity, the strength and peace of religion, you had felt that, if you were a Christian, you might hope to experience all this, but that as a Jewess it was impossible,—that there were so many books not merely to explain the Christian religion, but to give sympathy and comfort in every affliction,—that there were churches to frequent, and so many home-speaking, heart-appealing prayers to help them to lift up their thoughts to God, that could you but be a Christian, you might be comforted and even happy,—that you had been tempted most strongly to adopt the Christian faith, but that your promise to your dying mother

to keep true and faithful to the Hebrew religion withheld you,—and, moreover, that whenever you asked any
questions concerning religion, your friend had entreated
you to seek information from your own,—that in her family, as in others of your Protestant friends, religion was
actually taught, made a rule of life, and you could not
recall any Jewish family in which this was the case, even
your own,—that I was the only person who ever spoke
to you on the subject. Why was this? What caused
the great difference? Even where you are now, you
had sometimes asked the meaning of certain forms, and
never could get a satisfactory answer.

You have, indeed, asked me most important questions,
my dearest Annie, and I will endeavour to reply to
them. I agree with you in the many and far superior
advantages of the Christian over us. Religious books
adapted for our youth and sympathising in our feelings,
we have not indeed. With the sole exception of one
Synagogue in London, our houses of worship cannot be
to our youth as the Christians' are to theirs; but for
home-speaking, heart-appealing prayers, the BOOK which
gives these to Christians, gives them equally, ay, and
gave them first to us. The Bible is the source, the
foundation, the example of all prayer, and that is OURS.
It is from the study of and belief in this, that the peace
which passeth all understanding, the peace to which
Isaiah alludes, when he says, in such trusting faith,
"Thou wilt keep him in *perfect* peace whose mind is
stayed on Thee, because he trusteth in Thee;" and then
appealing to his countrymen, conjures them, "Trust ye
in the Lord for ever, for in the Lord Eternal is everlasting strength;"—from the Bible it is that this perfect
peace is derived, for there, and there alone, we learn to
know our God, and knowing, to love Him; there we

find our surest guide for conduct and feeling, strength for life on earth, and hope and belief in life in heaven; there we find the model of every prayer, and the things for which we should pray to become acceptable to God, and reasons for every form and ordinance to which we still adhere. It is not the actual creed which marks the difference in individuals or families. It is the *study* or *neglect* of the Bible. The spiritual, the consoling and strengthening piety to which you allude, as characterising your friend and her family, does not proceed from the fact of her being a Christian, but from her having made the Bible her sole rule of action. If you were to see more of the world, you would find that, as there are unhappily many nominal Jews, so there are very many nominal Christians, and both proceed from the same cause, indifference to all serious things, and utter neglect of the Bible. Unfortunately, circumstances have so placed you, that the only serious thinkers and spiritual minds among whom you are thrown are Christians, and therefore you very naturally suppose the difference must lie in the superiority of their creed. But, my dear Annie, how does it come, if the necessity, the strength, and purity of religion are only taught amongst the Christians, that *I* should so earnestly have besought you to make it your own, and from my own experience have written of comfort and strength? I am no Christian. Nay, I have been the last four years associating with such unenlightened members of the Greek and Roman churches, that, had I been narrow-minded enough to judge *only* by them, the Christian would be to me but a term for superstition, irreligion, and utter ignorance of God's word, compared with which, the most ignorant of my own faith would seem infinitely superior. I do not write this from any feeling of prejudice, but simply to prove to you that we must judge effects by their *real*, not their *apparent causes;* that it is not being a Christian, even a Protestant Christian, which will make us spiritual and teach us the true value of piety, but the earnest and prayerful study of that Holy Book which was given to *us* first, and which, therefore, ought to be treasured as a mine of peace and hope peculiarly our own.

Dearest Annie, study this Holy Book with prayer and love, before you decide on being a Christian. I am not astonished at the strong temptation which assailed you; but I am unspeakably thankful, that, even in death, your beloved mother had power to withhold you, and deeply grateful to Mrs. Balfour for referring you to a Jewish friend. Your situation from childhood, with regard to religion, has been a peculiar one. The kind, but very aged relatives with whom you lived till fourteen, had escaped from Portugal to the West Indies, and only came to England, when already too advanced in years for toleration and freedom to alter previous habits. In Portugal, as you know, to be even suspected as a Jew exposed our ancestors to all the horrors of the Inquisition, sequestration, torture, and often even death. The religion of their fathers, therefore, was instilled with such impenetrable secrecy, and so burdened with caution and the constant dread of discovery that, to do more than attend to its mere elements, and keep the mind faithful to the doctrine of the Divine Unity and the perpetuity of the Jewish Faith, in contradistinction to the bewildering dogmas of saints, martyrs, infallibility of the Roman Church, masses, etc., was impossible. To become spiritual was equally so; for the Bible was a forbidden book to the Catholics, and therefore equally so to the secret Jews. Those, therefore, who from some imminent pressure of danger fled to other countries, were unable to throw off the caution of centuries. They could not realise that the yoke was so far removed from their necks, as to permit the *public* practice and *open* confession of their faith. To speak of, or impart it, by means of free reference to, and discussion on the Bible, . had so long been an utter impossibility, that it was scarcely unnatural, that they should suppose it impossible still, when in reality no impossibility existed. This is the reason why so many of our ancient Spanish and Portuguese families, when they came to England, adhered so very strictly to the *form*, to the utter exclusion of the *spirit* of their religion, and never spoke of nor attempted to teach it, except by desiring a soulless obedience, which had no power, when the youthful mind began to inquire for itself. We must regret this, but we can scarcely wonder at it. They could not teach the spirit of their faith, for they knew it not themselves. It requires long years of rest, of freedom, of equality, of intellectual exercise, so to raise and purify the mind, as to enable it to attain spirituality itself, and teach it to others. We see this truth borne out in the present improved state of the Jewish nation. They are beginning, nay, for some years have begun, to break from the stagnation, which was the natural consequence of their escape from dangerous positions in Portugal to the rest and security of England; and the mind and heart have so far awakened and advanced, as no longer to be satisfied with lifeless forms, but are prepared and eager for the reception and inculcation of that pure spirituality which, equally with the ordained form, is inseparable from their fathers' faith.

The long years of concealment and persecution, from the effects of which it requires almost as long an interval effectually to break, are the real and only reason of the grand distinction in the religious education of Protestants and Hebrews—I should say *was* the reason, for it no longer exists, and the Bible is taught and treasured as it ought to be, by Jews as well as Christians. Your early years were not indeed thus privileged. Not that your aged relatives were mere formalists,—they venerated, loved, and were supported *individually* by the spirit of their faith; but from never having been accustomed to speak of it, even to each other, they were entirely ignorant how to impart it to so young a child, and perhaps shared the opinion of their age, that it was a subject too weighty and solemn for the comprehension of a childish mind. Like many others even now, they very likely supposed, that what was necessary for you to know would come intuitively; that to see, that you attended to, and obeyed certain forms, and solemnised certain days, was all the religious duty incumbent upon them, and this I know they performed lovingly and well. You had their example even in the daily perusal of the Bible; but it was a Hebrew or a Spanish one, and therefore utterly incomprehensible to you. Your childhood, then, was not blessed with a religious education; and from fourteen to eighteen, an age when the impressions are strongest and the affections most intense, the too lowly spirit and trembling doubt in her own powers of your poor mother, prevented your receiving those earnest lessons of piety, which from her lips never would have been forgotten, and which might have spared you much of your present pain. Not that I would reproach her; the decision was mistaken, but it sprung from such a meek, fearful, humble spirit, that, while I contested with it, it only made me love her more. You tell me, that almost her last connected words were to

conjure you never to desert your faith, the full comfort
of which, she assured you, she was feeling at that awful
moment; to seek and love God in your youth; and to
regret, with tears, she had not spoken on the sacred
subject oftener with you, in her days of health and
strength. But she did not tell you why she had thus
refrained; and observing, as I know you have, her
earnest lowly heartfelt piety, you will perhaps hardly
credit me when I tell you that it was, because she felt
herself unworthy and incapable, and believed her child
a better Jewess than herself. The island, in which so
many years of her married life had passed, admitted no
Jews. She was literally compelled to adopt the semblance
of Unitarianism, and even change her name. She could
not adhere to a single ordinance of Judaism; and how,
then, could she impart it even to the children who were
with her? Circumstances of a most imperative nature,
and utterly impossible to be controlled or altered, compelled your father's residence in that island; but the
heart-break to her was, not its privations, and annoyances, and unhealthiness, though these were all hard
enough to bear, but the circumstance above stated,
which was known only to me and to her God. She was
too fond, too true a wife to annoy her husband with
either regret or murmuring; but I do believe, that
inward and constant suffering shortened her life by many
years. She returned to England, and to all the ordinances of her venerated faith as far, at least, as lay in
her power; but even the deep delight of this obedience
could not remove the painful impressions of the past.
On this subject alone my remonstrances failed to have
effect. How could she attempt, her letters would
reiterate, to talk with, or instruct her Annie in religion,
when her whole past life must deny her words? How

could she teach her that Judaism was all in all, when
her own example had taught the bitter lesson that it
must give place to circumstances? No, she would watch
over, shield, cherish, as only such deep love could, but
she was unworthy to speak to her of God. This was the
reason of your mother's silence; but what her religion
was to her, how truly she lived and died a Jewess, her
letters, through eighteen years, will prove. Will you
not, then, examine the faith she so much loved, while
advantages and privileges are yours, the absence of
which gave her such intense suffering, though it could
not shake her faith?

One thing let me entreat you: do not judge your
whole nation by the few families whom you may know.
A small country town is the very place to engender
prejudice and narrow-mindedness, both in favour of,
and against certain points. It strengthens error, because society is not extended enough to mark those
diversities of character and opinion which, if duly considered, must enlarge the mind, and purify it from all
too selfish dross. From finding few, with whom we can
exchange thoughts and ideas, we imagine our own opinions
infallible, and even by what we read may be led unconsciously to the same bias. From having no serious
books of our own fitted for our females and youth, those
who are inclined to serious reflection are compelled to
turn to works by serious Christian authors. There they
will find sympathy and pleasure, but so intimately mingled with the peculiar bearing of the Christian faith,
that unless fully and thoroughly versed in our own, it is
next to impossible not to share the writer's belief in the
excellence of his own religion, over and above that of
any other. In fact no religious work would be worth
reading, if this honest prejudice did not infuse it; for

to bring merely intellect and imagination to bear upon a subject so solemn, to the exclusion of *heart* and feeling, would render it a mere mockery unfitted for the service of either God or man. I have no doubt the indiscriminate reading of these books has increased your idea, that spiritual peace, and strength, and comfort are only to be found amongst Christians; but, dearest Annie, let the experience and the earnest lessons of a Jewess convince you to the contrary. In the constant study of the Word of God you will be very often startled to find, that a similar style of promise, narrative, and spiritual guidance, which you thought were only revealed in the New Testament, were found in ours ages and ages before; and that it is our utter neglect and disregard of these precious things which have so concealed them, as to cause the supposition that they were given to the stranger rather than to us. And is not this dreadful? Should we not do all we possibly can to remove the dross which long, long ages of persecution, and its concomitant mental darkness, have gathered round our purely spiritual faith, and individually prove that it is the study of, the belief in, and love for the Word of our God which will raise us in the scale of being, and give us every privilege, temporal and eternal, which we are told can only be found in the adoption of the Christian creed? Ask any enlightened Protestant, and he will tell you that the actual *doctrines* of belief are of little moment, compared with the *spirit* which he supposes that doctrine breathes, and which the preaching of Jesus and his apostles diffused over a benighted world. And that spirit (but wholly and entirely distinct from doctrines, on the precise nature of which not two congregations could be found to agree as early as the second century after its propagation) had its origin, its influence, its infallibility, in the wider spread and universal acknowledgment of that blessed Word, which for centuries before, for our especial benefit, God had inspired holy men to write.

This is a grave and important consideration, but one to which the serious and enlightened thinker, be his actual creed what it may, will unhesitatingly respond. Alluding to that intense and purely spiritual love of nature which pervades the works of modern poets, and renders them so infinitely superior in warmth and truth to the ancients, one of my favourite authors* thus writes : "Yes! the only difference between modern literature and that of the ancients, lies in our grand advantage over them in this particular. It is from the literature of the BIBLE, and the heirship of immortality laid open to us in it, that we owe our enlarged conceptions of natural beauty, and our quickened affections towards the handiworks of God. We walk about the world as its true heirs, and heirs of far more than it has to give. We walk about in confidence, in love, and in peaceful hopes ; for we know that we are the rightful sons of the house, and that neither death nor distance can interrupt our progress towards the home paradise of the Divine Father."

Christianity must, indeed, be dear to those nations and those individuals, who can enter into the full beauty and truth of this passage, for it has given them the Bible. But who will deny, that the Hebrew had it first, ay, and direct from that God who, when He designated Israel as His son, His first-born, proclaimed himself our "FATHER;" and when He passed before Moses and proclaimed himself "Merciful and gracious,

---

* William Howitt, Rural Life in England, p. 323.

long-suffering, and abundant in goodness and truth, keeping mercy for *thousands*, and visiting iniquity *only* to the third and fourth generation, forgiving iniquity and transgression and sin, and only so chastising, as to deter others from sin;" and again, through David, as one whose mercy is as immeasurable as the heaven is high above the earth, as a father who pities his children, and as far as the East is from the West removeth our transgressions from us,—surely taught us the thrilling truth, that God is Love, ages before the Apostles so simplified His glorious attributes to the duller comprehension of the heathen, as merely to designate Him by those three words? I do not blame the Christian for thinking that to him alone the glorious privilege of Biblical revelation is accorded, if he sees its rightful and original possessors indifferent to, and unhappily sometimes unconscious of, the gift. We cannot wonder, if the Divine Spirit of the Bible *appears* only known to, felt by, and acted on by Christians, that they should fancy a superior dispensation must have been vouchsafed to them, of which we too are ignorant as others; but O! the fault lies in us, not in them,—not, indeed, now as it was; for the word of God is resuming its destined and treasured place amongst us.

This brings me to the point I have touched on before, but which you may perhaps think requires a little farther illustration. I have referred to the non-spirituality of the Spanish and Portuguese Jews of a former generation; but you will think, perhaps, that this reason will not hold good with the families among whom you are at present thrown, as they are not Spanish, and, consequently, are not exposed to the danger surrounding the secret Jews. No,—but the debased and miserable condition, to which, the various and enslaving restrictions of Germany and Prussia subjected their ancestors, had the same degrading and darkening effect. How was it possible that they could obtain anything like elevation of mind, refinement of sentiment, and spirituality, or in more familiar words, poetry of feeling, when doomed to the very lowest and most restricting occupations? The Hebrews of Germany, as in many other countries, were debarred from all intellectual, or even, so to speak, social pursuits, and were confined to certain quarters of certain towns, their sole means of either subsistence or influence that of amassing and lending money, a pursuit of all others the most detrimental to the better part of our mingled nature, the most deadening to every energy and lofty impulse. This, however, was the fault of circumstances, not of individual or national character; but they could not, even in freedom and unshackled by any social restrictions, shake off in fifty, or a hundred years the habits and feelings of ten or twelve centuries. It requires time and that gradual advancement and enlightenment of the mind and species, which liberty and equality engender, to regain the holiness and spirituality, which are so essentially the breath of the religion of the Lord, but of which His just anger at our awful iniquities in the past has, through the treatment of the nations, for a while deprived us. We must remember, too, and draw our conclusions accordingly, that it is only within the last half century, that we have enjoyed even some portion of equality in England; and if we truthfully regard events, we shall find that we, Hebrews of both denominations, Spanish and German, have advanced in all the higher, holier, and refining attributes of man, according as we have been advanced in social consideration. We should remember this, dearest Annie, when we are inclined to draw conclusions disparaging to our own people and in favour of those, who have never been exposed to the enslaving restrictions and persecuting statutes under which we have so long laboured; not that I could wish you to elevate your own nation unduly above others, but only to do it simple justice, and examine *causes* carefully ere you condemn *effects*.

LETTER V.

FROM THE SAME TO THE SAME.

Charge of non-spirituality, promulgated both by Christian and Hebrew against the Jewish religion—Whether founded on truth or on error —Ancient and modern Judaism—An assertion, not a fact—Causes of human additions and their abuse—Distinction between ancient and modern Jews—Superstitious observances of some Jews, not belonging to, or a part of Judaism—Strange notions concerning spirituality—Examination of its real meaning—Mingled nature of man—Opinion of the ancient sages—Four elements, their respective. incitements—Necessity of strict adherence to the word of God— Superiority of simple truth over imaginative speculation—Use of the latter—Intention of Revelation.

I AM not at all surprised, my dearest Annie, at that which you tell me, because I have heard it myself so often; though how, or whence such a mistaken charge originated, is indeed incomprehensible. I allude, as you will of course perceive, to the accusation promulgated against us (and which you have heard repeated) not by Christians alone, but actually by many amongst ourselves, that the Jewish religion is *not* a spiritual religion; and that, therefore, those with whom you are at

present domiciled should think and assert it, cannot
astonish me in the least. We will try if we can discover
whether it is founded on truth or error. I am the more
encouraged to do this, from the deep and thankful joy
which your answer to my last has given me: "That it
did not tire you in the least, but gave you so much to
think about, it seemed to draw you out of yourself, and
make you happier." My own darling Annie, if there be
a portion of peace in the words of an erring fellow-mortal,
how inexpressibly will it deepen and increase as your
impressions on the necessity and comfort of religion
become more fixed, and gradually lead you to that
unerring Word which "never faileth, but giveth the
waters of eternal life to all who thirst."

Concerning this mistaken charge of non-spirituality in
a religion which proceeded from the mouth of God himself, that God whom we only know as a SPIRIT, without
form or substance, a pure essence pervading heaven and
earth, and whom we are expressly commanded to
worship in *spirit* and in truth, it appears to me that
Christians have adopted and asserted it, simply from the
mistaken supposition that modern Judaism is distinct
from ancient Judaism, and that we *now* receive and
follow the ordinances and superstitions of man, in lieu
of the words of the living God. They suppose this
partly from observation, and partly from the received,
but yet erroneous, assertions of books. Now, there is
no such thing as ancient and modern Judaism. Judaism
is the religion which God gave to his people Israel
through Moses, and which was to last through all ages
and for ever. It can be neither altered nor abolished,
neither modified nor improved. When our opponents
bring forward the constantly reiterated assertion, that
the Hebrews have mingled all sorts of petty and enslaving

customs and binding forms, which we cannot find in the Word of God, I answer, "It is quite true;" but human weakness and human error cannot tarnish the intrinsic beauty, nor interfere with the ordained perpetuity of the Mosaic system. And if we examine the origin of these human additions, we shall find that they proceed from the intense desire of our ancient sages to preserve the undying spark of religion alive within us by means of outward ordinances, which, by their constant occurrence, would bring our Creator to our thoughts, when, from slavery and misery, we were debarred from all more spiritual communion. At first, indeed, the outward ordinance was sanctified, and vitalised, by the inward aspiration; but, as time rolled on, sinking us deeper and deeper into the abyss of wretchedness, through persecution and its natural consequences, ignorance and superstition, the very word of our God being constantly denied us, was it either strange or unnatural that men, still ardently attached to the name of Israel, and dying by thousands for their faithful adherence to the only spiritual truth which they could enshrine and comprehend, the Unity of God, should cling to the forms instituted by their sages, and at length surround them with a divinity and glory not their own? and that their being able to obey and follow them alone, to the exclusion of the more spiritual ordinances of the Lord, should lead them in their mistaken, but very pardonable darkness, to place them on an equality with, and then gradually *before*, the changeless statutes of the living God? It was comparatively easy to hurry over a Hebrew blessing at certain periods of the day, and to obey certain forms; but it was far more difficult to realise the innumerable duties, feelings, and thoughts included in these thrilling words, "Thou shalt love the Lord thy God with all thy heart, with all thy soul, and with all thy might;"* "Thou shalt love thy neighbour as thyself;"† "Thou shalt not avenge nor bear any grudge."‡ It was barely possible, in the debased state in which the mass were sunk, to comprehend the sublime truths and spiritual doctrines of all the prophets; and therefore is it that the *religion* is charged with becoming a lifeless form and mere human will-worship, when, in fact, the semblance of such, for semblance alone it was, originated in the effect of persecution on the mind, *not* in the imperfect nature of our creed.

All true Hebrews and, in fact, all right-thinking Christians must deny the assertion of an ancient and a modern *Judaism;* but, my dear Annie, I quite allow that there is a distinction between ancient and modern *Jews.* That distinction has, indeed, been brought about by the circumstances so often reverted to; but it *nevertheless does* exist. To the ancient Israelites our God was revealed, face to face, if we may so speak, without irreverence. He brought them out of Egypt with a mighty arm and an outstretched hand; displayed before them miracles and wonders, which He only could perform; gave them His law amidst such awful demonstration of His stupendous power, that all beheld and believed; spoke to them in all the varied epochs of which we read in His holy word, spreading over some three thousand five hundred years, through men chosen and inspired for the office, so that we may say, they were in direct communication, through selected individuals, with their Father in heaven, even in times of the most awful national iniquity. He had called them His own. For the sake of His beloved servant Abraham, the faithful, He set apart his descendants to receive and

---

* Deut. vi. 5. † Levit. xix. 18. ‡ Ibid.

propagate a revelation, which was gradually to bring the whole world to a knowledge of, and obedience to, the Lord. Their own sins, constant unbelief, and repeated desertion of the Divine Law could not interfere with the furtherance of this gracious and unchanging purpose. They, indeed, brought down on themselves, both individually and nationally, the wrath of the Eternal, threatened already and from the first delivery of the Law, if they disobeyed; but His promise to Abraham, that in his seed all the nations of the earth should be blessed, by a knowledge of the Lord and His Commandments, was and is fulfilled, equally in their *dispersion*, as in their exclusive election in the Holy Land.

The ancient Hebrews were the sole repositaries of Revelation. Fewer in actual number than any of the heathen nations, their only territory, a portion of the world so small that, compared with the dominions of heathen princes, it would be scarcely larger than the smallest county of England compared with the whole of the British Isles,—yet in that small spot of earth the God of a thousand worlds had set up His one temple, and was worshipped according to the spirit and the ordinances which His infinite mercy had instituted, and which were to teach a knowledge of Himself (though darkened and mystified, by the impossibility of men's comprehending, of themselves, the purity and the spiritual doctrine of His Divine Unity) over the whole world. Until national iniquity tempted the Eternal's wrath, we find the Israelites quite undisturbed in the possession of their Holy Land, and preserved entirely distinct, and secure from the revolutions and changes continually occurring in the nations around them. The fame of their revelation spread far and wide; for the interference of the Deity, both nationally and individually, was so strikingly and wonderfully manifested, that even many of the heathens acknowledged His power with awe and reverence; and the word *Hebrew* or *Israelite*, was always associated with a degree of holiness and imagined power, distinct from any other race. .

Such were the ancient Jews,—men in direct communion through their priests and prophets with the Lord,—a selected nation like whom, as the oracles of Revelation, as the witnesses and workers of wonders, as orators and poets, inspired not only by the inward spirit, but the public proclamation of the Lord, to reveal His will and guide His people, there has been, and there is no other, standing apart like a sun, whose rays were to penetrate the darkness around, and transform it into day. And these rays are emanating still, though the fearful crimes and wickedness of the nation have dissolved the sun itself, and scattered its minute particles to the North and to the South, to the East and to the West, to the farthest isles of the sea, to the remotest climes of the land. In every Hebrew there dwells the undying particle of that deathless light, which at the end of days is to reunite, and form again that Sun of Righteousness, under which Israel shall dwell in safety, and the whole world acknowledge the ONE sole God.

The grand distinction, then, between the ancient and the modern Jews, is that the former were *visibly* the holy people of the Lord, the receivers and promulgators of the knowledge of Himself: while the latter, equally His holy people, equally His witnesses, are yet the persecuted of a world and, as such, tossed amongst and mingled with the nations, scarcely able to recognize themselves as the same people who were the chosen of the Past, and regarded by every other faith as a race abandoned and utterly cast off, and left by the wrath of the Eternal so entirely to the imaginations of their own evil hearts, as to have no claim whatever upon Him, save by embracing another creed.

And this is the great error, which we must guard against. There *is not* the difference they assert. The Mosaic religion, as taught and revealed in God's word, is as imperatively binding on the modern, as it ever was on the ancient Jews, and that it *appears* not to be so is the fault of circumstances before alluded to, but which can have no weight in our consideration of the question, "whether the Jewish religion be spiritual or not?" I grant (and with deep regret that there should be such a fact to grant), that in many parts of the world, particularly Poland, Gibraltar, Barbary, and Palestine itself, there are Jews, whose religion is so tarnished with superstitious notions, extraordinary forms and narrowing ordinances, for whose existence or even foundation we look through the law of Moses entirely in vain, that it might give a colouring to the idea, that there *is* no similitude between ancient and modern Judaism. But such changes are the simple effect of human error, and cannot bear upon the question at issue. If we ask an enlightened Protestant, whether he recognises in the strange superstitions of the Greek Church, or even in the apparent image-worship of the Catholic, the pure religion of Jesus, he would decidedly answer in the negative. Is it not then quite as unfair and erroneous to judge of the spirituality or non-spirituality of our religion, by the superstition of certain modern Jews, as it would be for us to judge the purity and spirituality of the Christian faith, by the Christians of Russia and of Spain?

I am quite certain, that were the subject placed in

this light before enlightened Christians, they would unhesitatingly withdraw their charge, and agree that
human error cannot interfere with or change the spirit
of a system organized by God Himself; so that they are
not justified in burdening JUDAISM with the sometime
superstition, sometime indifference, and but too often
utter want of nationality, in the modern JEWS.

Christians would grant this : nay, the very charge is
excusable in them, drawing conclusions as they must do,
so often from appearances. But what can we say for
those who amongst ourselves can assert any thing so
absolutely and scripturally, and even talmudically false,
as the non-spirituality of their thrice holy faith?   It is
to me so marvellous, so incomprehensible, that any Jew
can read his Bible and its commentaries, by many of
our earliest sages, and yet believe this, that the only
possible way to explain it is the supposition, that he
actually cannot know the meaning of the word *spirituality*, and, by a strange mystification of ideas, associates
it with the mere doctrines of the Christian creed, particularly that of the " Holy Ghost," and so rejects it as
anti-Jewish, and tending to mislead him. This is the
only tangible and rational reason I can find for this
extraordinary error, which I have known take possession
of some minds so strongly, that the very word " spirit,"
or " spirit of God," even in only a poem, terrifies them
from the perusal, or causes its condemnation as too
Christian for the approval of any Jewish mind.

Grieved indeed should I be, if any one were to attempt
to impregnate your mind with these mistaken notions.
Full of poetry and feeling as it is, the very idea that the
Jewish religion consisted only in obedience to certain
laws, would terrify you away from it to another, where
your high and earnest aspirations might find vent.   But

I trust to prove to you how utterly unfounded is the charge, how completely every form and ordinance of our holy faith, even those instituted after our dispersion, which we are permitted to obey since the sacrifices and temple-service ceased, must be infused with that vital breath of piety, which is in fact the essence of spirituality, to mark it as an accepted offering, or rejected mockery in His sight, for whom it is observed.

We will first examine the real meaning of this often quoted word. I need not remind you of the mingled nature in which it pleased our Creator to form man, that we are expressly told in Holy Writ, " that the Lord God formed man of the *dust of the ground,* and breathed into his nostrils the *breath of life."* And from this breath man became a *living soul,* an utterly distinct creation from all which had gone before; for God merely *spoke* to the waters, and the earth, and the air, and on the instant they teemed with *life;* but the gift of the LIVING SOUL was for man alone, and imparted by the *breath* of his Creator. It is this undying soul, or spirit, which unites man with the Deity, and so utterly divides him from all other animated creatures. The existence of this spirit would, were it separated entirely from its clayey tabernacle, be an existence of love, and purity, and adoration, similar to that of the angels and ministers of heaven.

The earthly body in which it is enclosed, our ancient sages declare to be composed of the four elements which are the component parts of this, our terrestrial world— fire, earth, air, and water—" the nature and tendency of which are opposed to each other; but by the word of God peace reigneth amongst them and maintaineth their existence. When, however, the termination of our earthly existence arrives, He withdraws that peace, the various elements degenerate into their natural discord and opposition, and soon destroy the body, which returns to the earth, whilst the spirit returns to the God who placed it therein."* This is a curious and ingenious commentary on the simple words of Scripture, telling us that God made man of the dust of the earth, and perhaps was needless for a simple explanation, but knowing your discursive and imaginative mind, the idea is more likely to do you good than harm.

The element of FIRE, they say, incites "pride, overbearing, haughtiness, wrath, envy, jealousy, covetousness and ambition," all those passions which, if encouraged, "*burn* as a continual fire within us," *consume* every higher feeling, and embitter our whole *inward* life, however the outer one may seem prosperous and happy. The element of AIR tends to all those petty levities and abuses of speech, which, though only *words* conveyed to and fro by the BREATH or *air*, do so much mischief, not merely in our social intercourse, but to our own souls, in engendering many vices which God condemns. The mischief produced by *words* is incalculable, and even more dangerous than that by actions. The latter we can guard against: the former is invisible and impalpable, but most deadly. How much of discord is produced in families who ought to be so united, how much of angry feeling inflamed, how often coolness and separation between intimate friends are engendered and widened, how constantly is enmity excited, all from WORDS which, if we could but examine or enquire into their foundation, would literally dissolve into nothing! But once spoken, who can recall them, or who can remove the sting, which sometimes even simply an un-

---

* Four Sermons by Rabbi Abraham Belais.

guarded expression will produce? The slanderer, the calumniator, the liar, even the prevaricator, characters the most despicable and the most mischievous, are all produced by *words*, merely words; and these, our ancient sages say, are the offspring of air. FIRE excites the inward feeling of sin, to which AIR gives words.

The third element is less satisfactory to my ideas than the previous ones and the fourth; but I will record it notwithstanding. WATER, they say, incites the mercenary craving for worldly treasures and pleasures, which overwhelm us by a *torrent*, and excite to innumerable meannesses in money transactions, taking bribes, and oppressing the poor and unprotected, necessarily causing the transgression of such commands, as " Thou shalt not steal," " Thou shalt not covet," " Thou shalt not oppress," " Thou shalt not take usury." What these peculiar vices have to do with, or how they can originate in, the element of water, our sages may perhaps satisfactorily for themselves explain; but to me the idea is rather unfounded, even in an Eastern imagination, which allows greater license than any other. They are much more likely to originate in the influence of the fourth element, EARTH, which, they say, incites to indolence and laziness in work, a contented acquiescence with merely an *animal* nature, and, as the natural consequence, a distaste and indifference, if not actual repugnance to the service of God, and the consideration of all serious things, shrinking from prayer and thanksgiving, considering attendance and offerings at the house of God a burdensome and wearying task, and engendering all the vices and miseries thence proceeding. This is, indeed, the natural effect of a mere earthly nature. The breath or spirit which God breathed into man, and so made him a living soul, is the only distinction between us and the

beasts of the field. If that immortal spirit be so deadened and silenced within us, as to have neither voice nor .
power: it follows that we must become like the mere
animals, and utterly incapable of a lofty aspiration, pure
desire and heavenly thought. The less the spirit works
within us, the more do we give ourselves up to those
enervating indulgences and those animal pleasures
which, though perhaps not actual vice at first (if the
neglect of the precious gifts intrusted to us can ever be
anything else), sink us deeper and deeper into the vortex of dissipation, and sin must follow. The more this
earthly nature is allowed to predominate, the less inclination and the less power have we to exercise and cultivate the intellect or mind; and the cultivation of the
MIND, if united with the right government of the HEART,
is the surest and best method of the elevation of the
spirit above the body, as our God ordained.

The theory of the four elements, as combined in the
body of man, I do not at all fancy you will quarrel with,
my dear Annie; only remember, that the Scriptural
account of the creation, which must be received as the
only divine account, and therefore the only one demanding our implicit belief, is " that God formed man out of
the dust of the earth, and breathed into his nostrils the
breath of life." I am earnest on this point; because a
mind like yours, unless carefully regulated, and always
referred to the unchangeable Word of God Himself, is
likely sometimes so to wander in the alluring and pleasant fields of the imagination, as at length to lose itself
in the endless labyrinth of conjecture, and find neither
rest nor comfort in the simple record which the Bible
gives; and, believe me, it is only TRUTH which will support us in affliction, and guide us steadily forward in
prosperity and peace.

Speculation is well for health and leisure, truth may seem too stern and simple then; but come sickness, come sorrow, and O how gratefully we welcome her angel form! Not that I would either check or condemn imagination, I value it too highly as a precious gift from God Himself, and I think those thrice blessed on whom it is bestowed. That it may be a dangerous gift I grant; so is beauty, so are riches, so is successful ambition; but we do not value these therefore the less, nor withhold our children from seeking their possession. Blessings and gifts are dangerous, not in *themselves*, but in their *abuse*. If we carefully train the heart, and urge and guide the mind to love truth yet more than fancy, we need never fear the undue influence of the imagination. It will, as it was intended, make us infinitely happier, ay and better, but never lead us wrong.

The ancient sages, whose notions we have been considering, used both their capacious intellect and their peculiarly *vivid* imagination, in illustrating certain simple texts, so as familiarly to instruct and delight the masses of their countrymen. They never intended these various illustrations and commentaries to take the place of that venerable Word, which was their foundation, but merely as an intellectual exercise to amplify and define.

Whether or not we agree in the idea of the four elements, this simple fact is evident, that we are composed of two natures, and that, would we seek to become deserving of the love and favour of our Father who, when He breathed His essence within us, destined us for happiness, and virtue, and immortality, we *must* give the spirit greater ascendency than the earthly; and to do this is the intention of all Revelation; the seeking it is to be SPIRITUAL, and the peculiar frame of heart and mind which it produces is SPIRITUALITY.

Is it likely, then, that the very religion, which God in His mercy revealed to man, should be deficient in the one important point which is the aim of all? Even earthly lawgivers invent codes which will secure, or which seek to secure, as far as their limited understandings will go, the elevation and bettering—in other words the spiritualising—of their species, by regarding and punishing every earthly propensity, when it injures a fellow-being, as a crime against the state. Would our God do less? or reveal a law, obedience to which deadened the spirit and vivified the animal? It is almost impious to suppose it; but my letter has grown to such an unconscionable length, that we will leave the farther consideration of this momentous subject till my next.

LETTER VI.

FROM THE SAME TO THE SAME.

Farther doubts—Charity towards every creed—Examination of the
nature of the sin we commit in leaving one faith for another without
examination—Error of believing the word Bible synonymous with
the Pentateuch—The latter not sufficient of itself to prove the
spirituality of Judaism—First command of Judaism, and its first
doctrine of belief, compared with the opinions of contemporary nations—Its simplicity and yet inconceivable vastness—Groundwork
of Judaism essentially spiritual; its vast importance in the first
ages, difficulty of acquirement—Hebrews at the period of the
Exodus not a spiritual people—Intention of the law—Workings
and intent of Christianity and Mahomedanism—Review of the progress of natural religion—How far it was possible to advance without Revelation—Fearful effect of indifference—Alleged absence of
prejudice of the purely Divine authority for, and acknowledged necessity of, the doctrine of unity.

You tell me, dearest Annie, you are quite clear now
as to the real meaning and the real intent of spirituality,
and that my communications on that subject interested
you more deeply than you can express. You entreat
me to *prove* that our holy religion is spiritual, as I feel
it, and say that you have heard and read, that no book
of divinity can be spiritual, unless it explain the Old
Testament by the light of the New, and that the revelation on Mount Sinai was one of fire and blood, consist-
ing merely of types and shadows of the purer light to
come, not being perpetual, or a reality in itself: that
such thoughts will come, and you cannot answer them.
Nor am I at all astonished that they should come. Your
mind is at present in a state of restless inquiry, and

things, even sentences, which you may have read, or even merely heard in a more quiescent temper, and have then forgotten, return to perplex and unsettle you. You tell me, too, that you were much struck with the verses I have quoted at different times, they seemed so exactly the comfort that you wanted; but you always supposed that they came from the New, not the Old Testament, and were, especially, the privileged possession of Christians, as they were so frequently quoted in Christian books, and those of your own people, with whom you have ventured to speak on the subject, knew nothing about them. Again let me warn you, my dear girl: do *not* judge of the Jewish religion, or of the Jewish people, by the very few whom you happen to know; but always remember there are *nominal* members of every creed, and that, were your circle wider, you would find nominal Christians exceeding the number of nominal Jews, and so divided amongst themselves, that, were you really bent upon deserting your faith, which I do not believe you are, you would find it difficult to decide which of these various thinkers and speculators it would be safest and best to join. I do not write this from any feeling of disrespect or uncharitableness; as conscience dictates, so it is right to worship; and if our Father in heaven looks with an eye of love, and has compassion on *all* His creatures, bearing with error itself in the mode of service for the sake of the love and zeal borne towards Himself, how dare we, weak, finite mortals of a day, judge harshly of one another? My only wish is to remove a degree of prejudice which has arisen (from circumstances) in your mind against your own people, and which, therefore, inclines you to love another better. You will very probably ask me, if I consider all religions alike in the sight of our Father in. heaven, and the earnest worshippers of each equally acceptable to Him, why am I so desirous that you should remain a Jewess? Because, dearest Annie, it is a widely different thing to be earnest and faithful to the creed we have imbibed from infancy, to deserting it, without examination, for another. To assert that which in our own hearts we disbelieve, even before man's tribunal, is a fearful sacrilege; what must it be when such a false proceeding rests between our own consciences and an all-seeing, all-penetrating God? He has told us in His Word such and such things are truth, and must be observed perpetually. If we neither know, nor desire to know, anything of these solemn truths, how can we, without falsehood, say we *disbelieve* them, which, if we adopt and make public profession of belief in a new revelation, we must do, though we may not actually say so in distinct words? To believe or disbelieve a narrative, we certainly ought to know every part of it. How foolish we should seem, to declare that we do not believe one account, and adopt another, without knowing anything of either. Even in the common occurrences of life, this proceeding would expose us to laughter and contempt. How much more solemn then it becomes, when it relates to our position with our heavenly Father, and our destiny through all eternity! It is for this reason, and feeling the heavy responsibility devolved on me to watch and guard you, that I so earnestly entreat you to examine your own faith. If, when you have stated every doubt and prejudice, my answers fail to make manifest the fulness, and the comfort, and the beauty of our spiritual faith; if, after due and patient examination, your heart and mind shall decide in favour of the Christian: I will not keep you back, grievous as it would be that so wide a barrier were flung between us. Annie, darling, the peace of your conscience is more unutterably precious, than my transitory joy. If, indeed, the Jewish religion is not enough to satisfy your yearning affections, fill your aspiring mind with adoration, comfort every sorrow, enhance every pleasure, and so point with light-clad finger to the immortal spirit's eternal home, that the very darkness of the grave becomes illumined : then, dearest, seek another and more satisfying creed; but oh! do not decide on this, till you have proved the revelations of your God to Moses imperfect, His Word untrue.

The study of the Law *alone*, as distinct and wholly unconnected with the Prophets, I acknowledge will not satisfy our longings for a *spiritual* religion; because, though even there, there are very many verses and statutes of a purely spiritual nature, we might be apt, in the imperfection of our wisdom, to overlook them, in the *seemingly* more important ordinances, which demanded, if I may so speak, *palpable* and visible obedience. The historical and prophetic books give us the real *spirit of the Law*, instruct us as to the *feeling* and *temper* which would render the sacrifices and other formal observances acceptable to Him, who is a spirit in Himself, and whose essence fills the universe. But then the Bible must not be considered, as it unfortunately too often is, synonymous *only* with the Pentateuch. The same Almighty and Merciful Being who inspired Moses to write those five books, inspired other holy men to write the remainder, and, in consequence, one part is quite as holy and quite as binding as the other.

The very first command in the Jewish ritual is belief in the unity of God. His proclaiming himself to His people as the one sole Deity, without division either in form or essence, as a Spirit filling heaven and earth, a

jealous God, prohibiting the worship of any other, marking the maker of idols as subject to His wrath and the
judgment of His law, was in itself a groundwork, or
frame, of spirituality, the extent of which can only be
realized, by a glance over the worship and belief of every
other nation. Even Plato, one of the wisest and purest
thinkers, and Aristotle, a philosopher equally renowned,
could not arrive at such a pitch of exalted spirituality
as to embrace the pure doctrine of Unity, which the
most ignorant amongst the Hebrews grasped and believed. It seems as if the idea of the omniscience, the
omnipotence, and the ubiquity of the Deity were beyond
the range of even their extraordinary intellect; and they
composed a theory of the Logos, and the spirit thence
proceeding, dividing and yet uniting the Godhead, in a
manner remarkably, though not exactly, similar to the
Trinity of the Christians. It is impossible to study
their curious theory, without being struck by the evident
incapability for the human mind, however richly gifted,
to attain, without divine revelation, belief in the purely
spiritual doctrine of the Unity of God. Here are men
whose marvellous wisdom had raised them so far above
their age, that they believed in a Spirit, or Godhead, far
superior to the idols to which the masses bowed down,
and beheld, faintly gleaming indeed, but still distinct,
the fact of our Immortality: yet the one omniscient and
ubiquitous God of the Hebrews was to them incomprehensible; and they, therefore, set up a theory which, by
dividing his essence, seemed to endow Him with greater
power than as One alone.

Accustomed from our infancy to repeat our belief that
"the Lord our God, the Lord is ONE," we are not in the
very least aware how much of spirituality is included in
that brief sentence. Nor, in fact, can we realize it, un-

less we look back on the extraordinary worship of the
heathen nations from whom we were delivered, and the
strange and varied religions (so to speak) which even at
this present day characterise the savage inhabitants of
Asia, Africa, and America, on whom the light of revelation has not yet dawned.   Even in these the *spirit* craves
for something beyond itself, and so they bow down to
the sun, or moon, or stars, or images embodying some
aspirations of their own imaginings.   But the idea of
the God of the Hebrews is too sublime, too purely
spiritual, to be received without direct revelation.   We
do not regard it thus; because, having been handed
down from generation to generation through the apparent instrumentality of man, we forget WHENCE it
originally proceeded—from the mouth of God Himself.
In its simple truth, "there is but one God," a child can
believe, and understand it.   In the vastness, the concentration of attributes, the marvellous truths which the
idea combines, it is a subject impossible to be attained
in all its fulness, save by the most spiritual, the purest,
the wisest, and yet the humblest of men.   Thought
loses itself in the immensity of the contemplation.   The
purest intellect, the most vivid imagination, *cannot* embrace all the perfections, all the combinations of what
we are apt to consider contradictory attributes, such as
unswerving justice and yet unfathomable mercy; prescience in the Deity, yet free will in man; omniscience,
not of this one little world, but of the hundred other
systems which roll round us, visible only as the lights
of night; omnipotence, at one and the same moment,
to guide the hearts and actions of millions and millions
of human beings, each apparently following his own
inclinations and his own passions, to further God's own
immortal will; ubiquity, to fill heaven and earth, every-

where at the same moment, yet with each individual, as caring for him alone; combining in Himself mercy, wisdom, might, the perfection and concentration of glory; the pure light, in whose light alone we shall see light; the Spirit, from whose inspiration all our best actions spring; the Fountain of life, whence life shall flow for us everlastingly; salvation to all who look to and believe in Him;

> " A ' refuge' for all in the tempest of life,
> A ' shadow from heat' and a ' fortress in strife,'
> The ' strong habitation' where all may resort,
> The ' rock' which for ages the faithful have sought;"

the sole One who was, is, and ever will be. In the mere enumeration of these attributes, these varied designations to bring down the incomprehensible majesty of the Eternal to the feeble conceptions of man, thought becomes bewildered, and the brain actually aches in the vain desire to penetrate the infinite. How then could the mere human nature of man comprehend the mighty theme? how, even the immortal spirit, unless it had been revealed? And how can any one deny, that, regarded thus, even the doctrine of Unity, simple in its element as it is, becomes inconceivable, even to the most spiritual nature? and therefore, that to believe in the Eternal, as He is revealed in His word, demands the acquirement and encouragement of that peculiar temper of the mind, which in my last letter I defined as spirituality?

You see, then, that the very groundwork of our religion, the acknowledgment of and belief in one God, is essentially a spiritual principle. Its vast importance is proved by the constant care of Moses, and all the succeeding prophets, to preserve the people from the infection of idolatry; and the great difficulty of acquiring it, is marked by the continual relapses of the nation into the visible worship of images. Humanity had not attained that perfection, which would enable it to distinguish its twofold nature, and deaden the earthly by the superiority of the spiritual. For Abraham's sake, God selected a people who would be enabled to do this, by a Divine revelation; but they required time, prepared as they were by such startling and awful manifestations of the still invisible Being, who was henceforth to be their sole object of adoration. The Israelites who quitted Egypt were not a spiritual people; they could not be; for suffering and bodily misery had deadened every purer aspiration, and made them long for mere physical relief. But the law was given to make them spiritual; and, through them, to extend the same exalted feeling over the whole world; and this beneficent intention is working even now. Christianity and Mahomedanism are both labouring towards the same end; and both these great religious systems proceed from ours. Yet, far advanced as they are in bringing all nations to a knowledge of the Lord, still, even they have not yet attained to the pure spiritual doctrine of the Jew. True, the disciples of Mahomed believe in, and three times each day declare, "There is but one God;" but that belief is so blended with a strange imagining of heaven, the spiritual idea of immortality so clothed with the peculiar delights of eastern desires, that it is impossible for the Hebrew to imagine for a single moment the attributes of the one God of Mahomed can be the same as those revealed by Moses, even though we believe, from our inmost heart, that Mahomedanism, even as every other religion, is working the will of the Eternal, in *preparing* all people for that blessed day, when the *veil shall be re-*

*moved from all nations, and the covering cast over all
people shall be destroyed.* Christianity, again, approaching infinitely nearer to us in its spirit and its laws, and
acknowledging the same guiding book, and therefore
the same God, far advanced as it is in spirituality and
enlightenment, and in holding forth many a bright example to us of true and beautiful piety, still, even it
cannot embrace the doctrine of the one sole indivisible
God, cannot realise the perfection and unity of His attributes, without the intervention of a mediator and a
holy spirit, distinct from, yet united to Himself. It
often appears strange, that, where we have so much, so
very much in common, the Christian idea of the Godhead should be so distinct from that of the Hebrew;
that, where a religious system has advanced so *very* near
the sublimest truth, it should yet pause, incomplete, and
present a stumbling-block, which the enlightened Jew
can never over-leap. It would appear still more strange,
if I did not firmly believe it ordained in fulfilment of
that word, which has declared, we should be a distinct
people for ever, and which (humanly speaking) would be
still more difficult of accomplishment, if the Christian
idea of the Eternal were in all points like our own.

This has been, I fear, but a grave, perhaps uninteresting discussion, dearest Annie; but it is necessary in
the examination of a question so important as the spirituality or non-spirituality of a religion, to begin from
the very beginning. It would be an interesting task to
trace the advance of natural religion, from the savage
who creates images, bringing, as it were, his gods, or
mental ideas, before his sight. Then comes the worship
of some species of animal: witness the idols of Egypt.
In both of these, we see the supremacy of the senses, to
the utter silencing and deadening of the spirit; for this

idol-worship was always accompanied by rites and ceremonies of an obscene and brutal nature. Then, a step
in advance, came the worship of the sun, and moon, and
stars, far more intellectual than the last, both in the
actual objects of adoration and the mode of worship.
Then came the belief of a great Spirit, an invisible but
all-pervading Deity, and objects of creation were worshipped only as His emblems. Zoroäster taught the
doctrine of an infinite God; but unable to attain the sublime idea revealed to the Hebrews, he circumscribed
and bounded the Eternal power, by the introduction of
two equally great, but antagonistic principles—Ormuz,
the principle of good, of which light was the type, and
Ariman, the lord of evil, whose emblem was darkness.
Here we see a very great advance towards a spiritual
worship, that is, the inculcation of principles to which
the inward spirit, not the outward senses, can respond;
but, from its being merely the invention of man, seeing
the light at a great distance, and from the infirmities
and weakness of his finite existence, he was unable to
grasp it in its perfected fulness. Very soon after Zoroäster's death even this spiritual advance merged into a
species of idolatry. From being taught to venerate light
as the type of the Spirit of Good, it became itself the
object of worship; and the adoration of fire followed.
The highest grade to which unrevealed religion can attain, is the belief in an all-pervading Spirit, and in His
employing certain inferior spirits of good and evil to em-
body His attributes and execute His will. This was the
worship of many of the European nations before the
spreading of Christianity, and it is the religion now of
many American Indian tribes. This is demanding more
from the spiritual and intellectual part of man than the
worship of certain portions of creation; because, in the

latter worship, its objects were visible and *palpable* to bodily sense; and in the former, imagination, the peculiar attribute of our spiritual nature, alone could give them life, and verify belief. This was as far as man of himself could attain; and we see the wide distinction between such an idea of the Deity, and that which He Himself revealed to Moses. I have already called your attention to the principles of the two great systems, Christianity and Mahomedanism, which, grafted on the Mosaic revelation, have been permitted so to spread over the earth, as to forget their origin and believe in individual infallibility, and in the utter rejection of that people and that law, without whom both systems must fall meaningless to the ground. And surely we Hebrews must feel and acknowledge, that the Divine Unity revealed to Moses, clothed as it was with such soul-speaking, consoling, encouraging attributes as we have before quoted, and dilated upon with, if possible, even still greater fulness by the later prophets, is the sublimest, most purely spiritual, most truly exalted notion of the Deity to which man, while on earth, can. attain; utterly inconceivable to him unless Divinely revealed, and impossible to be realised in its perfection of extent and glory, unless the spirit is elevated above the outward senses, and the immortal soul is allowed voice and communion with the Fountain of living waters whence it originally came, and which, by means of Revelation, purifies it, or at least places in its power the means of purifying, for a return unto Himself. Of course, Christians will say this is mere prejudice in favour of my own, and it may be; but still what would my religion be worth, if it were not? Reverence towards, and conviction of the truth of our own, in no way implies disrespect towards others. Those who entertain the same prejudice in favour of their own, as I do towards mine, believe me, dearest Annie, I respect and even love; for there is a bond of sympathy between us, which the mere free-thinker never can attain.

Of all characters, the most dangerous associates for the young are those, who declare themselves free from prejudice on any one topic, especially on matters of religion. Specious and plausible, they may take our resting-point from us, but they give us none on which to rest, in return; and instead of having *no* prejudices, they are more prejudiced than any, and for the most fearful of all doctrines, that of unbelief. Indifferent to all, they examine none; and what must follow, but their adopting a religion (so to speak) of their own imaginings, and plunging into all the miseries, contradictions, and perplexities of mere deism? That I am not prejudiced in favour of the sublime doctrine of Unity, without reason, is, however, proved by the very simple fact, that it is considered so important an element of religion founded on Revelation, that the Trinitarian himself believes in it, and would feel it the greatest insult to assert that his religion inculcates a plurality of gods, or division in the essence of the Holy One. The reconciliation of Trinity and Unity is the grand mystery of the Christian faith, with which we have nothing to do. I only refer to it, to prove to you, that the sublime idea of Divine Unity revealed by Moses, is equally acknowledged by Christians, though, from the peculiar reading of the same texts to which they are accustomed from earliest childhood, they cannot realise its fulness and completeness in itself, as that ancient people to whom it was by God Himself revealed.

LETTER VII.

FROM THE SAME TO THE SAME.

Powers of comprehension increase by exercise—Uses of sorrow—Second grand principle of Judaism equally spiritual as the first—Love even for a fellow-mortal, a spiritual feeling—Adoration the highest grade of love—Its definition—Effects of the law, if fully obeyed—Gradual preparation for the command to love God—Its disobedience causing sin—Love of God and love of man, proved to have the same spiritual origin—Love for the absent—A link between spirit and spirit—Vast importance of obedience to the command, "thou shalt love the Lord thy God"—Its comfort as a sustaining principle, especially to woman.

I AM very much pleased with your letter, my dear Annie. It is written with that open candid spirit, I so loved in your childhood, blended with that advance of mind and intellect, which I felt sure would be yours in youth. I am not at all astonished that you are surprised at yourself, that your powers of comprehension and thought seem so deepened and extended, and that the consciousness of this change makes you so much happier. A trial fearful as yours, and on such a disposition, could not fail, at first, to stagnate every mental as well as physical energy, and utterly disincline you for those lighter avocations and amusements, which you alone thought about before. Without some powerful impulse, this disinclination would have sunk into listlessness and indifference; your sweet disposition has saved you from this, by urging you to listen to the voice of affection, even though at first it seemed to speak harshly and uncongenially. You have, indeed, begun to think (human

love would say) too soon by many many years; and my
heart is full of tears, when I think how early your sweet
flowers of youth have faded; but I know this is a wrong
regret, my beloved Annie.   Deeply as I love you, earnestly, and by any sacrifice, as I would have guarded you
from all sorrow or care, yet our Father loves you more;
and if He has seen fit to try you thus, how may I repine?
Though life may not be to you again, as it seems in
the first beautiful freshness of our earliest youth, it will
have deeper, purer, more lasting joys.   Its very pleasures of seemingly a trivial and social kind (for you will
take pleasure even in trifles again, though you now feel
as if you never could) will be enjoyed with more zest
and depth, though more quietly than in former years.
The principles which, in a right mind and well regulated
heart, sorrow instils, will shed a light and beauty over
the simplest thought.   The teacher is, indeed, sad and
stern, and in her actual presence we can but weep and
feel; but when she has departed, leaving but the pressure of her hand on our heart, the trace of her step in
the decreased buoyancy of ours, we acknowledge that it
was indeed an angel friend, and bless the thoughts and
powers which she has left.   You are beginning to feel
this, dearest Annie, though but faintly, for her presence
is still with you; and in the stern bestower of suffering
how can we recognise the Angel of Mercy?   But let
time pass, and the wound be healed, and you will regard
her as I do.

You tell me you never thought of the doctrine of
unity before, as I have brought it to your mind, and you
are much struck with it; that the idea of one God appears such a very simple and easily conceived belief;
but that the ideas which seemed to flash into being from
the perusal of my letter, almost bewildered you with

their vastness and comprehensiveness; and that you quite felt, that the very first principle of Judaism adapted itself to the spiritual and intellectual part of our nature, and if studied and considered as it ought to be, must check the too great indulgence of mere sensual pursuits. The very next grand sustaining principle uphold the first. We are first instructed in the pure spirituality of the Divinity whom we are commanded to worship, and then desired to love Him, with all our heart, and soul, and might. And this is a command *impossible* to be obeyed by a mere earthly nature. The very affection we bear to a mortal has its seat in the soul. In its depth, its endurance, its unselfishness, or rather in the self-abnegation it inspires, in the mighty conquests, the earnest striving after some perfection, for the sake of a beloved one, all of which are included in the feeling of love, we read its spiritual and immortal nature. It is utterly and wholly distinct from mere sensuality. To realise love in its purity and fulness, it must be excited towards a being, either actually higher, and purer, and better than ourselves, or towards one whom our imagination has gifted with such attributes, and round whom we have thrown a halo not his own, but which dwells in our own souls and more spiritual nature, and so yearns to find a vent. We may caress beings lower than ourselves; we may like even mere animate things; but we cannot *love*, in the real meaning of the word, either one or the other. You will ask me, perhaps, what then is the feeling we bear towards children and young people? Love, undoubtedly; but love for the immortal, and the intellectual, and the exquisite beauty of sentiment and guileless truth which, if love is called towards them by other than their natural relations, we may be sure they possess. Even here, it is still a spiritual principle, acknowledging and loving the image of God in His infant and youthful creation, unrecognised, perhaps, indeed as such, but proved to be such by the fact, that lower natures never experience such an emotion, and children (except their own) are rather annoyances than objects of love, and youth, with its pure, fresh, springy feelings and inquiring mind, is entirely misunderstood. You may be sure, dearest Annie, when we do really love children and young people, there is something to reverence as well as to caress. The outward form may call for the caress; but the internal spirit alone can inspire reverence. In what are children our inferiors, except in experience, the sad, stern teacher which affection would avert from them as long as possible? Have they not the same immortal souls, the same human nature, the same capabilities of joy and suffering, which will produce the same results? and far, far more disinterestedness, and guilelessness that even thinks no evil, and lofty impulses and kindly actions, than those of older and, in worldly parlance, wiser years? Even in the love warmly excited towards children and youth, then, it is *spirit* attracted towards *spirit:* we trace and love something good, and pure, and holy, and these are attributes of the divine Soul, not of the earthly shell. Of course, the more clearly these attributes are defined, the more perfection to which they have attained, the more intensely we love; and this is the reason why we feel the emotion much more strongly towards those higher, and wiser, and purer in the scale of being than ourselves, than towards those who have still to attain the same position, though the essence of both feelings is the same. There is no emotion so powerfully illustrative of our mingled being, as that of adoration, the highest grade of love. It is the immortal soul recognising qualities and attributes in another, the faint likeness of which is impressed on itself, but which is felt, as if the earthly shell so closely enshrining it prevented it so fully attaining; but still it encourages the adoration or love, because, in doing so, it seems to attain a portion of the purity and goodness which it admires, and, imperceptibly at first, but surely, advances towards the same.

In almost every nature there is this longing for something to worship, and if it have not legitimate, or revealed, objects of adoration, it will create them. It was this feeling which, in the mass, made Odin a god, Mahomed a prophet, and allowed Luther his supremacy; invested Dante with a halo, gave Cromwell kingly power, and Napoleon the empire almost of a world.* In all these, it was the recognition of master minds. Admiration was first excited, then reverence, then love; and once love, obedience was a matter of course. It follows, then, that the strong feeling of admiration is not only purely delightful in itself, from its permitting the ascendency of the spirit over matter, but a feeling which ought to be encouraged and inculcated, from its leading up to reverence and adoration. It must be something in the spirit which inspires it, either vast superiority of the mind, or of the moral qualities, or of holiness, and to these the mere animal can never attain. Our soul, or life, we are expressly told, is the breath of God, which He breathed into us; and, therefore, it is not only divine, but reflects His attributes, as a tiny globule of dew does the rays of the immeasurably distant, immeasurably brilliant sun,—clogged and checked by the influence of the grosser body, but still enabled to

---

* See Carlyle's "Hero Worship," where this principle is most fully and forcibly worked out.

attain such perfection, even on earth, as will permit it distinctly to realise the bliss awaiting it, when it returns unembodied to its parent Fount, and to conceive, with a vastness and clearness perfectly incomprehensible to a less lofty nature, the attributes, and the perfection, and even the economy of God.

To obtain this perfection, this triumph of the spirit over its earthly weaknesses and animal propensities, God, in His infinite mercy, revealed Himself, and instituted a worship, obedience to which could not fail to obtain the end desired. We cannot, perhaps, realise this now, because the law, in its various statutes, and still more in its spiritual ordinances, never was fully obeyed; but we feel its truth, by noticing those whose minds are embued with its pure spirit, and observing how nearly they attain perfection, and how much more open they are to the perception of holiness, and loveliness, and the good, not only in the animate but the inanimate creation around them. Perceiving how strong and purifying was the capability of worship, or adoration, or love, in the spirit of man; how it yearned towards satisfying its higher nature, by contemplation of something still higher; and how that yearning led man into a thousand errors, both in the objects and mode of adoration, the Lord God of Abraham first revealed His stupendous might, proclaimed his consoling attributes, His glorious perfections, for the very conception of which it was necessary for man to give the spirit ascendency over the earthly; and then, when sight and hearing* had added

---

* By "sight" we allude, not to the similitude of God, but to the various signs by which He revealed Himself before the Exodus from Egypt, and the thunders and lightnings of Mount Sinai in the delivery of the law, and by "hearing," to the trumpet which sounded long, and waxed louder and louder, and to the almighty voice of God.

their evidence to the internal conviction of the mind, and not till then, did the Lord, in His infinite mercy, command His people to LOVE Him with heart, and soul, and might, marking, in that very command, His religion spiritual above all others; for what mere animal could love that which it has not seen, and that which it can only conceive by the power of the mind? Yet God knew it was in the power of man so to love, or He would not have ordained it.

For comprehending all that is comprised in that emphatic sentence, I must refer you to other books, my dear Annie. It would delay us too long to enter upon it here. Your own vivid imagination and strong powers of reflection, will also enable you to enter into its full force, scarcely requiring my feeble explanation to bring it home to your heart, or my representations to bid you acknowledge, that the Revelation which first spoke these words, as man's guide in his aspirations towards his Maker, and followed them with, "Thou shalt love thy neighbour as thyself," as his guide in his conduct towards his fellow-man, must be all-sufficient in itself.

I have heard many say, they cannot understand this feeling as experienced towards our Creator, that it must be such a totally distinct emotion from love towards a fellow-creature, that it ought not to be classed under the same denomination. I never could understand this imaginary distinction, and always regretted to hear it brought forward, proving, as it does, that even real earthly love, so to speak, must in that case be utterly unknown. It is, indeed, the highest and purest kind of love, mingled so intimately with reverence, that we are sometimes apt to suppose it is all the latter, and none of the former. But this is a very mistaken error. It is no unknown deity, concealed in the dense veil of mystery and darkness, with which some of the heathen nations have robed their principal idol, that we, Hebrews, are commanded to love. He has revealed Himself to us as the concentration of all perfection, combining in Himself, and in His rule, every attribute and every quality which, possessed in the faintest degree by a fellow-mortal, all high and noble natures would at once reverence and love. Power, and wisdom, and purity, and goodness in a mortal, sometimes create the feeling of awe above that of love; because we fancy one so far above us cannot enter into our weaknesses and faults, or at least can give us no love in return. We cannot, we dare not, feel this in our communings with our Father in heaven. Veiling His perfection, His might, which in itself must appal us, He has not only called Himself our Father, but proclaimed Himself to be LOVE,—declared that our hearts are open to Him,—that He can read their inmost throb, and will heal their most secret wound,—that He has compassion on our weakness, ay, and will forgive again and again our sins, if we will but turn again to Him and love Him,—that He loves us better, bears with us more tenderly than our dearest earthly friends; for they cannot read the constant, yet darkly hidden struggles of our own heart, the circumstances, the temptations which may have caused us to err, or the misery and pain which follow momentary sin; but our Father can; and yet He loves us, feels with us, and will forgive. If a fellow-mortal could do all this, should we not lavish on him our best and purest affections? feel that we could indeed rest on such deep love? could tell him all our thoughts, wishes, joys, and griefs? secure of such perfect sympathy, that there would not be a throb unread? and of such compassionate tenderness, that every pang will, by his influence, be healed? or, if it be better for us that we should suffer longer, his sympathy will strengthen to endure? Who will deny that they can feel all this; and why not towards our God? We need not fear that such intimate communing will engender undue familiarity, or irreverence in His service. In loving and regarding Him thus, we only obey His first command; and if it were to remove or lessen the reverence we must also bear towards Him, if love were incompatible with the awe called forth by such perfection, would God Himself have commanded it? Dearest Annie, do not let such a mistaken notion gain possession of your heart, so fitted as it is by nature, or rather by God's grace, for such an exalted and purifying emotion as the love He ordains. Do not be persuaded into the idea, that the love of God is so utterly distinct from the love we bear a mortal, or that the consciousness of His love towards us cannot have the same consolatory and strengthening influence as that of a fellow-creature. I do not tell you that it will be attended by the intense delight, the peculiar joyousness of earthly affection; because, while on earth, we must cling to our fellow-beings. Interchange of thought, of mutual interests, expressed approbation, merited regard, all bring a sensation of enjoyment unsurpassed by any other feeling, while our sojourn is on earth. Youth craves for this—cannot realise belief in any other kind of satisfaction for the yearning heart, and, *while* it possesses it, asks no more. Nor does Revelation prohibit this feeling; nay, in commanding us to love God and our neighbour, it deepens and spiritualises it till it becomes immortal. Ask any one of any creed, who has really sought with heart, soul, and might to love the Lord, and he will tell you, the love he bears to his own especially beloved ones, and his fellow-creatures as a whole, is deeper, more intense, more prayerful, than it ever was before.

I think those who would throw so wide a barrier between the love we bear each other, and the love we are commanded to bear towards God, only argue from the sensations they experience when in constant intercourse with those they love. But what is the feeling when divided by the wide ocean, or opposing barriers of land, when year stretches on to year, and we change sometimes from youth to age ere we meet again? what is it then we love? The eye may have lost the form on which it may have loved to linger; the ear listens no more to the encouraging voice; hand no more clasps hand; we have no longer a kindly bosom on which to lean; the fond caress, the spoken word, which, happily timed, have power to raise the depressed, strengthen the weak, encourage the suffering, forgive the erring, all have passed ·from us; but do we cease to love? What is it that conspires to make letters, those winged messengers, bearing our thoughts, feelings, joys, griefs to those far distant, so powerfully secure of sympathy, encouragement, and love? Is this merely an animal sensation? Or is it not rather spirit, loving spirit, and by means of the immortal MIND, traversing space and annihilating time itself, in its enduring love for, and faithful communing with the object of regard? Those who feel absence to be the grave of love, of course cannot understand this purity of spiritual affection, and to them it might be difficult to explain the love our religion ordains towards our God. But to you, and I think to many others of an equally ardent, equally feeling temperament, the argument stated above will not be without weight. If the spirit within us thus enables us to love and commune with a brother spirit through space and through time: why is it so utterly impossible to feel the same, though, of course, in a much higher and more reverential degree, towards the Lord of the SPIRIT OF ALL FLESH, our Father, Saviour, and God? for under each of these appellatives He has revealed Himself to Israel? We cannot say we do not know Him; for, if we read and believe His book, we must know Him better than we can any earthly friend; for He is Truth, and His attributes are unchangeable and eternal. We dare not say we are unworthy to love a Being of such infinite holiness and transcendent perfection; for He has commanded us to love Him,—commanded all Israel, without distinction of either sex, age or rank, worthiness or unworthiness; and if we do not endeavour to love Him, we not only deprive ourselves of most unspeakable comfort and satisfying strength, but actually sin against His word, and expose ourselves to His wrath by disobedience. It is not, indeed, a disobedience which will bring down on us His judgment through the instrumentality of man; because it lies only between the heart and its God. But, if we believe in the Bible as God's word, we must feel that to disregard and disobey the command, "Thou shalt love the Lord thy God with all thy heart, and soul, and might," is as sinful a disobedience in His sight as disregard or contempt of any other law. So important do I feel it, that I believe perfect obedience to it and faithful adherence to the Divine Unity, will render us acceptable as Israelites still, even when, thrown into positions unavoidable in our captivity, obedience to the more palpable and visible ordinances of the Law is wholly unattainable. I am aware that this is a bold departure from modern Jewish ideas; but I am borne out in it by all the prophets, even Moses himself, in Levit. xxvi. 39, to the end, and Deut. xxx. 6; and far from encouraging laxity in obedience to the statutes and ordinances of the Law, which it might be said to do, it urges and impels their strict observance, as the *only* means of manifesting the love we feel, and so brings them to our minds, so entwines them with our affections, that every ordinance, ay, every festival, is kept and hallowed in the heart, even when the outward observance may be impossible.

It is only those who do not love God, who disobey His law, and feel His ordinances a weight and annoyance; and therefore it was He commanded us to love Him, that all His service might be one of thanksgiving and joy, and entwined with the strongest and purest feelings of our nature. The very essence of His revelation is LOVE. His attributes, His compassionating tenderness towards us, the emotions with which He desires us to regard Him, all are love,—love alone; and how then can any one declare the Jewish religion is *not* a spiritual creed, and that it addresses itself to mere animal obedience, not to the spirit's aspirations, or the heart's desires? I do not think you will continue to believe thus; and, trust me, those who do assert it may follow indeed the forms and ceremonies of their fathers, and perhaps periodically read the Pentateuch; but the Psalms and Prophets must be to them utterly unknown, and the *spirit* of the law, a meaningless word. To women, especially, a religion in which love is the vital essence is imperatively needed, and, therefore, am I so earnest in endeavouring to display its true spirit to you. Were you even very happy, as is natural to your age, and surrounded by kind and affectionate friends, answering your every thought, and enhancing your every pleasure: still, dearest, there would come a day when you would need it, crave for it, as every woman must. The female heart can scarcely ever find perfect sympathy on earth.

It has griefs, cares, even emotions, almost incomprehensible to itself, and which, if confessed even to our dearest friend, frequently return unanswered to the recesses of our own souls, as if the medium of words had given them a grosser meaning, and the mere surface, not the depth, were seen. But lift up such emotions, either in a written or voicelessly breathed prayer, and how fully are we answered, how blessedly consoled! But how could we do this, if it had not been revealed, that God is love, loves us, and has commanded us to love Him? We could never dare to bring up the seemingly petty things, which form man's existence of either joy or sorrow, before Him, unless commanded by revelation so to do, and guided also in the way of obedience. All creation, indeed, proclaims Him to be a God of infinite beneficence and might; but when we look on the work of His hands, how trifling and unimportant must we feel, and how could we suppose One so mighty would care for us? Without revelation, we must be lost in an abyss of doubt, error, and mystifying speculation, leading us farther and farther from the sole Rock of refuge, the only strength and consolation which mortals can have —the consciousness that God has love, and compassion, and care for all, even for the most insignificant of His creation. It is for this reason I am so very anxious to make manifest to you, that the revelation vouchsafed to our fathers is a revelation of love, and so display it, that your *heart* may feel, and respond to its truths, as well as your understanding. I know that by many Christian writers the Mosaic system is always alluded to as a law of fire and blood; but this notion proceeds from the popular error, that it is a law impossible to be obeyed in all its minutiæ, and that it consists of mere form and ceremony, heavy and burdensome, without any appeal

to the affections to give it life and breath. My letter is
already too long to enter upon this subject now. It has
been already proved erroneous, I think, by the command
we have been considering, and will be answered still
more clearly, as we proceed to consider the reasons for
many of the seemingly puzzling ordinances, the intention of others, and the spirit which must pervade them
all, to render them acceptable offerings to God. For the
present, dearest Annie, I am sure I have given you quite
enough to think about: so farewell.

LETTER VIII.

FROM THE SAME TO THE SAME.

Doubts as to the Divinity of the Bible—Natural when youth first
begins to enquire for itself—How regarded by various characters—
Impossible to prove any truth, without granting some imaginary
laws—Laws of nature, what are they?—Miracles of nature—Imperfection of the results of reason compared with those of faith—Superiority of a firm religious belief above every other blessing—Personal
evidence of Sir Humphry Davy disproving the idea that faith is
merely superstition—Faith and intellect both needed in the study
of the Bible—Summary of proofs of its divinity—Existence of the
Jews—Universal acknowledgment of the Bible—Perfect agreement
of all its parts—Belief of the Deist, why adopted?—Mere Deism
proved impossible—Moral laws of the Bible followed and obeyed,
however unacknowledged—Conscience, how formed?—Perpetuity of
the Bible laws—Causes of the decrease of persecution traced to the
increased knowledge of the Bible.

I HAD been expecting the contents of your last letter,
dearest Annie, from the very first of our correspondence,
though I would not touch upon it, till you brought it
forward yourself. You tell me you have shrunk from

doing so, feeling as if it were so very sinful, even to think such a thought, much more to give it words, that it is scarcely a defined feeling, more like a floating idea; but that it will come to disturb you, when you would gladly rest on the consoling doctrines, I have brought forward. It is the miserably doubting questions, "How do we know that the Bible is indeed the word of God?" "How can we prove, that all which is written there is Divine, and so ought to guide us in our knowledge of Him, and our conduct towards each other?" "What proof have we, that we are the people of whom Moses wrote, or that all he recorded ever happened?"— that every time you take up your Bible to try to read it, and feel its truth, these thoughts will come, and you find so much in it to perplex and bewilder you, you have often put it down in despair, and sometimes found yourself longing to believe in the New Testament, parts of which, seemed so much more simple and clear than the Old, but that the new views I had given you of the Jewish religion made you long still more ardently, to feel the same towards it as I do. Do I think, that with such sinful doubts of a book, I feel to be so holy and inspired, you ever shall?

I do indeed think so. The very restlessness of enquiry, the desire to find the truth, the candour, yet humility, with which you acknowledge every doubt, all make me very hopeful, that our Father will in His own good time permit "His countenance to shine upon you, and give you peace." Do you think the doubts you have ventured to put into words, have come to you alone? that they are not equally the trial of all, who are beginning seriously to look into what they believe, and to know the foundation and reason for the hope that is in them? My dearest Annie, few, very few, even amongst those placed in far, far more favourable circumstances for the growth, guidance, and encouragement of religion, than you have been, but have felt at the beginning of their individually responsible career all that you describe. That there may be hundreds, nay thousands, who have not, is no proof to the contrary.

The nominal religionist never looks into the subject, nor thinks a serious thought. The formalist is satisfied to do as his fathers did before him, never enquiring wherefore. The bold and daring, without being actually impious or unbelieving, feels so strong in his own strength, that he would imagine it cowardice to bow to any guiding law, believing his principles and his conscience are all-sufficient for his safe-guard, forgetting that conscience is an *effect* not a *cause*, and that if there were no Divine Laws governing the world, to mark the distinction between right and wrong, there would be *no* conscience, nor would there be in fact any need for it. The presumptuous and the superficial, declaring they will believe nothing without proof, that Faith is a folly and superstition, unfit for any but women and fools, who deem their shallow wisdom so supreme, their intellect so extensive, that it can penetrate even the wisdom of the all-wise, *must* reject the Bible; for to such it must be as utterly incomprehensible, as utterly useless. But it is only the superficial, who thus sit in judgment, so to speak, on the word and the attributes of the Most High.

The profound thinkers, the natural philosopher, approaching higher and higher the courts of wisdom, penetrating deeper and deeper into the secrets of nature, are those who *believe* the most, feeling the utter impossibility of *understanding* one fraction of the wonders and the mysteries which, even in this inferior world, are

ever around them. It is the extent of human weakness
and ignorance to assert, as, unhappily, only too many
do, that they will believe nothing without proof, take
nothing for granted. There is not a science in which it
is possible to advance one step without granting some
truth, without some imaginary, or rather unproved
laws, on which to build their after-theories. Whatever
they may say that they prove, they prove nothing, without supposing certain laws or axioms, which it is *impossible* to prove. For instance, the often repeated declaration that the miracle of staying the course of the sun
and moon at the word of Joshua, lengthening the day
by the pause in the earth's career, was impossible, because it was contrary to, and would have occasioned confusion in the laws of nature. Now what are these laws
of nature? What human wisdom can explain or define
them, farther than what man's senses have revealed to
him in their daily action, or his imperfect wisdom may
have penetrated as to their course, and rule, and effect,
and the apparent consequences of their suspension? He
cannot, he dare not, declare that he can explain, why
nature's course should be as it is, and not arranged differently. Say what he pleases, assert his wisdom as he
may, he *must* acknowledge certain natural laws, though
he *cannot prove* them to be really such as he believes
them, before he can build a single theory on the *proofs*
of whose truth he lays so much stress. Why then
refuse to grant as much in the science of religion? Because to do so, man's boasted wisdom must be humbled;
his pride, his strength, his consciousness of power, must
bow down to the same holy guide which is open even
to women and to children. He must acknowledge that
there are simple assertions in that Divine Book, which
even his penetrative intellect cannot attempt in this life

either to explain, or to reconcile with much that is passing around him, and rather than so humble himself, he
will reject it altogether. It demands childlike faith,
and so, in his weak presumption, he proclaims it unfitted
for the intellect of man.

How different are the views of a philosopher. "In
my opinion *profound minds* are most likely to think
lightly of *human reason.* It is the pert superficial
thinker who is .generally strongest in every kind of unbelief. The deep philosopher sees chains of causes and
effects so wonderfully and strangely linked together,
that he is usually the last person to decide upon the
impossibility of any two series of events being independent of each other; and in science so many natural
miracles, as it were, have been brought to light, such
as the fall of stones from meteors in the atmosphere,
the disarming a thunder-cloud by a metallic point,
the production of fire from ice by a metal white as
silver, and referring certain laws of motion of the sea
to the moon, that the philosopher is seldom disposed to
assert confidently on any abstract things belonging to
the order of natural things, and still less so on those
relating to the more mysterious relations of moral events
and intellectual matters." The same deep philosopher
asserts: "By *intellectual* superiority, I mean that of
man's spiritual nature; for I do not consider the results
of *reason* as capable of being compared with those of
faith. Reason is often a dead weight in life, destroying
feeling, and substituting for principle calculation and
caution." Again:—"I envy no quality of the mind or
intellect in others, be it genius, power, wit, or fancy;
but if I could choose what would be most *delightful,*
and I believe most useful to me, I should prefer a *firm
religious belief* to every other blessing; for it makes life

a discipline of goodness, creates new hopes when all
earthly hopes vanish, and throws over the decay, the
destruction of existence, the most gorgeous of all lights;
awakens life even in death, and even from corruption
and decay calls up beauty and divinity; makes an instrument of torture and of shame the ladder of ascent
to Paradise, and, far above all combinations of earthly
hopes, calls up the most delightful visions of palms and
amaranths, the security of everlasting joy, where the
sensualist and the sceptic view only gloom, decay, annihilation, and despair." *

These, dearest Annie, are the views and opinions of
one of the profoundest thinkers, of the wisest philosophers, of the most practical and penetrative chemists,
that ever existed. His extraordinary genius, not content with following a beaten path, ventured deeper and
more daringly into the secrets of the natural world, the
combinations of apparently opposite natures, the marvellous mysteries of effects from certain causes, linking
the cause with the effect in almost all his discoveries,
and so penetrating science as more than once to endan-
ger his life in its pursuit:† yet this great and wise man,
whose profound intellect very few in any age can vie
with, or, at least, surpass, raised above all weakness or
superstition, tells us that the "results of reason cannot
be compared with those of faith," and places a firm
religious belief far above every other earthly blessing or
heavenly grace. Surely, then, he is in himself a proof
of the utter falsity of the notion, that faith is nothing
worth, a mere superstition, fitted only for weak and
prejudiced minds. If an intellect like Sir Humphry

* Sir Humphry Davy's Salmonia.
† By inhaling certain gases to discover their effects.

Davy could pronounce it superior to reason, surely we may so believe it, and use every effort to make it our own.

You will wonder, perhaps, why I have chosen to make this digression, instead of answering your questions at once? Because I wished to impress upon your mind, that you must bring FAITH, as well as INTELLECT, to the study of the Bible. Unless satisfied from the first that there is much in the Holy Scriptures which, in this existence, we may not hope to understand, their perusal will do more harm than good. You will be constantly losing yourself in idle speculation, in the darkness of error and mystifying doubts. And verses, hailed by the believer as conviction strong of an infinite Love and infinite Mercy, will be turned by the sceptic into one bearing upon his own spiritless unbelief. Not that I wish you to adopt my views of the divinity of the whole Bible upon faith *alone*. Intellect and reason will both help us here, though, to my own heart, the existence of the Jewish nation, regarded in all its varied phases, is the strongest, most unanswerable, if not all-satisfactory proof that the Bible *must* be the Word of God. *Man* of himself could not have written that of futurity, which every passing century fulfils.

" How do we know the Bible is indeed the Word of God?" you ask me. And in reading my reply, remember, I can but give you my individual opinion. Would that there were any one book of our own to which I could refer you instead; but whilst our teachers and ministers, both of ancient and modern times, would pronounce us unbelievers and heretics, if we ventured to question the reasons of our faith, they have left us nothing, except in language and theory far too abstruse and weighty for woman's comprehension, to which we can refer to satisfy the momentary doubt.

To me the Bible is proved to be the Word of God, in the first place, from the proof already quoted—the undying existence of the Jewish nation, though they have encountered misery upon misery—been several times, humanly speaking, on the brink of extermination—are fewer in number than any other religion in the known world—are scattered from north to south, east to west, as witnesses of the Most High, exactly as written by Moses and the later prophets—and have endured trial, persecution, and dispersion, so exactly according to the prophecy of Moses, that the account would seem as if written *after* these events took place, not centuries and centuries *before*. Secondly, From the universal acknowledgment of the divinity and perpetuity of the Book by every people who believe in Revelation, however diverse and contradictory their doctrines or actual creeds may be. Thirdly, That the age and writers of the Old Testament have *never* been made matters of either question or dispute, that even our persecutors themselves, and those more kindly, but equally dangerous converters of the present day, though they believe the *Jews* are rejected, never deny either the genuineness or divinity of the Old Testament. Fourthly, It seems to me clearly proved to be the Word of God, from its extraordinary adaptation to the various characters and diverse feelings of man, and from the perfect harmony and agreement of all its varied parts. Pentateuch, historical books and prophets, all are so perfectly one, so completely the reflection of one almighty and all-guiding Mind, that though the individual character of some of the writers may be discerned, the lessons they inculcate, the attributes they give to God, the warnings with which they threaten, the rewards they promise, the domestic and social life they picture, are so exactly the same, that not the smallest contradiction, even by the most prejudiced, can be discovered, while each book retains sufficient individual peculiarity, utterly to prevent the supposition that they were all the work of one man. Now, mere human opinions, and discussions or explanations on the same thing, always differ so widely, that we scarcely ever find two persons either to think or to impress alike; and therefore we are justified in believing, that nothing but the Divine inspiration could have caused the *perfect agreement* of the whole canon of Scripture, so that not the slightest contradiction, either in theory or practice, doctrine or spirit, can be discerned; and yet not only were the writers of widely different characters, but they lived in different ages, and were placed in positions utterly dissimilar. Again, what mere human invention could have compiled laws which, even to this day, are guiding the whole civilised world? The ceremonial law, indeed, is peculiarly ours; but the moral law given to *us* has extended wherever Revelation is acknowledged. You may be, and no doubt have often been told, that there are hundreds and hundreds who, though they are withheld by some strange feeling of shame (in itself a proof that their ideas are wrong) from publicly denying the Bible, are still complete deists in heart. Yet these very men, in spite of themselves, bear witness to the Divine inspiration of the moral law. They acknowledge, they say, a God. Why? Because all nature proclaims it; but as for priestcraft (for so they denominate the Bible and its earnest commentators), it is beneath their dignity as men, and so they scorn it.

But I would ask them, why it is they never steal, nor bear false witness, nor do murder? Why it is they shrink from a dishonest or dishonourable act? Why are they so earnest to protect the injured? Why do

they refrain from maltreating even any enemy? Why
do they keep so strong a guard upon their passions, lest
they should betray them into error or crime? The law
of the country may act in some degree as a *restraint;*
but it would not make them regard their transgressions
as sins to be avoided in their own heart. Conscience,
they will reply, conscience is enough for any man, to tell
him what is right or wrong. Alas for such deluders!
*Their conscience, such as it is, has been formed by that
very Divine Law which they reject.* The Spartans considered it no crime to steal, and they were comparatively
a civilised nation. Human life was considered of so
little moment, that the weakly infant, and the helpless
aged, were alike left by their own nearest relatives to
die, as useless any longer to the State. Why, if conscience be so all-powerful, were not these crimes prohibited in Lycurgus's otherwise refining laws? But to
leave the nations of remotest antiquity where, the deist
may say, human nature had not sufficiently advanced for
conscience to distinguish between right and wrong, let
us glance over the savage nations of the present day;
because, if conscience be inherent, it *must* have voice
and power with them equally as with us. Is it not with
them the greatest virtue to revenge an injury by murder, it matters not how inflicted? The laws of their
state may prevent appropriation of a brother's property;
but they consider it no sin, nay rather a triumph, to rob
and defraud the stranger. They will torture a fellow-
creature without the very smallest feeling of compunc-
tion, and would be astonished if told, that in doing so,
or in avenging, or in slaying, or defrauding, they were
committing a sin. Then how is it, that conscience is so
silent with them, and so loud with us? If man had no

need for a Divine law, surely we should find the case of all nations the same.

Again, if the laws and restrictions of the Bible were of human compilation and invention, is it not a marvellous fact, that they should have remained unaltered through thousands of ages? The Egyptians, the Greeks, the Romans, all compiled laws; but there is not a trace of them remaining: they perished with the nations to whom they belonged. Modern states have each their individual code, liable to be altered or modified, increased or annulled, according to the varying conditions, demands, and necessities of the people which they govern. The code of one nation, however civilised, will not do for any other. We hear of the laws of France, and of the laws of England; of the statutes of Spain, and of those of Italy; and we think of something as a distinct possession peculiar to each country. But the laws of the Bible extend over the whole world where a revealed Deity is acknowledged. The Christians will tell you, that their whole system will fall at once to the ground, if the Old Testament be denied. The Mahomedans acknowledge and believe in the inspired mission of Moses, and the sublime doctrine of the Unity which he taught. The very means which Mahomed adopted for the formation of a new religion, are to me proof of his strong belief in the mission and legation of Moses. He received all the laws of the Koran, he declares, from the mouth of the angel Gabriel. Now why should he have taken the trouble of asserting, and trying to prove this, if he had thought, that the laws and word of a *man* would be sufficient for him to obtain, fix, and transfer spiritual authority? If he had believed that Moses, as merely a *man*, acquired all the power to create a nation and an entirely new religion: surely his ambition would have prompted him to have accomplished his spiritual and temporal schemes by his own individual hand and mind, without any reference to a divine guide or help. The Christians again assert, that Jesus united in himself god and man, otherwise he, as a man, could have had no power to alter the Law of Moses, which proceeded from God. God, they say, might alter or modify His will or law as He pleased; but a mere man could not. Now, is not this in itself convincing, in what a divine light the Word of God given through Moses and the Prophets must have been, and must be considered, even by the two great systems, which are spreading revelation over the world, and so constantly endeavouring, but always without success, to vilify and exterminate the Jews? Of course there are exceptions to this fearful treatment of a people, for whom those moral laws were compiled, and to whom that pure knowledge of the Lord was given, from which all nations and all people are benefited. The more the Bible, the whole Bible, is made the guiding star of the land, and the Old as well as the New Testament studied, the more consideration the Jews receive: the less we read of persecution. It is where religion is a mere word, where the fearful vices and passions of men set up a demon of hate, and cruelty, and wrath, and call it an angel of light, where men so bury the word of God from the eyes and hearts of the masses, that they are scarcely aware of its existence, much less of the sublime doctrines it inculcates, and so are unable to discern that the demon, their superiors call *religion*, is *not* such as the Bible teaches,—it is in such lands that persecution rages, not merely against the Jews, but from Catholic against Protestant, Greek against Catholic, sect against sect. But when once the Bible is appealed to, and read by all, then peace and charity twine hand in hand, and persecution is stilled. Will not this very fact prove, that there must be something superior in the spirit of that Holy Book, to the mere device of the best and wisest man? I will leave your other questions till my next, dearest Annie. The subject is such a momentous one, that I would rather divide it than weary you, as a longer discussion at present, I fear, may do.

LETTER IX.

FROM THE SAME TO THE SAME.

Every ordinance of the Bible bears the stamp of the same beneficent Deity, who is revealed in creation—We bear within ourselves the proof that God is a Deity of infinite love and goodness—Superiority of the good over the bad in producing happiness—God's word to be proved Divine must agree with His attributes, as revealed in nature and in man's organisation—Conviction that virtue is superior to vice, does not constitute conscience—Various ideas of right and wrong—The Israelites when they quitted Egypt could not have framed their law —What the law inculcates—Human laws merely temporal, lasting only as founded on revelation—Are modern Jews the people of whom the Bible speaks? examined and proved—Prophecy of Moses —Promise to Abraham—Prophecy of Psalm xliv.—Prophecy of Isaiah xliii.—The Bible without the Jews, a record, not a witnessed truth—Jews bear witness to the farthest boundary of the past.

" How can we prove, that all the laws which are written in the Bible are Divine, and therefore ought to guide us in our knowledge of God, and our conduct towards Him and towards each other?" is our next consideration, dearest Annie. To my heart, the answer is very simple: Because all which we are commanded therein to do and to feel tends to make us *happier* and *better*, and so bears,

on every ordinance, the stamp of the loving and beneficent Deity, whom Creation reveals. Because by obedience to the spirit pervading the whole Bible we are
purified from the grosser part of our mingled nature,
and are enabled to give to the spirit, soul, or mind,
higher and higher ascendency; and, though still liable
to the imperfections, and trials, and pains of earth, we
have gained a position, which enables us to look on even
these things, in the light of Heaven; and in the most
troubled lot to feel thus happier, than the prosperous
who know not God.

We bear within ourselves the proof, that God is a
Deity of infinite love and goodness, in the fact, which no
one can gainsay, of the superiority of the *good* over the
bad in producing happiness. Even a child, ay, even an
untutored savage after some self-conquest, some act of
kindness or forbearance, some courageously spoken truth,
is conscious of a very superior feeling of happiness to
that, which is his when passion has been indulged, safety
obtained by a lie, cruelty committed, forbidden pleasures
secretly obtained, even though, perhaps, at the *moment*,
the satisfaction in the last may seem greater than that
which attends the pursuance of the first. It is *after-*
wards, when the mind is calmer, the soul alone with itself and its invisible, and, perhaps, still unknown God,
that the vast superiority of a good action or feeling over
a bad is made manifest. All will acknowledge this.
Even the man, who has run a successful career of wickedness, will never confess himself, either in words or by
semblance, to be happy. The votary of pleasure and
excess, wearied and dispirited, craves for something beyond what he has grasped. The indulgence of hate, the
gratification of revenge,—how fearful is the troubled
storm within, which marks their progress! Can we hesi-

9*

tate a moment in deciding which produces the greater amount and purer quality of joy, the act of *revenging* or of *forgiving*, of punishing or pardoning, of obedience or disobedience? That there are natures too low and degraded to understand these loftier emotions may be true; but it will not bear upon the question of their truth or falsehood. And that the better and purer we become, the happier we are, is an unanswerable evidence that our Maker and God, He in whom we live, breathe, and have our being, *is* a Deity of purity, and truth, and goodness, loving and taking pleasure in all things that tend to the same, and that enable His children to make manifest the likeness in which they were made. Now, had the Deity who made us been other than our purer inward self reveals Him, had He pleasure in evil, and wrath, and falsehood, were contention, and pride, and rebellion pleasing in His sight: the practice of the EVIL would give us infinitely greater enjoyment than the seeking of the GOOD, enjoyment not only at the moment, but in its retrospection through a life. But the evidence of ages proves the utter falsity of such an idea, and shows clearly that, where there is a predominance of sin, there is an equal predominance of misery, alike in individuals and in nations; and, therefore, if we only look within ourselves, and examine the biography of others, and trace how virtue engenders happiness, that its pursuit will give us peace and tranquillity, even when subject to, and suffering from the imperfection of earth, and the faults of individuals,—that a career of vice *never* yet has brought either peace or joy, though its feverish excitement may *seem like* the latter: we bear within ourselves, in our own being, the proof unanswerable, that He who made us is equally a God of infinite goodness as of infinite love.

I hope I have made this clear to your mind, my dear Annie; for it is an important item in the consideration of your question, viz., "How do we know that the laws in the Bible are divine?" If we grant, that from our own inward feelings we know and acknowledge our Maker to be all goodness, and love, and truth, the proof of the divinity of the law, professed to be of His ordaining, must rest in its agreement or disagreement with these attributes; and this agreement is pre-eminently the case with the law given through Moses. It would detain us too long, to enter into a minute examination of the grounds for this assertion. All that I wish you to do now is to read and think about the ordinances of our pure and holy law, and then to tell me, if you do not perceive that in all its commands it reflects those attributes, which our own feelings apply to God. To do this fully, you must consider the state of the world at the time this law was given. You will say, perhaps, that what I have written on our innate perception of right and wrong, or rather the superiority of our virtuous over our vicious inclinations in creating happiness, contradicts my previous assertion of the necessity of a Divine Revelation to mark the boundaries of right and wrong, and that without Revelation there would be no such thing as Conscience. This is still my firm belief; and I ground it on the fact of the fearful iniquity of almost every nation at the time of the delivery of the law, and of the very erroneous notions of right and wrong entertained by the uncivilised nations of the present day. The conviction, that to follow virtue is superior happiness to the indulgence of vice, I believe *is* natural to every human being, be he savage or enlightened, heathen or Hebrew, and that this inward conviction is the universal response to the attributes of the Deity.

But this does not constitute Conscience; for the Ideal, which in fact virtue is, is variously clothed and variously defined, according to the superior or inferior ideas of right and wrong entertained by different men; and, therefore, the consciences of minds enlightened by Revelation reject, as wrong and sinful, certain acts and certain feelings which the unenlightened perform and encourage, without the least idea that they are in any way committing sin; but these men have their own ideal of virtue, which they follow up, and consider far superior to vice. What, then, constitutes the difference? Simply, that Revelation has formed the *conscience* in the one, and that the innate idea of virtue is *not enough* to create it in the other. I do not tell you that the Indians and other unenlightened nations are not happy, and have not amongst themselves many a bright example of virtue; but we cannot compare either their amount and quality of happiness, or their standard of virtue, with those where the Divine Laws are acknowledged and obeyed.

When we read the history of the various idolatries and impure rites performed under the name of religion by the ancient nations, and of their strange and fearful notions of superior powers, is it not impossible that a nation of slaves who, from their long bondage, had also become impregnated with the awful notions of their task-masters, could have attained such sublime ideas of the Deity, and framed a law which the whole civilised world acknowledges, even though many centuries have passed since its delivery, without a direct inspiration, which springs from certain signs and evidences of Revelation? Why, if man had power to do what Moses did, does it so happen that such a law has never been given before or since? Why, if man knows of himself what is pleas-

ing in the sight of his Creator, and what is not, should
the descendants of Abraham, a mere handful compared
with the rest of the world, have been the only people
who compiled a law to that effect? It is only the presumptuous, the ignorant, and the superficial, who can
attempt a reply to these proofs, and they may indeed
satisfy *themselves*, but will convince none else. Their
wordy arguments may silence those who feel faith and
reverence for the Word of God so closely entwined with
their being, that they shrink in anguish from such
irreverent and fearful unbelief, and cannot continue to
converse on it. But silence is not conviction, when
even the very groundwork of argument cannot be the
same.

The proof to me of the divinity of the law of Moses
(I am alluding now only to the *spiritual* and the *moral*,
not the ceremonial law, because, though equally of
divine origin, that is, and will be for ever *peculiarly
ours*) is simply its perfect agreement with the attributes
of the Deity, not only as He proclaimed Himself to
Moses, but as He is recognised by the moral and intellectual nature of man; that it inculcates, in its minute
ordinances, veneration, love to God and to man, charity
in the widest extension of the term, forgiveness of
injuries, benevolence, not only in act but in feeling,
honour to parents, respect to the aged, tenderness to the
young; that it incites to the cultivation of wisdom, of
intellect, of every spiritual and ennobling feeling, all
that can tend to give the spirit ascendency over the
earthly, and prepare us for life eternal. It prohibits, on
the other hand, all that can prevent our attaining this;
and, therefore, alike in its commands and prohibitions,
guides us to the same end, and reveals the same all-good
and all-loving God who, while He grants man perfect

liberty of choice and freedom of will while in the mortal
clay, places before him the means of showing forth
the likeness of God, in which he is made, more and more
distinctly, and so securing his spiritual happiness in this
world and his eternal felicity in the next. No human
laws ever looked farther than the temporal tranquillity
and well-doing of a state. Those which have been
formed *since* the dispersion of the Jews, and the universal
recognition of their moral law, are still human statutes
based on those which are divine. But of the far-famed
laws of Sparta, Athens, and even Rome, mistress of a
world, there is not a single trace remaining; and is it
not, then, a striking proof of the Divine Revelation of
our law, that it should outlive all others, and that the
perpetuity of human statutes should be only as they
agree, or disagree with the law of God?

Your next question is, "How do we know that we are
the people of whom Moses wrote?" I answer, By the
recognition and evidence of a world; by the exact
fulfilment, both in our past history and present destiny,
of prophecies only to be found in God's Holy Word,
and only fulfilled in ourselves; by our adherence, wherever we may be scattered, to the ordinances, not alone
of the moral, but of the ceremonial law instituted
through Moses, and of which we are the selected and
faithful guardians. It is farther proved by the fact that
neither through the swords and fires of persecution, nor
plague, nor the thousand evil chances which have befallen us, have we been rooted out from the earth, or
decreased in numbers, even for a time, that no human
power can prevail against us, however we may fall before it, that, while nations and dynasties have been
encountering revolution on revolution, conquest, defeat,
change, extermination, we have remained in every land

a mere handful, compared with the nation who protects or enslaves us, but still existing unchanged in one tittle either of our characteristics or our laws. Nations who were cotemporary with us in antiquity have utterly passed away. The modern world presents a series of shifting scenes, of which the only changeless features are the Jews. Take the prophecy of Moses, contained in the 28th chapter of Deuteronomy, and compare it carefully with the history of the Jews, beginning with the siege of Jerusalem by Titus, and going through our dispersion in those lands where we were literally compelled, in semblance, to bow down before the images of the Catholic, things of wood and stone,—where, indeed, we found "no ease, neither did the sole of our foot find rest, but where we had a trembling heart, and a failing of eyes, and sorrow of mind, and our life hung in doubt before us, and we feared day and night, and had no assurance of our life." What nation, but us, have such things befallen; and how, then, can we doubt for a single moment our identity with the people whom Moses brought out of Egypt, and of whom, in this sublime prophecy, he spoke?

Even by the most prejudiced of our opponents, it is acknowledged, that Jesus was himself a Jew, and that his Apostles taught the gentiles, in simpler words, the knowledge of the Lord and of the Moral Law, already revealed to us. From us, then, the blessing of revelation certainly came, whoever might be the ministers to bear it, mingled with some human error permitted for a time, over the known world. "In thy seed all the nations of the earth shall be blessed" God said to Abraham centuries before the advent of Moses; and in our dispersion, in the wider spread of OUR Scriptures, in the immortal hopes, and glorious future destiny they reveal, in the ennobling aspirations they inspire, in their very revelation of a Father, who has dearer and tenderer, more enduring and more forbearing love, than any earthly parent,—is not this promise also fulfilled, and, in the revelation vouchsafed to the seed of Abraham, every nation blessed ?

In Psalm xliv., we read, "Thou hast given us like sheep for food, and hast scattered us amongst the nations. Thou sellest thy people for nought, and dost not increase thy wealth by their price. Thou madest us a reproach to our neighbours, a scorn and derision to them that are round about us. Thou madest us a byword amongst the nations, a shaking of the head amongst the people." Where shall we find this fearful prophecy·fulfilled, save in the past and present position of the Hebrews since the destruction of Jerusalem? and can we then doubt our identity? The Psalm agrees so exactly with the words of Moses, though written centuries afterwards, that we must believe it equally inspired, and that it relates to the same people ; for to none other, but the Jews, can it apply! It describes their position among the modern nations so exactly, that we must feel it to be a prophecy, though couched in the metre of a Psalm. It will not bear upon the position of the Hebrews, at the period when it was chaunted by the sons of Korah, in the very least. Then, though a nation apart, they were acknowledged and respected by the surrounding nations.* They were not considered either a reproach or a derision ; their priests were acknowledged, even by the heathen, as servants of the living God. Alexander, in the plenitude of his power, knelt, and reverenced the

---

* I do not allude to the Philistine inhabitants of the same land, but to the Syrians, the Egyptians, the Babylonians, etc.

Hebrew's God, when the High-Priest went forth to meet him. Naaman, the Syrian general, went to consult the Hebrew prophet, on the mere report of a little Israelitish maid. Benhadad, himself, the sovereign of Syria, directly he heard the Jewish prophet was in Damascus, sent to enquire "If he should recover from his disease." Now this proves very clearly, that the Psalmist could not have drawn his conclusions, of the reproach and derision with which his brethren would be regarded, from their present position in the sight of the nations; for when he wrote, probably in David's time, though few in number, they were considered one of the greatest, most valiant, and most honoured nations of the earth. He must have penetrated futurity, and so correctly, that only wilful unbelief, which I am sure is not your case, dearest Annie, can refuse credence to the assertion, that the Jews *are* the people of the Bible, alike in its narrative and prophecy.

I do not think you will require more to prove to you, that we *have* evidence of our being the people of whom Moses and, after him, all the historians, psalmists, and prophets of the Bible, wrote; but yet, I cannot resist calling your attention to one or two verses of Isaiah, as strongly confirmatory of what I have already brought forward. In the forty-third chapter, at the eighth verse, we read: "Bring forth the blind people that have eyes, and the deaf that have ears. Let all the nations be gathered together, and let the people be assembled: who among them can declare this, and show us former things? Let them bring forth their witnesses, that they may be justified; and let them hear, and say it is truth. Ye are MY witnesses, saith the Lord, and my servant whom I have chosen; that ye may know and believe me, and understand that I am He; before me, there was no god formed, neither shall there be after me. I, even I am the Lord, and beside me there is no Saviour. I have *declared*, and have *saved*, and have *showed* when there was no strange god among you; therefore ye are my witnesses, saith the Lord, that I am God."

Here the prophet first calls upon the unbelievers and sceptics, men who have unhappily had existence in all ages, and who are, indeed, *mentally* blind and deaf, though *physically* they have both eyes and ears, and tells them to summon all the nations and people, and to enquire who amongst them can declare this, and show us former things? The enquiry relates to the seven previous verses of this chapter which, you will perceive, if you refer to them, describe both the creative and the saving power of the Lord. He tells Israel that, even when he goes through fire and water, his God will be with him; that he shall pass unscathed; that He is the Holy One, and the Saviour of Israel; and so precious, and so beloved in the sight of God is Israel, that He hath given nations for his ransom, and people for his life. He bids him fear not, for "from all the quarters of the globe, will He gather the people whom He hath called by His name, and formed for His glory." It is this especial favour, these things, the prophet asks the nations, if they too can declare, as shown to them? If they can show those former things which, by creation and redemption, the Lord has revealed to Israel? So closely entwined is the belief of the modern nations with the Revelation vouchsafed to Israel, that they might perhaps think it easy to answer, and might forget that they are building up their structure on the Divine groundwork originally ours. But how could the ancient nations, to whom Isaiah appeals, reply? Did the idols to which they bowed form them? Could they preserve them in the fire and the flood? Did they know the One sole God and Saviour, invisible, but ever present in His works? Had they been saved by a strong hand and outstretched arm, and ransomed by the mighty power of a God? Let them bring forth their witnesses, that such things had been, or, when they hear of such things as revealed to them, let them, if they can, say it is truth. They cannot; for the sin and wickedness of these nations were too great for the blessing of Revelation to be vouchsafed to them, and therefore, all was darkness around them. Not so Israel; of them the prophet says, "*Ye* are my witnesses, and my especial servant, my first-born son (see Exodus iv. 22); I have revealed myself to you, that ye may know and believe me, and understand the mysterious and mighty truth that I, who spoke to you, am God; before me there was no other, and after me there shall be none; and I alone am thy Saviour. *I have declared* my name and attributes unto you. *I have saved* you from your Egyptian task-masters and heathen foes. *I have showed* you my wonders and miracles. When there was no strange god amongst you, I manifested myself in the cloud and the fire, which guided you in the wilderness, by a voice on Mount Sinai, before thousands and thousands of my people; therefore, ye are my witnesses, that I am God;" and these witnesses, the evidence of a world proclaims us still to be!

Wherever we may be scattered, wherever a copy of our Scriptures is found, there this sublime prophecy is fulfilled; and no effort of either sceptic or scorner can prove it otherwise. However the modern Jew may be considered as rejected and stiff-necked in unbelief, however the erroneous idea may be entertained, that the Jews must all acknowledge Jesus, ere the redemption of the world will be achieved: still not one will deny, that TO US ALONE in ancient times was God revealed, that to US ALONE the Scriptures were given. Degraded, sunk, scattered, despised as we are, no other nation or people have ever set themselves up as the chosen of the Lord. However new religions, grafted on the Jewish root, may have so extended as to conceal and forget their origin: yet wherever the Jew is, there stands the witness of the Lord, there stands the living evidence of the Scriptures, acknowledged to be the descendant of the people on whom Revelation was first bestowed, and without whom there could be no knowledge of a God, nor of His Word. If there were no Jews, then, indeed, we might doubt the Bible, for we should merely have a record but no witness. We should look upon it as we do on the ancient histories of Egypt, of Assyria, of Greece, or of Rome, records that may indeed be true, but of which there is no *living* trace. Nay, unless the Hebrew still existed, in himself the evidence of the past, we should have less evidence of the Bible's truth, than we have of the histories above-named. They have their monuments alike of architecture and sculpture to mark, that, however their records may be mingled with fable, still such nations must *have* existed. The Hebrews have no such monuments. They were to be themselves witnesses of a mighty, and stupendous, and purely spiritual truth; and such they are. Their long dispersion, a chastisement for their iniquity, is working out the Providence, as the Prophecy of God. He has placed them in every corner of the earth, even in the most remote parts, that, wherever knowledge of Him may be conveyed, there should be His witnesses. Is there one other people, one other nation, who can thus bear witness to the farthest boundary of the past? The Christians, or the Mahomedans, if they went no farther than their founders, would still leave from four to five thousand years in utter darkness. The creation of the world, the institution of the Sabbath (for however they may differ on the day, there is not a religion that does not observe a Sabbath), the Ten Commandments, comprising such a vast combination of spiritual and moral, domestic and social, individual and general duties—all would have remained unknown. Both these great systems have arisen on a previous Revelation, to which they could bear no witness, and of which they could bring no proof, had the people on whom it was bestowed been utterly exterminated as so many other contemporary nations. But even those most prejudiced point to us, and exclaim (little thinking that even in such exclamation prophecy is fulfilled): "Behold the WITNESSES of God's former mercy and present wrath!" Dearest Annie, have we not then all-sufficient proof that we are the people of whom Moses and the after prophets spoke? Do we need more than the evidence of our opponents, and the response of our own hearts—the history of the Past, and position of the Present? Characteristics of feature alone would mark us a people apart: while ordinances, Sabbaths, festivals, and fasts, laws, customs, modified, however, by the effect of the varying climates and character of the lands in which we are scattered, all so exactly accord with those written in the Pentateuch, and given to the descendants of Abraham, that to doubt our identity with the Israelites, seems as impossible as to disbelieve in our present existence. If I have made it as clear to you as it is to me, I shall, indeed, rejoice; but where the heart is full of the subject on which the mind is working, it is more than ordinarily difficult to throw it into words.

10*

LETTER X.

FROM THE SAME TO THE SAME.

Evidences in the ancient nations of the creation and deluge—The narrative of Moses does not deny the theory of the geologist and astronomer—Difficult for the finite to comprehend the infinite—Man as powerless to comprehend the wisdom of God, as an unborn babe to understand perfected manhood—Birth to the one and death to the other, likely to produce the same marvellous and graduating change—Comparison of the career of man and of the angel—Man can attain some knowledge of God in this world—Comfort of faith to the truly wise—The superficial pursuers of science alone deny the Mosaic record—The mixed multitudes could not have understood Moses, had he entered into astronomical definitions—Mischief of superficial science—Contrary effect of true philosophy—Creation the mere act of volition in the Almighty mind—Magnitude of the moral mission of Moses must have prevented philosophical disquisitions—The sun, moon, and stars are the same to earth now, as at the period of their creation—The record of Moses sufficient for us on earth—Difficulty of expressing that which we feel deeply—Science does not contradict revelation—They are inseparably twined—Pride, the origin of unbelief.

You tell me many, very many doubts are satisfied, my Annie; that on many points both mind and heart can rest more calmly than they have done yet. Thankful, indeed, am I that so it is, and still more at your promise to tell me all that puzzles you as you proceed. I cannot hope to explain all; but I trust to give you answers sufficiently *reasonable* to permit the calm and trusting acquiescence of faith, on the many, many things which in religion must, while on earth, remain unsolved. You agree with me as to the convincing evidence of the divinity of Revelation, and of our being the people whom God redeemed and ordained His witnesses; and you ask me, if the history contained in the Book of Genesis, and the narrative parts of the Pentateuch, are found elsewhere than in the Bible? If they are not contradicted by the discoveries of the geologist and the astronomer? and other questions, which I will notice in due order.

All the nations of remote antiquity, and even the histories of their mythology, possess certain legends and traditions, agreeing remarkably with the events of the Book of Genesis, especially the creation of man and the deluge. The aborigines of America, and the numerous native inhabitants of India, have certain traditions that tally so exactly with the Mosaic records, that we cannot doubt they relate to the same events. In fact, so curiously similar are the legends and some of the rites of the American Indians, and of some of the African tribes, to the narratives and observances of the Jews, that strange hypotheses have been raised upon them, pointing them out as the lost Ten Tribes of Israel. To the truth of the deluge the whole face of the earth bears witness. The discoveries of geologists do not do away with the Mosaic account of creation, though some minds, not wide enough to embrace the vast extent of the question, may assert it. Moses describes the works of God in language best fitted for the narrow, and, as yet, unenlightened comprehensions of the people he addressed. We cannot find a single word in his narrative that will *deny* the theory of geologists, that the world must have passed through many stages. The Hebrew word translated *"day,"* may equally signify any length of time. Man was not yet on the earth to mark its flight by any particular division; and to the Eternal, we are told, "a *thousand* years in His sight are but as yesterday when it is passed, and as a watch in the night." All those marvellous changes and revolutions, seemingly so stupendous to the finite comprehension of man, are the mere act of volition in the mind of the Infinite; and what might be an *era* in man's bounded reckoning, is but a *minute* in the reckoning of God. It is difficult, perhaps, in the finite and the bounded, to obtain just ideas of the infinite and boundless. Man is apt to measure wisdom and power by his own, when in reality he can compare them no more with those of his Maker, than he can the instincts of the worm that crawleth at his feet, or of the fly that flits round his head, with the powers dwelling in himself.

Or (as a juster comparison, perhaps, for into the worm and the fly, though their beneficent Maker has endowed them with all things necessary for their safety and enjoyment, He has not breathed a soul emanating from Himself) let those who would circumscribe the wisdom and the power of the Infinite by the reckoning of the finite, look upon the new-born babe, in whose infant limbs and infant mind dwell all the *capabilities* which time has so perfected in themselves. Surely, when compared with such, man might think himself a god! And as that child is utterly incapable of comprehending the wisdom of a philosopher, the power of the mind, the strength of manhood's frame, so is man equally unable to comprehend the wisdom, and the power, and the might, and the will of God. The child will, indeed, become the man, and so attain the powers to the new-born babe so utterly unknown; but, for man to understand the infinite, death must be to him what birth is to the child—admission to a world. The death of man gives birth unto an angel. Perchance, even as the child progresses to the perfection which the finite may attain, so may the new-born angel gradually advance, till the ways, as well as the works of the Infinite, are to him revealed, and he is made capable, in some degree, of comprehending the perfection he has till then only believed in and adored. The Babe is born to die: the Angel is born for life eternal. The Mortal circumscribes the power of the former: the Immortal is before the latter. The sphere of Man is bounded by Time: the sphere of the Angel is boundless through Eternity. The Angel then may, and will, attain the perfect knowledge of the wondrous workings, and mysterious ways of the Most High, in whose revealed presence he stands from the moment of his *immortal* birth; but Man, though he may do much towards the attainment of this thrice-glorious knowledge, *must* ever be liable to the pains, and imperfections, and chains of earth; and, therefore, to attempt to judge the wisdom, and power, and will of his Maker, by the bounded nature of his own even most aspiring thoughts, is a degree of presumption, ignorance, and profanity, most fearfully opposed to any true religious knowledge.

That man *can* attain some knowledge of his Father and God, even in this world, is proved by the words of the Almighty Himself; for "Thus saith the Lord, Let not the wise man glory in his wisdom; neither let the mighty glory in his might; let not the rich glory in his riches; but let him that glorieth, glory in this, that he *understandeth* and *knoweth me*, that I am the Lord, who exercise loving-kindness, judgment, and righteousness in the earth, that in these things I delight, saith the Lord" (Jerem. ix. 23, 24). Now, man can reach this knowledge, not by measuring the Infinite by the Finite, the Immortal by the Mortal, but by advancing farther and farther in the realms of wisdom; for the more he does so, the more will he feel how little he can attain, and the less will he be inclined to set up his own judgment, by which to understand the word and the ways of God. The more he acquires, the more he grasps the wealth of mind : the more thankfully will he rest on those blessed words "THE JUST SHALL LIVE BY HIS FAITH;" for the more intensely will he feel that, if his salvation depended on his wisdom, or might, or understanding, he is lost eternally. But, angel-tongued, those words sink into his heart, giving him hope, and strength, and comfort; for his deep researches and mighty wisdom have only taught him "that the results of reason are nothing worth compared to those of *faith.*"

You will think, perhaps, that this is all a wide digression from the question we are now considering, as to the truth or error of the Mosaic account of creation; but I want you to understand, at the very outset of our inquiries, that the discoveries of human wisdom, marvellous as they may seem, ought not, and cannot, weigh one tittle against the simple word of God. The geologist and the astronomer, who deny or doubt the Mosaic record, are standing merely on the threshold of science and wisdom. They have not advanced far enough to perceive the boundless sea of nature's mysteries, and solveless causes of certain visible effects, which must drive human reason from her throne, had she not Faith to rest on; that childlike faith tells them, there is no denial of their discoveries in the canons of the Scripture; that Moses adapted his narrative, and Joshua his words to the sun and moon, to suit the simple minds, long crushed mental powers, and outward senses, of the people whom they led; that though, as mind advances, it penetrates more and more into the mysteries of Creation, and discovers *more* than Moses taught, it is enough for their immortal hope, to take his book as their guide to Eternity, satisfied that if more were needed for their salvation, God would have revealed it. How could the mixed multitudes who had come out from Egypt have understood or believed their leader, had he told them the stars were suns, the planets larger worlds than our earth; or had they heard Joshua bid the "earth stand still," when before their very eyes the *sun seemed* moving? Our heavenly Father, infinitely more merciful than man, demands no more than can be given. He spoke to us through Moses, as we would to children, in the first stage of education; and such we are before Him still, despite the wisdom we have gained. His loving mercy has given us Creation, on which to use the mental powers with which the same love has stored our minds; but when such exercise turns us from Him as He is revealed in His word, bids us doubt Him, because our finite and imperfect faculties cannot reconcile our discoveries with His simple word, then indeed is knowledge to us what the serpent was to Eve,—robes of light clothe a form of darkness,—mist surrounds us, and on our bed of death, we vainly grope for some hold for our struggling soul. What are mere earthly science and earthly wisdom, then? The true philosopher who has advanced farther, deeper still, before whose discoveries those of the deist are as nothing, sees God gleaming through them all, and, as a little child, he rests upon his Father's word, and feels that, though research and discovery may bless his life, Faith alone of all his earthly possessions remains beside his dying bed, reconciles his Father's works with His word, and guides his released soul to everlasting life.

Thus, I cannot consider, that the Mosaic records are contradicted by the discovery of the geologist and astronomer. God spoke, and chaos gave place to order, darkness to light; water and earth were divided one from the other; grass, trees, herbs, flowers, rocks, mountains, and valleys—all that could beautify and fertilise, and render the world fit for the residence of the new Creation—took their appointed rests as we see them now; and whether this creation burst into being at once, or whether it was accomplished by various revolutions and changes on the earth's surface, and whether other animals, besides those with which we are at present acquainted, had their existence: all was equally the mere act of volition in the Almighty mind, and took no more time in His reckoning, than if we felt the wish for a certain flower, and saw it on the instant spring up before us. Time—revolution—change—are words peculiar to man. We cannot, we dare not, apply them to God. We see the earth, divided from the waters, bearing the grass, the trees, the flowers, the grain, each with seed within itself, to produce its fellow, exactly as Moses told us, and even the very animals as named by him: then how dare we say, his account is contradicted and rendered null? Even if we grant (which I am quite disposed to do), that various strata and gigantic fossil remains seem to tell of certain changes in the earth, of which his narrative bears no trace: these changes may have taken place in the period designated, for man's comprehension, as the "evening and the morning were the first day." Ages in the reckoning of Time, are but as a moment in the reckoning of Eternity, incomprehensible and stupendous in the magnitude of creation, if judged by the powers and work of man, but a mere act of volition in the Lord.

Again: of the sun, moon, and stars we are told, "And God said, Let there be lights in the firmament, or *expanse*, of heaven, to divide the day from the night, and

let them be for signs and for seasons; and let them be
for lights in the expanse of heaven, to give light upon
the earth, and it was so; and God made two great lights,
the greater light to rule the day, and the lesser light to
rule the night. He made the stars also. And God set
them in the expanse of heaven to give light upon the
earth and to rule over the day and over the night, and
to divide the light from the darkness." Such is the
narrative of Moses, in words so simple, so *proved* by
each revolving day and night to the senses of man, that
a little child can understand them. When that narrative was given, the human mind, except in certain chosen
individuals whose communion with their Maker made
them wise, was in its earliest infancy. To have revealed
to them the discoveries of modern science would have
demanded from them a stretch of faith not one could
have possessed, and unbelief must have marked the
very outset of the Mosaic Revelation. Long ages after
the period of Moses, the discoveries of Galileo were
deemed so impossible, so heretical, that he was not only
persecuted, but so bent himself to the dark spirit of his
age, as absolutely to profess publicly a recantation of
his own glorious discoveries. In the very infancy of
the world, ay, and amongst men who even actually *saw*
with their own eyes, *heard* with their own ears, and *felt*
with their own senses the stupendous manifestations of
their God, and could yet disbelieve and murmur,—how
could Moses, deputed for a much higher mission, have
entered upon the real *nature* and more extended intent
of those glorious lights which he *saw* divided light from
darkness, and ruled the day and night? He might not,
even himself, have known that which the advance of mind
has gradually revealed. Surely, his mighty task, to
preach the sublime doctrine of the Unity of God, to

11

make manifest His power and His love, to lead a stiff-
necked and constantly rebellious people forty years in
the wilderness, still hoping, still believing in the promised end, the possession of the land of Canaan; the
delivery of a Law like which there neither was then, nor
ever has been any other, adapted to the minute government of a disorderly multitude, entering not merely
into social and general government, but into domestic
and individual life:—surely this was sufficient demand
on any single mind, inspired as it was by the direct
spirit of the Almighty. If we reflect on all Moses had
to do, and did, we surely cannot be surprised if his
relation of the events which preceded the release from
Egypt be brief, and even, to some exacting minds, unsatisfactory. He told enough for guidance, in connection
with his own revealings, to prove the truth of God's
previously spoken word to Adam, Abraham, Isaac,
Jacob, and Joseph. He entered sufficiently into the
work of Creation, for the mind and senses of those
whom he addressed, leaving to after-ages, and more
perfected intellects, those discoveries which, however
they may increase our adoration of the stupendous
power and extended government of the Eternal, however they may prove to us that our earth, lovely, perfect as it is, is but an atom in the vast immensity of
works around us, *cannot* contradict His word, while
sun, moon, and stars remain as *man beholds them.*

Do not think that I am contradicting, or doubting,
the wonderful discoveries of astronomers, and that I
would confine man's ever-soaring mind to the child-like
relation of the first chapter of Genesis. No: I would
merely prove to you that it is quite possible to unite
the two, and that the one *does not contradict the other,*
as mere superficial reasoners but too frequently assert.

What is it we are told? That two great lights were
placed in the expanse of heaven to divide day and night,
and to be for signs and seasons, days and years; that
the larger light was to rule the day, and the lesser one
the night. He made the stars also. And after He had
made these lights, great and small, He set them in the
expanse of heaven to give *light upon the earth*, and mark
day and night. Can any one, dare any one, say this is
no longer the case, or has ever ceased to be so? The
planets may be all worlds, larger, more perfect, of more
angelic nature than our own; the fixed stars may be all
suns to other and even invisible worlds; there may be
(nay, there are) myriads and myriads more stars and
planets, with their attendant satellites, than even the
telescope discovers; our own moon may be a world; our
sun may be a star to other worlds; but granting all this,
how can it be said to *contradict* the Mosaic account of
creation, when before our very eyes, before the eyes of
our ancestors ages and ages back—ay, for six thousand
years, the sun, moon, and stars have done their work,
with reference to this little earth, as their Creator and
ours ordained; giving light by day and giving light by
night; ruling days, seasons, years, and remaining in the
expanse of heaven, where our Father placed them from
the beginning, to do His work and bless His creatures?
What their other purposes may be, we shall know when
our release by death from this world gives us entrance
to another. For that life, whatever, wherever it may
be, other laws, and other information will be provided,
as much superior in the amount of intelligence and
revelation concerning the works of our God, as the mind
of the wisest philosopher is superior to the dormant
capabilities of the new-born babe. While *on earth* the
simple record of Moses is sufficient for our belief, or

more would have been given. If, indeed, that *contradicted*, or even *circumscribed* the discoveries of advancing human intellect, we might have some slight excuse for refusing to believe it; but it actually does neither. In its simple truthful relation, it appeals to the outward senses and inward experience of mankind, from the youngest child to the wisest philosopher, and founds its assertion on the evidence of thousands of years.

It does not say such and such things were not: then, indeed, it might contradict modern discovery. It only says, such things were, and not even that there were *only* such; and it thus gives abundant room for all the exercise of mind, at the very same time that it proves its assertion by the natural laws, so to speak, of every passing day and night.

O! that I could but make this sublime truth as clear to you and other doubting minds, my beloved Annie, as I feel it to be; but when the heart is full to overflowing, when the subject is felt to be so important, so entwined with one's very being, as by all who seek to love God the justification of His Word, through his chosen servant, *must* be, it is impossible to write with the calm, cold, quiet reasoning, which perhaps it may demand. But to describe to you the cold shudder which creeps over me, when I hear, as I have sometimes heard, men of wisdom, of research, of discovery, speak sneeringly of God's Holy Word, and by a few words fling doubt and contempt on the faith of thirsting youth, or of guileless age, is equally impossible. So simple, so easy appears to me the union of Revelation and all science, that how any mind can reject the one as contradicting the other, is as utterly incomprehensible as it is fearful. Such minds have never been taught to believe in any other than themselves. The idea of a higher and ubiquitous

Power, who can unite seeming impossibilities,—of a loving mercy which can, at the same moment, so reveal His mighty works, as to give scope to the full powers of the human mind, and yet reach the comprehension of the most ignorant, enabling a child and a savage to *believe*, through the evidence of their senses, and the philosopher to revel in the glorious triumphs of his mind,—the infinite Love which commands, as the simple condition of salvation, *faith* which is equally attainable by every age and every mind, instead of wisdom, or knowledge, or discovery, of which, compared with the vast multitudes of human beings, how very few can boast, and how few, therefore, could be saved—such ideas must be to the deniers of Revelation utterly unknown. However wise, however learned, still that wisdom is wanting which is pronounced by God Himself superior to all—the knowledge of the Lord. Pride, fearful pride it is, that but too often originates unbelief, and turns the light of science and discovery to darkness, and in the end to despair. O! that I could feel I had provided you with a shield of defence against those unhappy scoffers who, by a few words, have the power to shake and destroy the guileless trust of years; that to your aspiring mind and loving heart the simple record of Revelation, and the vast immensity of the discoveries of Science, may become as inseparably entwined as they are to me; and that the farther you advance in the study of religion, the more forcibly you may feel that, instead of contradicting, one upholds and confirms the other. Once having bathed in the Fountain of living waters, however the mind may soar or dive in the wide regions of discovery, it remains true to its resting on the Word of the Lord, as a bird to its home, and every fresh discovery but deepens faith. Alas, for those unhappy ones who go forth in their own strength, plumed in their own pride! Your other questions must remain till my next, my dear Annie. My heart must throb less quickly, ere I can attempt to write on any other theme.

LETTER XI.

FROM THE SAME TO THE SAME.

Discoveries of science likely to lead to despair, save for the revelation of a Father's love—Beautiful unity between His word and works—Reason must convince the mind, as well as love the heart—The real existence of the characters of the Bible proved by reference to them, by the Arabs, and Mahomedans—Mahomed must have had some strong reason to refer to them—Palestine equally holy to the Mahomedan, as to the Christian, and Jew—Evidence of nature to the truth of the Bible—Fulfilment of prophecy—Superstition and prejudice—Many things in the Bible to startle us—Innumerable mysteries of daily life—Faith acceptable to God—How to read the Bible —God has given us perfect liberty of will—Different impressions of His word on different readers—Fault of man not coming from God —Denunciation of the prophet on the despisers of the law—Necessity of Bible laws to youth—Why should religion and the Bible be the only part of education to be received or rejected without study and examination.

THANKFUL, indeed, am I, my dearest Annie, that my last letter has given you so much pleasure, and that its views have found so powerful a response in your own warm heart and unsophisticated mind. It has, you tell me, awakened so many new ideas, "that the infinite love and tender forbearance of our heavenly Father towards the weakest and most ignorant of His children, is so proved in the very order of His Revelation regarding the work of Creation; at the same time, that the discoveries of modern Science so reveal the immensity of His power, and wisdom, and glory, that the mind almost loses itself in their contemplation; that you cannot understand now, how any one can deny the necessity of a Divine Revelation, as the very vastness, and sublimity, and inconceivable glory of the Deity, as disclosed in the discoveries of science, must, it appears to you, drive man almost to despair as to his own acceptance in the sight of a Being so far above him, had he not the Word of Truth to show him the path of life, and to tell him, that transcendently glorious as is His God in the evidence of *His works*, His WORD proclaims Him the Father, whose love for the weakest and the humblest is infinite as His power, everlasting as Himself."

Yes, dearest Annie, it is indeed so; and I thank you for the expression of such a thought. I knew, that once awakened to the beautiful idea of Unity, the complete connection between our Father's WORD and WORKS, you would acknowledge the necessity of, and delight in, the study of the one equally with the other. But though truly I rejoice that so it is, we must not *only* rest on faith and feeling, we must bring forward all the evidences, and answer all the doubts we can, that reason may convince the mind, as well as love affect the heart.

Evidence of the existence of the characters in the book of Genesis, and of Moses himself, is found, not so much in the belief of Jews and Christians (because in the one, it would be heresy and blasphemy to contradict it, and almost as much so in the other, as the Old Testament is of equal sanctity, and equal importance to the Christian as to the Hebrew), but in the testimony of

the Mahomedans, ay and of the Arabs, centuries before
Mahomed himself appeared. From time immemorial,
they count their proud descent from Ishmael, the son
of Abraham, and (a striking proof of the truth of Moses'
record) adhere to the sacred covenant of Abraham, at
the age, when the Bible tells us Ishmael was received
into it, that of thirteen years. Mahomed confirmed
this rite; and to this day it is part of the Mahomedan
religion, and.is in itself a striking proof of the truth of
Scripture. To the Arabs, the acknowledged descendants of Ishmael, no divine revelation was vouchsafed.
All they retain and venerate, regarding Abraham, and
Ishmael, and Moses, must have had its origin in tra-
dition, handed down from father to son, till Mahomed
collected and compiled them in a book of laws.

Now, from the despicable light in which the Jews
were regarded at the time of Mahomed, it would appear
that, unless he had had some very strong reasons for
a reference to the characters of their books, it would
have been more to the glory and virtue of a new religion
not to have had any thing to do with a people so debased. Whether Mahomed was acquainted with the
Hebrew Scriptures or not, his constant references to
Abraham and Jacob, Joseph and Moses, and even to
Job, are equally powerful evidence of the truth of the
Bible, and the existence of these characters. If his
knowledge came from the traditions of the Arabs, these
traditions must have had a very strong foundation in
Truth, to have outlasted so many centuries; and they
agree too remarkably with the Pentateuch, to permit a
thought of either springing from falsehood. Truth
alone is *enduring* and *unchangeable*. Falsehood varies
with every passing breath. If Mahomed was really
acquainted with the Hebrew Scriptures, he must have

had internally a very strong conviction of their sacred truth ; or he would not have allowed a book, which he declared to have been given to his care by an angel from heaven, to contain reference to the characters of those Scriptures, and so many strikingly similar laws. The first grand doctrine, the Unity of the Eternal, and the constant communing between man and his God, the covenant of Abraham, the strict prohibition of certain meats, the toleration towards strangers, (for that was the true spirit of the Koran, though it made its way by fire and sword,*) and various other minute ordinances, both spiritual and ritual, are strikingly like those given to the Jews. Again, the extreme veneration borne by the Mahomedans to the memory of Abraham and Moses or Moussa, surely is in itself evidence of the existence and the sanctity of both characters. Palestine is Holy Land to the Mahomedan, as to the Christian and the Jew. Travellers relate, that the Mahomedan will point out the sites of those solemn scenes of Scripture, in which Abraham, and Jacob, and Moses were actors, with as much earnestness and veneration as the Jew himself. Surely, this is a speaking testimony of a most solemn truth. Nay, is not Palestine itself, with its thrilling associations, bearing on almost every rock, and mount, and glen, and river, names and memories sacred not to the Jew alone, but to every faith professing to be built on revelation,—Palestine, struggled for by Christian and Mahomedan, and still lying waste, as the Lord ordained, giving not to strangers the fruition, and the beauty, and luxuriance, which *were* given, and will again be given, to the Jews,—Palestine, still regarded with an eye of longing by the true Hebrew, as

---

* See Gibbon, Decline and Fall, vol. ix. Hist. of Mahomed.

his only home, by the Christian as indissolubly linked with the past,—is not Palestine itself, then, an evidence of the truth of Revelation, which no effort of the Sceptic can have power to overthrow, while that small portion of the earth exists? God has stamped His name, and the name of all His faithful witnesses, on that sacred Land—and till it be annihilated, its silent testimony to the truth of Revelation must endure.

The histories of Egypt, Assyria, Babylon, Greece, and ancient Rome, written as they were by heathen and unenlightened historians, all bear witness to the truth of the Bible, by a perfect agreement with its historical relations and frequent reference to the Jews as a holy and singular people dwelling apart; and the early traditions of each of these ancient kingdoms bear affinity, in a greater or less degree, to the record of creation and the deluge, as described by Moses.

Prophecy fulfilled, not only in the matter of the Jews, as we considered in a former letter, but in the kingdoms of Egypt, Moäb, Babylon, Idumea, Tyre, and some others, fulfilled so precisely, that the fox and the bittern, exactly as foretold, are now the sole possessors of what was once a mighty and populous city, the pool and the desert covering the palaces of kings—could this be, if the mere mind of man had written it? As the mere effect of chance, of a fixed necessity, a natural revolution of earthly kingdoms, is it not a marvellous accordance with the word of finite man that, even in the minutest point, it should not go beyond or stay within the line marked out? that, even to the appearances of Nature where, when the prophetic word was written, man saw but thriving cities, palaces, and courts, thronged with their human inmates, all should be fulfilled? If written *after* these occurrences took place, is it not marvellous that in two thousand years the fraud should never have been discovered and exposed? If, indeed, the Bible be the work *of* man, is it not strange that it should never have been *overthrown by* man? that no other book has *ever* risen like it? that, despite the constant attacks which in every age it has undergone from ambition, presumption, malice, infidelity,—despite the thousand daring spirits who either publicly or privately deny its divinity, —despite the still larger number to whom it is unknown, it has NEVER FALLEN, never ceased to be either *nominally* acknowledged or *truly* felt as the word of God, wherever Revelation, it matters not under what denomination, has extended? Superstition and prejudice, in favour of a constantly inculcated theory, are certainly strong; but superstition will not *fulfil* prophecy, nor prejudice court investigation, as all true believers do. Nor is it likely that superstition and prejudice, if on them alone the belief in Revelation depended, could have so existed through many ages and the varying revolutions of men and states, as to recognise in every age, in every land, and every creed which preaches God, the same volume as the only *divine* one, or build their theories upon the same *truths* of which that one same volume speaks.

I trust, dearest Annie, that these simple considerations will prove to you, that we may certainly appeal to the evidence of reason, as well as to the thrilling response of faith and love, to prove the divinity of the Bible. That there are many parts which, on a first, or even third or fifth perusal, will startle us, and excite the thought, "Surely such and such things are contrary to the attributes of our God, or contrary to our ideas of virtue in those who were His chosen and beloved servants;" customs that may *seem* revolting, rites that *may appear* useless,—that you will often feel this, *must* be at first. I shall not be surprised at any objections you may bring; but when we come calmly to consider them, I have no fear, but that you will feel as I do, that they neither contradict God's attributes, nor the consoling truth and beauty of His word.

We first must satisfy our reason that, despite much which has been brought against the divinity of our Holy Scriptures (learned and wise as may be those who swell the ranks of infidelity), the Bible still remains unchanged, unequalled, recognised either as a whole, or by belief in the existence of its characters, by all who acknowledge a God,—borne witness to by the testimony of Nature and Science, as well as by the heart of man,—proved that the Pentateuch and Psalms, and some of the Historical Books, could not have been written by the Jews *after* their captivity in Babylon; because the pure Hebrew in which those books were written became at that period so mangled and corrupted by the introduction of the Chaldaic phraseology, that they bear, in their very language, intrinsic witness of their previous existence. The Jews could *no more* have written the laws of Moses *after* their return from Babylon, than they could *before*, when their constant proneness to idolatry *must* have deterred them from instituting such severe and awful judgments upon it, had it been merely the work of man. And when our *reason* is satisfied on this head, we must bring *faith* to aid us. As merely the word of man, man would be justified in rejecting the Bible, if there were any part he could not by either reason, analogy, or reflection satisfactorily understand. As the word of GOD, he is *not*, and *never* can be thus justified; because he must know and feel that, in the daily occurrences of life, the wonders of Nature, nay, the very beautiful mechanism of his own frame, the marvel of his birth and death, the workings of his mind and will, there are *innumerable* mysteries which to solve is, in this present existence, utterly impossible; and therefore, if thus it may be with the revealed *work* of the Eternal, so it may equally be with His revealed *word*. When satisfied that we may go to the Bible for guidance, because *it is* the voice of God, and reading there that, when Abraham *believed* in the Lord, "his faith was counted unto him as *righteousness;*" and that "the just *shall live* by his *faith;*" "Look unto me, and be ye saved, all ye nations of the earth:" we feel at once that faith *is* acceptable unto the Lord; and, as Abraham believed when God spoke to him by a distinct voice, though the Revelation was so mighty, and seemingly so impossible to human reason in a childless, aged man, so must we do, when we listen to the voice of God, as recorded in His holy word. And if, when we have tried all that puzzles us by the attributes of God, and by other efforts of the understanding, we are still not satisfied: all we have to do, is to rest calmly on the belief that we shall know it all hereafter, when our intelligence, bounded by the finite and the mortal as it is *now*, shall have attained that glorious perfection which will enable us to perceive and adore the *ways* as well as the *works* of the Eternal.

It requires little faith to believe in the DIVINE origin of the Bible, because its proofs are so striking, so unanswerable, and so multiplied; but we *must* bring faith to its *perusal*. If we come to its hallowed pages with a scornful and defying mind, judging human nature in the Past by human nature in the Present; the customs and passions of the East by the habits and cool calculation of the North; circumscribing the power and love, the justice and mercy, of the Omnipotent and Infinite, by the limitable faculties of the weak and finite; believing, that to be the chosen and beloved of the Eternal, man must be the faultless and perfect emanation of Himself, not the frail child of clay, utterly forgetting that God is Truth, and as Truth, His ways cannot really contradict His attributes, however they may appear to do so to short-sighted man:—if we come with such a spirit to this sacred duty, better, far better not to come to it at all! The perfect freedom which our God has given us to choose the good, or choose the evil, the unchecked liberty of our own free will to seek His love or tempt His wrath, is ours, even in the simple matter of the perusal of the Bible. God will not interfere by a miracle to display its divinity to him who wilfully, and without examination, rejects it; but to him who seeks its everflowing fount of living waters by fervent prayer and loving service, He will display its fulness more and more. There must be always a disinclination to His service, a presumptuous denial of the necessity of divine guidance, an irritation against the pressure of obedience to minute ordinances, a desire to follow the "inclinations of the heart and delight of the eyes," instead of the commands of the Lord, in all who reject the Bible; and to such spirits the Book *must* remain not only sealed as to its real meaning, but as giving back the reflection of their own mistaken fancies, and so lead them farther and farther from the only path of safety, even while it leads the believer through the thorny path of earth to the holy rest of heaven.

But these widely contradictory impressions received from the same volume spring not from God. They come from man's *free choice*, and to himself alone we must look for their original cause. Some are satisfied to retain the idea, that they *cannot* feel towards it as others do; that where so many see beauty, and divinity, and fulness, they see nothing but darkness, and mist, and imperfection. Where others see a divine unity, and harmony, and connection throughout, they perceive only disunion, and discordancy, and contradiction; they make no effort, either by examination or persevering study, to think otherwise; they never think of analysing the spirit with which they approach the volume; of discovering whether they are anxious to believe or disbelieve, whether they are not amongst those to whom the prophet says, "Woe unto them that are wise in their own eyes, the prudent in their own sight, who call evil good and. good evil; who put darkness for light, and light for darkness; who put bitter for sweet, and sweet for bitter; who justify the wicked for reward, and take away the righteousness of the righteous from him; therefore as the fire devoureth the stubble, and the flame consumeth the chaff, so their root [or *motives* of action] shall become rottenness, and their blossom [*the actions themselves*] shall go up as dust; *because they have cast away the Law of the Lord of Hosts, and despised the word of the Holy One of Israel.*"

Can any language be clearer than this, to show us the fearful state which *must* await those who despise the Word? But do not think, my dear Annie, I write this in condemnation of any of my fellow-creatures. God knows, my heart is so full of tenderness and compassion towards all those, be their actual creed what it may, who are standing on that fearful precipice of unbelief— rejection of the Bible as the voice of God (and so our unerring guide for every feeling), that with the energies of my whole being I would work to save them. They can have no abiding principle, and so no rest. If they have, it is from that very Word which they despise, and which, inciting them to all good and virtuous deeds, saves them in spite of themselves. All that is good, all that is high and holy, all that is self-denying, and forgiving, and forbearing, all that incites to steadiness and truth, every pure and noble quality within us, has its origin in obedience to the laws laid down, and in admiration of the attributes of God, proclaimed by His word, the Bible. We may neither know nor recognise it as such; but such it is proved to be, by comparing the morals of those lands where God is *known*, with those where He is *not*.

By the young, especially, of both sexes, this unerring guide is imperatively needed; and therefore is it, that I am so anxious you should recognise and feel its fulness and divinity. As long as we are children, the commands and instructions of our parents are all-sufficient guides, whether founded on a recognition of the word of God or not: we never ask or seek for more; our conscience is satisfied with obeying and trying to please them, and we are happy or unhappy as they are satisfied or not. As we leave childhood, and attain a completely new existence (for such is youth), we become conscious of a craving for something more. On one or more subjects our opinions may differ with those of our parents or older friends. Startled at our own boldness, we hardly know by what test to try them; and unless we have been so trained as to know *what* guide to refer to, we must be tossed on a sea of painfully conflicting feelings. The authority of parents and guardians is diminished— is become merely nominal. We give them, indeed, the respect, and love, and deference due; but we have become, with regard to our inward self, our own masters.

We mingle with the world,—we hear sentiments, and

perceive actions totally at variance, perhaps, with those
we have been taught are right; and yet those who may
thus speak, and thus do, may be amongst the most
influential, and apparently the most amiable, of those
with whom we associate. There must then have been
either error in the instructions of our childhood, or in
the companions of our youth. How, then, can we distinguish which is the right and which the wrong, unless
we have some higher guide than that of man? We
see, perhaps, what is termed custom and habit, not only
permitting, but authorising, certain things which we
may inwardly feel are wrong. We are told, perhaps,
"O every body does it, or thinks it so, there can be no
harm in it;" and what is to save us from doing the
same, unless we can turn to an unerring guide, and read,
"Thou shalt not follow a multitude to do evil," and at
once we know our duty? We may ardently desire some
pleasure, some indulgence which we see others enjoying,
but which, from peculiar circumstances, or because our
awakening conscience bids us hesitate as to its real
nature, is prohibited to us. How are we to acquiesce
happily, or to be safely guarded from the temptation,
unless we *feel* that in His word God has said, "Thou
shalt not follow the inclinations of thy heart, nor the
desire of thy eyes," *if* there is even a doubt of their
leading to evil? We may witness petty malice, envy,
leading, even in polished societies, to a desire of annoyance, and so veiled, so seemingly natural in the present
state of things that, if we do not pause to think, we may
do and feel exactly the same; but if we have sufficient
faith to turn to our Bible for guidance, even for this we
read, "Thou shalt not go up and down as a tale-bearer
amongst thy people; thou shalt neither avenge, nor bear
any grudge, but shalt love thy neighbour as thyself."

12*

We may be laughed at for a scrupulous adherence even in trifles to truth, for refusing to join in the thoughtless amusements of youth, who in their wild spirits make even age and infirmity a theme for laughter. The principles imbibed in childhood will not be strong enough to guard us against doing the same; but we are safe, if we believe that GOD, not Moses, said, or rather says, for as long as the Bible lasts, GOD SPEAKS, " Ye shall not deal falsely, neither lie one to another. Ye shall not curse the deaf, neither put a stumbling-block before the blind. Ye shall rise up before the hoary head, and honour the face of the old man. In all these things ye shall fear (or have regard unto) thy God, that He is the Lord," marking even these comparatively little things. In youth, also, the very desire for the praise, and love, and admiration of our fellow-creatures, might lead us into error, unless we have that higher principle of action which, founded on God's word, tells us, that the praise of man is nothing worth, if upon it we cannot ask His blessing. It is in youth that conscience first stirs within us, teaching us that there are two opposing principles ever at work in the world and in individuals, right and wrong, or good and evil. We know it, we feel it throbbing in its newly awakened power through every nerve; but we cannot hope to define it, to mark clearly before us the boundary line which stretches between them, seemingly so narrow as almost to be invisible, (but in reality so wide,) unless we recognise the Bible as the voice of God, teaching us those things which are, or are not acceptable to Him. We cannot, we dare not rest on the word of man; because it is changing, shifting, varying with every breath of that bugbear to so many—public opinion. We are told, no doubt often, that all the high, pure, fresh feel-

ings of dawning life are pure romance; that the customs
of the world will not permit the continuance of lofty and
generous sentiments; that we *must* sometimes sacrifice
truth and honour, we must think more of ourselves than
others, and a long etcetera of similar worldly maxims:
and how is the young mind to retain its purity, how
endure the loneliness of such utter want of appreciation
and sympathy, unless he can turn believingly to his
Bible, and feel that as long as that book reveals the
attributes of God, and the attributes which in man God
loves, he may rest content and thankful that such sentiments *are* his own, despite the scorn and misapprecia-
tion of a world?

These are but a few of the blessings, which faith in
the Bible, as God's own inspired word, will bring to us,
dearest Annie; but they are enough to make manifest
my meaning that, without such belief, a youth can have
no fixed *principle* of life, no *sound motive* of action, but
must be liable to be tossed to and fro with every new
opinion he hears, be led into error and suffering before
he is even aware of their vicinity: and once urged to
despise the Word, its guidance, its beauty, and its consolation, are lost to him for ever, unless, indeed, the
grace and love of God bring him back with an humbled
and enquiring spirit to its hallowed pages. It is because
I feel so very strongly its deep importance, that I have
so earnestly endeavoured to convince your *reason*, as
well as to excite your affections to it, as DIVINE. Without such belief, it can never be to you, what your character so intensely needs. To look on some parts as
Divine, and some as human, never clearly comprehending which is which, must lead you deeper and deeper
into confusion and error. Very many do this, because
they will not give the subject the calm and steady ex-

amination which it demands, and which, moreover, they will gladly and earnestly bestow on every other that may appeal to their interest or inclination. It is strange, anxious as man always is for the future of *this* world, how little he cares for, or concerns himself about the future of hereafter. Why should religion be the only part of education, on which there is no need for instruction? Why should the Holy Scriptures be the only Book to be received, or condemned, *without* study and examination? In general when we wish to prove the truth or falsehood of an assertion, we examine carefully and deliberately all the pros and cons; we analyse, comment, compare, weigh, reflect, and only pronounce a verdict on conviction. Why then should not men do this on the important question, of the divinity or non-divinity of their only guide to salvation? But who of the presumptuous deniers of the Bible ever did so? Who ever took so much trouble on a subject on which their happiness rests, and salvation depends, though, for temporal concerns, it is done almost daily? Dearest Annie, notwithstanding all I have written, I know there must be still much in your young mind to answer, ere it can rest calmly. Whatever they be, doubts, or merely questions for information, write them as fully and freely as I have endeavoured, and will still endeavour, to reply.

LETTER XII.

FROM THE SAME TO THE SAME.

Impossible at first to realise pleasure in the perusal of the Bible—
Necessity of perseverance—Pentateuch not sufficient in itself to give
spiritual comfort and individual guidance—Prophets explain the
spirit of the law—Use of the Psalms—David an' inspired writer—
How to take pleasure in the Bible—An easy method of perusing
it—How to make even narration, comfort and example—Valuable
auxiliaries in its perusal found in various explanatory works—
Paucity of Anglo-Jewish works—Plenty of material in the old
writers—Effect of Keith's Evidence of Prophecy—The perusal of
spiritual works assists us to derive the full comfort of religion.

"You do, indeed, feel the necessity of some guide on
which to rest," you tell me, dearest Annie; "you are
satisfied with the verses I have quoted, the proofs I
have brought forward; but still, try as you may, you
cannot realize *pleasure* in the perusal of the Bible;" nor
do I expect, you will as yet; but persevere in it as a duty,
a daily duty. Accustom yourself to come to it, under
difficulties, and trial, and joy: and its strength, and
peace, and consolation, *will* all come. Trust my experience, and believe that, when I began to read, your
present feelings were all mine; ay, and even now,
many and many is the time, when it is even as if it
were sealed, when I cannot realise either peace, or pleasure, or instruction, and I persevere from duty, not from
love; but these are but *intervals* of weariness and pain,
in their darkest and longest duration; but they are only
a grain in the balance, compared to the fulness of peace

and comfort I have at other times experienced. You have only known the Bible as a Sabbath Book, brought out on the Saturday, to read a certain portion of the law, and put away again. Now, though the Pentateuch is the most important, as the foundation not only of the Jewish, but of *all* Religions, and, as such, is a portion of Scripture with which every Hebrew, male and female, ought to be as well acquainted, as with his own existence; yet it will not bring so much spiritual comfort and spiritual guidance to individuals, as the Psalms and Prophets, Proverbs and Ecclesiastes. We must *not* confine ourselves to the Pentateuch *only*, if we would really become "Israelites indeed." There is much, indeed, in the Prophets relating to the Future, which now we cannot hope fully to understand, and can only *believe;* satisfied that, as we see before our very eyes the exact fulfilment of some prophecy given at the same time, so we may rest assured of the fulfilment of the others. But there is quite as much, which is addressed to us individually even as the voice of God speaking to our own souls, under every circumstance of life. There, too, by the reproofs and threatenings addressed to the idolatrous and rebellious inhabitants of Palestine, we perceive the real meaning, intent, and spirit of every ordinance and that without *love* and willing service, even obedience itself was utterly worthless.

The Psalms, too, teach us the same thing, and should be regarded not only as forms of prayer and thanksgiving, but as guides in our daily, moral, and spiritual duty. It has been objected, that David was neither a law-giver, nor a prophet, but merely a man like ourselves; and his words and experiences, therefore, are of no more weight than those of any other man. But the fallacy of this opinion is proved, not only from the thousand and thousand years, during which those Psalms have been acknowledged as inspired prayer and praise; but because there never has arisen any other man to write the same, or sacred poems in any way resembling them. What man of himself has done, man may do again, if not exactly identically, at least with so much resemblance, as to show some points of similitude between them, and mark both to be the work of similarly gifted minds. Since the time of David, and his instituted choir of Levites, amongst whom were the sons of Korah and Heman, whose names we see at the head of some of the Psalms, no such compositions have ever appeared. Prayer and praise have been pronounced perfect or imperfect, as they borrow, or do not borrow, their expressions from the Psalms. ALL the writers of the Bible were inspired, and as such *are* the voice of God. If we needed the power of prophecy to prove it, many of the Psalms *are* prophecies, fulfilled since they were written, and being fulfilled now.

Do not imagine, dearest Annie, that when I say perseverance will teach you the full beauty and comfort of the Bible, I mean you to devote any length of time to its daily study, as you would to any other difficult pursuit. Accustom yourself to feel that your morning and evening prayer are *not* complete, unless you commence, or conclude them, with one chapter of the Bible, or two or three Psalms: and you will so associate it with the pure and holy thoughts of God, which must accompany earnest prayer, that even as in times of difficulty and distress you fly to prayer, or in time of joy to praise, so will you equally seek your Bible secure of aid, sympathy, comfort, and love, which without it you dared not believe your God would give.

Remember, I do not tell you, that you will always

derive pleasure, or even instruction, from this daily perusal. Many and many a time you will read with a wandering mind and wearied spirit, you will feel, as if the task were utterly useless; but it is *not* useless, only persevere, only trust and believe, even when you can derive neither comfort nor enjoyment: and both will come again, the more soothing, the more reviving from their late suspension. I could tell you of one, now deep in the vale of years, to whom the Bible has been not only a treasured companion in many a private hour, but her sole stay, her sole hope, her sole enjoyment, through a life of many and deep afflictions; and now, in her eighty-third year, she tells me, she never reads the Bible, especially the Psalms and Prophets, without finding something she had never noticed before, something yet more inexpressibly beautiful and inexpressibly consoling. What book of man's invention could stand this test? And this is the evidence of a Jewess, my dear Annie, and a Jewess of what is now termed *the old* school, not of a Christian, which, if at this distance I can guess your thoughts aright, you will have fancied that it is.

But though I tell you fourteen or fifteen chapters perused each week will open to you the inexhaustible fulness of the Scriptures, and that I would not have the Bible made a task-book for long hours of tedious study: I wish you very much to lay aside a brief half-hour in the day, or devote a portion of your Sabbath to reading the many valuable works written by good and learned men relative to, and explanatory of it. You will find, by doing so, your interest so much more excited. Subjects apparently obscure, from our ignorance of the times or customs to which they relate, will become clear. Verses we may have read often without remark, become suddenly fraught with matter for new thought; characters which, from the disjointed verses which have related to them, we have not been of ourselves able to combine under one life or picture, will become as interesting as the characters of fiction, with the addition of a sacred moral and living example, which may assist us in our daily paths. I will explain my meaning by an instance of my own experience. There was a time when, though I was more than usually suffering from ill health, and harassed with constantly pressing cares, I had many calls; and all spiritual comfort seemed to have departed from me. I could no longer realise what often before, and very often since, sustained me under similar trials, the conviction, that whom *God loveth* He correcteth; and that peace would come again. At that very moment (I cannot remember now by what touch of thought excited), the lives of many of our Father's chosen and beloved servants came one by one before me—Joseph, Moses, David, Elijah:—had they not all suffered, ay suffered intensely? had they not all been tried by sorrow? had not they endured exactly the same as is the lot of human nature now? They were not exempt; and yet how earnestly, how fervently they loved and served their God, and how deeply, how tenderly was manifested *His love for them.* Human trial was then no evidence that we were forsaken of Him, that He had turned aside His face in wrath, and left us to our own weakness and misery; and even as if an Angel had spoken sympathy, and bade me *endure*, for my Father loved me still, so did that one thought, created by a consideration of the *characters*, not merely the *verses* of the Bible, brighten my path of gloom, and strengthen me as none other could have done. Books, then, that will bring before us the biographies of the

13

Bible, are valuable assistants in the study of the Scriptures, also such as produce evidences of prophecy fulfilled, and such as describe the customs of many of the present eastern nations, and the geographical associations of biblical localities, all of which we may find in works not heavier, or more uninteresting than the researches of modern travellers. Would that I could mention any Anglo-Jewish theological works—would, as I have often felt before, that our Hebrew students would select for our females and youth portions of those mighty tomes of spirituality and learning which our ancient sages have bequeathed us, and not drive us to the aid of the stranger. Judging by what I have read in the "Hebrew Review," and the "Moré Nebuchim" of Maimonides, much might be compiled, which would be invaluable to our inquiring youth, and render their Bibles dearer than ever, through commentators of their own nation. Till that is obtained, if we would seek aid for serious thought, we must go to Christian books, choosing, of course, those which are more spiritual than doctrinal. The spirit of the Christian religion is equally the spirit of the Hebrew; for both owe their origin to the same Book. We have but clearly to understand our own, and a glance will divide our doctrinal points from theirs. Nay, more, you will find, the more you study and examine your own that, the very books which confirm Christians in their faith, will confirm you in yours. One especially, a very beautiful work, "Keith's Evidences of Prophecy," was once lent me, not with any wish for its religious doctrines to convert me (that I well knew from the upright character of the lender), but for the exquisite beauty of its language and sentiments. It is many years ago; for I was scarcely older than you are now, and just beginning to think for myself. Well do I remember the trembling with which I began its perusal—trembling lest my dawning hope and trust should be shaken by 'his completely Christian book. But both were strengthened, dearest Annie. It was a strange, an almost indefinable effect; but so it was. Every evidence of prophecy fulfilled proved so convincingly that others were still to be accomplished; and the truth, the perpetuity, the unchangeableness of my holy faith, the impossibility of its ever merging into another, stood before me clearer and more convincingly than they had ever done before. I have no fear, then, of your perusing similar works. It is easier, much easier, to divide your peculiar creed from that of the writer, than to attempt, or hope, to think seriously, and derive comfort from serious things, unless you accustom yourself to read, and take pleasure in books of a spiritual and meditative nature: not, indeed, to take the place of any other; I should be truly grieved if I saw you devote your fine mind and vivid imagination to them alone, and deserve that you should neglect my advice entirely if I desired you to do so. No, dearest, make the Word of God and its explanations the *groundwork* of every study; and from the lightest kind of recreative reading you will gather flowers, where others cull but dangerous weeds. This is a shorter letter than usual; but just now I have no time for more.

LETTER XIII.

FROM THE SAME TO THE SAME.

Selection of the Israelites incompatible with the Divine justice towards the other nations—A common objection easily removed—Man's perfect freedom of choice—Narrative of Cain—Man a responsible being from his creation—Offspring of Cain and of Seth—Causes of the flood—Noah, his righteousness—Renewed workings of evil—Rise of idolatry—Origin of the promise of the law—Abraham, scriptural account of his selection, his descent—Some knowledge of God preserved among the descendants of Shem—Distinction between the descendants of Shem and of Canaan—How man may obtain the grace of God—Belief in pre-election a fearful mistake—Causes of the variety in character and inclination—All men equally responsible—Ancient parable—The man who resists temptation more worthy than he who is not tempted—Canaanites not wicked from destiny, but inclination—God will not strengthen good inclinations, unless sought for by effort and prayer—Causes of the extermination of the Canaanites—Israel's selection increased their responsibility—Why selected?—The gift of eternal life not vouchsafed to them alone—Extract from Joseph Albo—Law of the Noachidæ—Divinity of the Mosaic code acknowledged by both Christians and Mahomedans—Why the Jews do not make converts—Heathen and savage nations, how saved—All systems of religion working God's will—Responsibility increased with greater spiritual privileges—Grateful feelings ought to attend the Hebrews' observance of the law—Spiritual joy very different to narrow-minded exclusiveness—Selection of Israel perfectly reconcileable with the attributes of God.

You tell me my last has given you so much comfort; because I appear to have felt all that you are feeling, and that I am not surprised or grieved at anything you write. I have not *quite* forgotten that I was once young; nor am I, my dearest Annie, so exacting as to imagine, or even to wish, that the experience of long years and heavy cares should be yours all at once. Do you think a knowledge of religion comes by instinct, and without inquiry or examination? It is the error of many, but an error nevertheless. I wish you to tell me exactly every doubt or question that passes through your mind, and therefore shall at once enter on the subject you have alluded to with such evident hesitation in your last:—"The very selection of the Israelites appears to you incompatible with the uniform justice and impartiality of our heavenly Father. Why should one people have been thus favoured, when all mankind are equally His children? Was it not permitting only a few to inherit eternal life, and dooming all the rest to perdition and to sin?" You must remember that, though, when Adam sinned, the good in man succumbed to the evil, and his earthly nature became more powerful than his spiritual, yet still God left him a perfect *freedom of choice*. It was quite in his power to give the good sufficient ascendency, so as to attract towards him the favour of God, and so advance more and more in the path of righteousness. We are told this, first, by the words of the Eternal to Cain:— "If thou dost well, shalt thou not be accepted?" Here is a clear proof of the *capability* of human nature to do sufficiently well for the mercy of God to purify and accept it; "but if thou dost not well, sin lieth at the door." "The desire to do wrong may be thine (for such is the real meaning of the sentence, 'and unto thee shall be his desire'); but thou shalt rule over it." From these words we know that God had placed within man, from his creation, a consciousness of right and wrong, which made him a responsible being, and accountable for certain actions which his spirit, or soul, silently condemned. There was, as yet, no given prohibition against envy; but when Cain was wroth at his brother's offering being

accepted, either the voice of God distinctly heard, or
merely the whisperings of his soul, told him it was sin,
and warned him from its encouragement.   Then followed
the murder of his brother, which the same inward monitor
must have told him was fearful sin: else why did he seek
to conceal it?   The offspring of Cain appear to have in-
herited their father's evil propensities, while those of
Seth chose the better path, and called on the name of
the Lord: in other words, worshipped and believed in
Him.   Of these, Enoch so walked with God (that is, so
permitted the spiritual part of his nature to gain the
ascendency), that God took him, even without the pangs
of death.   Meanwhile men multiplied, and the offspring
of Cain formed unions with the purer offspring of Seth;
and from these a still more degenerate race descended,
till the whole earth itself became corrupted, and, according to the language of man, God repented that He had
made man, and ordained the fearful chastisement of the
flood.   But still, even in this universal wickedness, one
good man was found; therefore it is clear that human
nature still had the power to choose, and was not sinful
from *a blind necessity,* and because it knew no better.
Noah was a descendant of Seth, and was, the Bible tells
us, "a just man, and perfect in his generations," words
which appear to me to signify that his immediate ancestors, from Seth downwards, were all those who had
chosen the good in preference to the evil; and he was
acceptable in the sight of God, not only for himself, but
for the worth of his fathers; else why should it be so
emphatically said, he "was perfect in his *generations*"?
a supposition borne out by the deathless translation of
Enoch, his great-grandfather.   The righteousness of
Noah is proved not only by the fact, that his family
was the only one spared, but from his changeless con-

stancy and child-like belief in the words of God. The brief recital of Scripture would sometimes occasion the idea, that the ark was built in a very short time. Now, the very shortest interval must have been one hundred years—of course, a shorter period in that age than it would be now; but still, even supposing it five-and-twenty or thirty years of labour, how invincible must have been his faith and firmness to pursue the work, and, most probably, in the midst of those who scoffed and scorned it. The infirmity of human nature, we might almost suppose, would occasion intervals of doubt, and despondency, and questions as to the necessity of the work, even without actual unbelief. The course of nature went on the same; the bright sun shone, and the seasons revolved in their course; the mighty torrents remained chained in their rocky beds; man went on in his career, sinful, flourishing, and happy, without a sign or warning to reveal the wrath of God, except the words and work of Noah, which they were not likely to regard with more attention, than the heedless and erring of the present day would believe it to be the word of God, if told that the Bible condemned their evil course.

The flood took place, and sin for a brief, a very brief while, was exterminated from the earth. But once more in security, the evil awoke again, even in the family of Noah; and from Ham and his son Canaan originated the fearful systems of idolatry and increased crime, which spread far and wide over the world, and rendered it more and more difficult for man to realize of himself the good, and return unto the one sole God. The omniscience of God saw this; and when the sweet savour of Noah's righteous offering ascended, He said He would "no more destroy the earth for man's sake, for the imagination of man's heart is evil from his youth;" He would no more

smite every thing living as He had done. He saw that
even signal chastisement would not destroy the propensity to evil which, of course, the more it was encouraged,
the more powerful it would become.   Yet still interfering
not with men's *perfect liberty of choice,* He left them to
their own devices, foreseeing, in His omniscience, that
glorious day when, after ages and ages of trial and purification in human reckoning, the good would eventually
triumph over the evil, and a new and sinless existence
dawn for man.

Our ancient sages declare, that it was on account of
Abram's firm resistance to the idolatrous practices of his
father and countrymen, that God revealed Himself to
him.   This may, or may not be; but the Bible-record
simply gives us to understand, that God selected him
because he saw that his heart, like Noah's, was perfect
towards Him; and his first call was a trial both of faith
and obedience, which he had perfect freedom of choice
either to heed or neglect.   He descended in a direct line
from Shem, one of the two righteous sons of Noah; and
I have always thought that, in the descendants of Shem,
a faint and imperfect (but still some) knowledge of the
Almighty God was preserved, even though they worshipped household gods or idols as visible deities, or as
emblems of the Invisible.   My reason for this idea is,
that both in the case of Abraham's mission to Laban for
Rebecca, and Jacob's sojourn with his uncle, it is evident
from Scripture that the Supreme God was not utterly
unknown.   "Come in, thou blessed of the Lord," is the
greeting of Laban's house to the steward; and, again,
"The thing *proceedeth from the Lord;* we cannot speak
unto thee bad or good.   Let her be thy master's son's
wife, as the Lord hath spoken."   Now the mere recital
from the steward would not have been sufficient for such

an immediate and hearty recognition of Abraham's God, if there had not been some previous knowledge of Him. "I have learned by experience," says Laban, "that the Lord has blessed me for thy sake." The very fact of Abraham's, and after him Isaac's, great anxiety that their sons should be saved from a union with the Canaanitish nations, and marry among their own kindred, equally the descendants of Shem, is a proof in itself of the superiority, in point of moral virtue and some knowledge of the true God, of the latter over the former. The descendants of Ham and Canaan had chosen the pursuing of the evil. A review of the fearful idolatrous rites of those nations and their immoral and demoniacal customs would show you, how terrible is the extent to which human wickedness can attain. The descendants of Shem, on the contrary, though the imperfection of their mingled nature prevented their attaining those just ideas of the Supreme Deity, which would entirely prevent the worship of idols, and inspire a pure heart-service, only to be fully acquired by a Divine Revelation, yet had none of those obscene and polluting ceremonies which desecrated the nations around. They were a pastoral innocent people, unable, indeed, to refrain entirely from the worship of images, but still believing in a God above them, and obeying Him whenever His commands were revealed, as we have already seen.

Amongst these Abram was born and nurtured, and, as he broke from the trammels of image-worship, seeking with the earnestness of unusual intellect and purity the One spiritual God—to his countrymen so faintly known,—that God, in His mercy, and exactly in accordance with His afterwards revealed word, which promised to answer all those who sought and called upon Him, made Himself known to Abram; and, to try his obedience and his faith, He desired him first to leave his country and his kindred, and his father's house, and go to an unknown land; and that unknown land was inhabited by the Canaanitish nations, a most impure race, mighty and numerous. His very going amongst them was a trial of his faith and constancy which, in a mere summary glance, we are liable to overlook. I have not space in this letter to linger on the Patriarch's numerous trials. All I wish to prove to you, is simply that, in the case both of Noah and Abram, they were righteous, not *originally* from any election or special favour of God, but because they exercised the freedom of choice granted to *all mankind*, and pursued the *good* in lieu of the *evil*, which latter, as decidedly the easier course, was chosen by the multitudes. That they so used their free-will, and against every obstacle struggled to become righteous, gave them favour in the sight of their heavenly Father, preserved Noah from the flood, and gave Abram the promise of a Revelation, which was gradually to bless not only his immediate descendants, but the whole world. Now every man had, and has it in his power to obtain the unspeakable blessing of the love and grace of God. It is a great and a most dangerous mistake to imagine, that the good are the *elected* of the Lord—that we are good or evil as He creates us. The infirmity and imperfections of human nature, the hereditary dispositions often engendered in families, are causes of the wide diversity of character which we so often trace even in children. Some have more difficulty to resist evil propensities than others; but this does not make them less responsible, or less free agents in the sight of God, though their inward struggles to give the good ascendency render them infinitely more acceptable than those who have no such temptations to resist. Our ancient sages illustrate this by a parable; viz.: "That a king had once extensive wine-cellars, over which he placed certain keepers, some of whom inordinately loved wine and all intoxicating drinks, and the others were habitually temperate, from dislike to these liquors. When, after some time, the cellars were examined, and all found correct, the king, to the astonishment of his followers, rewarded the keepers who were fond of liquor by a double amount of wages to what he paid the naturally temperate." "Both, indeed, have been equally honest," was his reply; "but I reward them according to the trouble it has cost them to obey my commands. The temperate had little or no trouble, from their dislike to wine; but how great must have been the trial and difficulty to those fond of wine, and habitually accustomed to strong drink."

And thus it is with the naturally disposed to good and evil. Man sees but the outward conduct of his fellows. God sees the *inward* principle, ay, and the *circumstance* which so often produces evil, and judges and rewards accordingly. And, therefore, that our natural disposition removes or lessens our responsibility before Him, is a doctrine as mistaken as it is dangerous.

Now those nations whom God commanded His people to exterminate, were not evil from necessity; equally with the offspring of Shem, they had in themselves the power to have become worthy of God's grace and forbearance, instead of which, they gave sin ascendency, and became more and more corrupt. You will say, perhaps, that I have told you the hearts of all men are in the hand of God, and He could, by a mere act of volition, have turned them from their evil way. He could; but, dearest Annie, He will not do this, unless besought to do so, not only by prayer, but also by some *effort*, however imperfect, to make manifest a *wish* to pursue the good. Our Father only asks this, and His infinite love and mercy will do the rest. But, if no prayer is breathed, no effort made, and the free choice granted us plunges us into the abyss of sin, how dare we be so presumptuous as to imagine God will stretch forth his hand to save? He had sworn never more to destroy the earth and all mankind; but the fearful wickedness of the descendants of Ham was such, as, for the safety and purity of the other nations, to demand their extermination. Still God gave them *time to repent and amend.* The descendants of Abraham were not to possess the land God had promised them for four hundred years, "because the *iniquity of the Emorites was not yet full.*" In that period, had they repented, and become like the descendants of Shem (remember, it was still fully in their power to do so), we cannot doubt for a single moment that, though His word would have been fulfilled, as to the possession of the land by Abraham's descendants, its original inhabitants, instead of being exterminated, would have shared all the blessings given to the Israelites, and, without being under the same responsibility (for the law only rendered those responsible to whom it was given), might have become equally acceptable in the sight of God.

The people of Israel were chosen as the receivers and promulgators of the law, for Abraham's sake; but that selection, instead of decreasing their responsibility and stamping them as righteous above every other, only made them *more* responsible, and simply instruments in the Eternal's hand in eventually blessing the whole earth. "For thou art a holy people unto the Lord thy God; the Lord thy God hath chosen thee to be a special people unto Himself, above all the people on the face of the earth. The Lord did not set his love upon you, nor choose you, because you were more in number than any people; for ye were the fewest of all people; but because the Lord loved you, *and because He would keep the oath which He had sworn unto your fathers,* hath the Lord brought you out with a mighty hand, and redeemed you out of the house of bondmen, from the hand of Pharaoh king of Egypt. Know, therefore, that the Lord thy God, He is God, the faithful God, who keepeth covenant and mercy *with those that love Him, and keep His Commandments* unto a *thousand* generations." (Deut. vii. 6–9.) And again, "Speak not thou in thy heart, after that the Lord thy God has cast them [the nations] out from before thee, saying, For my righteousness the Lord hath brought me in to possess this land; but for the wickedness of those nations the Lord doth drive them out before thee. Not for thy righteousness, nor for the uprightness of thy heart, dost thou go to possess this land; but for the wickedness of these nations the Lord thy God doth drive them out from before thee, and that *He might perform the word which the Lord swore unto thy fathers,* Abraham, Isaac, and Jacob. Understand, therefore, that the Lord thy God giveth thee *not this good land to possess it for thy* righteousness, because thou art a stiff-necked people." (Ibid. ix. 4–6.)

Surely, dearest Annie, these verses are sufficient to disprove the idea, that we were chosen for any special merit of our own; but only from the promise made by the Eternal to our father, who, from his goodness and piety, had so attracted His loving-kindness that He promised favour and mercy even to his *thousandth generation.* This promise would equally have been made to any other individual who, like Abraham, had of his *own unbiassed will* chosen the path of good. It was *no* preordained election. We were, indeed, from Abraham's time an *elected* people; but Abraham's goodness was the effect of his own free choice. Nor did this selection give us, as some might suppose, any *temporal* advantages over other nations. If we compare the extent of our territory and dominion with those of Babylon, Persia, Greece, and Rome, we shall perceive that we were in truth but a handful, as well as a people apart. Through us, indeed, Revelation was to extend over the whole world, and with our *spiritual* privileges no other nation could vie; but these privileges, while they marked us as favoured for Abraham's sake, so increased our *responsibilities*, that it was no *easy* task to gain the immortal goal which revelation placed before us. It is quite an erroneous notion to suppose that the Jews *alone* were permitted and enabled to inherit eternal life. Joseph Albo, an eminent rabbi of Soria, in Spain, who lived in the fifteenth century, a period when the Jews were subjected to the heaviest persecutions, wherever they were scattered, and when, therefore, if there were any exclusive notion of their immortal inheritance, we should certainly find it, yet, in his celebrated Sepher Ikkarim, or Book of Principles, enumerates, among the six Articles of Faith, which he declares *absolutely incumbent* on all professors of the Divine Law of Moses, the following remarkable passage:—the fourth item of the creed is "*That the proper observance of any one of the commandments of the Law will lead man to perfection:*" and on this he writes, "If this were not so, the Law of Moses would operate as a cause to deprive men of that perfection, which our rabbis of blessed memory called 'Eternal life in the world to come.' The purpose of all the commandments of the

Law of Moses is to enable *all mankind* to attain that perfection. And as the observance of *all* the commandments is obligatory *only* on the Israelite, it would thence result that, if the absolute condition of eternal life be the observance of all these commandments, the rest of mankind would become excluded, and the Law of Moses would be the cause of their exclusion. But this would be an effect *contrary* to the intention of that revelation. The truth, therefore, is, that the observance of any *one* of the commandments for God's sake, and with a perfect conviction of their divine origin, will lead man to eternal life. Consequently, the Noächidœ [which is a term signifying the whole human race] can, by means of their law, attain eternal life. And accordingly, our Rabbis of blessed memory [that is, some of our very earliest, most pious, and most ancient fathers] assert that THE RIGHTEOUS AMONG ALL THE NATIONS OF THE WORLD HAVE A SHARE IN THE LIFE TO COME."*

Now, dearest Annie, is not this a triumphant refutation of the charge so often brought against us, that we are a proud exclusive race, denying to all mankind the spiritual promises given to us, and that though we believe the Hebrews alone are to be saved, we make no effort to bring others over to our creed? As long as I can remember myself, the belief of Rabbi Joseph Albo was entwined with my very being, and so enabled me both to love and venerate the righteous of every other creed. Still, I longed for some witness stronger than my feelings, to prove that such was the vital spirit of the Jewish creed; and the joy, therefore, with which I perused the commentary of Albo you will imagine, when

---

* Hebrew Review, vol. i. p. 56, translation from R. Joseph Albo's "Book of Principles."

I found I was following and obeying, not the dictates of the heart alone, but those of my religion.

The law of the Noächidæ prohibits "idolatry, fornication, bloodshed, robbery, blasphemy, and eating the flesh cut from a living animal, and commands the propagation of the species." Now, this law is obeyed as Divine, by every religion throughout the universe to whom God is revealed; and from *our* law it originally came. Wherever God is known and acknowledged, the Law of Moses is always declared Divine. It is clear then, that, if the salvation of the righteous among the nations depends on their acknowledging any one of the commandments of the Law of Moses, and obedience thereunto for "God's sake, and with a perfect conviction of their divine origin," we have no need to make converts. We are, indeed, the first-born, first-beloved; but *all* who look to Him, and love God according to the law they follow, are our brothers, and equally with us heirs of immortality! You will ask me, perhaps, How will this hold good concerning the many *heathen* nations at the time of the delivery of the law, and the very many countries, now, the inhabitants of which are savage barbarians, utterly ignorant of God, and who have not even the law of the Noächidæ to guide them. I answer, that I believe, and the spirit of my religion authorises the belief that, as a God of infinite love and justice would NEVER create any being to be eternally destroyed, even they must have had, and must have, powers within themselves to win immortality. The miracles, wonders, and public manifestation of the God of Israel at the Exodus from Egypt, and His visible government of His people in Palestine, extended over the whole world; and, as I have said in a former letter, both people and law, even by the heathens, were acknowledged to be of God; and many of the commandments were *unconsciously* adopted and followed. They were at liberty to seek the Holy Land, and enquire of the Lord. Strangers, and even eunuchs, were promised a place in His house, which, instead of being exclusive, was open unto all men; and we know that very many came, and took back to their error-benighted homes tidings of the God of Israel, which gradually spread, faintly and disfigured indeed, but still sufficiently, even in their darkness, to win eternal life. We are repeatedly told, both in the Law and Prophets, to "*love the stranger*," that is, to treat him with kindness and goodwill, and set aside for him equal portions as free-will gifts, as we did for our own widows, and orphans. This was not only to teach us benevolence from man to man, but to spread the knowledge of the God, who had ordained these things, far and wide over the world.

With regard to the many nations of the present day where the *revealed* Word of God has never penetrated; where they *appear* to be left entirely to their own imaginings, I say, that as our Father's creation, we still cannot, we dare not believe, that their destiny is to linger on the earth for a few years of trouble, with feelings as strong in them as in their more enlightened brethren, and then to pass away for ever. The absurdities and the more revolting parts of their religion alone reach us. If we were to examine deeply into the inward faith of the Indians of America and the Hindoos of Asia, we might find ideas that would startle us with their sublimity and truth. Both have *visible* images of worship; but the "Great Spirit" of the one, and the "Brahma" of the other, are the undoubted acknowledgment of the One Supreme God, and are worshipped and contemplated inwardly as an IDEA far above the minor deities, which are multiplied according to their wants and fears. Even in those countries where we cannot trace this, we may rest assured, that God has placed within every immortally created being a power to distinguish in some degree between right and wrong, an impulse towards some virtue, and an opposition to the pursuits of vice; and that He demands no more from them than He knows they *can* perform.

I do indeed rejoice, when I hear of the efforts of those noble pure-spirited men, whom the worldly so often deride and contemn, the missionaries, who seek to preach even their gospel to benighted lands, and so win them to some knowledge of the divine commands. I know many would loudly condemn this as an entirely anti-Jewish idea; but believing as I do, and as my Bible authorises me to believe, that all the present systems of revealed religion are working God's will, and gradually bringing nearer that glorious day, when all darkness, all error shall be removed, and when, *our* chastisement being ended, we shall be restored to our own land, and all nations flow unto us, and acknowledge with us that God is One; and believing, too, that unless the earth is brought in some degree to know God, this will not be accomplished: I *must* rejoice at every effort (be it of individuals or nations) to remove ignorance and reveal the Bible, or (as in the case of the Koran) *some part* at least of Revelation.

There is no greater or more deluding error, than that into which some enthusiasts fall, of pluming themselves on their superior religious enlightenment as an especial election of the Lord. Where He gives more, He demands more; and our increased responsibility, instead of rendering our task *easier*, may make the path to heaven yet more difficult, than it is to those to whom less has been revealed. I do not allude to the holy pride and grateful joy with which every spiritually minded Hebrew *must*, or *ought* to, look back on the infinite love and mercy shown unto his race from the beginning,—that Revelation was given to *him first*, that from him, from his Scriptures, all the comfort, the fulness, the blessings of religion have proceeded, and are still proceeding,—that, however low his estate, however persecuted his condition, however denied the fact of his being still the chosen of God, yet nothing can remove the holy truth of his being one of that seed of Abraham, in whom all the nations of the earth should be blessed. But this truly spiritual joy is a widely different feeling from that narrow-minded and unscriptural exclusiveness, which is unhappily the fashion of too many in the present day. The former recognises, in every man who seeks to love and serve God according to the light his guiding law bestows, a brother destined like himself for immortality, and seeks, by his own firm adherence and faithful obedience to the law of Moses, to make its divine character more and more acknowledged. The latter wraps himself up in an imaginary righteousness, and would deny heaven and religion to all except those who think exactly like himself, forgetting that, even if it be so very righteous to think as he does, it is no credit to himself; for if he had not been so instructed, he would not have thought so; and if he be so superior in religious knowledge, he may be, nay he is, more *responsible* in the sight of his Father in heaven, but not more righteous than the followers of God and virtue among the less enlightened.

This has been a very long letter, dearest Annie, and I fear less individually interesting than some others; but your question combined subjects of such vast im-

portance to a clear comprehension of the very foundation of your religion, that I found it impossible to treat
them either briefly or lightly.

I want you clearly to understand, and fully to feel,
that the charge so often brought against our holy faith,
that a rigid exclusiveness and uncharitableness prevent
all efforts on our part to make converts, is an entirely
mistaken one. We never attempt the fearful system of
interfering with other religions, or to seek to turn man
from his own faith; because WE DO NOT BELIEVE that
the salvation of the nations is *only* to be obtained by
their becoming Jews. We do not believe that God has
mercy, and has opened the gates of His heaven to the
Jews *alone*. You will, no doubt, often be told by the
nominal Jew, as well as by the nominal Christian, that
this is only an individual, *not* a Jewish notion; but do
not let your faith be shaken by such remarks. Our
Bible tells us, that the law of Moses is incumbent on
the Israelites alone, not on the nations of the earth; and
our ancient fathers (men with whose deep learning and
profound wisdom, who of the present day can compare?)
have told us in clear simple words, "THE RIGHTEOUS
AMONG THE NATIONS OF THE WORLD HAVE A SHARE IN
THE LIFE TO COME."

You are satisfied, then, I hope, that the selection of
the descendants of Abraham is perfectly reconcilable
with the attributes of justice and mercy in our heavenly
Father; that instead of "permitting only a few to inherit eternal life, and dooming the rest of mankind to
perdition and sin," it was to be the seed *in which every
nation of the world should be blessed, a promise fulfilled*
and still FULFILLING; that, though it revealed more, it
demanded more; and therefore, instead of unduly ele-
vating us in our own estimation above every other, it

ought to make us more humble, more lovingly obedient to our God, and more universally forbearing and charitable towards man, than any other people in the world.

Consider well these important truths, and, above all things, remember, dearest Annie, that man is not originally righteous or evil from the *favour* or *disfavour* of his God, but from his own free choice; that our Father has placed within all His children the power to resist evil and pursue the good; and that, therefore, we dare not plead hereditary disposition or untoward circumstances, as an excuse for persistency in wrong, when once we *know* the *right*. That some have much more difficulty in overcoming evil inclinations than others, that some are good almost unconsciously, simply from disposition, I allow; but we must never forget that GOD reads the heart and reins, man only the outward conduct; and therefore the righteousness that man perceives and reverences, may be less acceptable to God, and reap less reward in heaven, than the worth obtained by the mighty conquest of the evil which so fiercely struggled for ascendency within, and the *reflection* of which, perhaps, has *alone* been visible. The various dispositions found in man are of *earth*, and often hereditary; the free-will to choose is the voice of God, speaking through the emanation of Himself—the immortal soul.

LETTER XIV.

FROM THE SAME TO THE SAME.

Imperfection of the characters of Scripture—How to reconcile apparent contradictions—Scriptural characters merely human and exposed to human frailties—Position in the past unable to be judged by the present—Liability of all men to fail in faith—Error always followed by suffering—Jacob's trials—Joseph's boyish character, and effect of adversity—Proneness of human nature to judge harshly of others—Charge against Moses refuted—Consequences of his hasty deed—His character so purified by forty years of exile, as to render him a fit recipient of the Eternal's revelation—His natural impulses —Consolation of his mingled character—Sins of David—Why chosen in lieu of his brothers—Apparent contradiction of his selection, and after-faults—His selection exposed him to heavy temporal trials and dangers—Fearful chastisement of his sin—Individual responsibility —No such thing as fated evil—Reconciliation of Nathan's seemingly contradictory words—Death of David's infant, and why—Easy for the believer to reconcile apparent contradictions in the Bible—Religion given to enable us to conquer sin—Greater reward for the penitent than for the naturally righteous—Extract from the Fathers —Accordance of Scripture characters with the words of the Bible —What God requires of us—No man utterly reprobate.

"THE characters of Scripture sometimes appear to you scarcely deserving of the high estimation in which all believers in the Bible hold them," you tell me, dearest Annie; "that even Abraham was twice guilty of deception; and from a feeling [as it appears to you] almost like cowardice, Isaac did the same; Jacob was certainly even more guilty; Joseph, in his youth, reported evil of his brethren; Moses slew a man and hid him in the sand; and David was guilty of two most fearful crimes"—facts that appear like objections certainly, but which rather ought to comfort than disturb us. If God did show favour only to the perfect, we must despair; for we could never hope to become like them: and, in fact, from a consideration of human nature now, we should be inclined to believe, that the characters of the Bible must have been a completely different race of beings, and elected by the Almighty as recipients of his favour, and not as being (which in my last I endeavoured to prove to you) equally free-will agents with ourselves. If we acknowledge the Bible to be divine, a revelation vouchsafed to guide us, now that the immediate inter-ference of the Eternal is removed from us, we shall easily be enabled to reconcile these apparent difficulties by the simple fact, that God would not have shown such especial favour to those characters, and proclaimed them through all succeeding generations as His servants, elect, and even friends, if they had not been deserving. We read the *outward* frailties: God saw the *inward* heart. We judge the Past by the thoughts of the Present, a very mistaken thing to do; because, though the emotions and feelings of humanity are through all ages the same, human nature is always *advancing*, and what we con-sider even a *crime* now might have been merely a failing then. All the characters to which you refer were *human*, liable to suggestions of the evil, equally with the im-pulses of the good.

It is true, Abraham and Isaac failed in faith; but at this distance of time, and from the brief record of the Bible, we cannot tell the extent of the danger which menaced them, and so tempted them to a departure from the exact truth. You think they ought not to have doubted the power of the God who had so revealed Himself to them; but it appears to me, that it *is this very* failure of faith, where our path does not lie clearly before us, to which this imperfect existence is so very liable. In great things, or in lesser ones, if it be *clear* that only God can help us, we go to Him directly, but seldom where we fancy the aid of man, or our own efforts will do. We ought to remember, too, that Abraham and Isaac were surrounded by nations who knew not God nor His commandments, and therefore had no restraint upon their passions or inclinations. It was far more natural, that they should resort to stratagem to elude the impending evil, than believe, without a direct promise to that effect, that God Himself would interfere in such a *seeming* trifle. But that it was *wrong*, both they and we are taught by the issue. Their stratagem *produced* the very evil which they had hoped it would avert.

If, dearest Annie, the faults and failings of these great men had passed with a mere record, and no notice had been taken of them by some chastisement evinced, we should, perhaps, be justified in believing that it was scarcely compatible with the attributes of the Eternal to choose such men for his favoured servants; but there *never* was a fault committed, which did not bring some suffering, which then, as now, is the constant accompaniment of error. God did not permit any evil to happen to Sarah, because He had *promised* Abraham to be with him wherever he went; but, during the time that he was ignorant of her fate, he must have endured the bitterest *human* emotions of anxiety and dread, without even the power of appealing for God's help, for he had trusted in his own strength and wisdom, and had failed. Jacob's deceit was followed by a series of sufferings, which we very often overlook, when we speak of him as merely the favoured ancestor of Israel. First

came the dread of his injured brother's vengeance; then
his hasty flight from his father's house, and painfully
weary journey; then Laban's constant deceptions—the
renewed dread of his brother—the deceit practised by
Simeon and Levi on the Shechemites, troubling the
temporary quiet of his household, and exposing him to
very great danger; again, the early death of his beloved
Rachel; and his last and most fearful trial, the effect of
deceit again on the part of his own sons—the supposed
death of his darling Joseph, and long separation from
him. When we think of all these trials, must we not
intensely feel that, however *spiritually* blessed, because,
in the main, his *heart* was right with God, his human
error met with human retribution? and that, though the
revelations vouchsafed to him must have inexpressibly
comforted and sustained him, still his earthly life was
one of *constant trial,* equal in severity and continuance
to any of the present day? Did we perceive, that the
men whom God especially favoured were carried through
this life without one of the sorrows and cares, which are
the heritage of all men, we might then, with some
show of justice, object to the faults which their history
records and assert that, to our imperfect vision, it *seemed*
like injustice so temporally and corporally, as well as
spiritually, to bless individuals who had just the same
faults and imperfections as those, for whom there is now
no visible interference. But, when we look attentively
into the inner and outer life of these scriptural characters, we must acknowledge their life on earth was just the
same blending of joys and sorrows, cares and anxieties,
dangers and oppressions, as human life is now.

It seems a somewhat harsh judgment, to bring forward, as an alloy to the beautiful character of Joseph,
the petty failing of his early youth, that of "bringing

15

to his father. his brothers' evil report." To me, it is
a still more perfect illustration of human nature, than
had he been depicted without one fault. What is more
natural than that the over-indulged and petted favourite
of a then weak old man, should sometimes complain of
the unkind treatment, and the ill-conduct of his elder
brothers? That it was wrong, all must allow; but it
was human nature. Favouritism and over-indulgence
might have had the same evil influence on Joseph, as
they always have, even to the present day, in families.
We do not see the true beauty of his character until
adversity developes it. Had he remained with his father,
his character *might* have deteriorated, not advanced.
His very dreams would, perhaps, have increased the
evil of individual presumption, already engendered by
indiscreet favouritism, had not the Lord, in His ever-
acting mercy, *overruled* the cruel enmity of his brothers,
for Joseph's individual benefit; not only in his *temporal*
elevation, which, remember, did not take place, till he
had been some years in servitude, and in prison, but in
the improvement and perfection of his character. It
is a mistaken idea (but produced, I think, from the stories
written from the Bible for children), to suppose that it
was on account of any striking virtue in the early youth
of Joseph, that he was made the favourite of his father.
The Bible expressly tells us, " Now Israel loved Joseph
more than all his children, *because he was the son of his
old age.*" He was also the son of his beloved Rachel,
and very fair to look upon; and no doubt, he possessed
many of those sweet and attractive qualities, which are
so engaging in early youth, but which might never have
reached such exalted virtue as his after-years displayed,
had it not been for the sad but beneficial lessons of
adversity. When torn by cruel task-masters from the

doting love of his father, compelled to serve in the
house of Potiphar, falsely accused, and flung into prison
without even being heard in his defence, the thought of
his early home must then have returned to his mind;
and how bitterly *might* he have felt that he had, perhaps,
increased the irritation of his brothers by the too presumptuous relation of his dreams, which must, in his
imprisonment, have seemed so impossible to be fulfilled.
That Joseph's natural disposition was peculiarly sweet
and noble, is proved by the *effect* of adversity upon him.
But we have no right to quarrel with the failing of his
early youth, unless we saw that his life had been one
continued stream of prosperity, from beginning to end,
or could point out one individual in the past, present, or
the future, who, formed of dust as well as spirit, did not
inherit the imperfection of the one, as well as the perfection of the other, so as to be subject not only "to the
ills which flesh is heir to," but to its weakness and its
faults.

How sad it would be for us, dearest Annie, if God
judged us as we judged each other; if He took note of
those little things, with which even the most righteous
have to contend, as to let them over-balance all the
good of deed, and thought, and feeling, to which our
mingled nature *can* attain!   It is not only with the
characters of Scripture we sometimes cavil; but if we
look well into our own hearts, we shall be startled to
find, how often we are striving to discover some petty
fault or slight failing, in those who bear the character
of unusual goodness, something which would bring them
down to us, and so lessen the uncomfortably restless
feeling, which would urge us to *rise to them*, a sensation
which, however undefined and unconscious, *always* attends the contemplation of superior *goodness*.   With

regard to the grave fault said to tarnish the character of Moses, and to raise the objection, that God should select one guilty of murder for the giver of His Law, we reply, that God saw the *circumstance:* we see but the *deed.* God read the *heart,* the whole train of feeling before and after: we read but of the fearful glance and upraised arm. If we believe in God as a being of unalterable truth and perfect justice, as His word reveals Him: we *must* rest content that, evil as the actual *action* was, the *heart* was perfect with Him; that no sin towards God entered his heart—no previously encouraged envious or angry thought, as in the case of Cain. It was simply an irrepressible burst of natural indignation, a passionate impulse, at seeing a countryman, probably a bond-slave, utterly unable to protect himself, smitten by an Egyptian.

Understand me, dearest Annie, I am not defending the *deed;* for though, in the time of Moses, the laws against murder were *not* accurately defined, yet "whoever sheddeth man's blood, by man shall his blood be shed" had been said and acknowledged as a prohibition against murder ever since the time of Noah. It was a sin in itself; but its origin was a noble feeling of saving an injured brother from a cruel oppressor; and the spirit of the words, "Vengeance is mine, saith the Lord, and I will repay it," had not yet entered the mind and heart of man. Had Moses escaped without any notice of his sin, and *directly* afterwards been favoured with an especial Revelation from the Lord, we might be startled; but flight alone saved him from the consequences of his mistaken deed. The wrath of Pharaoh *was* excited against him, as it would have been against any other man. Even his countrymen, for whom he had interfered, reproached him with cutting words:

"Who made thee a prince and a judge over us; intendest thou to kill me as thou didst the Egyptian? And Moses *feared*, and said, Surely this thing is known. And when Pharaoh heard this thing, he sought to slay Moses. But Moses fled from the face of Pharaoh to the land of Midian." And there he dwelt, forgotten, alike by the Egyptians, his countrymen, and, it would seem, even by his family, for forty years,* performing all the lowly duties, and sharing all the toils and cares of a shepherd to his father-in-law,—he who had been brought up in all the enervating luxury of an Egyptian court. Who can say then that, if he sinned, he was not punished? And who may declare the purifying thoughts and meditations, which in those long years of exile might occupy his heart, and so render him a fit messenger for the word of the Eternal? Forty years was a long period of exile for an involuntary sin, but not too long for his character to attain that purity and elevation, and great self-control, which was necessary for his important mission. The *natural* character of Moses was evidently impetuous, perhaps, even of passionate impulses. We see this, not only in his slaying the Egyptian, but when he flung down the two tables of stone, in his fierce anger at the idolatry of the people (enough, certainly, to rouse his wrath), and when he struck the rock instead of speaking to it, as God had commanded. Natural irritability, in this last instance, had even power to drown the whisper of faith. "Must *we* fetch you water out of the rock?" he angrily said,

---

* The chronologists of the Bible differ so remarkably, that it is scarcely possible to obtain clear dates and length of periods; but that Moses was forty when he slew the Egyptian, eighty when he saw the burning bush, and a hundred and twenty when he died, they all agree; and, in that case, forty years must have elapsed in his exile.

instead of reproving them for tempting the anger of the
Lord, as in the previous instance he had done; and
God said, " Because ye *believed* me not, to sanctify me
in the eyes of the children of Israel, therefore ye shall
not bring this congregation into the land which I have
given them," thus proving, that even in his favoured
servant Moses, the faithful of his house, a prophet like
whom there never was, or will be another, disobedience
and unbelief, even in one solitary instance, might not
pass unnoticed.   Yet the Bible tells us, " Now the man
Moses was very *meek*, above all the men who were
upon the face of the earth," and this is *no contradiction
whatever* to his being naturally impetuous.   The one
was the imperfection of his human nature, the other
was the effect of the spirit's ascendency over the
earthly, and obtained by prayer and struggle, probably
in that long forty years' exile to which I have before
alluded.   That he was, indeed, the very meekest of all
men, we cannot glance on his various trials, provoca-
tions, and insults, even from his own family, without
feeling; and that two or three times natural impetuosity
should break forth, is to me such consolatory proof of
his being *human* like ourselves, that I hail them with
gratitude instead of objection, and love to contemplate
his character the more, from the fact that its beauty
and consistency are those to which *all* men can aspire.
He does not stand before us freed from all human feelings, impulses, and affections; his heart is full of them,
and so we hail him *brother*, even while we feel the deepest reverence for that *spiritual worth*, which marked him
the chosen and beloved of God.

The sins of David were of a deeper dye; but surely we
cannot read his agonised repentance without feeling that,
if he sinned as *mortal*, he repented as only those can

whose hearts are right with God. When Samuel called the family of Jesse to the sacrifice, struck by the imposing appearance of Eliab, Jesse's eldest son, he said in his heart, "Surely the Lord's anointed is before me." God answered, "Look not on his countenance, or on the height of his stature, for I have refused him; for the LORD seeth not as man seeth; for man looketh on the outward appearance, but the Lord looketh on the heart." This, perhaps you will say, is exactly that which you find it so difficult to understand. There must have been some imperfection in David to attempt the committal of such heavy faults. We do not hear anything of the kind in Eliab, and yet he was rejected, and David chosen. Eliab was in a private station, and his errors and faults were only of consequence to himself in his individual responsibility before God; but if we believe that God's word is TRUTH, we *must* be satisfied that David's heart was more perfect with God than his brothers', or he would not have been chosen. His being chosen in no way distinguished him by the bestowal of temporal happiness and honours, as the epithet "anointed king" so often, but so erroneously supposes. Nay, from that very hour, his life became one of trials and dangers which, had he remained the lowly shepherd boy, he would probably never have known. If you carefully read over his life, you will find it one series of sorrow and disaster, even after his elevation to the throne. You will say, perhaps, "What has that to do with his faults?" Only so far, that as his being spiritually favoured by God did not exempt him from *human suffering*, so we have no right to imagine that, because he was more holy, in some respects, than the generality of his fellows, he was to be entirely exempt from human *imperfection*. His piety, his faithfulness, his unwavering trust in the loving mercy of his God, however severely tried, were displayed throughout a long life. His sin was the ascendency, for the time being, of the mortal over the immortal, the clay over the spirit. Of the fearful extent of the temptation, we, of less impassioned and colder calculating climes, cannot have the least conception. Excuses, indeed, there are none; and though God, in His untiring mercy and in accordance with His promise that for the truly repentant there is forgiveness, pardoned, yet He chastised not only David, but the partner of his crime, in the bereavement of their first-born. The suffering endured by David and his wife on this occasion is touchingly narrated by the sacred historian (2 Sam. xii. 14–25); and his intense repentance and anguish are seen in the fifty-first Psalm, like which, for remorse, prayer, and self-abnegation, there is not, and never will be, another.

Nor was the death of Bathsheba's infant his only chastisement. We are expressly told, "But the thing that David had done displeased the Lord;" and when Nathan's exquisite parable of the ewe-lamb had opened David's eyes to the enormity of the crime, and, in great wrath, he exclaimed, little thinking he was passing sentence on himself, "As the Lord liveth, the man that hath done this thing shall surely die; and he shall restore the lamb four-fold, because he did this thing, and had no pity:" Nathan, after emphatically declaring, "Thou art the man," proceeds to pass a sentence upon him from the Lord, which was fulfilled to the very letter. Read the whole of the twelfth chapter of 2 Samuel, and particularly notice from the seventh to the thirteenth verse. Every denunciation there contained was awfully accomplished. First came a repetition of the many favours which he had received from God; and that, had they been too few or too trifling, He would have added to them yet more—words which, to a feeling and affectionate heart, must have been fraught with absolute agony. And then came the denunciations of the tenth, eleventh and twelfth verses, whose exact fulfilment, because divided by two or three pages from the sentence, we are sometimes apt to overlook. "The sword" did "not depart from his house," and "evil was," indeed, "raised up against him in his own family." In the very next chapter, we ' have the account of Amnon's horrible sin, and Absalom's fearful, but perhaps natural revenge. Imagine the variety and combination of suffering to a father, and one affectionate as David: the ruin of his daughter, the murder of one son by another's hand, and the banishment of that other, who had been from his very birth his darling. Nor was this all. In his banishment, Absalom harboured those rebellious and ambitious thoughts, which ended in stealing the hearts of the people from his father, and setting up the standard of revolt. David, aged and oppressed by many sorrows, none greater than this conduct of his child, was compelled to fly from Jerusalem, and became exposed to all the evils and anxieties of war and flight, which did not end, till his darling, his beautiful Absalom, between whom and his father's heart not even revolt and sin could come, paid the forfeit of his rebellion by an early and most painful death. Was not, indeed, the sword then unsheathed from his own home, and evil raised up against him in his own family? And still more—read the latter part of the eleventh, and the twelfth verse of chapter xii. and then go to the twenty-first and twenty-second verses of the sixteenth chapter of the same book, and you will, I think, be almost as much startled as I was, by the perfect agreement of Nathan's prophetic threatening with its fulfilment. In the mere reading of the history of David, this accordance is likely to pass quite unnoticed. We regard the detail merely as painful afflictions, perhaps strange, in the life of one whose piety and general goodness ought, we think, to have exempted him from human trial. But how different does it appear, when we see it in connection with his sin. Amnon and Absalom were each, indeed, *individually responsible* for their *individual* sins. We must ' not fall into the unfortunate error of supposing that, *because* God ordained that David should suffer from the sins of his house, these young men were *fated* to act as they did, and so were not free-will agents.' They had equally free-will to choose the good, and conquer the evil, as any other person. You will say to this, perhaps, that whether David had sinned or not, their evil inclinations would equally have gained ascendency, and he must, therefore, have suffered just the same. But this is an objection easily obviated. Their evil inclinations might have been the same; but if David had not so sinned as to need signal chastisement, they would have been turned aside from touching *him*, recoiled upon themselves alone, and even this prevented, for David's sake, till he was removed to another and better world. But, as a punishment for his great sin, God permitted the evil *already* chosen by Amnon and Absalom to be the instrument of wrath in His hand against their father, causing him the same intensity of suffering as he had caused to others, and infinitely more, than if his sin had been punished by instant death. In that case, indeed, justice would have demanded an instant account of the trespass before that awful tribunal whose sentence is for everlasting. But the good found in David, the quick remorse and instant confession, "I have sinned against the Lord," in those brief words acknowledging not only the magnitude of his offence, but his perfect conviction of the justice of his sentence, were acceptable to the Merciful Reader of all hearts; and therefore Nathan said, "The Lord also hath put away thy sin: thou shalt not die," words that allude entirely to the sin and its consequences in a *future state, not* that it was to bring no painful consequences in this world. In the latter case, it would seem like a contradiction, to assert that a sin was forgiven, and yet to punish for it. David's remorseful confession *did not* annul the previous sentence pronounced against him. That remained in full force, and was, as we have seen, fully accomplished. It merely gave him hope and confidence, that the mercy of God had so far forgiven him, that his sin would not be visited upon him after death, by the punishment of excision.

How truly the prophet read human nature, when he said, "Because by this deed, thou hast given the enemies of the Lord great occasion to blaspheme," not only in his own time, but through all ages, in the very remark, that the sinfulness of his chosen servants casts a reproach upon the judgment of Him who, we are told, is all-righteous and all-just.

I have regarded this subject at great length, my dear Annie, because I consider it such a very important one. As I have told you before, if we commence the perusal of the Bible with a determination to disbelieve and cavil at all that does not accord with our finite understanding: we had better at once close the sacred volume, and not attempt to read it, until the grace of God grants us a better temper. If, on the contrary, we acknowledge it divine, and, therefore, that God *is* that transcendently holy, true, just, long-forbearing, and infinitely loving Being which his Word records Him: we shall find it as easy to reconcile *apparent* contradictions, as

sceptics do to bring them forward. Concerning the
failings of His favored servants, however, there is
neither real nor apparent contradiction. Human nature
cannot be so wholly spiritualised as, while on earth, not
to inherit and display some of the imperfections of man.
Our religion was formed for, and given to beings of a
mingled nature; and, aware of the fearful temptations to
sin, the natural passions and evil imaginings of His children, God, in His infinite mercy, promised even greater
favour to the *repentant*, than to those whose natural
dispositions are sufficient to guard them in a greater
measure from sin. "There is more joy in heaven over
one sinner that repenteth, than over ninety and nine
who have not sinned" is a sentiment found in the Gospel;
and therefore supposed to be the spirit of the Christian
religion, in contra-distinction to that of the Jewish.
But this, like many other similar assertions, is a great
mistake. It was the essence of the Jewish religion
first, and thence, and by *Jews* was preached to the
Christians. "In reference to the *purity* of *thought*, our
sages give the preference to him who has led a righteous life throughout; but in reference to the *reward*
which Revelation promises, the Rabbinical commentators
allow *more* reward to the penitent, commensurate with
his continued struggle to escape from sin and adhere to
the good." "Therefore, our sages say, the position which
the truly repentant occupy, the naturally righteous
cannot reach; since by mastering their habitual vicious
passions, their struggle with the evil imagination of
man's heart is greater, and the victory more glorious."*
Is not this the exact spirit of the verse of the Gospel

---

* Biblical Expositions, by Rabbi Abraham Belais, compiled from
the ancient fathers.   Pages 44 and 88.

quoted above? And how, then, can we say, it is peculiar to the Christian religion alone? If we would but look for it, how much should we find in both faiths upon which to agree, instead of those petty differences which, when brought forward, do but shut man's heart against his brother, and puff it up with self-righteousness and unholy pride.

In accordance with this Divine compassion for the natural frailties of man, God's chosen servants were, in all points, like ourselves, a mingling of the spiritual and the earthly, or, in plainer words, of good and evil. The spirit, indeed, with them gained an ascendency which it is difficult to attain, now that the direct interposition of the Almighty in man's affairs is no longer visible; but the earthly part of man was in its *first stage*, in its actual infancy, and subject to yet greater weaknesses and stronger temptations than *ought* to be the case now, that human nature has had so many centuries in which to advance. God Himself says, "The imagination of man is evil from his youth." David says, "Enter not into judgment with thy servant, O Lord; for in thy sight shall no man living be justified:" and Solomon, whose wisdom was a direct gift from God, repeats, "There is no man so righteous on earth that doth good and sinneth not." If, then, the men whom God selected for His especial service had been *perfectly righteous:* they must either have contradicted the words, declaring all men are naturally inclined to evil, or have been chosen from a superior and differently constituted race of beings, and so be to us, neither comfort nor example. Instead of which, they were in all things like ourselves; and we are not justified in refusing reverence and admiration for their spiritual worth, and other high and beautiful characteristics, because they had imperfections like every other man. In common with their brethren, they suffered the consequences of sin every time they were led astray. God did not interfere supernaturally to protect them, or to forgive, without some chastisement marking His displeasure. The descendants or seed of Abraham, He promised, for *Abraham's* sake, to bless; but he did not mark them from their birth, as men whose righteousness was to procure His favour. His blessing consisted in instruction in the right, that they might be aided in conquering the evil, and helped forward in the pursuit of good, but not in exemption from those temporal ills which man, while he remains man, must encounter. Abraham, Jacob, Joseph, Moses, all were of mature age, had had experiences of life and time, to prove that they had either repented and atoned for evil, or had naturally chosen the good, before a direct revelation marked them as especial instruments of God. David, though anointed by Samuel in early youth (a ceremony which does not appear to have been regarded by his father or brothers as anything more than an especial blessing of the prophet, earned by his early piety, and endowing him with the prophetic spirit; but which was not considered as marking him out for their future king*), encountered even more temporal trials,

---

* The account of Samuel's visit to Jesse, does not give me the idea that he publicly proclaimed its intention. The words he is recorded to have said, as each of Jesse's sons passed before him, were evidently spoken in his heart, even as he had heard the voice of the Lord addressing himself. Had David been then elected as future king, Eliab would hardly have so roughly addressed him when he came to the camp; nor in fact was he safe from Saul's persecution, nor would he have been so completely the unknown youth and lowly shepherd, as he was considered, till the acclamation "David hath slain his tens of thousands, and Saul his thousands!" excited the jealousy of the king.

than either of the characters above-mentioned; but even in his faults, his spirit of piety never failed. In every circumstance of his life, sorrow or joy, failing or thanksgiving, prayer or repentance, his treasury of Psalms shows how the spirit obtained ascendency, and devoted his whole heart to God; and this is what God requires of us. For the attainment of this spiritual blessing—love and devotion towards our God, He gave us His law, and showed us how to subdue the evil, and adhere to the good. He does not demand, for the attainment of His favour, that faultless righteousness which man demands. He knows that, while of earth and on earth, we must in some degree be earthly, in individual liability to error and its individual suffering, as also to trials, brought about by GENERAL as well as individual imperfection. He demands the *heart;* " My son, give me thy heart" He says, by the mouth of Solomon; because He knows, that if that, indeed, by given, the very failings of humanity will tend to draw the soul yet closer to Him, and gradually, yet surely, to subdue the propensities to evil. The law was revealed to help us to give Him our hearts. The prophets show us how to do so still more. The characters of the Bible give us example as well as precept, to prove that, if the spirit be right with God, imperfection will bring repentance, and repentance, pardon. The spirit of our religion teaches us, that the penitent and regenerate are yet even more acceptable to their Father, than the more naturally disposed to righteousness; because they will cling yet more lovingly and faithfully to the beneficent Parent, whose unfathomable love has so forgiven them. Do we then need more, to explain away the apparent objection of imperfection in the characters favoured of God? Dearest Annie, look not either in yourself or others for perfect righteousness.

If you do, you must despair, and fall farther and farther from your only hope, and never-failing trust. Seek to know God, and so to love Him, as to give Him your whole heart.

This we can do, or He would not have desired it; though we must not think, that it will guard us entirely from occasional failures of duty and even from graver faults. Yet, if we do so love Him, the misery and repentance we shall feel, when earth's imperfections have for the time gained the ascendency, will not only give us humble hope for forgiveness, but render us more and more circumspect and desirous of conquering the evil, than if we had never felt the inclination to do wrong. Be assured of this that, as there is no character, however perfectly righteous in the eyes of his fellow-man, that does not feel within himself the evil inclinations and imperfections of his earthly nature, so there is no man, however *seemingly* plunged in sin, that has not some redeeming quality in the sight of God, some generous impulse, some noble affection, some spiritual aspiration · which, had it not been crushed by the tyrant Circumstance, proceeding from general imperfection, would have led to good,—hidden from man, but known to, and cherished as the latent seed of salvation by, the universal God. "There is, indeed, no man that sinneth not;" but, believe me, there is no such thing, except in instances very "few and far between," as utter irremediable, death-consigning depravity before God.

LETTER XV.

FROM THE SAME TO THE SAME.

Doctrine of evil inclinations essentially Jewish—Proved such from the Word of God—Impossible to discuss the subject without approaching controversy—Belief of the Jews concerning the effects of the sin of Adam, and physical death—Belief of Christians on the same subject —Why denied by the Hebrews—The soul a pure emanation from God—Individual responsibility an important principle of Judaism —Inculcated by the Law and the Prophets—Possibility of attaining righteousness—What is needed to purify and render it acceptable— Extract from Ezekiel—Christians' idea of infinite sin and infinite atonement—Moses' self-sacrifice refused—The principles of Judaism reject vicarious atonement—Explanation of David's and Solomon's verses concerning man's inherent sinfulness—No contradiction to the words of the Law—Allude to the penalty of sin in this life— Those of Ezekiel to the individual judgment hereafter—Conse-quences of sin in this world on the family of the sinner—The choice of man no ordinance of God—The Hebrews' immortal hope—Evil finite, good infinite—Extent of God's love illustrated—Man's right-eousness not of itself sufficient for justification—Jewish faith in-culcates happy feelings—Awakening to the consciousness of inclina-tion to evil, proof not of increased sin but advanced spirituality— What characters deny the natural inclination to sin—God and His service to be associated with man's every thought and deed.

"Is not the doctrine of the universal prevalence of evil, or perhaps you should say, inclination to sin, more Christian than Jewish?" you ask me, dearest Annie, after acknowledging the comfort you derive from the views contained in my last. The doctrine, as there enlarged upon, is undoubtedly, undeniably, and scrip-turally JEWISH. If the earthly nature of man did not

16*

incline him more to the evil than to the good, we should not have such verses recorded, as those I have quoted as spoken by God Himself, and by David and Solomon,—implied by every other holy man,—and so commented upon by our ancient sages, as for them to declare that there is even greater reward laid up for the penitent than for the naturally disinclined to sin; because of the greater difficulty the former has to subdue himself than the latter. Now, if inclination to evil were not inherent, that is to say, if man were so constituted that every wrong thought and deed were difficult to realise; that his nature was such as always and unwaveringly to pursue the good; and that the evil was chosen from pure contradiction, and wickedness encouraged even as we now seek to strengthen and encourage the good: there could need no promises of mercy to the penitent, because there would be no mingled nature to bring forward. There would be no occasion for those innumerable gracious promises towards sinners; because, if man's nature were all spiritual, or angelic, there could be no such thing as sin. There would have been no need for a law, and instruction in the way of salvation; because man would have had all the elements for obtaining it in himself.

It is difficult to enter upon the full consideration of your question, my dear Annie, without approaching points of difference which I would rather have avoided. Controversy is peculiarly painful to me. Once clear on my own faith, my great wish is always to find matters of *agreement* instead of difference,—the one tending to enlarge the heart with universal love, as much as the other closes it with the fearful armour of self-righteousness and exclusive appropriation of heaven. Yet to young inquirers like yourself it is absolutely necessary that they should be clear on the groundwork of their belief, and on the distinction between it, and that of the religions among which we are so indiscriminately thrown. The more closely they approach in essentials, the more important must it be to distinguish the dividing line. Of course, as a Jewess, as I have told you before, there is no help for it, I *must* be prejudiced in favour of my own, and perhaps may not give you the correct rendering of the Christian belief, not from wilful error, but from positive ignorance. Besides which, there are many variations of the same thing, even in religion, and *individuals* may deny my *general* assertions from individual ideas. All I can attempt is, to endeavour to mark the dividing lines between the Jewish and Christian ideas of man's natural inclination to sin, by a general view of what I have always understood to be the vital principles of the latter faith.

The Jews believe that the sin of Adam so far changed man's nature, as to give the earthly the dominion over the spiritual; that the pleasures, the desires, the various inclinations of the body would thenceforward always be stronger than the voice of the soul; that to love God, to truly believe in, and so to worship Him as to conquer every earthly temptation for His sake and become pure on earth, as we believe our souls will be in heaven, would *never* be fully obtained, and even to be attained in any degree would involve a task of pain and struggle, and constant relapses into weakness and infirmity; that this change would descend to Adam's race, and mark all men as being subject to the same ascendency of the evil, and *therefore* the punishment of death was the destined portion of all humanity. Had the consequences of Adam's sin been confined only to himself, he alone would have been chastised; but the imperfections and evil inclinations extending unto all generations, justly subjected them to the same close of their existence. You will be very likely to suggest that, if we believe in immortality, death is *not* a punishment; but this is more an enthusiast's, than a rational idea. While in this world, life is so dear, that we find it preserved even in the most destitute and painful positions. Very few can so realise the joys of heaven, as to welcome the dark, terrible, and unknown passage to those promised joys. Even the most truly pious, the most sincerely righteous, have been known to regard death with awe and trembling, if not with actual dread; and it is quite a mistake to imagine these feelings either to be cowardly or erroneous. They are the *natural* and *intended* emotions with which the dictates of God's unerring justice should be regarded. All men sin more or less; and to all men comes the same purifier, robed as an angel of light, or spectre of horror and darkness, according to the disposition of the soul; but still a dispenser of suffering *physically*, as in the parting of soul and body in the dying, and *mentally*, as in the anguish of bereavement to the survivors.

The Christian creed is, that not only did Adam's sin bring death into the world, but condemned his own *soul* and that of all his unborn descendants, even the spotless babe, to everlasting perdition; that man has no power whatever in himself to pursue the good and strive for heaven; that unless baptized, and so, through his sponsors, receiving Jesus, he is lost eternally; that *only* the acknowledgment of the infinite atonement can bring salvation, and without such acknowledgment, every effort after righteousness is futile, and the most earnestly pious lover of God and man is condemned, without hope of redemption or escape, while the greatest and most impious sinner may be saved, if he only declare his belief in Jesus.

I do not tell you this is the belief of all *Christians.*   I know many who would shrink from it; but it is un-doubtedly the general doctrine of *Christianity,* and so accounts for the anxious desire of its followers to convert all people to the same saving creed.

The Hebrews deny that the soul is touched by Adam's sin.   As a pure emanation from God, sin cannot touch it, except that of its companion, the body.   God breathes the breath of life into every new-born babe; the soul is from Him; it does not descend as heritage, like the body, from one being to another.   The whole of our guiding books inculcates and reiterates the sublime theory that "EVERY MAN IS RESPONSIBLE FOR HIS OWN ACTS;" that he *has* the power within himself to subdue the evil, suffi-ciently to attract towards him God's grace and aid to give the good sufficient ascendency; and that purified and accepted by the infinite mercy of his Father in heaven, who does not demand more from His children than His wisdom and goodness knows they can bestow, he can obtain salvation and acceptance before God. The whole intent of our law was to teach man what is acceptable to, and would make him a worthy servant of the Lord, and what is evil and displeasing in His sight. If man had no power to keep this law, would the all-just and all-loving God have desired him so to do? I have read and heard, that "being under the law" exposes the Jews to even greater and more appalling perdition, than those who do not recognize it; as it is, and was always, *quite impossible* for them to observe it as God commands. Does not this appear a very fearful thing to assert? as if our ever-loving Father would *command* that which all the while He *knew* His children *could not obey,* and leave them in utter darkness, without ever expressing it in words, as to the sole condition of their acceptance?

It is impossible to read the book of Deuteronomy and the Prophets, particularly the eighteenth and thirty-third chapters of Ezekiel, without being convinced that to walk in the paths of righteousness and turn from the evil *is* in every human being's power, and that *we do not* need anything more than the promised love and mercy of our God to purify our feeble efforts, so as to obtain forgiveness and salvation. "Therefore I will judge you, O house of Israel, *every one according* to his ways, saith the Lord God. Repent and turn from all your transgressions, *so iniquity shall not be your ruin.* Cast away from you all your transgressions, whereby you have transgressed, and make you a new heart and a new spirit; for why will ye die, O house of Israel? For I have no pleasure in the *death of the dead*, saith the Lord God; *therefore turn and live ye.*" Now, if we *could not* turn from our transgressions, and seek a new heart and a new spirit, would the God of Truth and Justice make our so doing the SOLE condition of our salvation? We of course feel it can be only education and habit, the reading of the Old Testament by a different light, and the not-rending of the veil which God Himself has thrown over the nations, that prevents all men from acknowledging the clear and simple truths, encouragement, and comfort which this chapter reveals: while *they* no doubt imagine and regard us as equally blind, not to see and feel the absolute necessity of the condition of salvation, so important unto them. I would neither seek to shake their belief, nor condemn, nor even interfere with it. All I wish to do, is to enable you, as a Jewess, clearly to understand your own.

I have been told, that without the infinite atonement God could certainly have forgiven the sin of man, but would have failed in justice. Now it appears to me, that there is more justice in the Jewish belief, of every man being made responsible for his own acts, than his receiving it through the sacrifice of another; and for this reason. In Exodus xxxii. there are these remarkable verses:—"Moses said unto the people, Ye have sinned a great sin [the making and worshipping of the golden calf], and now I will go up unto the Lord, peradventure I shall *make atonement for your sin*. And Moses returned unto the Lord, and said, O this people have sinned a great sin, and made them gods of gold. Yet now, if thou wilt forgive their sin,—and if not, blot me, I pray thee, out of thy book which thou hast written. And the Lord said, Whosoever hath sinned against me, him will I blot out of my book."

Now here is a complete offering of the self-sacrifice of the innocent, body and soul (for "blot me out of thy book" meant utter annihilation), as an atonement for the guilty, and its as *complete rejection*, couched in words which most forcibly illustrate the Jewish doctrine of belief, that every *soul* is responsible for its own acts, and *cannot* release itself from individual responsibility by the atonement of another, though that other be said to unite God and man. As Jews, we dare not accept belief in vicarious atonement, without forswearing our religion. Its grand principle is, that the consequences of Adam's sin, in the sinful inclinations and physical sufferings of this human frame, belong only to *this life*, and touch not the soul, God's immortal gift to every individual. That soul stands in judgment *after* death, not for Adam's sin; but for its own while united to the body, and receives forgiveness, not through the intercession and meritorious sacrifice of another, but from the changeless and endless mercy of its God, who has promised, not only that our transgressions will be removed from us as far

as the east is from the west; but that as high as the
heaven is from the earth (that is immeasurably), so
great is His mercy towards *those that fear Him*, and that
that mercy should be extended unto *thousands*. The
ways of God, we are expressly told by Isaiah, are not
our ways, nor His thoughts our thoughts; therefore, even
if we knew it, we dare not judge of the sentence it may
please Him to pronounce on the souls of men, by our
bounded thoughts and finite views.

You see, then, though the groundwork of both faiths
is the same, the superstructure is very different, and
ought to be clearly defined to every young Hebrew.
The Christian believes that every thought and act of
man is clogged with sin. The Hebrew cannot do so;
because his Bible tells him that there are thoughts,
actions, ay, and even feelings, which *are* pure, and holy,
and acceptable to his God. There are recreations and
employments which the Jewish creed can regard as innocent and healthful, both before God and before man.
The verses, "There is no man that sinneth not"—"In
thy sight shall no man living be justified"—"The soul
that sinneth, it shall die," *do not* contradict this assertion.
David meant, that by his own unassisted efforts after
righteousness and endeavors to conquer sin, he could not
be justified before God; because he must have, in *addition*, a most determined faith in God's righteousness and
changeless promises, so to purify his endeavours as to
gain for them that acceptance, which they could not of
themselves obtain: while "There is no man that sinneth
not," and "The soul that sinneth, it shall die," do not
follow one another as a pronounced doom on man, which
requires some infinite union of atonement and redemption to avert.

The words, "The soul that sinneth, it shall die," are

not uttered by the Eternal as a distinct and unconnected
sentence on *all men,* as which they are so often quoted
in defence of the necessity for atonement. Refer to the
eighteenth chapter of Ezekiel, and you will see that they
are used merely in reference to, and to prove, the incor-
rectness of the received idea, that the *children* were to
suffer for the sinfulness of their parents. "As I live,
saith the Lord God, ye shall not use this proverb any
more in Israel. Behold all souls are *mine,* as the soul
of the father, so also the soul of the son is mine: the soul
that sinneth, it shall die. But if a man be just, and do
that which is lawful and right, ... he *is just,* he *shall
surely live* before me, saith the Lord God. If he beget
a son that is a robber, a shedder of blood, ... he shall
surely die: his blood shall be upon him. Now if he
beget a son, that seeth all his father's sins which he hath
done, and considereth, and doth not such like, ... *he
shall not die for the iniquity of his father,* he shall surely
live..... Yet ye say, Why doth not the son bear the
iniquity of the father? When the son hath done that
which is lawful and right, and hath kept my statutes and
hath done them, he shall surely live. The soul that
sinneth, it shall die. The son *shall not* bear the iniquity
of the *father,* neither shall the father bear the iniquity
of the son: *the righteousness of the righteous shall be
upon him, and the wickedness of the wicked shall be upon
him.* But if the wicked will turn from all his sins that
he hath committed, ... *he* shall surely live, he shall not
die. ... Have I any pleasure at all that the wicked should
die, saith the Lord God, and not that he should turn
from his wickedness and live? But when the righteous
turneth away from his righteousness, ... shall he live?
All his righteousness that he hath done shall not be mentioned: in his trespass that he hath trespassed, and in his

17

sin that he hath sinned, in them he shall die. . . . . Again, when the wicked turneth away from his wickedness that he hath committed, and doth that which is lawful and right, *he shall save his soul alive.*"

Now, is it not very clear from these verses, that *it is possible* even for the greatest sinner, through God's infinite mercy, to turn from his evil ways and save his soul alive? and that it is equally possible for man, even though his body inclines him to its own sins and infirmities, still to be *naturally* righteous, and so attract towards him the favour of his God? that also the words so often quoted, simply mean each *individual* soul that so sinneth as to reject all God's promises of mercy and forgiveness if he repent, shall *individually* die? For we are simply told that neither the righteousness of his father, nor that of his offspring, will avail to save him; and, in the same infinite justice, that if a man be individually righteous, he shall be rewarded for his own righteousness, and the iniquity of a sinful parent, or a sinful child, shall not be visited upon him. And this is no contradiction to the words of the law, in which God says, He will visit the iniquity of the fathers upon the children. It would appear so, superficially considered; but the threatening of the law, and the comfort of the prophet, have been so ably reconciled in a sermon by the minister of the British Jews,* that I cannot resist (I will not say quoting, for I do not know the exact words, not having heard or read his sermon) giving you his sense in my own language.

It is clearly evident, that the frequent use of soul, death, and life, in this chapter of Ezekiel, alludes to the *existence after death*, to the immortal emanation breathed from God into man. He would not say *all souls are*

---

* Rev. D. W. Marks.

mine, if He alluded to the body, because He had before sentenced, that "Dust thou art, and unto dust thou shalt return." The body is not *of* Him, though His creation. The soul or spirit *is His*, and to Him must return. No sin can touch that soul or spirit, but *its own*, while united to the body. It is not only pure from Adam's trespass, but from those of its immediate parents, and its own offspring. The body is the heritage of man, as the soul is the immediate and direct gift from God. The judgment, then, to which Ezekiel alludes, is that which will be the portion of each soul, in the world to come, *after* death has closed its bodily existence here. The sentence spoken by God through Moses, alludes to those trials, infirmities, and temptations, which are ever the consequences of man's sinfulness *in this world*, and which no individual righteousness *can* avert. Do we not see, as the inevitable rule of this world, the sins of parents visited on their innocent offspring, either in a stigma on their name, depriving them of all connection, and rendering the obtaining of honest employment painfully difficult, if not impossible? exposing them to evils of every description, and increasing the natural propensity to sin, by the example of those whom they are called upon to honour and obey? Yet even they have the power within themselves to choose the right, and, according to the difficulty of that choice, and their trials on earth caused by their parents' sin, *not* their own, so will their reward be great hereafter. That they should suffer on earth the consequences of the iniquity of their parents, is *not* the ordainment of God, but the choice of man. Those who sin, *know* their children will suffer from it. The feeling *has* been so strong as to check the progress of iniquity. The becoming a parent has awakened very many to the sense of their immortal

responsibility, startled them into a conviction, that the
present is *not* all, that they no longer belong to themselves *alone.* The thought of the *soul* of their *child*
has first roused them to think of their own; and meditations, how to teach religion and good to their offspring,
have taught it to themselves. Bad habits have been
broken off. Home has been made indeed home; and the
world and all its dangers, and temptations, and snares,
have been gradually deserted, from the time that an
angel from God has descended on the domestic hearth
in the shape of an immortal babe. That becoming a
parent has done all this, not one, but very many instances in the annals of mankind have fully proved; if,
then, the sins of parents be visited heavily, it is because
a still stronger power to resist the evil, and choose the
good, *has* been granted to them than to others. They
do not persist in sin, because *ignorant* of what will,
what must be, its effects on their children. God has
not only told them this, but given them increased powers
of resisting sin, and stronger incentives for the pursuit
of virtue.

They know, all men know, the consequences of sin,
that the act of one individual may recoil in its consequences with *suffering* on *many:* then, if they persist,
surely the deed is theirs, not the ordaining of Him who
has given them the power to resist. That the innocent
should suffer in any degree for the guilty, might, and
would, seem strange and unjust, *if this world were all,*
and no reward were laid up with God for those who
love and seek Him, and yet suffer, on earth. We cannot
study revelation without feeling convinced of the consoling truth, that we are not only individually responsible, but that our God will judge and have compassion,
not only according to the good deed accomplished, but

the sin resisted, the suffering borne, the strength of the temptation, and the force of circumstance. Once let this belief be fully obtained, and there is neither darkness nor gloom on the face of the earth. Evil, and its necessary consequence, suffering, are *not* God's ordaining, but man's free choice. Heaven and its unutterable joys, its rest, its fulness, man may aspire to; but its perfection of felicity, as much above our deserts as the heaven is above the earth, is God's free-loving gift. Evil and good both bring forth their own fruits; but the one, confined to man and earth, is finite, and commensurate with its parent. The other, springing from and returning to God, is infinite, and so *must* be as far superior to the mere *deserts* of even the most righteous, as God's mercy is to man's. He does not love and grant us immortal joys, according to the measure of human love and service, but according to His own. "They shall be righteous in my righteousness, their righteousness is of me, saith the Lord," are words repeated continually, difficult I fear to be understood in their fulness, unless *realized* by the heart's interpretation awakening the mind.

An illustration may, perhaps, be necessary, to explain it more clearly. We are expressly and repeatedly told, that the love borne by our God towards man is as a father's for his children, a mother's for her helpless infant. When Zion (figuratively weeping for the children of Israel) said, "The Lord hath forsaken me, and my Lord hath forgotten me:" God's gracious reply was, "Can a woman forget her sucking child, and not have compassion on the son of her womb? Yea, they may forget, yet will I not forget thee." And again: "As one whom his mother comforteth, so will I comfort you." Now, if we reflect a moment on the intense love borne by a mother for her babe, long before it can give her even a look of recognition, much less a word of infant fondness in reply, on the cares, the thoughts, the feelings it calls forth: you will, I think, my dear Annie, more clearly understand what I mean. The mother loves her child according to the vast capabilities of love found in *her own breast, not* according to what her child is able to give her; she cares for it, guards it, thwarts it when it seeks, as pleasures and playthings, what might prove injurious; asks, indeed, as it becomes old enough, love, obedience, and service in return; but, however imperfectly such may be rendered, she continues to love and judge from the fountains in her own heart, not from the merits of her child. Thus it is that our Father in heaven loves and cares for us. We cannot measure His love by ours—we cannot judge of His judgments by *our* judgment; for we human beings are equals, possessing no greater capabilities for love and righteousness than he whom we judge; but in God's word we read that in His righteousness we shall be made righteous, meaning that our feeble efforts after righteousness will be so purified by His as to render them acceptable. In His love our love will not be deemed wholly unworthy. In His salvation we shall be saved with an everlasting salvation; and in Him, the Lord, shall all Israel be justified, and shall glory.*

I think, then, our religion gives us sufficient reason to rest calmly on the belief that the phrase, "The soul that sinneth, it shall die," means nothing when *considered by itself,* but can only be taken in connection with the whole of the chapter in which it was found; and that that connection proves it simply to mean that

---

* Isaiah xlv. 17, 22, 24, 25, and many other portions of this prophet.

each individual soul is responsible for its own acts, and will be condemned or forgiven *individually*, not for the iniquity of another, be he parent or offspring; that Solomon's declaration, "there is no man that sinneth not," did *not* mean that no man could be considered righteous; because Abraham, Jacob, Joseph, Moses and David, Josiah and Hezekiah, and many others, were all proclaimed and blessed as righteous by God himself, but simply, that even the most righteous in this life are occasionally liable to sin, and naturally so inclined to evil as to require some effort to pursue the good. More than any other faith, then, ours points to virtue and holiness, as the goal not only to *be pursued*, but which God Himself has pronounced as attainable by man. It does not crush us with the fearful thought of hereditary and all-blackening sin, from which no effort of our own can free us. It permits us to trace beauty, and innocence, and truth, where others see nothing but evil. It grants us that blessed feeling of grateful joy, when our conscience whispers that some fault has been conquered, some evil inclination battled with, some painful truth spoken, some good deed performed; and therefore we may hope God will in His mercy strengthen us more and more to become acceptable to him. Dearest Annie, seek, strive, pray, to become that which our God *may* bless, and doubt not, unconscious as it may be to yourself, such you will become. Do not be disheartened, if you become more and more awake to the consciousness of inclination to evil; or if you appear, instead of becoming better, to have more faults and errors both in thought and deed than you had, *before* you began to think seriously. It is not that you really have, but only that you are becoming more aware of them, than you were before when you were ignorant of their existence. The very fact of your being aware of them, should comfort you by the conviction that the light of religion *is* shining in your heart, illumined by the grace of God, in answer to your earnest prayers and striving; for without that light, believe me, we never trace our faults and failings. It is only those who pass through life without a thought of God, who deny that the universal inclination to evil is stronger than the desire for the good. *Morally* righteous, following the received principles of honour and rectitude, having no temptation to do any very great wrong, or commit any startling sin, passing through an easy comfortable life, with no misfortune, perhaps, to startle them from their quiet security,—such are the individuals who believe that nothing more is needed, either for this life, or to gain the next. But they are mistaken, dearest Annie: our Bible tells us *more is needed.* The righteous men whom God loved and favoured, were not, indeed, free from sin; but they loved Him, sought Him in every thought and action, and, by prayer and striving, brought His grace to dwell within their hearts, and sanctified their lives to Him. Their very sins brought them yet nearer, by the unfeigned penitence, the deep humiliation which followed, preventing a recurrence of iniquity, and giving virtue and holiness a lovelier and more consoling light, from the former strife and tears. To be Israelites, indeed, we must be spiritual; and to be spiritual does not mean an entire freedom from human weakness, or even graver faults, but simply to give the spiritual ascendency over the earthly, and even in this world so to "walk with God," as to associate Him with our every thought and deed.

Many have said, that this leads to irreverence and familiarity; but they are wrong; for if it did, God would not have commanded His people to love Him with all their heart, and soul, and might, obedience to which can only be paid by such constant association. Nor would our sages have declared, that "man is to impress on his mind, that whatever he does is to be with the intention to glorify his Creator. His rising, his walking, and all *his occupations are to have that aim.*" This, then, is the true spirit of our religion, and this is spirituality. The degraded position which, for so many years, we have occupied all over the world, has naturally tended to prevent our realising this truth, as it was incumbent upon us to do. The mind must have space and opportunity to shake itself free from the cares, desires, and pains of the body, before the spirit can obtain ascendency; and this, in the age, or rather climes (for the *age* unhappily is never *past*), of persecution, was impossible. But in those blessed lands where the Hebrew is at peace, where the mind may be free, and mark its immortality, there is no excuse for us, if we do not strive, heart and soul, to evince the pure spirituality and divine truths of our holy faith, not by *words*, but by *deeds;* not alone *generally*, but *individually;* and the youngest, the humblest of those who bear the Jewish name may do this, dearest Annie. Not great deeds or mighty sacrifices are demanded: place God before you in the quiet routine of daily life, and you will not fail.

LETTER XVI.

FROM THE SAME TO THE SAME.

The ordinance of Sacrifice regarded by Christians as primary, by the Jews as of secondary consequence—Origin of this institution—Oblation an immemorial usage—Sanctified to the Lord—Maimonides' definition of the intention of sacrifices; their less importance than prayer—Made of too much consequence by the people—All Jewish writers agree in declaring the ceremonial secondary to the spiritual institutions of the Law—Sacrifices outward helps to inward devotion—Conditions for our acceptance in the time of our captivity—No mention of atonement offering—Why the Jew cannot accept the sacrifice of Jesus—Oblations condemned in the Psalms and Prophets, because unaccompanied by inward devotion—Reproof of Samuel—Views of David on oblation—Of Isaiah—Jeremiah—Ezekiel—Hosea—Joel—Amos—Micah—Habakkuk — Zephaniah — Zechariah — Malachi—Word of God confirms—Maimonides.

"Do not the Christians believe, that the numerous sacrifices specified in the law prove that vicarious atonement *was* a part of the Jewish code, and typified that sacrifice for the redemption from universal sin, in which they believe?" is the first on your list of questions, my dear Annie, and I am glad you have asked it; for I trust to be able to remove the mistaken idea, which I perceive, you have derived from your perusal of Christian authorities only. You say that you do not ask it, because you think a vicarious atonement *needed*, as you can rest, satisfied and happy, on the Jewish idea of individual responsibility, which I set forth in my last. You only want to know, if sacrifices were of so much importance as they are said to be, and that no prayer could be acceptable, and no sin atoned for without them: what is the present condition of our nation in the sight of God, now that sacrifices are impossible? A very natural question, *if* sacrifices were indeed of the vital and saving importance with which, in the Christian renderings of the Old Testament, they are regarded. But our Bible and its commentators tell us, that the sacrifices in themselves were of *very secondary* importance, compared with the *spirit* which was to pervade the offering. Their institution was *not to atone for sin*, but had its origin in the exceeding love borne by our Father towards the people, whom he had chosen as the teachers and promulgators of His law. It had been the custom, from time immemorial, for the imaginary deities of the heathens to be propitiated by the sacrifices of certain animals in the temples, and certain persons were also set apart for the priesthood, or temple-service. Before man attained to that advance in the scale of being which would enable the 'mass to acknowledge an Invisible Spirit as God, and, even when revealed, to give Him the *spirit-worship* which He demanded, as the soul of all religions, an oblation or offering seemed the natural and palpable return for, or recognition of, benefits received. Except in certain statutes relative to customs which we shall presently consider, and which to prohibit was absolutely necessary for the purification of His people, God interfered not with the habits and ceremonies which had become natural, except to sanctify them to Himself. The prohibition of sacrifices in those days, Maimonides tells us, would have been as impossible to be obeyed as would a prohibition of prayer in the day of trouble at the present time. God had already instructed His people in the knowledge of Himself; had proclaimed His pure Unity and His glorious

attributes, so as to be received and understood by all
Israel; had revealed His superiority to the gods of
other nations, by such signs, and miracles, and wonders,
as none but the Omnipotent and Eternal Creator could
display: and this done, and not till then, His mercy
ordained a form of worship, which would alike tend to His
glory and the sanctification of the worshippers, and yet,
not so rudely interfere with previously contracted habits
as to render obedience difficult or impossible. The mere
worship of the spirit was not only utterly impossible
then, but always: the mass of mankind must have some
visible and palpable ordinances of religion, in some to
inspire, in others to strengthen spiritual feelings; and,
of course, in the comparative infancy of the world and
of man, forms to attract the eye and occupy the hand
were imperatively needed. This was the origin of the
magnificent workmanship of the Tabernacle first, and
of the Temple afterwards, of the solemn service and
the imposing rites, of the rich and peculiar attire of the
officiating priests, of the ceremonies which attended the
performance of their temple-duties, and of the various
ranks, from the lowliest Levite to the sainted office of
the first high-priest, through whose Urim and Thum-
mim, in the earliest stage of the Jewish theocracy, the
Eternal's will was visibly revealed. Sacrifices had the
same origin and the same intent, to aid, by *outward*
help, *inward devotion*. They were to attend not only
confession *of sin*, but ceremonies of *rejoicing;* but in
both they were *secondary* to the temper of the heart
which was to accompany them. On this subject I cannot do better than quote to you Maimonides's own
words:—

"Reverting to our former proposition, we proceed to
observe, that oblations or sacrifices are a part of divine

worship only according to the *secondary* intention of
the law;* but invocation, prayer, and similar duties are
a part of worship approximating to the *primary* intention, and necessary to the attainment of it. The Divine
Lawgiver has established a great distinction between
these two kinds of worship; for although oblations and
sacrifices are offered in honour of the ever-blessed God,
they are nevertheless not to be offered as before the
giving of the law, when every man might offer what
sacrifices he pleased, and at whatever time and place
he chose; or, if he pleased, might erect a temple and
assume the priestly office; for all these things are now
prohibited. A particular house had been assigned to
these services, according to what is said, 'Thy holy
things thou shalt take, and go unto the place which the
Lord shall choose.' (Deut. xii. 26.) And to offer sacrifice
in any other place is pronounced unlawful; therefore it
is written, 'Take heed to thyself, that thou offer not thy
burnt-offerings in every place that thou seest.' (Ibid. 13.)
Nor are any permitted to bear the sacerdotal office, but
those of a certain family; all these things being to
check every kind of improper worship, and to prevent
the practice of every thing which the Divine Wisdom
judged proper to be abolished. But *prayer* and *depre-
cation* are duties which *every one* may practise in *any
place whenever he pleases.*

---

* Maimonides explains the primary intention of the law as relating
to the purification of the mind and spirit by mental exercises and
spiritual worship, and the secondary as relating to the outward forms
of worship, and those observances necessary for teaching men the
virtues and duties incumbent on a state, whose ruler and governor
was the Lord. In the first, of course, prayer and mental devotion
were included; in the second, oblations: the one was between the soul
and its Maker; the other was the outward obedience of the state—the
invisible impulse of devotion made visible and real.

18

"It is also, for the reason just stated (the secondary intention of the oblations), that we find the prophets so often reproving men for their too great eagerness to offer sacrifices, and inculcating upon them that they ARE NOT the first and independent object of the law; nor has the Divine Being any need of them. Thus Samuel, 'Hath the Lord as great delight in burnt-offerings and sacrifices, *as in obeying the voice of the Lord?* Behold to *obey* is better than *sacrifice*, and to hearken, than the fat of rams.' Isaiah also inquires, 'To what purpose is the multitude of your sacrifices unto me? saith the Lord. I am full of the burnt-offerings of rams, and the fat of fed beasts, and I delight not in the blood of bullocks, or of lambs, or of he-goats.' And Jeremiah says, 'I spoke not unto your fathers, nor commanded them in the day when I brought them out of the land of Egypt, concerning burnt-offerings or sacrifices; but this thing commanded I them, saying, *Obey my voice*, and I will be your God, and ye shall be my people.' (Jer. vii. 22, 23.) These words of Jeremiah have, however, given rise to a very general objection; for almost every one is ready to urge, 'How could Jeremiah affirm, that God did not ordain burnt-offerings and sacrifices, when it is well known that the greater part of the precepts of the law relate to them?' But the meaning of his words is what has been already intimated, and is the same as if he had said, 'The primary intention of every part of the law is, that you should know ME, and forsake the service of other gods, that I may be to you a God, and that ye may be to me a people; and the precepts which enjoin oblations, and command you to worship in my house, are given to *instruct* and to *assist* you in this duty. But these *designs ye have defeated*, and have had regard only to the *outward worship;* for ye have doubted my existence, as it is said, "They have belied the Lord, and said, It is not He." Ye have served idols and burnt incense to Baäl, and have gone after other gods, and have come to my house, and have cleaved to, and had respect *only* to the temple of the Lord and to the oblations, *which were not the first and principal object of the law.'*"

I fear this long extract will have wearied you, dearest Annie; but before giving you my own ideas on this important subject, I was anxious to place before you those of Maimonides at length.* Maimonides, though persecuted for some of his notions in his own time (as is unhappily the case with all those who have ideas in advance of their age), is now universally acknowledged as one of the *most orthodox writers* we possess. His Talmudical research was immense, and his knowledge of the Hebrew Scriptures of course perfect, not only in themselves, but in their Talmudical interpretation. In some of his writings we can unhappily trace the fierce exclusiveness, revengeful feeling, and narrow-mindedness, which cruel and continued persecution had rendered the characteristic of some of the Jews of the middle ages. But these very failings (failings of circumstances, not of *nature*, or of the Jewish religion), ought to render the opinions of his larger mind and nobler self of still greater value. We see him at times claim brotherhood with the fiercest and most exclusive of the Talmudical Jews, and yet displaying the real spiritual meaning and intent of the sacred canon, as only an enlarged and spiritualised intellect could have displayed. It was as if the mild lustre of

---

* Reasons for the Laws of Moses, from the "Moré Nebuchim" of Maimonides, translated by James Townley, pp. 182–186.

the perfection of the Holy Scriptures triumphed even over the lurid mist of persecution on the one side, oppression on the other, and intolerance on both; and that, when engaged on that holy study, all of age and circumstance passed away, and he was permitted to explain them, indeed, in the spirit of him whose name he bore. And like which Moses, his grateful countrymen sometimes say, there never was another, even in his earthly and uninspired nature, till Moses Maimonides arose.

The opinions of such a man must then be of immense importance to all those attempting to explain the Scripture in an orthodox Jewish light. In fact, so completely do *all* the Jewish writers of past ages, portions of whose works I have been enabled to peruse, confirm my repeated assertion, that the ceremonial was *secondary* to the *spiritual* religion inculcated by Moses, that the worship of the heart and mind came before that of hand and form, that "Wash you, make you clean, put away the evil of your doings before my eyes, cease to do evil, learn to do well, seek judgment, relieve the oppressed, judge the fatherless, plead for the widow" would *alone* make the outward worship *acceptable* to its Ordainer, that *without* attention to this religion of heart and deed, incense and sacrifice were abomination, oblations vain, the new-moons, festivals, and Sabbaths (though God could not do away with them, because His Word had passed that they were to be for everlasting) a trouble and weariness to Him, instead of a graciously accepted offering. I should sometimes feel inclined to smile, when I hear my opinions pronounced by both parties more Christian than Jewish, were it not for the deep regret which must attend the conviction, that those who make such an observation know so little, so very little, the true spirit of their faith, not only as revealed in the Bible, but as explained by our own sages.

We perceive, then, that instead of being *primary* (which, if they really were types of the Christian dispensation, the sacrifices decidedly would be), they were merely instituted as aids and helps to spiritual religion, as giving a kind of palpable and visible means of obedience to "a mixed multitude," who were not yet capable of attaining that mental and spiritual elevation, which would be in itself sufficient to lift the soul to God. But restrictions were laid upon these helps: no one could offer a *sacrifice* except in Jerusalem, where God had set up His temple; on *prayer*, however, there was *no* restriction either of place or time. This at once proves that prayer *was* acceptable, and repentance available *without* sacrifice; but oblations *without* prayer, and sin-offering *without* repentance, were an abomination.

In the twenty-sixth chapter of Leviticus, after a powerful description of the fearful fate of the disobedient which, word for word, has been fulfilled, we find the simple conditions which, even in our captivity, will render us acceptable to our still pitying Father, still forbearing God. Read from the thirty-ninth to the forty-sixth verse, and you will perceive not a word of either sacrifice or atonement, but merely that individual responsibility, which consists in an humbled heart, a conviction of iniquity, and a determination and endeavour "to do justly, to love mercy, and to walk humbly with thy God:" this will bring Him back to Israel; this alone is needed to render Israel once more acceptable to Him. Instead of being divided from Him, because we have no sacrifice to make our prayers acceptable, it was expressly prophesied, that "the children of Israel shall abide many days without a king, and without a prince,

and *without sacrifice*, and without an image, and without
ephod, and without teraphim" (all of which meant the
temple-service, ordained priests, and visible Revelation
of the Lord); and yet, during that time, which is the
same as that described in Leviticus xxvi. and Deut. xxx.
—our captivity throughout the nations—we have, in
these two consoling chapters, explicit and reiterated
instruction as to *all* that was needed to incline the
Eternal once more to us, and restore us to our own land.

If we acknowledged the sacrificial atonement of the
Christians, as being the great sacrifice typified by all
ours, the prophecy quoted above would remain unful-
filled, and, in fact, was not needed, because we should
still have a sacrifice and high-priest on whose merit and
intercession to rest. Remember, I do not wish to touch
on the Christian faith as regards *themselves*. As I have
said repeatedly, I trace the workings of the Eternal in
its progress, as a preparation for that great and glorious
day when we shall all know Him. I respect, from my
very heart, the true spiritual, believing Christian. I only
wish to make it clear to you, *why*, as children of Israel,
neither you nor I could accept the first grand doctrine
of the Christian faith.

That very many portions of the Psalms and Prophets
appear to condemn the sacrifices and other parts of the
ceremonial ritual, I quite acknowledge; but the condemnation was, as Maimonides expressly declares, *not*
of the *ordinance* itself, but of the fearful *spirit* in which
it was offered. This is clear from the simple fact, that
there is *never* a condemnation of the *outward* rite, without being followed by an allusion to the *inward* feeling
and social deed which *ought* to have sanctified the rite.
The offering, to *man*, appeared obedience: to the Reader
of all hearts, it was directly contrary. "Hath the Lord

as great delight in burnt-offerings and sacrifices, as in *obeying* the voice of the Lord? Behold, to *obey* is better than sacrifice, and to hearken, than the fat of rams." Is not sacrifice obedience? many would demand. No; for it was the mere work of the hand, not the impulse of the heart, nor accompanied by prayer; *therefore* it was so utterly useless as not even to be considered obedience. "Sacrifice and burnt-offering thou didst not desire," says David; "my ears hast thou opened; burnt-offering and sin-offering hast thou not required: then said I, Lo I come, in the volume of thy book it is written for me, *I delight to do thy will, O my God; yea, thy law is within my heart.*" And, again, in his agonised remorse, he exclaims, "Thou desirest not sacrifice, else would I give it; thou delightest not in burnt-offering. The sacrifices of God are *a broken spirit. A broken and a contrite heart, O God! thou wilt not despise.*" Now, in neither of these Psalms did the faithful servant of the Eternal, and true follower of the law, intend to contradict, or do away with the ordinance of the sacrifice. He merely meant, that his ears had been opened by the perusal of the law; and he learned that the sacrifices were not of that primary importance which probably his family, less enlightened than himself, had considered them to be; that, though ordained and permitted, because an ancient custom, God delighted not in them, as He did in a willing heart anxious to do His will; and all the spiritual and social ordinances of the law were, in His estimation, to be postponed to the deep repentance for sin which produced a broken spirit and a contrite heart; but that, nevertheless, *they were* to be observed he proves in the eighteenth and nineteenth verses of the same fifty-first Psalm, "Do good in thy good pleasure unto Zion; build thou the walls of Jerusalem: *then*

shalt thou be pleased with the sacrifices of righteousness, with burnt-offering and whole burnt-offering, then
shall they offer bullocks on thy altar." And this is no
contradiction to the previous words, "Thou delightest
not in burnt-offering." It simply means, that were the
temple and city of the Lord purified from the constant
sins and idolatries of the people, and the sacrifices
offered in the spirit in which alone they were acceptable,
then would God be pleased with them. David says,
" God delighted not in sacrifice, but in a broken and
contrite heart;" but if that humbled and repentant
spirit *dictated* and attended the offering, *then* God was
pleased with it, as *obedience*, not for any merit in itself.

Isaiah's testimony to the truth of this supposition we
have already considered, in the Eternal's inquiry "To
what purpose is the multitude of your sacrifices unto
me?" And the concluding command, "Wash you, make
you clean, put away the evil of your doings from before
my eyes," etc., already quoted, and very many passages
to the same import, may be found in the same prophet.
In Jeremiah, as Maimonides brought before us, we read,
"I spoke not unto your fathers, nor commanded them
in the day that I brought them out of the land of Egypt
concerning burnt-offerings and sacrifice; but this thing
commanded I them, saying, *Obey my voice, and I will*
be your God;" and in a previous verse of the same chapter, we learn *what* these "ways" are, "Trust not in lying
words, saying, The temple of the Lord, the temple of the
Lord, the temple of the Lord are these! for *if ye thor-*
oughly amend your ways and your doings, if ye thor-
oughly execute judgment between a man and his neigh-
bour, if ye oppress not the stranger, the fatherless, and the
widow, and shed not innocent blood in this place, neither
walk after other gods to your hurt: then will I cause you

to dwell in this place, in the land that I gave to your fathers forever," etc. Is it not very clear, then, that sacrifice by itself was of no importance whatever, nor even the public hieing to the temple of the Lord? They were not even considered to be *obedience, unless sanctified* by the worship of the spirit, and strict attendance to the social duties. The God of changeless truth did not contradict Himself, when He said, "I spoke not to your fathers" etc.; for He did *not* command burnt-offering and sacrifice, as the *primary* intention of His law, which the people, by Jeremiah's words, rebelliously chose to consider them. They were but aids to *spiritual* worship and to the *heart's obedience.*

In the sublime prophecy of Ezekiel—where again and again we are told what to do, even when sunk in wickedness, to regain the compassionating love of our Father—there is not a syllable of sacrifice or offering, except in the concluding chapters, and in connection with the new and glorious temple, which will almost cover the land of Israel, that *all* nations may flow into it. Now, if sacrifice and atonement-offering were all in all, as they are by some supposed to be, surely we should find some mention of them in a prophet who, beyond all others, instructs us in those spiritual and moral duties which, even when scattered over the nations, will draw us near to God, cause Him to be "a little sanctuary in the countries where they shall come," and induce Him, in His infinite mercy, to "take the stony heart out of our bosoms, and replace it with a heart of flesh, which will enable us to walk in His statutes, keep His ordinances to do them, and be His people for evermore."

In Hosea, exactly in accordance with the other prophets, we read, "For I desired *mercy* and not sacrifice, and *knowledge of God, more* than burnt-*offering.*" "Therefore also now, saith the Lord God, turn ye to me with *all your heart*, and with fasting, and with weeping, and with mourning, and *rend your hearts* and not your garments, and turn unto the Lord your God; for He is gracious, and merciful, slow to anger, and of great kindness, and repenteth Him of evil. Who knoweth if He will return and repent, and leave a blessing behind Him, even a meat-offering and a drink-offering unto the Lord your God?" Here is not a word of an *atonement*-sacrifice to bring us back to our God; but that we have only to *repent and amend*, and then, when the spirit is humbled, and the heart purified, we may rejoice in our meat and drink-offerings; for they will be accepted as any other merely *outward* rite.

In Amos we find, "I hate, I despise your feast-days, and I will not smell in your solemn assemblies; though ye offer me burnt-offerings, I will not accept them, neither will I regard the peace-offerings of fat beasts. Take thou away from me the noise of thy songs, I will not hear the melody of thy viols. *But let judgment run down as waters, and righteousness as a mighty stream.*"

In Micah, "Wherewith shall I come before the Lord, and bow myself before the High God? Shall I come before Him with burnt-offerings, with calves of a year old? Will the Lord be pleased with thousands of rams, or with ten thousands of rivers of oil? Shall I give my first-born for my transgression, the fruit of my body for the sin of my soul? *He hath showed thee, O man, what is good; and what doth the Lord require of thee, but to do justly, to love mercy, and to walk humbly with thy God?*"

Habbakuk says, "The just shall live by his faith," needing neither atonement nor sacrifice for his justification, or it would have been as clearly specified. Faith would create that holy spirit of obedience to inward and outward religion, which inclines our Father towards us; and therefore, that brief line includes and signifies obedience to *all* the duties which the law and the other prophets enumerated and enforced.

Zephaniah, in the same spirit, reiterates, "Gather yourselves together, yea, gather together, O nation not desired; before the decree bring forth, before the day pass as the chaff, before the fierce anger of the Lord come upon you. *Seek ye the Lord, all ye meek of the earth,* who have wrought his judgment; *seek righteousness, seek meekness: it may be, ye shall be hid in the day of the Lord's anger.*"

Zechariah has repeatedly verses to the same effect, showing, like the twenty-sixth of Leviticus, the thirtieth of Deuteronomy, and all the Prophets already quoted, all that is required of us in our *captivity*, to regain the loving mercy of our God, and the *absence of which* rendered our observances of the *outward* ordinances an abomination in the sight of the Lord, instead of an acceptable obedience. "The Lord has been sore displeased with your fathers. Therefore say thou unto them, Thus saith the Lord of Hosts, *Turn ye unto me*, saith the Lord of Hosts, *and I will turn unto you*, saith the Lord of Hosts. Be ye not as your fathers, unto whom the former prophets have cried, saying, Thus saith the Lord of Hosts, *Turn ye now from your evil ways, and from your evil doings;* but they did not hear, nor hearken unto me, saith the Lord." (Zech. i. 2–4.) "And the word of the Lord came unto Zechariah, saying, Thus speaketh the Lord of·Hosts, saying, *Execute true judgment, and show mercy and compassion, every man to his brother; and oppress not the widow, nor the fatherless, the stranger, nor the poor; and let none of you imagine evil against his brother in your heart.* But they refused to hearken, and pulled away the shoulder, and stopped their ears, that they should not hear. Yea, they made their hearts as adamant stone, lest they should hear the law, and the words which the Lord of Hosts hath sent in his spirit by the former prophets; *therefore* came a great wrath from the Lord of Hosts. Therefore it is come to pass that, as *He* cried, and they would not hear, so they cried, and I would not hear, saith the Lord of Hosts; but I scattered them with a whirlwind among all the nations whom they knew not." (Ibid. vii. 8–14.) "But now I will not be unto the residue of this people as in the former days, saith the Lord of Hosts. For the seed shall be prosperous; the vine shall give her fruit. . . . . As I thought to punish you when your fathers provoked me to wrath, saith the Lord of Hosts, and I repented not: so again have I thought in these days to do well unto Jerusalem and to the house of Judah ; fear ye not. *These are the things that ye shall do, Speak ye every man the truth to his neighbour, execute the judgment, the judgment of truth and peace in your gates : and let none of you imagine evil in your hearts against his neighbour, and love no false oath; for all these are things that I hate, saith the Lord."* (Ibid. viii. 11–17.)

The prophecy of Malachi is but a reiteration of the same solemn truths, perhaps, even in still clearer language, showing why the "Eternal had no pleasure in them, and refused to accept an offering at their hand:" not because he had *annulled* the ordinance; but because the offered sacrifices were corrupt and polluted, men bringing to the altar of the Lord "that which was torn, and the lame, and the blind, and the sick," instead of the *most perfect* of their herds and flocks, which had been ordained, and with weariness, and with a contentious and contemptuous spirit, "Thus ye have brought an offering: should I accept this of your hand? saith the Lord." And yet they mourn, and weep, and cry out, because "He regardeth not the offering any more;" thus proving, that they looked to the *ordinance* alone, and utterly disregarded the spirit in which it was to be offered. The whole prophecy marks the different light in which the mere formalists were considered, compared with the spiritual Hebrews. The former, who prided themselves on their rigid adherence to the ordinances, and, with *seemingly* mournful humility, walked before the Lord of Hosts, were *reproved* and *condemned;* but "they that *feared* the Lord *spoke often one to another,* and the Lord hearkened and heard it, and a book of remembrance was written before Him, for them *that feared the Lord and thought upon* His name. And they shall be mine, saith the Lord, in that day when I make up my jewels; and I will spare them as a man spareth his own son that serveth him. Then shall ye return, and discern between the righteous and the wicked, *between him* that serveth God and him that serveth Him not." (Mal. iii. 16–18.)

Perhaps, dearest Annie, you will think, that these extracts relate more to the moral and spiritual duties of · our people, than to the question which originated this very long letter. But without them, I could not have replied to my own satisfaction. I wished to prove to you, not from Maimonides alone, but from the word of God itself, the true intent of the ordinance of the sacrifice; its very *secondary* importance to the *great moral duties* and *spiritual communion* between the soul and its God, which constitutes real religion; the real reason for its *apparent* rejection by its almighty Ordainer; and the reconciliation of the constant reference to it in the

Law, with the equally constant condemnation of it in the Psalms and Prophets. I can only *hope*, that all this I have done will be sufficient for your eagerly enquiring mind to rest more calmly. The law perused *alone might* favour the supposition, that oblations were of equal importance with the moral and spiritual statutes; and thence (*i.e.* from the perusal of the Law alone) has originated the too rigid trust in mere outward and multiplied ordinances, which has so unhappily tarnished Judaism. But, perused with the explanations of the Prophets—explanations found in the reproof of iniquity, and information as to what to do, and how to feel, to render outward ordinances acceptable, we need no more to instruct us in the religion which will lead us up to God. Fearing to weary you, however, I will leave the farther consideration of this important subject till my next.

LETTER XVII.

Law perused without the Prophets likely to mislead—Could not be
only a spiritual system—Ceremonial ordinances absolutely necessary—Useless performed alone—Mere form an abomination, not
obedience—Mission of the Prophets in life, and through their writings—Forms of religion most important—Welcomed by the true
spiritualist—The sacrifices not annulled—Ezekiel's last prophecy—
Witness to the same of the other Prophets—Grand distinction between
the Christian and Jewish ideas concerning the sacrifices—Objection
of their being a great waste of animal life considered—Special intent of the Law peculiarly marked in the minute detail concerning
oblations—Prevented avarice—Provided food and drink for the poor
—Encouraged social kindliness—Why only the best and purest were
acceptable—Why certain parts of the oblations were to be destroyed
—Reason of the severe chastisement for apparently trifling disobedience—For the peculiar animals selected—The general condition
of mankind dimanding the greatest care to distinguish between the
service of God, and that offered to idols.

I WOULD not wait for an answer to my last, dearest
Annie, because, the subject under consideration not
being concluded, I thought it better to continue it
without any farther break, than the conclusion of one
letter and the commencement of another. The law
could not be only a system of spiritual worship. In
this life humanity, however far advanced, *cannot* realise
a religion of the inward heart alone. It must have outward aids. And if, even in its advanced stage, this is
still the case, how much more necessary must it have
been, when man was in his rudest infancy, as in the
Exodus from Egypt! To provide for his wants, and

help him to realise the constant presence of his invisible
God, to institute a reverential form of homage wherewith to approach and serve Him, to render repentance
more palpable, and give its subject the means of proving
that the sin was felt, acknowledged, and by the deep
penitence accompanying the offering, *not* by the offering itself, in some degree atoned; to prove that every
blessing was felt to be a gift from God, and required a
sacrifice of thanksgiving, constantly rendering it incumbent on the people to offer public worship, lest the idea
of private devotions being sufficient, should render them
careless and indifferent; to impress the dull minds of
the mass through imposing ceremonies and a magnificent temple service, as far superior in splendour and
solemn rites to the heathen worship from which they
had been rescued, as *their* God was superior to the gods
they had thought omnipotent before: this was the necessary and important intention of the Mosaic system,
accompanied, indeed, by such a minute and reiterated
detail of the moral duties, individual responsibilities
and spiritual worship, as *ought* to have taught them
the real intent of the outward form, and how utterly
useless, nay how completely an abomination to the Lord
it was, if unaccompanied by an obedient spirit, and by
that unrestrained and loving service of the heart which
was the vital breath of every sacrifice and form.

Too soon, unhappily, men fell from the lofty position
in the sight of God, in which adherence to the true
spirit of the law of Moses would have placed them, and
they became contented with lifeless obedience to certain
outward forms. They trusted in the *oblation*, and looked
not to the state of their own souls, nor cared in what
spirit they approached the temple of the Lord. They
imagined the mere sacrifice was obedience, and com-

plained of its small effect in gaining for them the favour
of their God.   Then arose such men as Samuel, David,
and the prophets, from whom I have so largely quoted,
to teach them that sacrifice *by itself* was an abomination
instead of obedience, that, till the duties from man to
God, and man to man, were performed, their oblations
were rejected, their festivals and Sabbaths a weariness
and trouble ; for their very observance in that perverse
spirit increased the national sin.   Such was the mission
of the prophets when they moved in life amidst the
people, and such is the mission of their writings to us
now.   Oh, if we would but think so, would but study
them as we do the law, and impress their spiritual
teachings on our children as we do the mere outward
rite, how different would be the aspect of Judaism, how
blessed her hope, how near its fulfilment her expectation !

Do not imagine from this, that I believe the forms of
our religion are of no importance, and that the sacrifices
are for ever done away.   I believe that every form
which we can observe in our captivity is *imperatively*
incumbent upon us, that our religion is imperfect without it, and that every truly spiritual Hebrew, instead
of disregarding the outward ceremonies, will delight in
obeying them for the love he bears his God, welcoming
them as immediate instructions from Him, even as a
child obeys with joy and gladness the slightest bidding
of those he loves.   No real love was ever *passive ;* it
ever longs for *action* whereby to prove what it feels ;
and so every ordinance believed to be from the Lord
must, by the real Hebrew, be welcomed with rejoicing.
Nor do I think the sacrifices annulled.   I dare not
think so ; for in that case I must disbelieve the prophets.
In Ezekiel's remarkable prophecy, contained in the last

nine chapters of his book, wherein he powerfully portrays the restoration of the twelve tribes of Israel to their own land, and the flowing of all nations unto them, he describes the outward temple-service so exactly in accordance with that ordained in the law, only on a much more extensive, and yet grander scale, that we cannot doubt that the ceremonials of our faith will, for *us*, be the same as they were. And amongst these *outward* ceremonials *oblations* are expressly included; and not only Ezekiel, but almost all the other prophets advert to them as being *again* acceptable, when sin shall be purified from the hearts of the people, and "the Messenger," or Messiah, whom the Lord will send, "shall suddenly come to His temple . . . . and shall sit as a refiner and purifier of silver, and shall purify the sons of Levi, and purge them as gold and silver, that *they may offer unto the Lord an offering in righteousness. Then shall the offering of Judah and Jerusalem be pleasant unto the Lord, as in the days of old and in former years.*" This is from Malachi, the last of the prophets; and is it not clear, that instead of *oblations* making the people righteous and atoning for sin, they were utterly rejected, *unless* the people were sufficiently purified to offer them in righteousness?

This is the grand distinction between the Christian and Jewish ideas on the subject of sacrifices. The former, regarding their every mention in the Old Testament as a type of the great sacrifice on which their faith is founded, must consider them of such *primary* importance, that all heart-worship was imperfect without them. The latter, on the contrary, are taught, both by their Law and their Prophets, that they are merely *secondary*, but part of the outward and ceremonial rite, which was of *no merit or importance whatever in itself, and by itself,* but was accepted as obedience, or rejected as abomination, according to the *inward spirit* in which it was offered. The Christian believes they are done away with entirely, because, as mere *types,* they are merged in the *reality* of the sacrifice of Jesus. The Hebrew believes they are only annulled during our captivity, because *only in Jerusalem* was it legal to offer them; and that, when we are sufficiently purified to be restored to our own land, the outward rites will be the same as they were in the days of old, and with them, but merely as *part* of them (having no merit in itself), sacrifice of course.

I hope I have made this distinction clear to you, dearest Annie. I. am aware that many of our nation think I am wrong ever to enter upon topics connected with the Christian faith, when endeavouring to explain our own. Perhaps they are right in the main; but where there has been an indiscriminate perusal of Christian authors, I am aware, from my own experience, that it is difficult clearly to distinguish the respective renderings of the same subject, unless brought side by side with each other.

There is one objection connected with sacrifice, to which, as I have no doubt it has entered your mind, though not yet expressed, I will revert before we quite quit the subject. Many sceptics have, I believe, enquired, " Was not the ordinance of the sacrifice a most expensive and useless waste of animal life; and the instructions as to the killing, use of the blood, etc., wearisome and disgusting minutiæ, very little in accordance with the solemnity and importance due to the service of God?" In reading the Law, we must never forget what I have mentioned before, and I shall probably repeatedly have occasion to mention again: namely, its *special intent* to sever the descendants of Abraham from the idolatrous nations with whom they had so intimately mingled, to give them an imposing form of worship, in addition to a spiritual belief which, instead of rudely *interfering* with, or *prohibiting* previously encouraged habits and customs, would sanctify them, and yet make an impassable distinction between those customs which *could* be sanctified, and those which, by their horrible blasphemy and licentiousness, were an abomination, and occasioned the destruction of the nations that practised them. This intent is particularly visible in the oblations, and the minutiæ which attend them. Sacrifice itself was not only a remnant of an immemorial usage permitted to continue, but it was made the means of aiding man, in realising spiritual religion, and purifying his character from those grosser thoughts of selfish aggrandisement, and the dislike to part with personal possessions, in a more or less degree common to us all. The riches of the Israelites did not consist in gold and silver, in fine houses, and in all the nameless luxuries of modern times. The distinction between the rich and poor consisted in the more or less quantity of flocks, and herds, and land and its agricultural produce; as, for instance, respecting Nabal, the churlish husband of Abigail, we are told, "There was a man in Maon, whose possessions were in Carmel, and the man was *very great*, and he had three thousand sheep, and a thousand goats," and of course bullocks, and the fruit of the land in proportion. And in Nathan's exquisite parable he distinguishes the rich and the poor man, who dwelt in the same city, by this simple phrase, "The *rich* man had *exceeding many flocks and herds;* but the poor man had nothing *save one little ewe-lamb.*" Now the ordinance of the sacrifice expressly provided for this distinction of ranks and possessions, by the command, "Every man shall give *according to his ability; but none shall appear empty* before the Lord;" and the two young pigeons, which were the only offering perhaps the poor man could get, were as acceptable in the sight of his Father, as the two he-lambs without blemish, and the one ewe-lamb, and the three tenth deals of flour, which the *rich* man was to bring with him to the temple on the same occasion. But whatever the quantity, the *quality* of the offering was to be *without* blemish, the purest and the best of Israel's possession, an ordinance which, if *obeyed*, must effectually have removed those fearful vices, *avarice* and *covetousness*, and that *closing of the heart and hand* against all generous impulses, too fearfully the characteristics in every age of man. From their Father and King they held all their possessions, and it was but just that He should demand a portion of His own; and according to the purity of the offering, and the willingness of its bestowal, so was the heart of the offerer, right or wrong, with God.

It was no waste of animal life; and it is, indeed, a fearful misconception of the holy rite to imagine, that the great and holy God *needed* the blood of goats, and the flesh of rams, or that He was pleased with the slaughter of His creation. He had given certain animals for the food and sustenance of man. It was no useless slaughter, to bring the best and purest of them to His courts at certain seasons and certain festivals, and offer them up there; for it was an *express* and *imperative* command that the wholesome flesh should not be kept till it was impure, and so be destroyed and wasted; but it was directed to be distributed and eaten with rejoicing, *not* merely by the bestowers of the offering, but by the *poor and the stranger*, the *fatherless and the widow*, by all who, perhaps, except at these seasons, knew not how to get a meal. To *relieve* the poor, utterly to prevent famine, and misery, and their inseparable consequences, *crime* and *sin*—such was the real intent and use of sacrifices, and this use alone rendered them acceptable to their beneficent Ordainer. So frequent were the seasons and occasions for sacrifice, that it was utterly impossible for even the poorest and most unprotected Israelite to be wholly deprived of wholesome animal food. There were free-will offerings, trespass-offerings, thanks-offerings, sin-offerings, and peace-offerings, all of which gave food and drink in abundance to the poor, and *compelled* the rich to part with a portion of their wealth for that purpose. A command to distribute three times in the year certain bullocks, sheep, and goats, flour, wine, and oil, to the poor, would have been easily evaded, if left to the judgment and mercy of man alone. But made a portion of the service to the great and invisible God, and the very quality and quantity of the offerings so minutely specified, there was no evading it, save by direct disobedience. Again and again, we find in Deuteronomy similar verses to this, alluding to the oblations attending the festivals of the Passover, Pentecost, and Tabernacles, "And thou shalt rejoice before the Lord thy God, thou, and thy son, and thy daughter, and thy man-servant, and thy maid-servant, and the Levite that is within thy gates, and the *stranger*, and *the fatherless*, and the widow that are among you, in the place which the Lord thy God hath chosen to place His name there."

Regarding them thus, how baseless and silly seems the reasoning of the sceptic! Instead of being a useless waste, it was a provision, and rejoicing for the poor. It brought all ranks in social union before their common

Father, and provided a *vent* for the feelings of thanks-giving or penitence, which, in that comparative infancy of humanity, demanded something more than mere *spiritual realisation.* We find by the Prophets, that the causes of the rejection of the oblations were not *only* because men imagined that, if they sacrificed, it did not at all signify *what* feelings they encouraged, or what transgressions they committed; but also from their presumptuously offering the *refuse* of their flocks, the blind, the lame, and the sick of animals, and polluted bread, instead of the purest and the best. And these were rejected, not merely as insulting the majesty of Him who, as the giver of every blessing, demanded a pure offering; but that, as the Hebrews were expressly forbidden to eat any animal which was diseased, or deformed, such impure oblations could of course *not* perform the part to which they were destined, viz., to provide wholesome food for the poor. And thus that form, which to mere superficial observers *appeared* decided obedience demanding acceptance at the hand of the Lord, was, in His sight, a twofold abomination. We cannot read the Prophets carefully without being convinced of this, and therefore am I so anxious that you should study them as frequently and as attentively as the Law. The great mischief amongst us has been the exclusive perusal of the latter, it often and often happening, that the Prophets have never been even examined, until attention has been called to them by Christian friends; and what must be the consequence? So many passages will equally bear upon the Christian rendering (especially to the many of our female youth ignorant of the language of their ancestors), that they must be startled, uneasy, and doubtful, if not actually converted, unless provided with the invulnerable shield of *scriptural* conviction of their own faith, founded on as intimate an acquaintance with the Jewish readings of the prophets, as of the ceremonies and forms of their law.

The directions concerning the blood, fat, and inwards of the sacrifices, apparently so tediously minute, were, at the time of their bestowal, *absolutely necessary* to mark the wide distinction between the Jewish oblations to the Most High God and those of the benighted nations to their idol deities. Those parts which we were to burn and destroy, and the blood which was to be poured upon the ground like water, were the most important portions of the idolatrous sacrifices. With the blood, the most diabolical rites and incantations were constantly practised; the entrails and other inward parts were always used by the idol priests for their oracles and other divinations, as we constantly perceive in the histories of Greece and Rome—nations actually civilised compared with the Emorites and other Canaanitish nations, from whose horrible rites the Hebrews were to be so guarded. It appears, on a mere casual reading, a harsh and unneeded sentence, that the mere eating of the inward fat and drinking of the blood, of the fowl or beast brought as an offering, should cause "that soul to be cut off from his people;" but when the law was given, God knew, that these actions, simple as they *seemed*, marked a *relapse into idolatry*, and so called for a sentence as severe, as that pronounced against those who actually bowed down to idols instead of the true God.*

---

* "Blood was regarded as the food of demons, not only by the nations immediately bordering upon the dwellings of the Israelites, but by other idolaters in different parts of the world. Maimonides, in his 'Moré Nebuchim' (lib. iii.), has stated at large, the superstitions of the Zabii, in offering blood as a sacrifice to the infernal objects of their worship. R. Moses bar Nachman, on Deut. xii. 23, says, 'They gathered together

To prevent the relapse into the abominations of the nations, who for their wickedness had been cast out from Canaan, could any directions be too minute? or any threatened chastisement too severe? The very animals chosen for Israel's oblations, were to mark the division and prevent all assimilation. Cats, dogs, bats, mice, reptiles, all the unclean beasts, we find held in high esteem among the heathen. Lewis, in his Antiquities, says, "The swine was held sacred to Venus; the owl to Minerva; the hawk to Apollo; the eagle to Jupiter, and even the dog to Hecaté." The lion, wolf, dog, cat, ape, and even frogs, otters, rats, beetles, flies, serpents, and fishes, were held in idolatrous veneration by the Egyptians and other nations. Now all these God pronounced to His people as unclean, unfit either for food for them, or for oblations to Himself. Whereas those animals which He gave us for subsistence, and of which we were to offer unto Him, were those which many of the idolaters actually worshipped as gods, and which, in consequence, they would never permit to be slain.

Thus, dearest Annie, even while our Father's infinite goodness permitted a form of oblation something similar to that to which the mixed multitudes had been accustomed, instead of harshly commanding a service so utterly distinct that it would have been next to impossible in that age to obey, He so ordered it, as com-

---

blood for the devils, their idol gods; and then came themselves, and ate of that blood with them, as being the devils' guests, and invited to eat at the table of devils, and so were joined in federal society with them; and by this kind of communion with devils, they were able to prophesy, and foretell things to come.' Similar practices obtained also amongst the Romans, and the sacred books of the Hindoos exhibit the same traces of worship prevailing also amongst them." Townley's Maimonides's Laws of Moses, Dissertation v. p. 177.

pletely and entirely to sever it from idolatrous worship and sanctify it to Himself. Considered thus, we shall not find one direction too minute, one ordinance unnecessary or derogatory unto Him, or one sentence on those who disobeyed or disregarded them too severe. The proneness to idolatry was so continued, and so fearful, the difficulty, in that dark age of the world, for man to realise an idea of a spiritual, all-pervading, and yet invisible Unity, as his Maker and God, so great, that it is next to impossible for us now to regard the varied prohibitions, ordinances, and threatenings of the law, so as clearly to understand them; unless we take the trouble, to read and study those works which will throw a light upon the condition of general humanity at the period of the Revelation through Moses. This consideration, however, must be postponed to another letter. The subject of the sacrifices has already extended to a greater length than either you or I could have imagined; but if it has removed any doubt, and clearly explained the origin of their institution and importance in the law, and the reason of their being so continually reproved and even rejected in the Prophets, I shall not regret either time or trouble.

LETTER XVIII.

FROM THE SAME TO THE SAME.

Reasons for certain ordinances and prohibitions—Difficulty at the present time to realise the wickedness and practices of other nations at the period of the Mosaic revelation—Why God did not miraculously change the heart of Israel for the reception of His Law—The descendants of Abraham never entirely lost their mental and spiritual superiority—Twofold intention of the Law—Eradication of idolatry and faith in the one true God—Explanation of certain prohibitions—Offering of first fruits—Unlawful mixtures in cattle, seeds, and garments—Idolatrous practices—Prohibition of passing the seed through the fire—Practice common to all nations of antiquity, and traces of it discoverable even now—Prohibited amongst the early Christians—Law explains itself when carefully read—Part of the Shemang refers to the same intent—Eradication of idolatry in agricultural pursuits proves the divine mission of Moses—Various reasons for the distinction between the clean and the unclean beasts —Consequences of indiscriminate eating in the East—Habits of some of the prohibited animals—Reasons for some of the prohibitions so excellent, as ought to satisfy us for the remainder—Examination into religion necessary and legal—Every ordinance and prohibition accordant with the twofold intention of the Law—How to realise the magnitude of this twofold intent.

You tell me, dearest Annie, that my last two letters, instead of wearying you, have answered so many unexpressed doubts and thoughts, that you have expunged some of your intended questions from your list. To others, you begin of yourself to perceive the reply; but you will mention them, to have them clearly defined. So many of the ordinances in the law had appeared to you so minute and unnecessary, so wearisome to attend to, and at the present time so incomprehensible; but, from what I have brought before you concerning the customs of the nations from which we were to be utterly separated, you imagine they might have had the same intent, and could be as easily explained as some of the minute ordinances of the sacrifices which we have just examined. You are right. There is not an ordinance in our holy law, which had not an intention perfectly accordant with the mercy, and wisdom, and majesty of the Supreme, and with the preservation of Israel, as a select and holy people, who were to be His witnesses over the whole world, and to the farthest boundary of time; and now Maimonides's "Reasons for the Law of Moses" must again be my authority. But again, I must entreat you always to place before you the fact that, while many commands were given to us to enable us to become a pure and holy people, and to instruct us in those feelings and those actions which would be acceptable to our Father, most of the *prohibitions* related to the customs and practices of the idolatrous nations, especially those of Canaan, whose exceeding wickedness had caused them to be an abomination to the Lord, and compelled Him to destroy them. The terrible impurity, sinfulness, abominable practices, disgusting rites, and degrading worship, to which human nature had arrived, would appear actually incredible, were it not confirmed by the books of the Zabii, to whose translations into Arabic Maimonides refers, as giving him "so much insight into the reasons and causes of many of our laws."*

Accustomed to be surrounded by those to whom Revelation is known, perceiving the God of the Hebrews acknowledged by one or other mode of worship over all

---

* Townley's Maimonides, pp. 162, 166.

civilised lands, the moral laws of our Bible, either pro-
fessedly or practically, guiding almost all mankind,—it
is perhaps very difficult for some minds, unless gifted
with some degree of imagination, to realise the state of
the world and human nature at the time Israel was
chosen, and the law bestowed. To enable the Israelites,
and "the mixed multitude" that went up with them,
gradually to realise a pure faith and holy religion, many
ordinances and prohibitions were necessary to be given,
seemingly useless, and even burdensome *now*, because
the very *idea* of the practices which they were to prevent
is at present scarcely attainable; but then they were
absolutely necessary for the furtherance of the intention
of the Lord. It might be, and has, I believe, been
urged, that God might have so changed and purified
the hearts of Israel, as to have at once inclined them to
reject idolatry, and worship Him in spirit and in truth;
but, as I think I have before told you, He never works
by miracles that which can (humanly speaking) be
attained by natural and gradual means. Had His grace
so changed the heart of man, no reward would have
been needed to urge him to walk in the way of righteousness, and no goodness attached to the performance
of his duty, or no piety comprised in his love and
reverence for God; for all would have been done, simply
because he could not help it. This was not the intention
of the Eternal. As the descendants of the faithful
Abraham, the Hebrews, even in their crushing slavery
of Egypt, never entirely lost their mental and spiritual
superiority to the nations around them. The mass, no
doubt, imbibed, in some degree, the idolatrous notions
and impure customs of the Egyptians, else we should
not so frequently meet with such mournful records of
their relapses; but amongst them there were ever some

individuals whose examples and precepts would keep
alive within them the remembrance of their forefathers;
and even the mass, in the time of greatest trouble, we
find "crying unto the Lord."

To attempt any thing like a review of the Law, would
be impossible in the space of even one or two letters,
dearest Annie. All I wish to impress on your mind is
its twofold intent, and to notice a few of the prohibitions
which, judged by *present* experience only, appear so
trifling and unnecessary. For the twofold intent I will
quote Maimonides's own words :—

"It is clearly evident, from many parts of the Scriptures, that the first *intention* of our Law was to eradi-
cate idolatry, and to obliterate the memory of it, and
of those who were addicted to it; to banish every thing
that might lead to it, as pythons, soothsayers, passers
through the fire, diviners, jugglers, enchanters, augurs,
astrologers, necromancers, etc.; and, finally, to prevent
the most distant assimilation to their practices, still
more to the adopting and observing of them. Hence
it is expressly declared in the Law that, even as the
worship paid to the idol is an abomination to the Lord,
so is the oblation offered to it, and every practice in the
remotest degree similar. In accordance with this, but
placed *after* the eradication of idolatry, because, of
course, till that fearful system was subdued, no true,
just, and spiritual notions of the Divinity could be
attained, the intent of the Law was to bestow on us certain precepts, which were to deliver us from these great
errors, and lead us to faith in the one true God, teaching
us, that God who created all things is ever present in
the world; that He alone is to be worshipped, loved,
and feared; and that to fulfil His will, nothing difficult
or laborious is required, *but only to love and fear Him,*

since by these two things His whole worship is perfected, as we shall afterwards demonstrate. Hence it is written, 'And now, Israel, what doth the Lord thy God require of thee, *but to fear the Lord* thy God, to walk in all His ways, and to love Him, and to serve Him with all thy heart, and with all thy soul?'" Such are the words and quotations of Maimonides, a Talmudical as well as Scriptural student of quite the beginning of the twelfth century. Had they been mine, or those of any other Jewish writer of the present age, they would, by both parties, Christian and Jewish, be pronounced the sentiment of the former, not of the latter. As those of Maimonides, they must be *orthodox Judaism*. O believe me, dearest Annie, if we could but peruse portions of our venerable teachers, if our gifted Hebrew students would but give us translations adapted for our enquiring and thirsting youth: we should have no need to seek Christian authorities for a spiritual creed; we should find all sufficient in our own, and perceive how completely love and faith were the *primary*, and rites and ceremonies the *secondary*, consideration of our Law.

"Thou shalt not seethe a kid in its mother's milk" is one of the prohibitions which has given rise to a great variety of speculations. Its real meaning is, very evidently, to prohibit any, even remote, assimilation to one of the principal customs of the Zabii, who, when they had gathered in all their fruits, used " to take a kid, and boil it in its dam's milk, and then, in a magical way, to go about and sprinkle all their trees, and fields, and gardens, and orchards with it, thinking by these means that they should make them fruitful, and bring forth the more abundantly the following year." If we found that these words gave a command unconnected and distinct, we might hesitate to attach this explanation to it; but as the conclusion of the verse is, "The first of the first-fruits of thy land thou shalt bring into the house of the Lord thy God: thou shalt not seethe a kid in its mother's milk," we at once perceive that it is but part of a sentence, and must be explained in connection with the previous part. The Zabii observed several idolatrous customs connected with the first-fruits; the seething of a kid in its mother's milk was probably one of them; wherefore the prohibition contained in this verse was given to guard the Israelites against adopting a similar practice.

It was a custom of the Emorites, or Zabii, also to offer the first-fruits of the land to their idols, and eat them in their temple, declaring that, unless this rite were attended to, every edible tree would dry up and perish. To guard us against this, we were expressly commanded not to gather in the fruit of the trees for *three* years after they were planted. "When ye shall come into the land, and shall have planted all manner of trees for food, then ye shall count the fruit thereof as uncircumcised: three years shall it be uncircumcised, it shall not be eaten by you." And when gathered, the first-fruits of the fourth year were to be offered in the holy place of the Lord, and sanctified to Him. The grafting one tree upon another was prohibited, from the fearful and obscene rites which attended this practice amongst the Emorites, and for the same reason, all mixture either of seeds, or in garments, was not permitted to the Israelite. "Thou shalt not let thy cattle gender with a diverse kind; thou shalt not sow thy field with a mingled seed; thou shalt not let a garment mingled of linen and woollen come upon thee. The woman shall not wear that which pertaineth to a man, nor a man that which pertaineth to a woman. The priests shall not round the corners of the head, nor mar the corners of the beard." Now these prohibitions, trifling as they seem, and incomprehensible, perhaps, to many at present, have all a reason and intent. The first was to prevent all impurity and violation of nature, even amongst brute beasts which, unless driven together for impure purposes by man, always herd with their own kind; for the same prohibition we find often repeated, "Thou shalt not plough with an ox and an ass together." With regard to the intermixture of the seeds, it was the custom of the Emorites to sow barley and dried grapes together, believing that without such union there could not be a good vintage, which, as an idolatrous superstition, was among the abominations for which they were rejected by the Lord. The garment of linen and woollen was the usual dress of the idol priests, who were also in the habit of rounding the corners of their head, and marring the corners of the beard in a peculiar manner; and to prevent the remotest approximation, even in dress, to those priests of Baäl, these customs were prohibited to us. Again: it was the custom of the Zabii that, when a man presented himself before the image of Venus, he should wear the coloured dress of a woman; and when a woman adored the star or image of Mars, she was to be clothed in armour. They usually considered their gods and goddesses to unite the sexes, and so, to propitiate them, they presented themselves before them wearing a habit different from their sex. When worshipping the god of war, the women thought they could not please him better than by appearing in arms, and the men, in the presence of the goddess of love and beauty, than by assuming the dress of a woman; and when sacrificing to Venus, the same change of garment was adopted, to denote that they considered her both male and female.* The impurity and idolatry of such customs are so very evident, that once being aware of them, the reason of the prohibition above-named is too self-evident to need comment.

The prohibition so frequently reiterated, and the transgression of which was always death—passing the children through the fire as an offering to Moloch—has, I believe, often been passed over by mere casual readers as incomprehensible, and by sceptics, as folly, such things never being heard of. Now, instead of never being heard of, it was a most fearfully common rite in all idolatrous nations, especially among the Zabii. And remnants of it *may still* be found amongst the superstitions and legends of some of the northern nations. The opinion was declared and circulated that, if the people did not cause their sons and daughters to pass through the fire, all their children would die, and their property be consumed. Moloch was, I believe, a huge brazen idol, with the body of a man, and the head of an ox, and the punishment for transgressing this universal command, to pass the seed through the fire, was to make an offering of innocent babes to the idol, by heating the image, and placing the naked infant in its red-hot arms. To avoid this, and to propitiate the idol to grant them the lives of their offspring, nothing more was required than to lead the child through the fire. In Maimonides's own age, he tells us that a custom was still existing of nurses taking the new-born infants in their swaddling clothes, and waving them to and fro in the smoke of herbs, of an unpleasant odour, thrown into the fire.† Dr.

---

* Young on Idolatrous Corruptions in Religion, vol. i. p. 97, 105, quoted in note 33 of Townley's Maimonides.

† Townley's Maimonides, pp. 210, 211.

Morison, in a learned later work, dedicated to James I., declares himself to have been an eye-witness of a singular custom in Scotland, the taking a new-baptised infant, and vibrating it three or four times over a flame, repeating thrice, "Let the flame consume thee now or never."*
In Athens, which we should have supposed too far advanced in civilization for such fearful idolatry as that of the Zabii, there was a feast kept by private families five days after the birth of a child, when it was a custom for the visitors to *run round the fire with the infant in their arms.* In Rome, the country-people had private as well as public feasts, in honour of their goddess Pales, during which they jumped over great fires made of stubble and hay, imagining themselves to be purified by the *palilia.* No rite amongst the heathen was considered complete unless they had passed through fire, as a ceremony of initiation, or lustration. And even amongst the early Christians we find some traces of this superstition in the fact, that St. Chrysostom "blames, amongst other heathen customs then remaining, the lighting two great fires, and passing between them ; and the sixty-fifth canon of the Council of Trullo condemns the observing the new moon *with making fires before their doors and leaping over them."* The scholiast, in commenting on this canon, also says: "The new moon was the first day of the month; and it was customary amongst the Greeks to hold a feast on that day, and pray that they might be lucky during the continuance of the month. They also kindled fires before their shops and houses, and leaped over them, imagining that all the evils which had befallen them would be burnt away, and that they would be more successful after-

---

* Townley's Maimonides, note 37, p. 361.

wards. Some Christians falling into this heathen custom, occasioned the prohibition of the above-mentioned
canon. On St. John the Baptist's eve, also, the vulgar
were not to kindle fires during the whole night, nor leap
over them; nor draw lots, nor divine about their good or
evil fortune;* and we can trace the remnant of this
superstition even now, and still more strongly a very
few years back, in the celebration of All-Hallow-E'en,
alike in Scotland, Ireland, and the west of England.

If, then, we can trace the remnant of this extraordinary superstition through so many ages; if there is
scarcely a nation amongst the heathen, polished Rome
and gifted Athens included, and in many parts of Persia
to this very day, by whom, in one feast or other, passing
through the fire is not a ceremony of the first magnitude:
can we not easily imagine its universality and extent,
at the time when our law was given, and therefore as
easily comprehend the extreme necessity to reiterate the
prohibition to the Jews? and connect its transgression
with the threat of some punishment, equal in magnitude
to the evils which the idolaters held out, as befalling all
those who refused to pass their children through the fire?

Thrown amongst the practisers of such impious rites,
for so many years, and still surrounded with them in
Canaan, from their own disobedience, nothing but a
miracle could have so preserved them from imbibing
some portion of their habits, sentiments, and customs,
as not to demand the greatest care on the part of the
Law, to prevent their relapsing into the horrible degradation of the species, from which the love of God had
rescued them. It is for this reason, that the command
"Thou shalt not let any of thy seed pass through the

---

* Townley's Maimonides, note 37, pp. 360 and 361.

fire to Moloch; neither shalt thou profane the name
of thy God, I am the Lord," is so frequently repeated,
and so emphatically enforced with the threat of death
to those who disobeyed. "When the Lord thy God
shall cut off the nations from before thee, whither thou
goest to possess them, and thou succeedest them, and
dwellest in their land: take heed to thyself, that thou
be not snared by following them, after that they be
destroyed from before thee; and that thou enquire not
after their gods, saying, How did these nations serve
their gods? even so will I do likewise.   Thou shalt not
do so unto the Lord thy God; for every abomination to
the Lord, which he hateth, have they done unto their
gods; *for even their sons and their daughters they have
burnt in the fire to their gods.*"   It has always seemed
strange to me, that such verses should be so entirely
overlooked by those who assert, that there are so many
things in the Law to which no meaning can be attached.
They would in themselves explain them: and the more
we study the customs of the early idolatrous nations, the
more distinctly and forcibly must the intent of even
the minutest ordinance of the Law stand before us.

The very words we repeat every morning and evening,
"And it shall come to pass, if ye will hearken diligently
unto my commandments, ... *then* will I send rain for
your land in its due season," etc., had their origin, not
as a promise of temporal prosperity for obedience, as we
commonly regard them, but because agriculture and its
prosperous seasons were so closely connected with idolatrous worship by the Zabians, that it was supposed
impossible for the earth to produce her fruit, or the
heavens their rain, without the celebration of the most
impure and abominable practices.   Therefore, in addition to the *precise prohibition* of each of these practices,

God inspired Moses to declare, that the earth would yield her fruit, and the heavens their first and latter rain, *only* on condition of Israel obeying the commandments of the Lord, and serving Him with all their heart and with all their soul; for if their hearts were deceived, and they turned aside to serve other gods, and worship, as did the Emorites, etc., then, instead of the healthy season which the idols promised their worshippers, God would shut up the heavens, that there could be no rain, and the earth would of course cease to yield her fruit, and the people would perish quickly off the promised land. It was to make the multitude understand that, if they adopted the practice of the Canaanites, that adoption would produce the directly contrary effect to that which they supposed. In repeating this portion of our prayers, we generally regard it as merely alluding to a temporal reward: instead of which, it bore directly upon the practices of the idolaters, and incited us to avoid them. It proves also most forcibly the divine mission of Moses; for how could a mere man have ventured to promise and threaten the interposition of Heaven, in case of obedience or disobedience? The ambition of a mere human lawgiver or leader would have shrunk from any such test of his mission, knowing the impossibility of bringing the seasons and elements to aid him, and so be likely by such very appeal to disgrace himself before the multitudes whom he desired to lead. Moses, on the contrary, condemns and prohibits all the magic of the Zabians, by promises regarding the produce of the earth and of trees, of healthy seasons, and refreshing rain, which he neither could, nor dared have done, had it not been the voice of the Lord speaking within him. The practices of the Zabians were much too general and deeply rooted, to give way before the mere word of a man, unless that word were fulfilled by the evidence of nature herself. They might, perhaps, have believed him at the moment of his command; but instances of disobedience were too common, for that belief to have continued, as we know it did, *unless* the threatened chastisement had visibly taken place.

The distinction between the clean and the unclean beasts, also, had its origin not only in teaching us the most pure and wholesome food, but as a still farther preventive against the remotest assimilation with the idolaters. In Townley's Dissertation on the Mosaic distinction of animals, preceding his translation of Maimonides, he gives a threefold reason for the distinction: first, *to prevent idolatry;* secondly, to promote the health and comfort of the people; thirdly, to influence the moral character of the nation. The prevention of idolatry was assisted by this distinction of clean and unclean animals, in two or three different ways. In the first place, it prevented all social intercourse with the followers of idolatry; because, of course, if the Hebrews might not eat of the same food, they could not meet for scenes of dissipation, in which even the most earnest followers of good are sometimes liable to be led astray. In the next place, they were not likely to regard as *deities* those animals which formed their daily food, adored as they had been by the Egyptians. In the third place, by this distinction between clean and unclean, they were taught to regard with a religious detestation those very animals, alike of fish, flesh, fowl, and reptiles, which the idolatrous nations accounted sacred, and held in the highest veneration. Is it not clear, then, that even in the prohibited meats the intention of severing us entirely from the idolaters is clearly visible, and adds increase of weight and solemnity to ordinances which, had they only been instituted to teach us the most wholesome food, ought to call not only for implicit obedience, but for the deepest thankfulness?

The extreme usefulness of the prohibition of certain beasts, birds, and fishes, can only be realised in its full extent, by knowing the consequences of indiscriminate eating in the East. Almost all those animals which were forbidden abound in gross juices and oily fat which, thickening the blood and checking perspiration, incite all those maladies connected with leprosy—a disgusting disease so inherent to the people, that no precaution. for avoiding or checking it could be too severe. It was for this reason, also, that an inordinate use of the fat of even clean animals was so expressly forbidden; as in hot countries, where the digestion is naturally slow and difficult, such rich food engenders all sorts of diseases which not only affect the body, but, from the close connection in this world between the two, deaden the soul, and entirely prevent its attaining that purity of sentiment and spiritual aspiration which God has endowed it with powers, even whilst in the body, to attain. Levi Barcelona, a Rabbinical writer, says, "As the body is the seat of the soul, God would have it a fit instrument for the use of its companion, and therefore removes from His people all those obstructions which may hinder the soul in its operations; for which reason, all such meats are forbidden as breed ill-blood, among which, if there be some whose hurtfulness is neither manifest to us nor to physicians, wonder not at it, for the faithful PHYSICIAN who forbids it is wiser than any of us."*

I know it is urged by many, that this distinction of

---

* Townley's Maimonides, Dissertation X. p. 71.

meats was all very well in the country where the command was given, and where the *reason* was so obvious;
but that it does not hold good in our captivity, as there
are no longer idolaters from whom we are to be severed,
and the food is no longer unwholesome—not perhaps as
unwholesome as in Judea, but still far more so than the
food legally permitted; but one cause for their prohibition remains quite as strongly in force now, as at the
time of the ordinance,—it is, that we are only allowed
to eat of those animals who feed on clean and pure food,
such as grain, grass, fruit, etc. Almost all those that
were prohibited feed on carrion, and other filth disgusting even to think about. The filthy habits of the swine
I need not bring to your notice; but perhaps you do not
know, that shrimps and prawns, thought by some to
be so delicate a food, are literally the scavengers of the
ocean, feeding even on the dead bodies of the drowned,
and the putrefying and impure carcases of dead fish and
other animals. They are the same in the ocean, as the
carrion-birds are on the land; and surely our whole
nature must revolt at the idea of feeding on such animals, even without the prohibition to that effect. This
cause of the distinction between clean and unclean exists
in every country and every age, and it cannot be waived,
as many attempt to do. The law is still the same; and
obedience to the ordinance is therefore as incumbent on
us in our captivity, as it was in our own land.

This is but a brief notice of a very important subject,
my dear Annie; but I wish rather to suggest matters of
consideration and thought, and so lead you to examine
farther for yourself, than to enter into any lengthy dissertation. If we can find reasons for *some* prohibitions,
prove the cause of *some* animals being forbidden: have
we not sufficient reason for calm belief in the wise intent,

and certain usefulness, and equal necessity for the remainder, even if some of them should still seem impossible to be satisfactorily explained?

In the study of the Law, as in every other point of
religion, remember and act upon Sir Humphry Davy's
sublime axiom: "I do not consider the results of
reason as capable of being compared with those of
faith." In His infinite goodness our Father has made
many things clear to us, even in our present imperfect
state, has inspired men at various times with sufficient
wisdom to guide and instruct the mass, not only as to
the necessity of love and obedience, but as to the meaning, intent, and usefulness of so many of His ordinances;
so that, if we cannot receive the remainder on trust, we
are, indeed, undeserving of His love. As I have often
told you, I think it a very mistaken notion to accept
any religion without examination. The great drawback
to Jewish enlightenment has been the "being Jews, only
because our fathers were;" that is, following certain
rites, reading certain portions of the Pentateuch, observing certain days, and abstaining from certain customs
and certain food, *because* our fathers have done so from
time immemorial; and if any enquiry be made, either
briefly answering by a reference, not to God's word, but
to custom, or evading it, by saying that we must not
enquire too deeply, or that the subject is too abstruse for
youthful or female comprehension.*

This will never do in an age of enquiry and enlightenment like the present. Such replies, from their own
nation, are the very incentives to desertion, and the embracing of a creed which will, at least, attempt religious
explanation and instruction suited to the sympathies

---

* This is no exaggeration, as the author's own experience can testify.

and comprehension of the young.   Thank God, there is a reviving spirit abroad amongst us.   The fearful state of apathy and indifference, superstition and exclusiveness, is in some degree giving place to active enquiry, and *thence* proceeding, and so doubly hopeful, to earnest and spiritual piety; and therefore, though there is, indeed, still much to bid the anxious worker despond and draw back from every effort after spiritual good, there is more to hope than has yet been the permitted portion of the Jew.

LETTER XIX.

FROM THE SAME TO THE SAME.

Alleged severity of the Mosaic system examined and refuted—The
first religion to teach "Thou shalt not avenge"—State of human
nature demanded a perfect code of justice, severe in theory, essentially merciful in practice—Consideration of the verse "Eye for eye,"
etc.—Its real meaning—Necessity for the *lex talionis* at the period
of the ordinance—The award of justice not the encouragement of revenge—Great care in the Jewish Law to discover the guilt of the
accused—Commands forgiveness of injuries in individuals; as a
state, it punishes assaults—Sentence of death frequently threatened,
and why—No nation so impartially and so mercifully administered
justice—Examination of the subject—Mr. Theodores's article in the
Hebrew Review—Publicity of trial—Liberty of defence—Security
against false witness—Choice of judges—Various tribunals—Liberty of appeal from the lesser to the greater—No imprisonment or
torture—Great care in the examination of criminals accused of
capital crimes—Depositions of witnesses—Proceedings of the court
—Verdict in favour of the prisoner could not be revoked—Cautious
proceedings after passing the sentence, lest the innocent should
suffer—The word of God commands this especial care—Extract from
Deuteronomy xvii., xviii.—Minor offences receive equally careful
investigation—Superiority of the Hebrew over the modern criminal
law—Its system in the infancy of the world compared with the proceedings in the middle ages—Law prohibits the taking bribes—Intention of Hebrew justice to prevent sin, not so to disgrace the
criminal as to drive him to its continuance—Pain of false charges
—Jews make no effort to disprove them—Prejudice from ignorance
—Absolute need of Jewish literature.

WE will now examine your next objection, dearest
Annie: "Are not the laws of Moses terribly severe, and
do they not, by such a sentence as 'Eye for eye, and
tooth for tooth,' etc., appear to authorise the accusation,

that the Jewish religion is one of fire and blood, and of returning evil for evil; very inferior to the forgiveness of injuries, and general spirit of love and benevolence pervading the instructions of Jesus?" This objection is so constantly brought forward, not merely in speech, but in books, often, perhaps, only as a passing sentence, but still, with such a determined spirit of belief in its existence, that it really appears barely possible to stem the torrent, and prove its utter falsity, not from want of evidence, but from the difficulty of being heard, and, by a simple statement of the Truth, of prevailing against the mistaken and encouraged prejudices of centuries. Those who wish to burthen our Law with this charge, generally take the verse "Eye for eye, tooth for tooth, hand for hand, foot for foot," as a distinct verse, not only unconnected with any that comes before or after it, but as comprising in itself the whole spirit of the Jewish creed. They quite forget, that the same law also most imperatively declared, "THOU SHALT NOT AVENGE; THOU SHALT LOVE THY NEIGHBOUR AS THYSELF;" and that in commenting upon "Thou shalt not avenge," Solomon directs us, "If thy enemy be hungry, give him bread to eat, and if he be thirsty, give him water to drink." What more can we need, to evince the spirit of that religion of which the writer was not only a member, but with the very depths of which he was intimately acquainted by the gift of wisdom, derived directly from God Himself?

The twofold intention of our law will help us here, even as in the subjects already discussed. Long unaccustomed to any government but the sway of their own passions; their spirits crushed under life-long toil; their inclinations constantly leading them to relapse into the evil habits and customs of the benighted nations amongst whom they had for centuries been thrown; unable, in the first infancy of revelation, to realise those holy aspirations and yearnings after God for their own sake, which can only rise in an advanced stage of human nature, except in the actually inspired: it was absolutely necessary for the moral and spiritual improvement which the Eternal designed, that the law should contain a perfect code of justice, the impartial severity of which should strike the Israelites with sufficient awe, to deter them from any *wilful* committal of injury against each other, and from sin against the Lord. It is utterly impossible for any unprejudiced person strictly and steadily to examine the law, or to read that excellent article in the Hebrew Review, on the "Administration of Justice in the Hebrew Commonwealth,"* without being struck by its perfection of justice fenced round with mercy, and its perfect aptitude to the condition of the people at the time that it was given. Had its ordinances been obeyed as they were written, it is my firm belief that sin would not have obtained that fearful ascendency which the annals of Israel present.

If you read the twenty-first chapter of Exodus carefully through, and the nineteenth of Deuteronomy, you will perceive that those often-quoted words, "Eye for eye," etc., allude to, and in fact, continue, a series of instructions how to chastise *wilfully committed injury*, instructions, not for *private and personal revenge*, but as the grave and just award of the Law, administered by men appointed for the purpose, and whose cool and dispassionate examination of the subject laid before them, rendered it an impossibility for any sentence to be pro-

---

* By T. Theodores, Esq.

nounced on the offender, unless *two* witnesses could be found to swear to the committal of the deed and to the person of the accused, which must have removed even the remotest semblance of private revenge, and have prevented even those perversions of justice too often discoverable in modern law.

Whether or not this "lex talionis" ever was enforced in our history, neither the Scriptures nor the writings of Josephus inform us; but that it pleased the God of infinite wisdom and infinite love to ordain it is, or ought to be, quite sufficient to convince the true believer, that, at the time the law was revealed, it was *necessary* for the guidance and protection of man, or it *would not* have been enforced. The irascible and violent passions of eastern natures were constantly liable to lead them into the infliction of serious injury, unless checked by the dread of equal suffering for themselves. You must remember, that it was not then, as now when men's consciences are, in general, sufficiently restrained, and when even deists, by the influence of the very book they deny, are guarded from injuring their fellows. It required centuries for the spiritual influences and moral guidance of the Mosaic Revelation, so to impress men, that whether they acknowledged them or not, still they followed their ordinances, and would have thought themselves disgraced and dishonoured in their own estimation, if they stooped to the wilful infliction of physical injury even on a foe.

In the infancy of the Law and in the East, however, brute force was ever called upon to satisfy hate, or indulge passion, and it was *against this* the law was needed to provide; and no sentence, in that debased state of human nature, was so likely to effect the desired object, as the law of retaliation, enforced with all the solemn state and impartial examination of a public court of justice.

How, then, can this law be twisted and turned into the encouragement of revenge, and the returning of evil for evil? Surely, we might just as well say that in England, when any individual is brought up before a magistrate for an assault upon another, and is either fined or imprisoned according to the degree of the offence, whether it proceeded from previously encouraged hate or malice, or was the mere impulse of passion, that the fine or imprisonment is *not justice*, but *revenge*, and contrary to the spirit of the Christian religion, which demands not only forgiveness of injuries, but commands that if a man smite one cheek, the other should be offered, and if a coat be stolen, the cloak is to be given instead of demanding retribution. I do not write this in any disrespect to a religion of which the foundation is our own. I am only desirous of proving, that the law of retaliation is no more an encouraging of revenge, than the punishment of an assault in England. The fine and imprisonment would not have been sufficient for the extermination of the sin of social injury, in the infancy of mankind. As human nature advanced, the "lex talionis" would naturally fall into disuse, from the absence of all occasion for the chastisement. No man, with the least spark of morality or religion, would wilfully destroy the eye or tooth, or maim a hand or foot, for the gratification of individual evil desires; and in the case of an *accident*, the sentence will not bear at all. If, even for accidental murder, our law provided cities of refuge, where the criminal could live securely sheltered from the natural dislike of the friends of the slain; we may rest perfectly satisfied, that all *unintentional injury* not only passed unpunished, but demanded from the receiver of the injury that perfect forgiveness, which is implied in the commands, "Thou shalt not avenge, nor bear any grudge against the children of thy people, but love thy neighbour as thyself." Now we cannot feel the desire to avenge, or to bear a grudge, unless we have received *some injury;* and therefore, it is as clear a command to forgive and love as before, as if the word forgive had been specified. So careful are we to abstain from even the remotest feeling of a grudge, that our venerable teachers declare, that, "If we are asked for a loan by a neighbour from whom we may have previously asked, and been refused a similar favour, we are not to say, Here, take it, I am not like thee, and I will not refuse thee, as thou didst me;' for it would prove that, even in granting the loan, we harbour a feeling of resentment, and seek a degree of revenge, in laying our churlish neighbour under an obligation." "Man is entirely to dismiss every feeling of ill-will from his heart," the fathers continue, *"as the law not only extends to the actual deed, but to the inward sentiment;* and therefore, the mind must be pure, that the *actions may proceed from a worthy source."*

Are these the sentiments of the exclusive teachers of a law of fire and blood, dearest Annie? O do not do your holy faith such wrong, as to pronounce it such, without deliberate examination, not merely of the law, but of its commentators, the prophets and our ancient teachers. The more you study, the more I am convinced you will feel the justice of my assertion, that you might just as well charge the English punishment for assault with being private revenge, instead of the award of justice, as to accuse the Jewish religion of inculcating evil for evil, because the state of mankind, in the infancy

22

of the law, required the "lex talionis" for wilfully committed injury, instead of any other sentence.*

I agree with you, that the sentence of death is very frequently threatened in our law, and for what, judged by *present notions,* seem very trifling offences, particularly those connected with the eating of the prohibited parts of the sacrifices. But we pronounce it a trifling offence, because we are not generally acquainted with the exact nature of the sin in the sight of God. The punishment of death by man's judgment was not annexed to the eating of the forbidden animals, Maimonides tells us; but excision was denounced against drinking the blood, and eating the fat of the sacrifice; and the distinction is easily explained. The eating of forbidden food was disobedience, and man was individually accountable for it to his Maker. The partaking of the blood and fat, etc., was IDOLATRY; and, therefore, the most heinous crime which Israel could commit. The eating of the blood, etc., the Omniscient knew was *always* the proof of a relapse into idolatry, which, instead of being confined to individuals, extended to numbers, who only needed example for the people generally to resume former practices; and therefore idolatry was deserving of, and could only be checked by, the chastisement of death.

But though the low state of the people at the delivery of the Law demanded *apparently* severe chastisements for sin, no nation so ably, so impartially, and so mercifully administered justice. Death was, indeed, more frequently *threatened* in their code than in any other; but the Jewish commonwealth saw fewer *executions* than any

---

* In practice, compensation was awarded to the injured party for the damage done, but no revenge inflicted on the assailant.

country, ancient or modern, in the whole world. Mr. Theodores's admirable article on this subject in the Hebrew Review,* ought to be known and read, not only by every Jew, but every individual, whatever his creed, who is under the mistaken supposition, that the Law of the Hebrews is one of fire and blood.

"Every part of judicial procedure in the Mosaic Law, is founded on three principles: *publicity of trial; liberty of defence for the accused; and security against false testimony.* Hence a single witness counts as nothing. Two or three at least were necessary to establish evidence. The witness, on whose declaration a citizen was to be arraigned, must previously be conducted before the priests and judges, and there take a solemn oath that his judgment was correct." The magistrates then inquired diligently into the truth of the accusation, and, if proved to be false, the blow intended for the accused recoiled on the false accuser. The trial was to be held before every member of the community, whence false testimony was every instant in danger of being brought to light by some of the surrounding persons. Each of the contending parties was permitted to nominate his judge; and these two selected a third, "but the slightest motive was valid on the part of the plaintiff or defendant, to put aside the eligibility of the judges; and each had the privilege of rejecting the judge chosen by his opponent, provided he could substantiate his objection with proofs of the existence of relationship, intimacy, or any other connection by which the opinion of the judge might be influenced. Nor could two judges hostile to each other be seated on the same tribunal, lest their own enmity might produce wilful opposition in

---

* Hebrew Review, vol. iii. pp. 7 and 21.

their awards." For the validity of the verdict, of course, a majority was needed; and if two of the three were opposed, and the third declared himself unable, or was unwilling to incur the responsibility of the casting vote, two more magistrates were called in and, if necessary, two more, until a satisfactory majority could be obtained. Those minor tribunals which belonged to every city, and which were held at the city-gates or public roads, could pronounce on the payment of tithes, the estimation of vows, and other subjects of the same kind—could administer oaths, impose fines, and inflict corporeal punishment, theft, violation of deposits, and immoral conduct alike falling under their jurisdiction.

In addition to these local tribunals, there were the Minor Council of Jerusalem, and the Grand Council of the kingdom, to each of which the accused might appeal, if dissatisfied with the verdict of his own city—a privilege which protected him against the fatal influences that local prejudices so often engender. Another admirable point in Jewish justice consisted in the fact, that though the accused individual was arrested and detained till after his trial, there were no such things as imprisonment in dungeons, secret inquests or examinations by the torture, the awful inflictions of which often extorted confessions of guilt from the innocent themselves. In minor offences, the accused, though apprehended with all the necessary formalities, was generally brought before the magistrates without any delay. Only in cases of murder the accused had to wait the term of his trial; but his prison was a whole town, and his securities the magistrates themselves.

Careful as the Hebrews were to obtain impartial judgment in minor offences, their precautions and customs concerning the trying of capital crimes, idolatry and

murder, deserve yet warmer commendation. A man's
testimony against himself had no validity, unless supported by two other credible witnesses. The case of
Achan, as related in Joshua, was an exception permitted
only from the extreme urgency of the times. Nor was
the evidence of one alone admitted, even were that witness a prophet. Children under age, bondmen, men of
decidedly evil repute, and all such as were by any
infirmity precluded from the free use of their physical
and intellectual powers, were all disqualified from speaking as witnesses.* "The depositions of all legal witnesses were taken with the greatest circumspection, and
the least discrepancy in their details obtained a verdict
of acquittal for the prisoner; and it greatly invalidated
their evidence, if the question, whether they had done
all in their power to prevent the alleged crime, was not
affirmatively answered." The judges for capital crimes
consisted of twenty-three members, "eleven of whom
were chosen from various professions, in order to throw
light upon subjects wherein, besides a knowledge of the
laws, practical experience might be required." "During
the sitting of the court, the auditors and candidates
present were at liberty to ascend the judgment-seat, and
to employ all their eloquence *if they intended to speak
in favour of the delinquent; but no such right was
granted them, if condemnation were the motive of their
application.* At any stage of their proceedings, the
prisoner might interrupt the debates and demand attention to his defence; and he was ever allowed the benefit

---

* As were also women, the reason of which the author has already
dilated upon in her Women of Israel, which will account for the non-
mention of it here.

of a scruple, where a point of law rendered the decision difficult."

"If the majority of opinions was favourable to the prisoner, he was immediately set at liberty; but if, by the majority found guilty, the court adjourned until the third day. During the intervening day, the judges were to give their whole attention to the case in question, abstaining from wine, and whatever else might interfere with their serious contemplation. The third day found them reassembled; but only those elders who had found a verdict of guilty on the day of trial, could change their sentence into an acquittal. *The word of mercy once pronounced could never be revoked.* In case of great division among the judges, two additional elders were consulted, and then two more, till sometimes the number of the council amounted to seventy-one. A majority of *one* voice was sufficient for the release and acquittal of the accused; but it required *more than one* to pronounce sentence against him.

"Even after sentence had passed, and the criminal was carried to the place of execution, every precaution was taken to bring his innocence to light, if, indeed, he really were not guilty. The magistrates did not quit their seats. An usher, with a banner, stood at the entrance of the place of judgment; another officer followed the prisoner on horseback, and incessantly looked towards the judges. On the first intimation of any light having been thrown on the case of the unfortunate man, the usher waved his banner, and the officer instantly took the criminal on horseback with him and rode hastily back. Even at the prisoner's own request, he might be taken back; and this has happened no less than five times. But if no hope arose, the procession moved slowly onwards, preceded by a herald, who proclaimed to the people, 'This man is led to the place of execution for such a crime. The witnesses who have spoken against him are such ones. If any one can offer any defence for him, let him do it speedily.' But if none appeared, the culprit was exhorted to submit with resignation, and to confess his crimes. At a short distance from the place of punishment, a soporific was administered to him, which had the effect of making him less sensible to the horrors of death. And only then, when every chance of reprieve was impossible, sentence of death was passed in the following words: 'Thou hast caused us trouble, and therefore thy God causes thee trouble this day. *This day shalt thou suffer, but not in Eternity.*' The criminal was then stretched at full length for lapidation, and the witnesses through whose testimony this punishment had been decreed against him, approached with the missile (a formula most likely to prevent false witness, for many, who would not regard the swearing falsely, would shrink in horror from themselves being the instruments of death). Again; the divine sentence, 'I abhor the wicked man who slays the innocent,' resounds in their ears; and human justice demands its due."

Such, dearest Annie, was the admirable system of Jewish courts of justice. You will, perhaps, urge, that this system of the state does not do away with the severity of the actual law; and you may inquire, by what right the Jewish elders used so many precautions before pronouncing the sentence of death. I answer, By command of the same Law which ordains the punishment, "If there be found among you, within any of thy gates which the Lord thy God giveth thee, man or woman who hath wrought wickedness in the sight of the Lord thy God in transgressing his covenants, and hath gone and served other gods and worshipped them, either the sun or moon, or any of the host of heaven, which I have not commanded; *and if it be told thee, and thou hast heard of it, and inquired diligently, and behold, if it be true, and the thing certain,* that such abomination is wrought in Israel, then shall the sentence of death be pronounced. At the mouth of two witnesses, or three witnesses, shall he that is worthy of death be put to death; but at the mouth of one witness he shall not be put to death." (Deut. xvii. 2–8.) And again, " *One* witness shall not rise up against any man for *any iniquity, or for any sin, in any that he sinneth;* at the mouth of *two* or *three* witnesses shall the matter be established. If a false witness rise up against any man to testify against him that which is wrong: then both the men between whom the controversy is shall stand before the Lord, before the priest and the judges who shall be in those days; and *the judges shall make diligent inquisition;* and behold, if the witness be a false witness, and hath testified falsely against his brother, then shall ye do unto him as he had thought to do unto his brother; so shalt thou put the evil away from among you. And those that remain shall hear and fear, and shall henceforth commit no more any such evil among you. And thy eye shall not pity; but life shall go for life, eye for eye, tooth for tooth, hand for hand, foot for foot."

Is it not unanswerably clear from these verses, that the system of administering justice as recorded in the Mishnah, Talmud Babylon, and Yad Hachazakah by Maimonides (for it is from these venerable authorities, Mr. Theodores informs us, that he has compiled the article from which I have so largely quoted), has its foundation and its superstructure alike on the Word of God; and that the verses I have transcribed contain in themselves commands for every precaution which we find the courts of justice always taking; and not only in matters of life and death, but regarding minor *wilful* assaults and other offences? How then can any one so twist and turn the decrees of the Eternal regarding punishment into a law of fire and blood, of retaliation and revenge, demanding a milder revelation to do away with it? How can they quote "Eye for eye," etc., as the pervading spirit of a religion, when it was a mere judicial sentence, the award for a *wilful* injury inflicted upon another, and, even as such, *never* pronounced without such extremely careful investigation of the matters, such proven evidence, not alone of the *deed* itself, but of the evil *intention* in the heart of the injurer, that our history does not record, in any of its varied phases, a single instance of this law of retaliation having been enforced? Better, far better, for true justice, did the spirit of Hebrew jurisdiction (ay, even the law of retaliation, with all its restrictions) pervade modern courts, than the infliction of *fines*, which permits the *rich* man to go scathless, for his crimes of *inclination*, and crushes the heart, and imprisons the body of the poor, for crimes of *circumstance*. And when we remember, that this admirable system of administering justice dates its origin from the earliest age of Revelation and the lowest condition of mankind, and compare it with the criminal law of the middle ages,—the dungeons and the tortures, whose very mention pales the cheek and turns the heart sick,—ordeals by fire, water, and single combat,—the inquisition and its hideous train of secret spies, false witnesses, pitiless executioners— rack, flame, and cord—and remember that these practices were permitted, nay legalized, in countries *professing* to be guided by a faith whose mildness, equity, and love, held the Mosaic law of retaliation in abhorrence:—surely,

surely, even the most prejudiced will acknowledge, that
mercy and true justice were the attributes of the Hebrew
legislation, ages and ages before such words were known
to and practised by those professing a milder creed.

I could quote to you very many more verses in our
law, bearing on this important subject, and proving the
care taken to prevent any unrighteousness in judgment;
that we were neither to allow pity for the poor, nor regard for the mighty, to interfere with the correct course
of justice, nor by any means to accept a gift; as, in the
first place, the poor could not bestow it, and, in the next,
"a gift doth blind the eyes of the wise, and pervert the
words of the righteous." But I fear the subject may
already have wearied you: one other point, however, I
wish to bring to your notice, and that is, the care taken,
that infliction of deserved punishment should not disgrace
the Hebrew citizen after its infliction. He may have
committed some sin demanding the chastisement of stripes,
which the law expressly tells us were *not to exceed forty,
lest thy brother should seem vile unto thee.* Compare this
merciful restriction with the one, two, and three hundred
lashes, inflicted for the merest trifle in the armies and
navies of civilised countries, and say which is the more
merciful? In obedience to this merciful clause, prohibiting any punishment which would render our brother
vile in our sight—every man, "immediately after having
submitted to the sentence of the court, *resumed his position in society,* without difference as to rank or birth.
Since all laws were applicable to all the citizens, it would
sometimes occur, that the highest dignitaries had humi-
liating punishments inflicted upon them; but they did
not, thereby, forfeit their offices, with the sole exception
of the president of the Sanhedrin, whom such a sentence
would move back into the rank of the common senators."

The intention of Jewish justice was to remove sin, by so chastising as to prevent a recurrence of it in the individual sinner, and in his brother, from the effect of example. But it so united *mercy* with justice, that it never drove man to desperation and a continuance in sin, which the modern criminal law, unhappily, but too often does. A young man or a young woman commits some offence, and is sentenced either to hard labour or imprisonment; he or she is thrown back upon society with a character hardened in crime, and a conscience in some degree seared to conviction, the necessary consequence of compulsory association with irreclaimably vicious offenders. Still, on the release of such as these, better thoughts and nobler resolutions may return; and they might still have become innocent and virtuous members of the state, if, directly contrary to the spirit of *our* law, they had not become *vile* unto their brother,—that is, had they not lost character and caste, and, refused admission into any respectable society or a share of any innocent employment, been absolutely cast back into the vortex of sin, as their only means of subsistence, their only refuge from despair.

In the Jewish state, this fearful injustice was effectually prevented, by every man resuming the station he had occupied, and no man daring to cast shame in his teeth, because he had, under strong temptation, been led away to sin. It was in his power to remove even the remembrance of it, by a strictly virtuous life. All men were liable to the same infirmities, the same failings, and so none dared to despise a brother.

I cannot describe to you the pain it always inflicts on me, when I read or hear those misunderstood and misquoted words, "Eye for eye," etc., ever cast in the face of the Hebrew as the pervading spirit of his creed, and so universally believed, that even some of the most unprejudiced on every other subject, the kindest and mildest-judging, and the actual respecters of the Jews as the first-born of the Lord, have been led to adopt this false idea, and *will not* regard these words in any other light than as inculcating a spirit of revenge. And we have allowed them to persist in this charge, when every Hebrew ought so to feel the stigma, as to rise up and prove its falsity, by revealing the real spirit of his Divine Law—that Law which was the first to teach love to God and love to man; and such forgiveness, that not even a grudging thought should remain; and such care for the poor, the fatherless, the widow, and the stranger, as none other ever did; such a careful and particular investigation into every accusation, that none could suffer innocently,—that Law so severe in theory, because the state of the people needed it to save them from relapsing into idolatry, but so merciful in practice, "that a tribunal which passed sentence of death once in *seven years*, may be called 'sanguinary,'" was the remark of one of the fathers; and another rejoined, "It would still deserve that appellation, if it passed such a sentence once in *seventy* years." O! why is not the true, loving, beautiful spirit of our holy law more widely known and disseminated by the talent of its followers? Why will not *Hebrews* feel as *Hebrews*, and glory in bringing forth to the light of day the institutions, and the customs, and the spirit of their fathers? Many, indeed, have lately distinguished themselves in the law, and in the fine arts of the English world; but why will not these gifted spirits do something for Judaism as well as England? There is no need to neglect the interests of the latter, in attending to the need of the former. We want Jewish writers, Jewish books. Prejudices never can be removed, till the bright undying ray of knowledge flashes over the world, dispersing the mists of ignorance which centuries of hate and persecution on the one side, and of exclusiveness on the other, have accumulated, and this ray, kindled in the immortal light of MIND, must wing its way from North to South, and from East to West, through the silent yet eloquent minister, the press; and then there may be hope of justice for the Jew. There is none now, and the fault is our own! We make no effort to enlighten our neighbours as to the true spirit of the hope that is in us, though no struggle is too great to obtain a proper position and estimation in the Christian world. I am writing warmly, bitterly, perhaps you will say, though I hope not; but the subject ever makes my heart beat, and my temples throb, with the vain yearning to perceive the true spirit of Hebrew patriotism awakening in our people—that they would but feel; it is not enough to make the *Jew* respected, but to have JUDAISM rightly reverenced: and to do this, there must be a JEWISH LITERATURE, or the Jewish people will not advance one step.

23

LETTER XX.

FROM THE SAME TO THE SAME.

Immortality, whether or not its revelation forms part of the religion
of Moses—Belief in it more visible among Christians than Jews—
Doubts on the subject natural to youth, should be answered, not
evaded—Personal experiences—Temptation to desert the Jewish
faith—Reassured in its divinity and revelation of immortality—
Consideration of the subject of transmigration—How it obtained
admission amongst the Jews—Not a principle of Judaism—Entirely
disproved by the doctrine of resurrection—Ideas of man concerning
the soul's fitness for reward and punishment—Cannot pronounce
judgment on the ways and thoughts of God—Supposition as to gradations of rank in the superior intelligences—Man's work not com-
pleted on earth—Immortality the essence of the Bible.

I am not at all surprised at the contents of your last
communication, my dear Annie; though you do seem
to fancy that you ought neither to feel nor express any
remaining doubt, when I have explained away so many.
That I have done so, I am indeed most thankful; but
the subject you have now brought forward, we have not
yet considered; for, though anxious to do so, I preferred
waiting till you should advance it yourself. You tell
me, I have, in almost every letter, either directly or in-
directly referred to the belief in immortality as the
inseparable essence of our holy faith; but that you
cannot satisfy yourself as to whether it really was inculcated by the Mosaic Revelation, and, as such, was a
legalised point of our religion; or whether we have not
imbibed our belief in it from association with those in

whose guiding book it is revealed in direct words. That
the comfort of such a faith is so indescribable, so absolutely needed for a calm acquiescence in the Divine
government of the mysteries and miseries of this life,
that you cannot understand why the Revelation through
Moses should not have given more decided information
on this all-important subject; that your mind is sometimes in such a painful state of doubt and restless enquiry, that you find yourself wondering whether you
really have foundation for the belief in immortality, or
are resting on a mere fanciful and imaginary truth derived from the superstition of ages. If, indeed, the
religion given to Israel through Moses be Divine, as
you now find it impossible to doubt that it is, why does
it not reveal a future state, and desire us to look to
another world for the rewards or punishments awaiting
our obedience or disobedience in this? Moses appears
to you always to refer to temporal recompense and immediate chastisement; and you cannot help sometimes
drawing a comparison between the sentiments of your
Christian and Jewish friends. In the one, the thought
of, and belief in, immortality seemed so ever present,
that even the heaviest bereavements were soothed by
the hope, not only of the happiness of those who were
gone, but of an everlasting reunion; and, of course, thus
considered, Death lost its deepest horror: that amongst
your Jewish acquaintance it was a subject always
shunned, the thought of immortality so vague and undefined, so little able to console in bereavement, so
clothed in fanciful hypothesis, that it seemed to you,
that it could have no solid foundation, and really was
wanting in our religion; that you had also heard, that
the Jews believed in transmigration of souls, and had
been referred to a passage in David Levi's prayer-books

to prove it; and that in, consequence of all this contending and bewildering thought, you were feeling not only restless, but actually unhappy. All which had consoled and satisfied you, appeared to have given place to this one painfully engrossing subject; you could neither think of those you had lost, nor of death, as it related to yourself, without a shuddering dread, which made you long to embrace the faith of the Christians, and rest on their belief in atonement and immortality, which gave them so much comfort; but, knowing the Jewish faith as you do now, you felt that to embrace another was utterly impossible; you could not forswear your own, feeling so intensely not only its *divinity* but its *perpetuity;* and you conclude, by entreating me to tell you how to dispel these doubts, and whether your mind will ever rest again.

Yes, dearest Annie, it will rest, as it has never yet rested; for it will be the rest of satisfied enquiry, not of that state of simple quietude which, in childhood, is our own. All that you have expressed, I have myself experienced, and so, I believe, have all who have thought on the subject at all. The same arguments would bear on the subject of belief in immortality, as those I have already advanced regarding religion in general. Childhood adopts without enquiry the lessons it is taught. The indifferent, even the sceptic, will repeat to young children the promise of future reward for good conduct and of punishment for evil, and will unconsciously infuse some kind of idea of soul, and heaven, and immortality; and on this the mind rests quietly, till youth takes the place of childhood, and the mind, bursting into new intelligence, the conviction of new powers, new sensations, demands more from its parents and teachers, than they are sometimes inclined to give. Or it may be, that some youth, unconscious of the nature of their own restlessness, and thrown with those who think this life all, and pursue pleasure or gain, frivolity or labour alone, banish these enquiries in the turmoil of the world, and become careless and indifferent to the soul's healthful peace; others, again, too timid to express their desire for information, satisfied to go on quietly as they have done, refuse to listen to the inward enquirers, till they are so silenced, as to forget they have ever arisen; but some dispositions *must* be answered, and it is because those of their own faith will not answer them, that so many leave their native fold and seek another, where answers will be given. Be assured, that you are feeling what all have experienced, in a greater or less degree, more especially amongst those where liberty of thought is permitted and encouraged—a freedom unhappily but too often suppressed amongst the Jews; it resulted, indeed, from the baleful effects of persecution, which prevented all public or even home instruction in our faith; but it is inexcusable now, in these blessed lands, where we are not only permitted to dwell in peace and freedom, but even granted the liberty of the press.

Whence *arose* my ideas of the bliss of heaven, as so infinitely superior to the joys of earth, that even in my very happiest seasons death was no object of terror, I cannot tell you, except, perhaps, from the favourite book of my childhood, Gessner's Death of Abel; but I can remember one year especially, when just your age, and my life so happy that every day seemed to strew fresh flowers on my path, repeatedly asking myself, when the silence and solitude of night usurped the place of daily joys, "Were I summoned now, could I die willingly, and leave this world, so fraught with beauty, and love, and gladness, and seek another, believing it more lovely still?" The mental answer was invariably in the affirmative. Every beauty and joy here, in their very intensity, seemed but to shadow forth that which would be hereafter. The same year, I had some conversation on the subject with a young Christian friend, who declared she could never sleep at night, if the thought of death came across her mind, it was a subject so fraught with gloom and horror—a feeling I could not understand.

One reason for this happy view of death was, that at the time to which I allude, no thought of inward sin and constant liability to error had ever entered my heart. I had only so far quitted childhood as to be conscious of the intense happiness of existence; and through tracing every joy to a loving Father's hand, every beauty of nature to His creation, adoring Him, in fact, through His works and gifts,—*His word* was still to me a sealed book. I knew nothing of sorrow or sin, and religion with me seemed but another word for gratitude and love. I had, indeed, no doubts of the divinity and perpetuity of my own faith with which to contend; for though surrounded by Christians, and my most intimate friends earnest followers of that faith, the instructions and example of a beloved mother had brought the Jewish faith to my heart and mind, and by guiding me to God's word for instruction and comfort under every circumstance, had provided me with an invulnerable shield and support, which, though *then* unvalued, gave me all I required in my time of need.

A brief interval this intense capability of enjoyment and its indulgence, from many happy circumstances, lasted. But then came change, and anxiety, and sorrow—not heavy trials like yours, but those petty cares and vexations and disappointments—those yearnings for a continuance of the peace and joy I had experienced which

might not be fulfilled, that rendered daily life as sad
and wearisome as it had been gay. My thoughts naturally became more serious; and I found that in many
things, in thought even more than deed, I was constantly
tempted from the right path; that it was not such a
very easy thing to love and serve God as I had imagined; that it required a constant watchfulness over,
not only deeds and words, but thoughts and motives, to
prevent murmuring and rebellion. Death, which had
been such a happy thought in joy, became now a source
of dread and gloom; not that I had ceased to regard it
as the gate to bliss ineffable, but that I felt myself so
utterly unworthy of such bliss, that to die then I thought
would condemn me everlastingly. As if to tempt me
from my sole Rock of help and salvation, the belief of
the Christian came to me, as it has come to you, and
promised comfort and redemption, if I would but accept
and believe in the sacrifice of Jesus. So strong was
the temptation, that I often think the sin of apostasy
must have been mine, had not the infinite mercy of
my God so blessed a mother's instructions, as to lead
me to His word for my sole guidance and relief. It
was only to my mother I could have ventured to reveal
these tormenting doubts and painful feelings; and she
was then too ill to administer such relief. I could only
go to the Book to which her love had led me, and there
I found, indeed, all I needed—all, not only to reassure
me as to my hope in death, but the foundation of that
firm conviction of the sufficiency, the support, the inexpressible consolation of our holy religion, which I have
endeavoured to impart to you throughout our correspondence. I saw no need for embracing another faith,
when the religion of my fathers gave me not only all I
required both for heart and mind, but showed me that

if I deserted this, I could not embrace the Christian faith, for all that the Christian's taught of death and immortality was the Hebrew's centuries and centuries before.

Reassured with regard to my hope in death, and all that was needed for my salvation and acceptance, I was naturally led to the subject now so painfully engrossing you,—Whether, indeed, the belief in immortality owed its origin to the preaching of Jesus and his disciples, or was preached to and acknowledged by the Jews? I never rested till my mind was satisfied on this head. My Bible was my sole authority. At that time, there were actually no Jewish books in English to which I could refer; and from my long residence out of London, I knew no one of my own faith to whom I could appeal. Like yourself, I noticed, that to many the notion of immortality was vague and undefined, and their ideas of heaven and hell far more according to Milton than the Scriptures. The very charge of transmigration startled me as it has startled you; but, dearest Annie, God's word did not fail me: it reassured on this topic as on every other; and may He grant that I may calm and satisfy your mind, as His word did mine. I took notes of my researches at the time. Since then, more extensive reading, particularly of our own writers, has of course enabled me to enlarge more on the subject than I could have done in a first examination of it. A learned dissertation, indeed, I cannot give you; my only wish is to help you to think for yourself; and my very first object will be to endeavour to remove from your mind all idea of transmigration as a part of *Judaism*. That it may have entered the mind of certain Jews, and that their love of fanciful hypotheses may have induced them to propagate it as a portion of their creed, is not at all unlikely; but such a fact only proves the imperfection and fallacy of man, and no more interferes with the purity and holiness of Judaism, than the strange and childish superstitions of Romanism have to do with the religion of the true Christian. The idea of transmigration formed a portion of the religion of the Persians, as it may still do, and as we know it does, amongst the numerous tribes of India. By them it was transmitted to the captives of Israel, whom Nebuchadnezzar had carried from Palestine and scattered over his vast empire, imbibed, perhaps, at first unconsciously, but encouraged by the fanciful and visionary, and verses sought for in their holy Scriptures and traditions, to give it foundation and authority. The Book of Job, as one in which the manners, customs, and philosophy of the East were very vividly portrayed, was pressed into their service; and yet but one verse alone appears to be quoted in their defence, "Lo, all these things worketh God twice or thrice with man."

Now, the word they translate *thrice*, means *oftentimes;* and when taken in connection with the remainder of the chapter whence it is quoted, instead of favouring the groundless doctrine of transmigration, alludes to the preparation man undergoes, by the mercy of God, for immortality. In answer to Job's bitter ejaculation,— "Oh that one would hear me; behold, my desire is that the Almighty would answer me; and that my adversary had written a book:" Elihu, in meekness, yet feeling unable to resist the inspiration of the Lord, offered himself in God's stead; and, in a strain of impassioned oratory, almost equal to the prophets, reproves Job for his error in endeavouring to penetrate the ways of the Eternal, and lift the veil His wisdom has cast around His actions—displays God's infinite mercy in calling men to repentance by visions and afflictions, that he might deliver his soul from death—tells him *that* "*these things* worketh God oftentimes with man, to bring back his soul from the pit, to be enlightened with the light of the living"—words as clearly illustrative of immortality in the Eastern idiom, as if in English we had written— "God dealeth out trial and affliction oftentimes unto man, to prepare his soul for release from death, and for life everlasting with Him in heaven."

The progress of this strange belief amongst the Israelite captives of Persia, may, in some degree, be accounted for, by a consideration of their degraded state, as recorded in Ezra and Nehemiah. The precepts of the Law were almost entirely forgotten, the Sabbath profaned, and intermarriages so common, that "the children spoke half in the speech of Ashdod, and could not speak in the language of the Jews, but according to the language of each people." Besides these visible evils from their captivity, it was quite as likely they should inwardly imbibe the peculiar notions of the people amongst whom they dwelt; but, of course, these could not be so publicly known as to be mentioned by Ezra. On their return to Judea, some of the most daring might have sought to preach the doctrine of metempsychosis or transmigration, and, like other innovators upon their holy faith, obtained followers. Many of the priests and rabbins were exposed to imminent danger; and some even lost their lives in their endeavours to check the progress of this doctrine amongst the ignorant rabble, pronouncing it to be heathenish and unlawful. This fact, in itself, proves that it formed *no* part of Judaism. We are told, it existed in the time of Jesus, and it proves the degraded nature of the religion he came to destroy; but this is a mere assertion easily disproved. It might have existed then; but it was, like all the other sins of the people, a consequence of their *neglect* of the law and the prophets, *not* a portion of their creed. The Romanists believe in purgatory, and the efficacy of masses for the dead; but we do not deny that Christianity revealed immortality to the nations, because some of its followers choose to encourage visionary ideas concerning it, which Jesus did not teach. Then why should Judaism, as a religion, be burdened with the idle and unfounded sophistries of some of its followers? when those sophistries have no foundation whatever in the law of God?

No Hebrew who believes in that most important item of his religion, the resurrection of the dead, can believe in transmigration. Judaism taught the one, and therefore must condemn the other. How can the thirty-eighth chapter of Ezekiel, the nineteenth verse of the twenty-sixth chapter of Isaiah, and the second verse of the twelfth chapter of Daniel, be explained, if the soul can inhabit more than one body? To which would she attach herself, when the great trumpet shall sound, and the dead awake to judgment? The idea is so perfectly absurd, that I would not have entered upon its consideration, had I not feared you would burthen your holy faith with the idle visions of its followers. Much, very much, is charged on Judaism, dearest Annie, which is chargeable on the *Jews* alone. The one is of God, and written solely in His Word, pure, changeless, incorruptible, and holy as Himself; the other is of man, frail, finite, fraught with error and foolishness, the moment he turns from the Word of God to follow his own devices. That the doctrine may be found in the writings of the Hebrews, is very probable; but it must be found in the Bible to be Judaism: and, as it is not there, as its admission denies the important article of belief there laid down, the resurrection of the dead, rest assured that it is not, and never was, considered part of our creed.

You tell me, you have heard it remarked that, to be perfectly purified, the soul should be tried in every position of life, and that most probably it is so: and that, though but a casual remark, it annoyed and engrossed you, from its apparent accordance with the idea of transmigration. As I have proved to you that transmigration is contrary to Judaism, I hope you will be enabled to dismiss it, and believe with me, that any person who seriously entertains such an idea *must* reject the Bible. If man once begins to reason on the "ways and thoughts" of God according to his own, he must be lost in a labyrinth of error and groundless speculations, which can never find either rest or satisfaction. Our Law has taught us those spiritual and moral, social and domestic, duties, which will incline towards us the favour of our God. The prophets have enlarged upon this Law, and, reproving our idle adherence to mere outward form and neglect of our duties towards both God and man, have reiterated the spiritual feelings, the circumcised *heart*, which must accompany not only our specified hours of devotion, but our whole lives, to render us acceptable. We find not a word of being tried in every condition of life: God knows the nature of His creatures, but man knows not his brother. He cannot, even in the common occurrences and daily trials of life, judge his brother's feelings entirely by his own: and how may he then pretend to pronounce on the extent of his inward trials— on the workings of his heart—the struggles of the good with the evil—the internal resistance to temptation— the difficulty to become that which God loves, and man approves—or on the circumstances which have combined to make him that which *man* may condemn, but on

which God may have such compassion, as to raise him
even above those, who, in this life, have had no temptation to be led astray? Where would be that "mercy"
which God has repeatedly promised shall be for everlasting, not only on the individuals that fear Him, but "on
their children's children unto thousands," if man were
doomed to go through three or four lives, and so *win*
salvation? His final reward would be simple *justice*,
needing no intervention of that love and mercy which
God has so largely promised to His children. The belief
falls to the ground at once, if tried by the test of the
Bible. To those who weave theories for themselves, and
prefer the dictates of their own finite imaginings to the
words of the infinite God, nothing can be brought forward; for the very ground of argument is not the same.
But the true believer must reject these fanciful ideas,
this meting out God's mercy and manner of purifying;
for there is no foundation for them in his Bible.

That our work is not all done in this life; that there
are gradations of rank, in that superior existence to
which after death we shall attain; that we do not pass
from this world into the highest nature of God's angels,
but, according to the superior and more perfect nature
of our future attainments, must still do His will; that
according to the manner of our lives here, judged by
the ways and thoughts of God, not man, shall we take
our place in His heaven, and enjoy a greater or less
portion of felicity with the perfect capabilities of attaining more, and ascending higher and higher in the scale
of immortal beings, till our individuality is merged in Infinitude, I do believe most earnestly and unchangeably.
I do not bring it forward save as an individual idea; because I know it would be said, that Revelation gives me
no foundation for it. But I feel, that Revelation *does*

give me authority for its encouragement in the glorious attributes which it assigns to God, and which, without Revelation, we never could have known.

We will, however, postpone the consideration of this subject till we are satisfied, not only of the truth of our immortality, but that it was the very essence of the Jewish faith, running through the Bible from the death of Abel to the last words of Malachi, like a silver thread, so fine and subtle as sometimes to be invisible, but of such importance that, without it, the whole fabric would snap and fall, and the existence of the Deity, and the destiny of man be plunged into impenetrable darkness and despair—the law be useless—virtue and vice, mere names—and of such continuance and strength, that neither the assault of sceptics, nor the workings of time have had power to destroy it, or even diminish the lustre of its rays, gleaming up so softly and purely, yet so unfailingly, from the pages of the Bible.

LETTER XXI.

FROM THE SAME TO THE SAME.

Subject continued—Man created for immortality from the beginning—
Would have attained the nature of the angels, without death, if he
had not sinned—Cherubim with the flaming sword figurative of the
trials and death through which the soul attains everlasting life—
Immortality originally an instinct; proved to be so, every nation,
ancient and modern, heathen or polytheist, having some ideas of,
and belief in a future existence—Instinct needs revelation to make
it a principle of being—Instinct stronger when man was in direct
communion with his Maker—Why it was not made a specified part
of revelation—Prayer and sacrifice common to the Israelites before
any law was given—Prayer never enjoined, but always part of the
Jewish system—Enjoined in direct words in the New Testament, as
is immortality revealed, and why—Known to the descendants of
Abraham long before the Law was given—So referred to, and forming the groundwork of the Law—Proved to have been the heritage
of the Hebrews by the proclaimed attributes of God—Death of Abel
proves the actual revelation, or visible confirmation of the instinct of
immortality; illustrates the words of Malachi; and the doom of Cain,
those of Ezekiel—Humanity in its infancy taught more by illustration than by precept.

My last letter was so much shorter than usual, dearest
Annie, that I have no doubt it was unsatisfactory, and
therefore I write again, without waiting to hear from
you. The subject we are considering cannot be com-
pressed in the limits of one or two letters, I shall, therefore, arrange and divide it as appears best suited to the
sense, without any regard to the forms of correspondence. .

When God breathed into man the breath of life, a

living soul, which was the likeness of Himself, in which
He made man, He endowed him with that *instinct of
immortality*, which marked him, even in his state of
innocence, as the germ of a still higher and more perfected being. That, even if he had not sinned, he was
destined to be translated to the nature of the angels, we
know by the Scriptural description of the garden of
Eden, and the after-reference to the tree of life, when
God said, "And now, lest he put forth his hand and take
also of the tree of life, and eat and live for ever; *therefore*, the Lord God sent him forth from the garden: and
he placed at the east of the garden of Eden the cherubim and a flaming sword, which turned every way, to
keep the way of the tree of life."   In what way man
would have attained that purer being to which he was
evidently destined, had he retained his innocence, no
one may pronounce; but that it would have been without the pang and trial of death, no one can deny, without
denying the Mosaic record.

The allusion to the tree of life, I myself believe illustrative of the ease and delight with which immortality
would have been obtained,—that had he continued obedient and faithful, had he permitted the spiritual to conquer the temptations of the earthly being, God would
have permitted the clayey shell to exhale, and the spirit
to ascend, with as much ease and pleasure, as man could
stretch forth his hand to the tree of life, and pluck of
its fruit and eat, leaving behind him a pure race a little
lower than the angels, as we are told God had originally
created him. But when he had sinned, though the
spirit could not die, for it was the breath or emanation
of the Eternal, the path of life was as difficult to tread,
and immortality to gain, as if, indeed, the cherubim
with flaming swords guarded the gates of heaven, and

turned every way, to keep the way of the tree of life. We cannot now approach the gate of heaven, save through the fiery portals and the dark passage of death. Often and often humanity proves the truth of those exquisite lines of Cowper—

" The path of sorrow, and that path alone,
    Leads to the land where sorrow is unknown ;"

and disease and suffering, the broken heart and stricken frame, the sword, the water, ay, and the fire itself, in the thousands and thousands of martyrs' deaths, have all been passed, ere immortality, or, in the emphatic language of the Scripture, *life* is gained. Well, then, may the cherubim's flaming sword turning every way figure forth the trials and death, through which Adam's sin caused man to pass, ere he could take of the tree of life and eat and *live for ever*.

From the moment the soul or spirit entered the beautiful dwelling, which God's own hand had created for it, I believe man was as conscious of his immortal relationship with God, as he was of the power of mental volition and physical movement. It was an instinct of his nature, requiring, in the earliest stage of the world, neither revelation nor reasoning, to bring it to his mind, breathing in his every feeling, every power, and as completely part of himself, as his undying soul. The proof of this natural instinct, I find in the fact, that there is scarcely a country or nation, ancient or modern (except those in the very lowest stage of barbarism), in which this belief cannot in some degree be traced. I do not even allude to the philosophers of the ancients, Socrates, Aristotle, Plato, Longinus, and many others, whose writings bear the strongest testimony to their belief in immortality, but to the nations at large, in whom, however visionary, however unfounded, however varied, still the belief, that this life was not all, pervaded and formed an important item in their respective creeds. That the idea of the future was vague, fanciful, formed perhaps from their national characteristics in this world, matters little. All I uphold is simply, that there is a natural instinct in every created being, bidding him look forward far beyond the limits of this life, rendering him restless and craving, and inspiring him to the performance of those deeds which the laws and customs of his nation or country pronounce praiseworthy. The Greeks and Romans believed their heroes and martyrs became gods; the Norwegians, and many of the Hunnish tribes, assigned to their warriors distinguished honours in the Hall of Odin. The Indians of America place food and wine in the coffin, and sometimes sacrifice a horse and slaves at the funeral of a chief, to supply him with provision and attendants, according to his rank and his long journey to an unknown land. If we were to review all the other nations, we should find similar superstitions, and all illustrative of the same fact—the instinct of our immortality. There are said to be individuals who declare they have never felt it, and assert themselves to be so perfectly satisfied with this life, as neither to care for nor believe in another. It may be so; but such will not alter or remove a general truth. There are many who so pertinaciously cling to one pursuit, or one object, as to be utterly lost to the finer and purer feelings and pleasures of our nature, and are utterly astonished, that enjoyment can be obtained from such a simple thing, as the sight of a beautiful country, a fine picture, or a piece of sculpture, the hearing of thrilling music, or eloquent poetry; but that their capabilities for such enjoyments are so deadened, that it would seem as if they had never existed, will not convince others of the non-existence of such feelings, but simply prove individual disuse of them.

Granting, then, that the testimony of all mankind, ancient and modern, savage and civilised, tends to prove that *there is* an *instinct* of immortality within us—needing, indeed, Revelation to give us divine assurance of its truth, and the test of reason for those sceptics who do not think faith in God's word sufficient, and demand proof from investigation and analogy: it follows, that this instinct must have been still stronger when man was in direct communion with his God, than it could be, when his sins had cast a barrier between his soul and his Maker, and he was led farther and farther from Him in the pursuit of his own fanciful and presumptuous devices. It is urged, that in the Mosaic revelation, nay, that throughout the Old Testament, there is no mention of immortality in direct words, and, therefore, we have no ground for receiving it as an article of belief; and yet the very persons who urge this acknowledge, that all those Hebrews who were beloved of God believed in it, taught it, and had divine revelation, individually, for the grounds of their belief. Now this is very like contradiction. There is no more mention of this solemn truth being *directly* revealed to Abraham, Moses, David, etc., than to the mass of the people. It was the privilege, the heritage of the latter, equally with the former. It was not made an article of creed, or a *specified* part of revelation, because its instinct was already so strong in the descendants of Seth, that it was as inseparable from them, as the necessity of *prayer*, and the ordinances of the sacrifice, neither of which, in the early stages of humanity, was either taught or commanded: prayer, in fact, we never find commanded, either throughout Genesis,

or in the Law, because it was part of man's nature—the
natural vent for the aspirations of the soul, by which
alone man can commune with God. No one with the
exquisite specimens of supplication which the Old Testament presents before him, can refuse to the Hebrews
either the privilege, or the practice, or belief in the efficacy of prayer, and prayer in all its varied phases, invocation, intercession, self-abnegation, entreaty; and yet
to bring up our petitions before God was not *commanded*
in the Jewish dispensation, as in the Christian—was not
taught in direct words, because it was already, and had
been from the time of Seth, the vital breath of those
individuals from whom God's chosen race descended,
and was by them, of course, transmitted to their sons
and immediate followers. The Law gave opportunity,
and appointed days and certain places, for the public
exercise of this spiritual instinct, but its secret and
individual practice it did not even mention: so completely was it already part of the worship of the nation.
We have specimens of it from the king to the private
female, from the lawgiver to the captive, from Noah
and Abraham to Esther, Ezra, and Nehemiah, besides
instances innumerable in the Psalms and Prophets: and
who then can say, because there is no direct command
to pray in the Old Testament, that it formed no part of
the Jewish dispensation?

In the New Testament we find the exercise enjoined
in direct words, "Pray always," "pray evermore," "pray
without ceasing." Too long petitions were justly rebuked,
and a model given; but why was this? Because the
nations to whom Christianity was preached, as preparatory to a knowledge of the God of Israel, were sunk in
ignorance and heathenism. Many worshipped idols—
and all, the devices of their own hearts. The divine in-

stincts of the undying nature and imperative desires of the soul, had long been either lost in, or blended with, such darkly erroneous notions, that they absolutely needed clear, brief, emphatic words to enforce them; and this is the reason why we find the duty of prayer *commanded* in the New Testament, and not in the Old, which was intended only for the instruction of the Jews.

Sacrifice is another strong proof of these spiritual instincts, as we find it *offered* and *accepted*, ages before it was made a national ordinance. Abel, Noah, and all the patriarchs offered sacrifices, and built altars, without any command so to do. God, indeed, told Abraham, when the patriarch asked how he should know that he should inherit the land, "to take an heifer and a she-goat and a ram, all of three years old, and a turtle dove and a young pigeon" for an offering; but this very direction proves the previous existence and practice of such a rite in the family of Seth, or we should find the method and order of the sacrifice as clearly specified to Abraham, as it was afterwards in the Law, when the long residence of Israel in Egypt had deadened that natural prompting of devotion, or amalgamated it with the somewhat similar but idolatrous rites, which were abominations in the sight of God. How could Abel and Noah have known that sacrifices were acceptable if offered in proper spirit, as a visible acknowledgment of the Divine supremacy, had there not been some *instinct* within prompting the rite?—It may be urged that, though the Mosaic record does not mention it, there *may* have been a revelation of God's will to that effect, *as* it is said there was against murder and adultery, and commanding the obedience of the Sabbath; and, therefore, there *may* equally have been a revelation of Immortality. But whether there really was this unrecorded revelation, or that prayer, sacrifice, and observance of the Sabbath proceeded from those divine instincts which God in His wisdom implanted in man, directly He endowed him with a living soul—the fact, that prayer was the vital breath of God's elect, and an essential part of the Jewish dispensation, though we can never once find it actually *commanded*, and that sacrifice was offered and accepted ages before it became an ordinance, remains the same, and bears with equal force and clearness on our own assertion, that equally with the necessity of prayer, so the BELIEF OF IMMORTALITY, was the *very essence* of the Jewish Faith—and that, without it, the Law itself would neither have been *given* nor *obeyed*. If we separate this Divine and glorious instinct of the soul from the Old Testament—we are at once lost in utter darkness. The Creator is not what He revealed Himself—a Being of such infinite love, that neither heaven nor earth can contain it; of such forbearing mercy, that sin itself is forgiven through sincere repentance; of such perfect justice, that He has given tests of obedience and service, according to the capabilities of His most frail children, not according to His own. He is none of these, if we aver that to the Old Testament immortality is unknown, but His very word is false. Those who deny to the Jews this glorious belief, know not what they do, nor the fearful charge they bring upon their God. Adopted without examination, ignorance and prejudice so fold themselves round it, that they believe it indisputably true; whereas they might well pause and shudder to find, that by its encouragement they actually *disbelieve* and deny the attributes which the Eternal proclaimed as His own, when he passed before Moses; and they must look upon the Old Testament as a revelation of injustice, tyranny, and wrath, instead of the love, truth, and justice, com-

passion and forbearance, which, read by the light of belief in immortality, it is.

This is a strong assertion, you will say; but, indeed,
it is a true one. We must doubt, nay, disbelieve, in
God Himself, if we disbelieve in immortality as the vital
breath of Judaism. There can be no intermediate path.
The Law was given, visible revelation was vouchsafed,
and prophets were granted to a people in whom the instinct of immortality had never been utterly extinct,
however choked up in the *mass* by temporal misery and
spiritual darkness. We *know* that it was the essence of
the Old Testament, *exactly as we know* that prayer was
an offering acceptable to God, and resorted to by all
ranks and conditions of men, not only because we are
told so in *direct* words, but because we read the *petition*
and the *reply;* and we cannot read the words of Moses,
David, Solomon, and the prophets, without perceiving,
unless wilfully blind, that their belief in immortality was
as strong as their belief in, and practical illustration of,
the efficacy of prayer. Prayer was *not* commanded, yet
they prayed; sacrifices were *not* enjoined *before* the Law,
yet they were offered; and we may just as well deny
these facts, though the whole Bible proves them, as to
say, because immortality was not revealed in direct words,
it formed no part of the Jewish dispensation. We must
never forget, in considering this important subject, that .
from Adam to Noah, from Noah to Abraham, and from
Abraham to Moses, even in the awful night of Egyptian
bondage, the witnesses of the Eternal and retainers of
those instincts and casual revelations which, till the Law
was publicly given, could alone have been their moral
and spiritual guides, never failed. God preserved an
unbroken line of His people, even in the midst of the
corruption and insincerity which devastated the whole

earth. Compared with the vast multitude of the voluntarily sinful, and those who were comparatively innocent from actual ignorance, the line of faithful witnesses was indeed but a spider's thread gleaming, in its delicate yet visible texture, through a dense and widely-extended pall; but still it *was* there, and it was to these the Law was given, not to men to whom the God of Israel, and the instincts He had given, were unknown. If the Jewish dispensation had been intended for the darkened multitude, the command to pray to God alone, and the revelation of a future life, would have been given as clearly as we find it in the New Testament. Like the benighted nations to whom the Apostles preached, they must have been taught from the very beginning. But the descendants of Seth were prepared by the revelations and instincts already vouchsafed. The groundwork of belief in immortality, the necessity and efficacy of prayer, and the acceptance of sacrifices, was already there, and on this groundwork the superstructure of the Law, and its explanations by the prophets, were raised; and, admitting such groundwork, we cannot acknowledge the superstructure to be imperfect and incomplete: we dare not do so; for if we do, we *deny* the truth and perfection of our God.

The sacrifice offered by Cain and Abel in the fourth chapter of Genesis, the acceptance of the one and rejection of the other, prove undeniably that there must either have been a *direct revelation* from the Lord, ordaining not only the sacrifice, but the spirit in which it was to be offered, for it was not the nature of the offering, but the secret sinfulness of Cain, which caused his to be rejected, as is proved by the Eternal's reproof;—or that He had given with the immortal soul the instinct of worship and spiritual love. The accepted sacrifice of

Abel proves this; and his *death* was the actual *revelation*, or the *visible confirmation* of the instinct of our *immortality*. The knowledge of good and evil, right and wrong, had been indeed dearly purchased by Adam and Eve; but that very knowledge must now have brought comfort in the midst of agony. They knew, and had known from their birth, that one son was righteous and the other sinful. God Himself had marked that it was so, by the acceptance of Abel's offering, and His reproof of Cain. And yet the righteous *died* and the guilty was doomed to drag on life, a fugitive and a wanderer, through weary years. What must this have taught? Death, the threatened punishment, the invisible terror, the inevitable doom of Adam's heritage, had been upon the earth, and snatched away the *only* righteous, and the guilty lived. If death were annihilation, what was Abel's reward? What incentive had Adam to bring up his children for the good, not the evil? But to Adam and to us that first death was the visible, the palpable, revelation of immortality. No word was needed to confirm the instinct which God Himself had implanted, as inseparable from the immortal soul. And did the Bible give us no other proof, allude to the subject by neither word nor record again: the death of the *only righteous* whom the earth had seen, is enough for the believer to rest, heart and mind, in thankfulness and peace. But it is *not* the only record. It is but the commencement of that silver thread to which I have before alluded, as running through the Bible, holding its varied web together, and in its very *first* event after man's fall, illustrating, with thrilling truth, the words of the *last* prophet through whom the Lord declared that those who loved and served Him should be *His* on that day, and in that world where He makes up His jewels, and when the dif-

ference between the wicked and the righteous alone shall
be discerned. And the sentence passed on Cain illustrates with equal force the words in which Ezekiel alludes to eternal life, and the time granted to the sinner
for repentance,—"For I have *no* pleasure in the death
of the wicked, saith the Lord, but rather that he should
turn from his wickedness and live." Are not then both
these verses, though written ages and ages afterwards,
powerfully exemplified in the very first Biblical record
after the fall? Abel was righteous; and therefore, though
it entered not the Divine economy so to interfere with
man's free-will as supernaturally to shield him from the
fury of his brother, a home was prepared for him in
heaven, where he shines as "one of the jewels of the Lord."
Cain was sinful, and therefore he *could not die* till his
sin was repented of and atoned, and so the everlasting
chastisement which must have been his had he been taken
from earth at the hour of his crime, was averted. God
had no pleasure in his death, but gave him time that he
might turn from his wickedness and live—for ever; for
such is the meaning of the prophet.

Where illustration ·and doctrine so· exactly agree,
though at opposite ends of the same Holy Book, and
written at widely severed epochs, to' my mind it seems
scarcely possible to doubt farther. In the early stages of
the world, man was taught yet more by illustration than
by precept. The instinct of immortality placed within
Adam, received undoubted confirmation from the events
of his own family. He was taught that, though death
in its actual physical agony, and in the fearful mental
suffering of the bereaved, was in very truth the chastisement for sin which the Lord had decreed, it was yet
to the righteous an entrance into life eternal; that death
was the cherubim's flaming sword, but that passed, the

tree of life was gained, and man could live for ever;—
and that lengthened life on earth might be the portion
of the sinner, enduring such trial and temptation as to
purify him for heaven, as was the destiny of Cain, whose
very sentence proved immortality as clearly, as his
brother's permitted death. From Adam this conviction
passed to Seth; and from Seth downwards to the chosen
repositors of God's Almighty will; and this, in some
measure, prepared them to understand *spiritually* as
well as *temporally* the promised rewards, and threatened
punishments, of the revelation on Mount Sinai.

LETTER XXII.

FROM THE SAME TO THE SAME.

Subject continued—Charge against Moses's non-revelation of Immortality proved false—How it has arisen—Powerful evidences in Deuteronomy, of Moses's reference to the life and death which are eternal—Causes why belief in Immortality was not made an article of salvation in the Exodus from Egypt—Bestowal of the Law presupposes a purer state of existence—Impossibility, from our social position and the gift of free-will, for all the righteous being rewarded, or the sinful visibly punished on earth—The Law granted to prepare us for an immortal existence—Too spiritual a belief to influence the mass, either then, or now—Obtained stronger ascendency as humanity and intellect advanced—The writings of David, Solomon, and the Prophets, prove Immortality the essence of their faith—Moses's prayer—Extraordinary agreement of the first and last prophets of Israel—Witness of Balaam to Israel's destined Immortality—Distinction between the sentence pronounced on crimes between man and man, and between man and his Maker, proving the same fact—Moses's last address suited to the comprehension of the enlightened, and agreeing in its immortal meaning with all the afterwriters of the Bible—His revelation of Immortality proved and illustrated by his own death.

No, dearest Annie, the charge so often brought against Moses, that in his ministry and the books revealing it we can find no mention of immortality, is *not* a true one. To the believer, convinced that man was aware of his immortal nature from the period of his creation, and still more from the first event recorded in his family, the Law, especially Deuteronomy, speaks in the clearest terms of that life and death which are eternal. To those who take up the books of the law alone, and read it as entirely a detached thing, unconnected with either Genesis or the Prophets, its ordinances are all temporal, and its commands and prohibitions merely local and of definite duration. Taking the mere letter, to the utter exclusion of the spirit, the charge *may* seem correct. To the Hebrew, however, it cannot. He ceases to be a Hebrew, the moment he disbelieves in immortality as the essence of his creed. Had we no writings left us in which the *inner* part of the actors of the Bible, men living under the law, and obeying its every precept, or suffering the penalty of its disobedience, were displayed: we might, indeed, be accused of making an assertion which we cannot prove. But with the words of Moses in his individual supplication before God—of David in his rich treasury of Psalms—of Solomon in his Proverbs and Ecclesiastes—of all the Prophets—of the writers of the Apocrypha—of our ancient Fathers—from the Babylonish captivity through every age—all of whom knew and acknowledged no faith but Judaism, no law but that of Mount Sinai, no revelation but that which their ancestors beheld—*we know* that immortality must have been preached, taught, and believed: or how could it have formed, as it does, the essence of their writings, the reflection of their inward thoughts and aspirations? A Jew could not write of theology, unless immortality was its groundwork. The extracts of our metaphysical writers in the "Hebrew Review," will prove this convincingly; and whence could this firm belief have sprung, except from their own faith?

There are many causes which account for the *apparent* omission of the inculcation of immortality, as an article of belief, and an incentive of action, in the laws of Moses. In the first place, the very selection of the people and bestowal of a guiding law presupposes another state of

more perfect being: else, why the great care to become
purified and righteous, and capable of realising those
higher feelings and nobler pleasures which earth could
neither satisfy nor give? As a nation, the judgments
of God were often permitted to be visible: with respect
to individuals, this never was, or could be. The social
state and gregarious nature of man would entirely prevent a realisation, while below, of that happiness which
God promised as the reward of the righteous. However
bearing in his own breast the elements of bliss and peace,
springing from a conscience perfectly at rest, the infirmities and faults, the suffering and trials of those around
him, especially in any near or dear connection, the liability to all the petty, but not less engrossing sorrows of
social and domestic life, *must* prevent all perfect joy.
To have realised on earth the promised reward of worth
and virtue, man must have been constituted differently,
and have possessed *in himself* and *for himself,* the capabilities not only of feeling, but of acting. Each individual must have been created to be his *own world,*
distinct and apart, needing neither domestic ties, nor
social help, and, if right *within,* utterly incapable of
suffering from *without.* Could we have imagined such
a being, we might also have imagined that this life
would have been sufficient, and that worth would have
brought its own isolated individual happiness, and sin its
equally isolated misery. But man was not thus created;
and therefore, liable as he is to all the deeper suffering and intenser joy of a social and gregarious being,
there must be something beyond this life, to which alone
he can look for that *individual* happiness of which
God's law assures him as the effect of virtue and obedience. As a social being, he cannot divide himself
from his fellows, and their influence on outward circum-

stances, or inward feelings, may make the most truly
righteous so sorrow-stricken, that only his own integrity
and trust will give him strength to struggle on, and enable him never to quit the path of light; and the same
social influences may so surround the wicked, with enjoyment, luxury, and ease, that not till the awful hour of
death, except in the occasions of torturing remorse of his
own mind, would he wake to the consciousness of sin, and
all the horror of a too late desire to make atonement.

That man has free will, no one can deny (however the
believer must feel, that God, in His inscrutable wisdom
and. infinite mercy, overrules it to the furtherance of
His own Divine economy); and therefore, this earth must
be, even to the individually righteous, a scene of probation and trial *which, if that were all,* needed neither the
restrictions of religion nor the acknowledgment of God.
Happiness or misery springs from the effects of man's
free will,—not the free will of the sufferer, but of those
connected with him, either in his domestic or social state.
To mark the good for undisturbed happiness below,
would interfere with that free will, and so disturb the
order of earthly things, and the supreme government
of the Eternal; yet, if there were no other state of
being, this visible distinction on earth *must be,* or God's
word would be false, and there would be no distinction
between vice and virtue.   What was the use of a guiding law, obedience to which was to purify and bring
reward, and disobedience to which was to compel chastisement: if this life were all, man's social nature were
to remain the same, exposing him to suffering and
misery from the imperfection of others, *not* his own?
If we were created but to live out a brief space of joy
or woe, vice or virtue, ease or sorrow, and be annihilated: what would distinguish us from the brutes of the

field, whose birth and death are the same? Why should we be burdened with restrictions and ceremonies, ay, and an ever-speaking conscience, if we were born but to die? What can it signify how we act, when between the wicked and the virtuous there is no visible distinction, and the former's span of life is often both longer and happier than the latter? It is folly, almost blasphemy, to pursue the argument farther.

God granted His Law as a *preparation* for our immortal being. To help us to distinguish between those things which were acceptable to Him, and those that were not; to enable us to attain a higher and more spiritual existence even here, and so awaken us to those more ethereal and subtle aspirations, influences, and capabilities of the soul, mind, and heart, which grosser natures know not, and mere animal education never can produce; and, by constant communing with, and reference to, the INVISIBLE, but all-emanating, all-governing Spirit of the universe, who had, in thrilling attributes, proclaimed Himself our God and Father, we not only were enabled to realise, but to keep alive the consciousness of our immortal soul which that God had breathed into us, by which to know and worship Him, in contradistinction to the influences of a mere earthly nature which, had we possessed it *alone*, would have made us in every respect, save that of actual frame, like unto the brutes of the field, endowed with certain instincts that prompt us to seek and find the largest portion of present enjoyment, and so utterly unconscious of right or wrong, as to need no instinct as to the which to choose.

That man was an immortal being, Moses had no need to teach; for, like the necessity of prayer, it was already known to all the descendants of Seth; but to make it an article so imperative that salvation depended on its acceptance,—-to hold forth its pure but, save to a favoured few, almost inconceivable rest and felicity, as the sole incentive to obedience in the vast mass of unenlightened, persecuted men, who went forth out of Egypt, would have argued an entire ignorance of human nature incompatible with either the wisdom, or the mercy, or the justice of Him, who, in making the slaves of Egypt a holy people, sought but their happiness, and, through them, the happiness of the whole world.

Nor is there any contradiction in this assertion. There are very few, if any, it does not signify of what denomination, who disbelieve in a future state of existence, however the belief may be coloured by their own imaginings; but how very few are there who can place this belief always before them, and act upon it as their incentive for action, their soother in earth's trials, and as the motive for universal charity and forbearance, because in their immortal souls all men are brethren ! *Individuals*, indeed, there are, and perhaps as many known to God as the "seven thousand," who in Israel's greatest corruption had never " bowed the knee to Baal;" but I am alluding to the *mass* amongst the nations. Christianity has, indeed, taught immortality, and in direct words ; but do we, can we, trace the *belief* as *inciting* and *influencing* the *multitudes*, though the *creed* itself is there ? And if a belief so purely spiritual cannot, even in these days of enlightenment and superior wisdom, be said to incite and influence the masses (though they believe), how could we expect it in the oppressed and suffering Israelites in the time of Moses? Groaning under their brutal bondage, so overwhelmed with work that the body had no rest in which the mind might breathe and struggle to throw off the shackles of its animal sufferings ; lowered and debased, till they could almost forget that they were *men:* who, but misguided enthusiasts, could imagine that a revelation of immortality could have been required and welcomed as an incitement to obedience and worship, as those more tangible promises of rest and peace in a country of their own, which a merciful God held forth? Could we ask the hundreds and hundreds of unhappy victims to the fearful system of overwork in London, which thought should bring the greatest comfort—the hope of heaven, or the body's needed rest, the mind's re-creation, and the heart's enjoyment:—can any one doubt what the answer would be? Ay, and they would still be Christians, still believers in immortality; and their Father in heaven would not judge of them harshly as the enthusiasts of earth; for He knows our nature, and that while on earth, we need earth's joys.

That the multitudes, then, at the exodus from Egypt, needed, and were governed more by temporal than by spiritual promises, is no proof that they did not believe in a future state. God, in His mercy, inspired Moses so to lead and threaten, as would most easily impress their lowered nature. If miracles performed before their very eyes, the awful revelation of Sinai itself, were yet insufficient to keep them believing and obedient: so simply spiritual a doctrine as that of heavenly reward must have been meaningless and vain; and our Father never demands more from His creatures than He knows they can bestow. The Law was to purify and spiritualize them, and, by the deepening and encouraging of the soul's inward breathing, gradually to give such scope and life to its impulses, as to need no divine Revelation of its nature and destiny; for every individual possessed it in himself. We know this is the case, by the clearer and clearer views obtained and written on this subject, as man's nature advanced and his intellect matured. Had there been any *new* Revelation vouchsafed to David, Solomon, and the Prophets, we might have denied that there was any reference to immortality in the Law; but such was not the case. In the writings of these holy men we see the *essence* of the creed they professed, brought forward even the more forcibly from their prophetic knowledge, that the day was advancing when the unhappy people would have no earthly resting-place nor earthly comfort, and when their only hope and incentive for adherence to their Law would rest on their firm, unchanging, enduring, and death-defying belief in immortality, a belief which their whole after-history proves.

Do not, then, be startled and pained, dearest Annie, at the accusation so often brought against our Holy Law and divinely inspired lawgiver. That God did not command *faith* in so purely spiritual a belief, as after-reward and punishment, as necessary to the acceptance of the people's prayers and service, only proves the infinitude of His mercy, *not* the imperfection of His law. But to say, that Moses never alluded to this sublime and ever-existent doctrine, is an utterly mistaken charge. In his very prayer before God, when the people had sinned in the matter of the golden calf, we find these words: "Ye have sinned a great sin; and now I will go up unto the Lord; peradventure I shall make an atonement for your sin. And Moses returned unto the Lord, and said, Oh, this people have sinned a great sin, and have made them gods of gold. Yet now, if thou wilt forgive their sin— *if not, blot me, I pray thee, out of the book which thou* hast written. And the Lord said unto Moses, Whosoever hath sinned against me, him will I blot out of my book."

Now the prayer and the reply must have been reported to the multitudes—or they would have thought their leader had deceived them, and not attempted to make atonement for them. And both the prayer and the reply must have been incomprehensible, had they not already known and believed in that futurity to which Malachi alludes in almost exactly the same words as Moses, though ages had elapsed between them:—"And the Lord hearkened and heard it, and a *book of remembrance was written before Him*, for them that feared the Lord, and that thought upon His name." Would it not be very remarkable, that Moses and Malachi, the FIRST and the LAST prophets of Israel, should so exactly agree, were not the writings of both divine, and that which was taught by the last, was also taught by the first? We can find no record of Moses having been *told* of the existence of this book; and yet he made the being blotted from it, and so losing his individual immortality, as an atonement for the people (an instance of self-sacrifice, with which no other history, sacred or profane, can compete). Therefore, that there is no revelation in exact words of a future state, is *no* proof that the people did not both know and believe in it; while their being satisfied that Moses *did offer* to atone for them, though the atonement was refused from God's perfect justice, is equally convincing that the book of remembrance, to which he referred, was also known to them.

Again, we find in the exclamation of Balaam—"Who can count the dust of Jacob, and the number of the fourth part of Israel? Let me die the death of the righteous, and let my last end be like his,"—a confirmation of the same fact. There never was any such visible distinction between the *physical* death of the righteous and the wicked, as could call for this exclamatory prayer from the prophet. He looked beyond. Heathen as he was by race and birth, God had singled him out to proclaim to the people the glorious destiny of Israel; and he could of course perceive that which was the *heritage of Jacob*, the light of immortality, so gleaming through the dark shadows of natural death, that he concluded his prophecy by the imploring adjuration, "Let my last end be like his!" If death were supposed to be annihilation, what could it signify whether it were that of the heathen or the Israelite? Both were liable to the same suffering, the same pain; but the one had but a faint instinct of another life, which the terrors of death might choke: the other had its confirmed realisation, brightening more and more as the dark portals neared; and this Balaam knew, or we should not find that earnest prayer unconnected as it is with his prophecy either before or after. It was, as if so overpowered by the glorious destiny revealed of Israel, even in his death, that the petition, "Let me die the death of the righteous, and let my last end be like his," could not be restrained, and its utterance marked at once his realisation of the immortality promised them.

The very difference in the sentences awarded to certain crimes, marks the fact, that a future state was already known. Those crimes that did violence to man, interfered with the civil law, and so disturbed the peace and harmony of the state, Moses invariably threatens to punish with death as inflicted by the civil statutes. To instance one verse among very many, "He that stealeth a man and selleth him, or if he be found in his hand, *shall surely be put to death.* And he that curseth his father or his mother shall *surely be put to death.*" These were, so to speak, palpable crimes, liable to the judgment of man, for it was a *community* they injured. "But he that sacrificeth unto any other god, save the Lord only, he *shall be utterly destroyed.*" The expression here is so different from that previously quoted, that it can only mean destruction here and hereafter; and again, alluding to the observance of the Day of Atonement, he continues, "for whatsoever *soul* it be that shall not be afflicted in that same day, he shall be cut off from among his people; and whatsoever *soul* it be that doth any work in that same day will I destroy from among his people."

Now it is evident, that these different expressions allude, not only to different degrees of sin, but to distinct chastisements. The harmony of social life might not be interrupted, nor man injured by his fellow, without such punishment as would prevent the recurrence of the sin, and serve as an example to others. Circumstances often and often occasion social crimes, particularly the sins of theft, and even murder. Those who commit them may have never been taught right from wrong; or the desperation of unconquerable privation and misery, may have urged on to momentary acts, wholly foreign to the individual nature. In Judea, indeed, this was never the case to the extent it is in modern lands; but from our moral law *every other* has arisen; and therefore it was adapted for all necessities. But though God's infinite mercy would judge his frail children by the *circumstance,* as well as the *deed,* by the influences of example and education, and so have mercy when man has none: yet the laws of a social state could not make this distinction. It was an imperative duty for public criminals to be publicly chastised; otherwise there could be no restraint on the indulgence of men's passions and desires, and anarchy and misrule would reign alone. But, "though put to death" by the civil law of his country, for treason against that law, much might be found, even in that apparently depraved heart, to obtain for his *soul* the Eternal's mercy, and so save him from perishing everlastingly. But those *secret sins* between the heart and its God, could have no restraint by civil law; for they did no social harm, affected but the individual, and might in fact never be known to the state. To these, then, God says, "the soul shall be cut off," or " the soul shall die," that man may know, however he may hide his iniquity, and so escape the judgment inflicted on those who sin more openly: yet still his SOUL must stand in judgment before God Himself, and will live or die according to his *secret* deeds. Capital crimes are punishable at once, and the mental and physical agony attendant on such a fate may he deemed sufficient suffering to save the misguided and erring (not the wilful sinner) from everlasting death; while to those who live on a *lengthened* day, rejoicing in a seemingly triumphant course, in an unnoticed abandonment of their God, and secret oppression of their fellow-creatures, believing that because no judgment has befallen them, His threatenings and promises are alike without foundation, may find that it is to them, that fearful sentence, "That *soul* shall be cut off from his people," is applied, and learn at the footstool of their God its full and terrific meaning. That so the words of Moses were recorded, is confirmed by the evidence of David in the ninety-second Psalm: "When the wicked spring up like grass, and the workers of iniquity do flourish, it is, *that they shall be destroyed forever!*" A brief but exact commentary on our own assertion.

That "put to death" alludes to temporal punishment, and that the *soul* shall die, or be cut off, or be utterly destroyed, alludes to the sentence pronounced hereafter, is not merely my opinion, but that of all our ancient sages, whose various opinions on the subject of excision, or rather a brief notice of them, I may be able to obtain for you before we quite conclude this subject. If we once acknowledge that the belief in another state of being has been the heritage of man from his creation, confirmed by the death of Abel, the translation of Enoch, and all the promises made to the Patriarchs: we shall find innumerable passages in the Pentateuch that not only confirm it, but actually refer to it in direct words, and in none clearer or more emphatic than in Moses's last address to the people, and in *his own death.*

"See," he says, in Deut. xxx. 15, "I have set before thee this day *life* and *good, death* and *evil;*" and in the nineteenth verse, "I call heaven and earth to record this day against you, that I have set before you life and death, blessing and cursing; therefore choose life, that thou and thy seed may live."

The mixed multitude who had gone up from Egypt, and whom Moses addressed equally with the more enlightened Israelites, most probably regarded these words, as the mass would now, merely as alluding to the prolongation of life and felicity in the Holy Land. But the real descendants of Abraham knew that no man, be he righteous or wicked, could escape the penalty of Adam's sin; that *evil* could not be connected with that death, which, as Isaiah afterwards taught, *taketh the righteous from the evil to come,* and is an entrance into peace, and which, *before* the Law, was practically illustrated in the death of Abel, and, during the Law, in choosing the *only* righteous of the family of Jeroboäm, and the righteous. king Josiah, for an early death. Nor can that life be considered a *blessing* and *good,* which even to the righteous is, from his social nature, so often dashed with misery. The multitudes, indeed, could not enter into this consideration of the subject; the judgments and miracles performed before them as chastisements for

national sin, had impressed them with the idea, that
death by the hand of God immediately followed rebellion against Him; and their only chance of entering the
promised land, and prolongation of their days therein,
was implicit obedience; but that the Israelites, especially their priests and elders, princes and leaders—all,
in fact, who could throw off the mental and spiritual
darkness engendered by their long bondage in Egypt,
regarded the words of their Lawgiver as alluding to
eternal life and death, is proved by a constant reference
to a future state, being the very essence of all those
writings in the Psalms, Proverbs, and Prophets, which
disclose the *inner* man.

The very rendering of this mighty truth, proves that
intimate knowledge of human nature which Moses so
fully possessed. Had he addressed himself only to the
comprehension and capability of the more spiritually
enlightened, the mass would have had nothing on which
to rest; for to natures lowered as their own, immortality
as their *only* incentive to obedience would have had no
weight whatever. Individuals amongst them there were,
no doubt, who would, and did, receive and promulgate
it; but not such could an earthly leader single out.
Had he, on the contrary, addressed himself *only* to the
capabilities of the multitudes, and merely promised temporal rewards, the more enlightened must have doubted
his individual wisdom, and perhaps disbelieved even his
inspired mission; for they knew that "life" might be a
"curse," and "death," a "blessing;" and that it was not
in the power of the most righteous, by his righteousness,
so to choose life on earth, that "he and his seed might
live." But the words he chose gave incentive for the
choice of good, in both their temporal and spiritual
sense. Moses's own belief in immortality, not the

greatest sceptic will deny; but there is no record of that
sublime truth being *revealed* to him. If it had not been
known before, we know it would have been imparted
equally with those glorious attributes of the Creator
which, at His servant's own request, God proclaimed before him. Moses was not different from his fellows, until
selected and inspired by the Lord in his eightieth year;
nor was he inspired *without* instruction. All that God
imparted to him, to fit him for leader and lawgiver, his
impartial record has handed down to us; and equally
would he have done so with immortality, had it been
then for the *first* time revealed. It would not have
come by inspiration any more than his other spiritual
knowledge; and, therefore, even as Moses believed it,
so did every other descendant of Seth, whose spiritual
nature was not wholly lost in brutalising bondage; and
thus known and believed, there was no occasion for any
farther revelation or proclamation of its truth, than the
constant reference to it in the very act of bestowing the
Law and all the ordinances therein comprised.

The confirmation of this supposition—the seal, as it
were, placed on the real meaning of Moses's words—"See,
I have placed before you life and good, death and evil,"
we find in *his own death*. If the prolongation of this
life were the *only* reward awaiting the good, would the
just, the merciful, the long-suffering God have *annihilated* His faithful servant at the very moment, that his
toils were seemingly at an end, and the promised land
attained? If we believe in the divine origin of the
Bible at all (and I trust, dearest Annie, that on this
subject your mind is now quite at rest), we must believe
not merely in its lessons of moral guidance and spiritual
hope, but in the ATTRIBUTES OF THE CREATOR, which it
reveals. These attributes are of as much weight and

importance, in attempting to explain, not only the Bible, but life itself in all its varied phases, as revelation either of *precept* or *fact*. If we believe in God at all, without even the acceptance of revelation, we regard Him unconsciously, perhaps, as good and beneficent, pure and holy; and Deists themselves would reject with horror the idea of associating Him, even in a momentary thought, with injustice or falsehood, tyranny or wrath. This then must be the witness of the *soul's instinct*, the reflection of that image of God in which He made man. Even polytheists will make the good deities the superior, and the evil spirits as of minor power, which must, at the end of days, succumb to the good. The revelation of the attributes of Israel's God not only confirms this natural instinct, but gives full scope and comfort to the aspiring mind, and enables it to understand much of those bewildering incongruities daily passing around us which, without such revelation, must have remained in darkness.

If God, indeed, proclaimed these consoling attributes which the thirty-fourth chapter of Exodus reveals (and what Hebrew shall deny it without forswearing his own soul?), the death of Moses is an unanswerable evidence to the truth of our immortality, and to the real spiritual meaning of the words "life and good, death and evil." If Moses might not be reckoned amongst the righteous, who dare ascribe to himself the term, and so avail himself of the promises of God? Who can peruse his life, and not be struck with the exquisite beauty of his character, the union of perfect humility with the noblest magnanimity, the naturally fiery temper subdued into meekness "above that of all men on the face of the earth," the childlike faith, yet mighty mind, the forgiving tenderness towards all his brethren, especially towards those who sought to injure him individually, the earnest longing that all "men might be prophets," and so be guarded from sin and accepted before God, the self-abnegation which led him to offer his own soul as an offering for sinners? Neither sacred nor profane history can produce a character so perfect; for when we compare him with others, we are apt to overlook the peculiar situation and circumstances, which rendered the path of unerring love and duty so much more rugged and difficult to him than to private individuals. Yet, this great and good man, for the commission of one sin, one breach of faith, was forbidden to enter the land of promise, was only permitted to gaze upon it, and then had to die; and would this, could this have been, if death were indeed annihilation, and the only reward of the righteous be prolongation of life and prosperity on earth? Every attribute of our God so forbids us to believe it, that we scarcely dare encourage the thought without blasphemy.

The sin itself was not, indeed, the mere disobedience of striking the rock, when God commanded Moses to speak to it. The words of the Bible are, "Because *ye believe me* not, to sanctify me in the eyes of the people." We read the action, God saw the heart; and marvellous, incomprehensible, as it may seem in one so perfect, He beheld there a momentary want of sufficient faith. He also knew that, by striking the rock, the superstitious people would endow the rod of Moses with that miraculous power which belonged to Him alone, and so sanctify the earthly instrument instead of God. But, though the sin was greater than it reads, we know alike, by the *attributes* as well as the word of God, that it was not of such a nature as to demand the punishment of annihilation. If death be the end of being, Moses, for one sin, was to share the fate of his most sinful brethren. He who had sinned once, was to die before he had entered the promised land, even as the most rebellious and stiff-necked, who were ever turning back to apostasy and sin. Abraham, Jacob, David, Elijah, all had sinned; yet neither received death as chastisement. David triumphed over innumerable obstacles, and received the reward of his righteousness in some measure, even in this life. Elijah was translated to heaven without even the pang of death; yet neither of these characters can be compared with Moses. And can we believe for a single moment, then, that his death was either annihilation to himself, or believed to be such by his followers? The justice and the mercy, ay, and the truth inseparable from the Eternal, forbid the very thought. Who could have believed the words of Moses, that life was the reward of the righteous, death the punishment of evil, if they had not possessed not only the *instinct*, but the *revelation* of immortality to explain the death of their righteous leader, which, without such revelation, must have so contradicted his parting precepts as undoubtedly to call for heresy and unbelief?

As an *example* to his own age, as an emphatic lesson to those to come, his momentary unbelief was chastised, to prove, that not even the most righteous can avert the penalty of sin, which *must* bring sorrow. Had the Eternal passed over the fault of Moses, there would have been but too many to accuse Him of partiality and injustice: publicly committed, it was publicly to teach us that, when the visible interference of the Eternal is withdrawn, unless we have FAITH which no temptation can shake, our very efforts after righteousness are incomplete, and we must bear its penalty, in some degree of suffering. But if to Moses death but closed his eyes on the promised land, to open them on the ineffable blessedness of heaven, some enthusiasts may demand, What was his punishment? While on earth, as I have often told you, we must in some degree be of earth. Whatever degree of spirituality we may attain, there never yet was any mortal, who could put on immortality with such rejoicing security, as to have neither regret for parting from life, nor awe at the approach of death. Moses was, indeed, inspired above every other man, before or after him; but he was peculiarly and essentially *human*, notwithstanding. To his mortal nature, the thought of that promised land of rest and prosperity, in exchange for the toil, and pain, and suffering of his weary pilgrimage and thankless government, *must* have been fraught with human joy; and the sentence of death before he entered it, must have been endowed with just sufficient measure of mortal pain and disappointment, as would chastise and atone for his momentary unbelief. More, God's mercy neither needed nor demanded. The home He had prepared for His faithful servant in heaven, He knew far surpassed in glory and joy even the promised land on earth; and thither he was translated with but one momentary pang; for neither the infirmities nor diseases of mortality had crept upon him; "His eye was not dim, nor his natural force abated."

To my heart and mind, then, the death of Moses *before* entering the promised land, is the strongest confirmation not only of our immortality, but of its previous revelation and acceptance as an incentive to virtue, which the Bible gives; and had we that incident alone, it would prove, that by Moses and in him the doctrine was preached and believed. The Pentateuch, then, instead of containing neither allusion to, nor revelation of our immortality, contains both its precept and its illustration. The death of Abel, the translation of Enoch, the human trials and cares of all the patriarchs, had already taught that this life was not all, nor the removal from it an evil, and prepared men for the reception of a law which was to purify them for heaven, and reveal a life and death beyond this world. The death of Moses was the practical illustration, not only of the life and death he taught, but in itself a revelation of immortality based on the immutable and changeless attributes of God.

LETTER XXIII.

FROM THE SAME TO THE SAME.

Subject continued—Importance of the conviction that Immortality was inseparable from the gift of the Law—Constant reference to it in our prayers—Allusions to it in the psalms and prophets—Impossible to quote all the passages relating to it—Term *soul*, when used, always signifies an existence distinct from the body—The existence and attributes of the Eternal must be granted, or impossible to advance a step—Distinction between the human and the brute creation—Immortality proved the belief of the Hebrews by the *life* as well as words of David—His feelings and exclamations on the death of his infant—His resignation thus contrasted with his agony at the death of Absalom, both proving the same truth—Choice "of death by the hand of God" another witness, and received as such by the people—David's peculiarly human and loving character.

ONCE convinced that immortality was known to the descendants of Seth, dearest Annie, and, like the necessity and practice of prayer, the very essence of the Mosaic Law, though the verses which allude to it *may* appear capable of a temporal as well as spiritual meaning, one great point is gained. In fact, unless we acknowledge and perceive, that it really is the foundation of the

Mosaic system, the allusions to it in the after-parts of the Bible must be incomprehensible. David and the other Psalmists, Solomon and the Prophets, were all Israelites, living under the Law, teaching its precepts, and purifying its ordinances by vivifying their formal observance by the worship of the mind and heart. No new revelation had been vouchsafed to them; and how then could they have so known and written of immortality, if it had not formed the very essence of their creed? Even those who deny to Moses and the Pentateuch the revelation of this glorious truth, allow that it is repeatedly alluded to in the Psalms and Prophets; but the one assertion seems completely to contradict the other. Who could have taught the writers of the Psalms and Prophecies this sublime fact? Neither Jesus nor his apostles; for their advent was not till centuries afterwards. How is it, that immortality is th very life-spring and foundation of *all* the Jewish theological writers? that we cannot glance over our morning, evening, Sabbath or festival books of prayers, without seeing and feeling such reference to our future life, that we can no more separate its truth from our minds, than we can the fact of our *present* being? And these prayers are but compilations from David, the Prophets, and our ancient fathers, with some portions of more modern date. But all have the same reference—all the same immortal groundwork. It is but a weak argument to declare that David and the Prophets were inspired to preach it, that it was no part of their Law. Their writings were for the mass; and how could they have been understood, had the doctrine never been known and received before? It was not as if they taught it in directly explanatory words, as the teachers of the New Testament brought it to the minds of the unenlightened heathen. They merely allude to it as a spiritual incentive *already known*, but, from the iniquity of the people and neglect of their law, disregarded and uncared for. We have seen the infinite mercy which adapted the rewards for obedience, at the time of the delivery of the Law, to the comprehension and inclinations of the benighted multitudes. The same infinite mercy inspired the Prophets to adapt their promises and threatenings, not only for their own time, but for the dark future, when the *visible* manifestations of God's providence would be at an end, and the righteous amongst His children be liable to be temporally overwhelmed in the torrent of national iniquity sweeping down upon them, save for the hope of an unchanging belief in that life hereafter, to which the prophets so emphatically and continually referred. It was for this reason, that the prophets allude to immortality more clearly, and more constantly than the Law; but their allusions would have been of none effect, had not the truth itself been already known and generally believed.

To quote, or notice, all the verses in the Psalms and Prophets which allude to our immortality, would be useless in a letter, dearest Annie; though I should wish you, as a pleasant exercise, to search through these books, for all the allusions to a future state, transcribe them, and at your leisure give me your thoughts upon them. There is no better method of becoming intimately acquainted with the spirit of the Bible. The very searching for, and transcribing some parts, open the understanding almost unconsciously to others, and light seems to pour upon the mind, we can scarcely trace the whence or how, save that one verse often appears·to bear upon and illumine another which, merely *read*, we should pass carelessly by.

I have already told you my belief, that whenever the term " soul" is used, as in the verses—" The soul that eateth blood, even that soul shall be cut off from his people"—" The *soul* that sinneth, it shall die"—" When the wicked man turneth from his wickedness, and doth that which is lawful and right, he shall save his SOUL alive,"—and in many others, it alludes to the soul, or life, distinct from the body; and I am borne out in my belief, by the fact, that righteousness, however perfect, penitence, however sincere, never, in any age and under any government, averted death; or that wickedness (save in the signal manifestations of God's providence in the wilderness) was ever so cut off as to mark the distinction between him that committed it and the righteous; for, if this life were all, it was imperatively necessary that such should be the case, to prove the truth or falsehood of the Eternal's word. With regard to immortality the same argument may be used, as I brought forward when endeavouring to prove the truth of Revelation, and of the Bible as that revealed word—that it is utterly impossible to advance one step in the consideration of any subject, without *granting* some *presupposed* law or fact. There is not a single science which can build up its so-called *proven* theories, without granting some law or axiom which it **cannot** prove. Astronomers, chemists, all natural philosophers, declare such and such things are, and are positive as to the fact. On what foundation? Their preconceived ideas and granted axioms of the "Laws of Nature." And what are these Laws of Nature? Who can *prove* that they are what the finite wisdom of man believes them to be? And yet, though they cannot be *proved*, they must be *granted*, or all science is absolutely at an end. Exactly in the same manner must the enquirer into the Bible believe or grant there is a God, and that He is, as He proclaimed Himself, "merciful and gracious, long-suffering, and abundant in goodness and truth, showing mercy unto thousands, and forgiving iniquity, transgression, and sin," or he is stopped at the first outset, and plunged into darkness and despair. Try as he may, he cannot believe that he is of the same nature as the brutes, and he must *grant* that the distinction between him and them is, simply, that he has a soul and they have not. But if the gift of this soul does not in the least distinguish between his death and theirs—that like them he is destined for annihilation—there is no love or mercy in its bestowal, no necessity for a law to guide it, no happiness in the affections, no satisfaction in mental cultivation. Instead of being endowed and blessed above the brute creation, we must sink lower, and would seem rather to be objects of wrath than of love; for we have intense *capabilities of suffering*, without any assurance or realisation of joy. If man grant, then, which, unless he be an idiot, he must, that there is a God, and a gracious God; and that he is possessed of a soul, marking him as a being of a twofold nature: he must believe that he is destined for something higher, and better, and nobler than the cattle of the field. The word of Revelation which faith, based on reason or inquiry, assures him *is* from God, tells him of reward and punishment, joy and life for the righteous, death and misery for the wicked; but that same word and the history of life through all ages seem to contradict these promises. Death is the fate of all; there is no distinction in the earthly fates of the righteous and the wicked, save that only too often prosperity marks the latter, and suffering the former; and therefore he knows that, *if he believes in God*, and in *the gift of his own soul*, he MUST BELIEVE

IN A HEREAFTER, when that Divine word shall be fulfilled. His immortal soul receives this belief with its
very first awakening into consciousness. It can no more
be argued out of it, than astronomers and chemists can
be argued out of their belief in the laws of nature.
Neither one nor the other can be proved, yet both are
believed; and from the one spring the *discoveries* of
science, from the other, the *revelation* of immortality.

No man believing in God, and in the existence of his
own twofold nature, can read the Scriptures without
conviction that, wherever the life and death of the *soul*
is mentioned, it signifies the judgment of eternity; and
in innumerable verses he must trace the confirmation
of his immortality. Not only the written Psalms, but
incidents in the life of David, prove how firmly he believed in this consoling creed, and how it *must* have
formed part of the religion in which he was reared.

We have already noticed David's sin, and the fearful
effects that followed in the dissensions of his house; but
as these events were many years fulfilling, and did not
so immediately follow the sin as to appear a judgment
for it, except to the heart of David himself, God ordained the death of the infant, the innocent offspring of
parental guilt, to immediately manifest His displeasure,
by the infliction of bereavement on the offenders. Now,
if dea h were annihilation, it is against every attribute
of our gracious God, to imagine He would have created
a babe in His image, and breathed into it the breath of
life, to destroy it utterly for the sin of another. We
know by the offering of Moses of his own soul and its
rejection, that no man could pay the penalty of another's
sin: every one must bear his own. And, therefore, the
God of infinite justice would have chosen some other
method of chastising David and Bathsheba, rather than

bereavement, if that bereavement to them condemned the innocent to suffering or annihilation. But the Israelites knew though the *guilty* suffered, the innocent was taken to that heaven where he would dwell for ever, a stainless cherub, by his Father's throne. Had the babe lived, he would have individually suffered the effects of his parent's sin; for against the offspring of such guilt as that of David and Bathsheba, the Mosaic laws were justly severe; and, therefore, in removing him in his infant innocence to a better world, God's attribute of mercy was confirmed, even as His attribute of justice in the bereavement inflicted on David and his wife.

That so David himself regarded this event in his life, both his words and conduct prove. "While his child yet lived, he fasted and prayed, and wept before the Lord, that the young life might be spared. And the elders went in, and tried to raise and comfort him; but he would not be comforted; and when the child died, his servants feared to tell him, for they said, Behold, while the child was yet alive, we spoke to him, and he would not hearken unto our voice: how will he then vex himself, if we tell him the child is dead!" But they were deceived; for when he heard the sad intelligence, he arose from the earth, washed and anointed himself, and came into the house of the Lord, and worshipped, and ate bread; and in answer to the questions of his astonished servants made that reply, which is to me as consoling and convincing of his and every Jew's belief in immortality, as if immediately revealed. "While the child yet lived," he said, "I fasted and prayed; for who can tell whether God will be gracious to me that the child may live? But now he is dead, wherefore should I fast? Can I bring him back again? *I shall go to him,*

27*

but he will not return unto me;" and David comforted Bathsheba his wife.

Now if David knew nothing of the world beyond the grave, how could the idea of rejoining his child bring such consolation, as enabled him to conquer his own grief, and comfort his wife? If annihilation were to be the portion of his babe and of himself, surely, instead of anointing himself and appearing in the house of God, submissive, ay, and sadly rejoicing, he would have wept and mourned yet more. He was no stoic to find comfort in his child's death, if he could not have believed he was happier than he could ever have been on earth. He was peculiarly and painfully susceptible to the joys and pains of the affections; and to him, therefore, yet more than to other men, would the death of a child have been unmitigated anguish, if he had not had a secure hope of an immortal reunion. We know the bitter agony he endured on the death of his darling Absalom. Then, indeed, he wept and refused to be comforted, not that he had less faith in immortality than at the death of his infant, but that, when he thought on the fearful crimes of his favourite son, that very belief must have added incalculably to the misery of bereavement. His infant's soul was secure; but Absalom's—if the sinful might not enter heaven, how could he be comforted for him?

The second incident in David's life may not perhaps appear to bear so much upon our immediate subject as the previous one, though to my heart, judging it by the *attributes* of our God, it is so powerfully convincing, that if I disbelieved in immortality as revealed to, and the heritage of, my people, I must equally disbelieve in God. When David sinned against the Lord by numbering the people, a choice of chastisements was sent him through the prophet Gad—seven years' famine, three months flight before his enemies, or three days of pestilence in his land. And David said, "Behold, I am in a great strait: *Let us fall now into the hands of the Lord, for His mercies are great;* and let me not fall into the hands of man. So the Lord sent a pestilence upon Israel, from the morning even unto the time appointed; and there died of the people, from Dan even to Beersheba, seventy thousand men."

Now if this life were all, where would be the mercy and the justice of the Eternal in thus cutting off seventy thousand men, for what at first reading appears one man's sin?

But the doubt that may enter our mind as to why David was not individually chastised, instead of so many of his subjects, is removed by a consideration of the first verse of the chapter, in which, by the words, "And again the Lord's anger was kindled against Israel." We know that it was an era of renewed national iniquity, like so many which had gone before it, demanding one of those *public* manifestations of the Eternal's displeasure, which could not "discern between the righteous and the wicked" while below, but *after death* evinced those "great mercies" in which the Hebrew king so trusted. David had not sinned alone, as in the case of Bathsheba, or he, as then, alone would have been chastised; but he sinned in connection and in company with the people, and so received punishment in their deaths, and, very probably, the deaths of many of his immediate household.* Many might declare that the

---

* He had sinned individually in the act of numbering the people; but it was because of the *national iniquity* that God permitted his evil inclination such ascendency as to resist the pleadings of Joäb. David had power within himself to have conquered that impulse of evil, and refrained from the trespass; but, as he chose the evil, God punished him

death of his people was of little consequence to him, so
that he remained unscathed; but this is the opinion of
natures far too selfish to comprehend the universal love
which characterised David.   His strong belief that a
hereafter of bliss was laid up with God for the righteous and the meek who might fall in the chosen pestilence, *could alone* have dictated the words, "Let *us fall*
into the hands of the Lord, for His *mercies are great;*"
but if death were the entire end of existence, what mercy
could be shown in the doom he had chosen?   But to the
believer in immortality, the three days' pestilence *was*
the least terrible of either alternative; for it exchanged
earth for heaven for the righteous with the least and
briefest mortal pang, and, checking the sinful in his
iniquitous career, removed his evil example from his
fellows, and, perchance, permitted him to labour and
obey in some other sphere, there to earn his immortality; for even to the wicked there seems, to my mind,
no such doom as utter annihilation.

This, of course, is but a speculation, dearest Annie,
with which, at the conclusion of our scriptural review of
the subject, I may indulge myself and you; but it will
not do to bring forward that which must be purely imaginary with the holy truths revealed in the Bible.   It is
enough for us to know and feel that in every signal chastisement inflicted on Israel, both in the wilderness* and
in Palestine, immortality is clearly revealed, or a miracle
would have divided the righteous from the wicked upon
earth.   If we believe in a God, and in His revealed attributes, this must be: we must believe in one or the

---

by a national chastisement, which the people's iniquity had already
prepared against themselves.

* Alluding to the thousands who perished for the sin of the golden
calf, for Korah's rebellion, and for the various murmurings of the people.

other; and, as we *know*, and experience but too soon
proves and confirms, that while man has free will, and
is a social being, there can be no distinction made between the righteous and the sinner in this life, we *must*
believe that there is a life hereafter, when this distinction will be made, or deny that God is just and good,
and that His word is true. To display His power to
individuals, or to prove that no national iniquity ever
passed without some signal chastisement which would
unanswerably prove His power and judgment, and by
its awful and sweeping nature withhold from the committal of similar iniquity, those judgments which the
Bible records were absolutely necessary in the infancy
of revelation. To have divided off the individually
righteous, and only stricken the sinful, could not have
been, without interfering with the Divine economy, and,
moreover, removing all *spiritual* incentive from man.
Without belief in immortality, the consideration of
those tremendous judgments, must plunge the soul in
utter darkness; for they deny the attributes and the
word of God; but *with* such belief that His attributes
and word are immutable and everlasting, they console
and strengthen, for they are in themselves the confirmation of a higher and purer hereafter.

Nothing but a firm belief in his own and his people's
immortality, could have dictated David's exclamation,
" For the Lord's mercies are great;" for such a three
days' virulent pestilence, during which seventy thousand were cut off from the earth, there could be no
evidence of mercy, save to the heart of a believer. The
triumph of the spiritual part of David's nature occasioned his choice; for *before* the *anguish* of the trial
came, he only looked on death as for the righteous an
entrance into life. But when the destroying angel's

sword was unsheathed, and he beheld his subjects falling like leaves around him, and nought but the suffering of bereavement to the survivors, his *human* nature triumphed over the spiritual; and we find him clothed in sackcloth and falling on his face, in agony imploring, "Is it not I that commanded the people to be numbered? Even I it is that have sinned and done evil indeed; but as for these sheep, what have they done? Let thy hand, I pray thee, O Lord my God, be *on me* and *my* father's house, but not on thy people that they should be plagued!"

With these words before him, who can say that these three days of pestilence were not chastisement and suffering to David individually? Yet they do not contradict that belief in the "great mercies of the Lord," which his previous choice had professed. They do but prove the peculiarly human and loving character of the Hebrew king, unable to sustain his people's anguish; and who shall say that, in the moment of trial, the faith in God's mercy shall not so fail us, as to bid us also call out, in our agony, "O Lord, hold thy hand," and yet more in the sufferings of our beloved ones than our own?

LETTER XXIV.

FROM THE SAME TO THE SAME.

Subject continued—Extracts from the Psalms of David, and remarks
thereon ; evincing David's firm faith in a world beyond the grave,
the felicity laid up for the righteous, and the punishing of the wicked
—Explanation of the term "land of the living"—Objection that the
Psalms are the mere reflection of individual minds, no proof of a revelation, refuted—Literature of the Jews compared with that of contemporary nations—Open to the people; understood by them Im-
mrotality therefore generally beleived in—Sons of Korah and Assaph
—Consideration of the forty-ninth Psalm and of the seventy-third—
—Powerful evidences of the general Jewish belief in immortality.

In perusing the Psalms of David, we can scarcely fail
to be struck with their agreement, not only in sense,
but in imagery, both with the books of Moses and those
of the Prophets : "Let them be *blotted* out of the book of
the living," David writes of the enemies of the Lord ;
"let them not be written with the righteous,"—words how
exactly similar to those of Moses and Malachi, so often
quoted !   The distinction between the righteous and the
wicked, reiterated again and again, is incomprehensible
and false, if we disbelieve in its reference to another
life, inexpressibly and encouragingly consoling, if we feel
that it does.   "Know that the Lord hath set apart him
that is godly for Himself:" can we trace on earth those
whom the Lord hath set apart ?   Is it not but too often
through human suffering only that our imperfect nature
attains to that righteousness which is accepted by our God?
and were this life all, where then would be its promised

joy? "The wicked shall be turned into the grave, and all the nations who forget God; but the needy shall *not always* be forgotten, the expectation of the poor shall not perish for ever,"—words how clearly illustrative, that though on earth the needy may *seem* forgotten, and the expectations of the poor to have no foundation: yet earth is not *always*, nor this life for ever. "I have set the Lord always before me; He is at my right hand, I shall not be moved: *therefore* my heart is glad, and my glory [or soul] rejoiceth; *my flesh also shall rest in hope; for Thou wilt not leave my soul in* the grave, nor suffer Thy holy one* to see corruption. Thou wilt shew me the path of life: in Thy presence is the fulness of joy, and at Thy right hand are everlasting pleasures!"

Had we only these verses, dearest· Annie, we should need no more to prove David's strong and ever-present belief in immortality. They cannot possibly be understood in any other light. His heart is glad, and his soul rejoices, he says, from the consoling effect of placing God always before him in the occurrences of daily life. His flesh or body also shall rest in hope (that is, feel no fear of death); for God would not leave his soul in the grave, nor permit that essence which, in its divinity and pure undying nature, is designated in the Eastern idiom as the holy one, to see corruption. "Thou wilt show me the path of that life which leads to Thy presence, where there is indeed fulness of joy, and at Thy right hand are everlasting pleasures." The preceding allusions to the death of the body and incorruptible nature of the soul, *must* convince us, that it is no path of earth to which he refers, but to that life which is in the presence of God for everlasting.

---

* Image of God, or soul.

"Deliver my soul from the wicked which is thy sword,"
he says, in Psalm xvii. : "from men that are thy hand,
O Lord [meaning instruments in God's hand for the trial
and probation of the righteous], from men *of the world
who have their portion in this life*, whom thou fillest
with treasure, who are full of children, and leave their
substance to their babes. But for me, I will behold thy
face, in [or by] righteousness: I shall be satisfied when
I awake with thy likeness."

The Psalm here alludes to those men whose worldly
prosperity, notwithstanding their sinfulness, has excited
a doubt as to the justice of the ways of the Lord, and
which we find explained in the ninety-second Psalm.
"How great are thy works, O Lord, and thy *thoughts are
very deep*. A brutish man [one who has never sought to
cultivate the spiritual and undying part of his nature,
but given full indulgence to the animal] knoweth them
not, neither doth a fool understand this, that when the
wicked spring up as the grass, and all the workers of
iniquity do flourish, *it is* that they may be destroyed for
ever." Their portion, then, however enviable in appearance, is only for this life; and from them David entreats
that his soul may be delivered, lest it should be led to
follow in their paths: for himself he asks but to behold
God's face (a figurative term denoting God's presence)
through his own efforts after righteousness, meaning the
same as the words we have already quoted—"I have set
the Lord always before me. . . . . I shall be satisfied *when
I awake* with thy likeness." Now as there is no reference to sleep, these words evidently signify, "when I
awake from this life, the likeness or presence of my God
will be all-sufficient for me." He asked not the treasures even of the children of the wicked, for their portion was but for *this life* (the very term marks a firm

belief in another). He asked only to obtain such right-eousness as would enable him to behold God before him, even upon earth, and when he awoke to everlasting life to trace and behold that glorious "likeness" in which his soul and the soul of every man were made.

In the twenty-first Psalm, which is a burst of thanks-giving for victory and spiritual confidence in future suc-cess, David exclaims, of himself, "The king shall joy in thy strength, O Lord; and in *thy* salvation how greatly shall he rejoice! .... He asked LIFE of thee, and thou gavest it him, even *length of days* for EVER and EVER. *His* glory is great in *Thy* salvation: honour and majesty hast *Thou* laid upon him. For Thou hast made him most blessed for EVER: Thou hast made him exceeding glad with Thy countenance. For the king trusteth in the Lord, and through the mercy of the Most High he shall not be moved." A thanksgiving how unlike that of a mere human conqueror, tracing strength, glory, honour, majesty, and salvation, all from God alone; and how strikingly illustrative of that life which was ever present to the heart of David! He asked life, and we know, by its gift in length of days for *ever and ever*, it was not the life of earth, but of eternity.

In the twenty-seventh Psalm, after an emphatic de-scription of the differing sentiments and pursuits and destinies of the righteous and the wicked, we read, "De-part from evil, and do good, and dwell [or *live*] for ever-more. For the Lord loveth judgment and forsaketh not his saints. *They are preserved for ever;* but the seed of the wicked shall be cut off. .... I have seen the wicked in great power and spreading himself like a green bay-tree. Yet he passed away, and lo he was not: yea I sought him, but he could not be found. Mark the per-fect, and behold the upright; for the *end* of that man

is *peace*. But the transgressors shall be destroyed together, the *end* of the wicked shall be cut off. But the
salvation of the righteous is of the Lord."

Can one word of these emphatic verses apply to earth
and time? If suffering *must* be the portion of the righteous, as we know it is, what joy or comfort could there
be in the thought that he was to be preserved on earth
for ever? Besides, the promise that he should be preserved for ever in one verse, and the command,—"Mark
the peaceful *end* of the upright," in another—is a contradiction impossible to be reconciled, if only supposed
to refer to *this* life. But we know that preserved for
ever, applies to the life beyond; and that the end of the
upright is full of peace, because he knows death to him
is but his birth into a better world, while to the wicked
even his end is cut off, a powerful expression for the doom
beyond the mere physical cessation of existence.

" For thou hast delivered *my soul from death*," David
says, in the fifty-sixth Psalm; "wilt not thou save my
feet from falling, that I may walk before God in the *land
of the living?*" And in the hundred and sixteenth
Psalm we find the same expressions, only so much more
enlarged upon, that we cannot doubt to what "land of
the living" they refer. "The sorrows of death com-
passed me," he says, after a burst of thanksgiving to the
Lord for having heard the voice of his supplication, "and
the pains of the grave got hold of me, I found trouble
and sorrow. Then called I on the name of the Lord;
O Lord, I beseech thee, deliver my soul. Gracious is
the Lord, and righteous: yea, our God is merciful. The
Lord preserveth the simple: I was brought low, and He
helped me. Return unto thy rest, O my soul, for the
Lord hath dealt bountifully with thee; for Thou hast
delivered my soul from [the fear of] death, my eyes

from tears, and my feet from falling. I will walk before the Lord in the land of the living."

Now, "the sorrows of death, pains of the grave," and troubles here alluded to, are evidently *mental*, and have to do, not with sickness and physical infirmity, but that weakness of humanity to which even the most pious are occasionally liable, when death and the grave are fraught ·with the gloom of leaving earth, instead of with the joy of entering heaven. David was human, liable to all the despondency and suffering of his fellows, even in those very things from which, from his constant efforts to know, love, and serve God, he might have been supposed exempt. The hundred and sixteenth Psalm describes his combat with his *inward* self, at the anticipation of death and the grave, the lot of all; the fifty-sixth, whence the same words are quoted, alludes to his outward vexations and annoyances, from the enmity of man, which led him to God for relief from them, even as in the hundred and sixteenth he beseeches relief from himself. In the fifty-sixth—"I will not be afraid what man can do unto me," he says, "for Thy vows are with me, O God; I will render praises unto Thee, for *Thou hast delivered my soul from death.* Wilt Thou not save my feet from falling, that I may walk before God in the land of the living?"

The enmity and dangers from man, painful and annoying as they were, still were endurable, for they were but of earth, and God's vow or promise was "to deliver his soul from death." There could be no comfort in the supposition that this deliverance was merely a longer life on earth, exposed to all the same annoyances from man, and to end at last in annihilation. This promise prompted the urgent prayer, "Save my feet from falling into the paths of sin"—tempted so to fall, from those petty stings from man which chafe the spirit into irrita-

tion and rebellion, far more than those in reality heavier
trials which can be traced to, and so received submis-
sively from, God.   He prayed to be saved from falling,
that he might indeed walk before God in the "land of
the living."   If earth were the land of the living alluded
to, even if his feet fell, he would still walk there till his
appointed time; and the sinner would have an equal, if not
greater, share of earthly joys.   But the land of the living
which he prayed to enter, was that heaven, the dwelling
of the righteous, where "the Lord dwelleth with him
that is of a contrite and humble spirit, to revive the
spirit of the humble, and to revive the heart of the contrite ones."

In the fifty-sixth, this conviction gives him comfort in
the midst of trials from man.   In the hundred and sixteenth, it has the same effect in a worse trial of despondency and dread.   Trouble, and pain, and sorrow almost
overwhelmed him; but his faith did not fail him, and he
called on God, and God answered him with a renewal of
that conviction of his immortality which had comforted
him before.   It is very mistaken to imagine that a mere
temporary reprieve from the mortal sickness of death
could have called forth the heartfelt thanksgiving and
spiritual trust in the Lord, with which the whole psalm
teems.   If it were, we should find some reference to
relief from *physical* pain and sickness.   The thanksgiving is for a *spiritual* benefit, even as the complaint
is for spiritual desertion.   The prayer and thanksgiving
of Hezekiah for increase of mortal life are so differently
rendered, that it is impossible to believe that David
alludes to the same thing.   "Return unto thy rest, O my
soul," he says, "for the Lord hath dealt bountifully with
thee.   He hath delivered thee from death, my eyes from
tears, and my feet from falling: I will walk before th

Lord in the land of the living." Here is no supplication that he *may* do so, but a firm conviction that he will. His soul might again return to its rest; for the faith in its deathless nature, which no physical pain, no mental depression could remove, had, through God's grace, returned.

"I will pay my vows unto the Lord, now, in the presence of all His people," he says, in the fourteenth and eighteenth verses of the same psalm—words as clearly alluding to *this life*, and a public thanksgiving for the mercy previously received, as the ninth verse refers to heaven as strongly as if it had been written, "I will walk before God in the land of *souls.*" But clearer proof than all the rest we find in the fifteenth verse,— "Precious in the sight of the Lord is the death of His saints." How could this be, if death cut the righteous off for ever, removed from earth the sole witnesses of God, and gave to the wicked unlimited dominion, which could not be, if the same fate attended all? Nothing could give sufficient strength and endurance to dawning righteousness, if not for the immortal hope of the righteous who had gone before. How could the deaths of the only ones who by loving service obtained the appellation of His saints, be precious in the sight of the Creator, if such deaths were the annihilation of soul and body, utterly separating them from Him as from their fellows? The verse is, in its brief but emphatic sentence, a complete explanation of the real meaning of David's spiritual pain, and its triumphant consolation, and in itself a direct revelation of immortality. God, in His infinite mercy, rejoiced in the death of His saints; because that earthly death relieved them from earthly sufferings, and permitted the soul's reunion with its kindred spirits in the land of souls, and in His presence for everlasting.

Very many more of David's Psalms might be quoted, as bearing equally on this important subject, dearest Annie; but I trust you are now sufficiently interested, to seek for them yourself. I will only quote two verses from my favourite hundred and third Psalm, where, after describing man as one "whose days are like grass, and as a flower of the field, so he flourisheth; for the wind passeth over it, and it is gone, and the place thereof shall know it no more," he continues, "but the mercy of the Lord is from everlasting to everlasting upon them that fear Him, and His righteousness unto children's children, to such as keep His covenant, and to those that remember His commandments to do them. The Lord hath prepared His throne in the heavens, and His kingdom ruleth over all." Now, if we deny David's belief in immortality, there is a complete contradiction in these verses. If man be *only* as a flower of the field, over whom the wind passeth and findeth him not, how can the Eternal fulfil His word, and show towards him everlasting mercy? The longest measure of human life is not a hundred years; and even if mercy were shown him every day of those hundred years, it could not be considered as fulfilling the promise from *everlasting* to *everlasting*. It is also to "those that *fear* the Lord, keep His covenant, and remember His commandments to *do* them," that everlasting mercy is promised, in contradistinction to the wicked, whose lot is only in this life. In this world, as we have so often reiterated, there is no distinction between the righteous and the sinful, nor ever was, nor ever can be; and therefore we *know* the mercy promised must allude to that other state of existence which is the portion of the righteous, or the words are utterly void of meaning. It appears to me, also, that the nineteenth verse is not so wholly unconnected with the preceding eighteenth as the full stop might lead us to suppose; but that it is for the seekers after righteousness, made perfect in His mercy, that the "Lord hath prepared His throne in the heavens," and thus fulfils His promise of "showing mercy from everlasting to everlasting to those that fear Him."

The only remaining Psalms to which I would call your attention are the forty-ninth and seventy-third, the one said to be written for the sons of Korah, and the other by or for Assaph, and so bearing additional witness as to the fact of immortality having been known to and taught by the Hebrews, ages before the advent of Christianity. The remark has, I believe, been made, that these Psalms, Proverbs, etc., are but the opinions of erring mortals like ourselves, and will not *prove* more than our own ideas may suggest to ourselves. But they *do* prove more. Compare the opinions of the Hebrews on all spiritual matters with the opinions on the same subjects of all the contemporary nations, and then let the sceptic reply how and why they should have so advanced in such purely spiritual feelings and notions as all the Psalms and Prophets reveal? Why do we not find the same revelations of heaven and immortality, the same aspirings of the panting soul after its God, the same earnest longings after righteousness, and firm belief in the mercy that would distinguish between the upright and the ungodly, in other nations as well as the Israelites? How does it happen, that we have no record left of the spiritual as we have of the temporal history of the Egyptian, Babylonian, Grecian, and Roman Empires, whose dominions were so vastly more extensive, whose power was of so much greater magnitude, and whose advance in the temporal arts and sciences equalled, if it did not surpass, the little land of Palestine? How is it that, in all the many ages which have elapsed since Moses, and David, and the Prophets, we have *never* found a writer or writers to give us what they have? If the writers of the Bible were mere men, in all respects (I will not say as we are, for that would be an entirely unfair criterion) such as the nations existing at the same era: how is it that, as time advanced and men's minds matured more and more, there has never been another book compiled to take their place? And how is it that the Bible alone, of all the writings of the same age, will still bear upon the wants and aspirations, the moral and mental feelings of all humanity? Mortal indeed they were, liable to all the frailties and sins, not only of their mingled nature but of their darkened age; but their spirit had been enlightened by the revelation of God Himself, to mark His chosen, and through them to fulfil His promise to Abraham, that "in his seed all the nations of the earth should be blessed."

The sons of Korah and Assaph were musicians and Levites, forming the choirs employed in the Temple-service. Assaph himself, and no doubt Korah, were living in David's time, and some Psalms are supposed to be the joint production of the minstrel king and his chief musician Assaph,—that is, the words were by the one, and the music by the other. Those Psalms, headed "For the sons of Korah, or for Assaph," are, however, considered by some to be of much later date, to have been composed and sung by the *descendants* of those Psalmists whose name they bear,—a supposition founded on the seeming reference of their subjects to events in the history of their people, posterior to the existence of Assaph and Korah individually. Whatever be their date, the forty-ninth and seventy-third bear so strongly on the belief in immortality, that they prove beyond all question, that it was the essence of the Jewish creed, and that to be so, it must naturally have been revealed; or why should the Jews have known it more than contemporary nations? *

The forty-ninth Psalm is supposed to have been written during the Babylonian captivity, more than five hundred years before the advent of the Christian era. Its translation in the English Bibles is, however, very obscure. The best rendering is that in page 109 of the Daily Prayer-Book of the British Jews; but that it refers to, or rather is, an emphatic description of the differing fates of the righteous and the sinful in the hour of death, is evident, even in its most confused translation. The very fact of its being chosen by the ancient compilers of our prayers, as the hymn for mourners after bereavement, proves this very convincingly. "I will incline my ear to a parable," the Psalmist says, after calling on all the people to attend, "and disclose my *dark saying* on the harp. Wherefore should I fear in the days of evil, when the iniquity of my oppressors encompass me? *Of those who trust in their wealth, and boast themselves in the immensity of their riches, none can by any means redeem his brother, or give to God a ransom for him* (for the redemption of their souls is precious, and it ceaseth for ever), *that he should still live for ever and not see the grave.* For he seeth the wise man die, and the fool and the brutes to perish to-

* It may be urged that Socrates, Longinus, and other heathen philosophers, believed and preached immortality without revelation. They did; but it was not till the dispersion of the Jews had promulgated *their* doctrines in some measure over the lands of their captivity; and no one can compare the mere *speculative* theories founded on *reason* and *analogy* of the heathen, with the *confirmed belief* from divine revelation, which the allusions to this solemn subject and the spiritual aspirations of the Hebrews so clearly betray.

gether, and leave their wealth to others. Their inward
thought is, indeed, that their palaces shall continue for
ever, and their dwelling to all generations, so they call
their lands after their own names." Is not this an exact
description of the men of this world, seeking, toiling
after the riches and treasures of this life alone, laying
up precious things, as if they could carry them away with
them? or seeking the poor honour of building palaces
to their own fame, and calling their possessions after
their own names, that even, seeing that death comes to
all alike, and will not spare them, nor their brother, nor
their children, however large the ransom for their lives
which their riches may enable them to offer unto God,
they still pursue their worldly course? "But man's
honour [the mere worldly honour and earthly distinctions above alluded to] endureth not, he becometh like
the beasts that perish;" because it was the *animal* propensities, whose gratification he sought alone, to the
utter neglect of the spiritual, and, therefore, how was
the soul fitted to appear before God? "Such is their
way: fools to themselves, and yet their posterity ever
applauds them!" And are not the winners of mere
worldly triumphs and treasure now, as then, the objects of popular applause? "Like sheep they are laid
in the grave; death feeds on them; but the upright
shall have dominion over them in the morning [of the
resurrection], when their form shall moulder away in
the grave, their dwelling." " *But God will redeem my
soul*," he continues, changing his style from the descrip-
tive to individual apostrophising, which is so often the
case with our Hebrew writers—"But God will redeem
my soul from the power of the grave, when He shall
receive me, Selah. Be thou [here the Psalmist is addressing his own soul], be thou not dismayed then,

when a man [who is not righteous] is made rich, and the glory of his house is increased. For when he dieth, he shall carry nothing away, nor shall his glory follow him. For though *he* doth *here* delight his soul, *thou* shalt be called happy *hereafter*, whilst he shall follow the generations of his fathers, who never saw the light [of heaven]. Man who is in honour [that is, in worldly rank and earthly treasures], and understandeth not [the ways of God by seeking after righteousness], is like the beasts that perish."

Is not this Psalm the exact commentary of those verses of the ninety-second Psalm which I have already so often quoted, dearest Annie? It is in itself so clear an illustration of the argument, that when the wicked prosper, their prosperity is merely of this world, and that the promised reward and blessing of the righteous are laid up with God, as the portion of the undying soul, that it can require no farther elucidation. I shall be truly glad, if it be as clear to you as it is to me; for a Psalm appointed for an hour of bereavement ought to have no dark or hidden meaning, but clearly and forcibly give us confirmed comfort in the thought, that immortality is the very groundwork of our creed.

The seventy-third Psalm is, in Bagster's Bible, appropriated to Assaph, and said to bear date* about the time of the destruction of Sennacherib's army, seven hundred years before the Christian era. If the date and the author be both correct, Calmet is wrong, and Assaph could not have been contemporary with David. This, however, signifies little. All we wish to prove is, that

---

* All the assumptions concerning the age of the Psalmists are merely arbitrary, and not capable of proof. Since they were inspired, as we believe, their predictions of future events are easily accounted for.—L.

immortality was known to the Hebrew, ages before the
advent of that religion, which is said to have been the
first to proclaim it, not only to the gentiles but to the
Jews.   Like the forty-ninth, the seventy-third Psalm
first alludes to the prosperity and triumph of the wicked,
which had excited the envy of Assaph, notwithstanding
his internal belief, that " God is good to such of Israel
as are of a clean heart."   It is a true picture of the
inward doubts and struggles of a holy and righteous
man, who, despite his constant endeavours to love and
serve God, is himself overwhelmed with trial and care,
and perceives the wicked, who know not, and care not to
know God, flourishing and happy.   "Verily," he continues, in the momentary weakness of his *human* nature, "I have cleansed my heart in vain, and washed my
hands in innocence.   For all the day long have I been
plagued, and chastened every morning;" and so his feet
had almost gone, and his steps had wellnigh slipped.
And the thought of the prosperity of the wicked, and
suffering of the righteous, was *too* painful for him,
"until I went into the sanctuary of God, and then understood I their end.   Surely thou didst set them in
slippery places; thou castedst them down to destruction.
How are they brought into desolation, as in a moment!
they are utterly consumed with terrors.   As a dream
when one awaketh, so, O Lord, when thou awakest, wilt
thou despise their image.   Thus my heart was grieved,
and I was pricked in my reins [reproached in conscience].
So foolish was I, and ignorant: I was as a beast before
thee [even for permitting the doubt of thy justice to
enter my mind].   Nevertheless [in spite of my doubt
and sin], I am continually with thee: thou hast holden
me by my right hand.   *Thou shalt guide me with thy
counsel, and afterwards receive me to glory.* Whom have

I in heaven but Thee? and there is none upon earth that I desire beside Thee. My flesh and my heart may fail; but God is the strength of my heart, and *my portion for ever*. But those that are far from Thee shall perish; Thou hast destroyed all them that go astray from Thee; but it is good for me to draw near unto God: I have put my trust in the Lord God, that I may declare all His works."

Will not this psalm prove the strength and comfort which the Hebrews realised in the reflections on, and belief in, a future state, dearest Annie? Do we need more to convince us that it *must* have been revealed, and formed part of the inward religion of every Hebrew? It is folly to argue that it was only known to a chosen few, and that the Jews, as a people, remained in ignorance as to this important point till ages afterwards. Their very Law was a mass of contradiction without it, and those psalms which formed part of their temple service, or helps to their devotions in their captivity, were perfectly incomprehensible. The press, or the literature of a country, is always the only sure criterion of the ideas, not of a few, but of a nation. The only literature of the Jews was sacred, and confined to subjects of such a lofty and spiritual nature, that it bore an impress of advance and enlightenment wholly unlike the literature of contemporary kingdoms. That literature emanated from God's Law, and, therefore, all it breathed was taught in that holy Law, and was thus the possession of the whole Jewish nation. The iniquity and terrible darkness on all sides surrounding their little spot of holy ground might, nay must, have had its effect on but too many, in rendering them utterly regardless of their glorious heritage; but this will not do away with the impression which all their literature leaves, that immortality was known and taught even before the delivery of their Law, which without it is as incomprehensible and useless, as with it it is perfect and eternal.

LETTER XXV.

FROM THE SAME TO THE SAME.

Subject continued—Proverbs and Ecclesiastes bear equally powerful evidence of the received revelation—Character of Solomon; his outward and inward experiences compared with those of David—Extracts from Ecclesiastes, and comments thereon—Ecclesiastes, a reflection of the inner man, querulous soliloquy—How regarded by the infidel and the believerb—Provers, not individually tinged—A book of instruction to the people—Extracts and notices therefrom—Its constant references to life and death eternal, and perfect agreement with the other portions of the Bible—State of Judea during the monarchy—The people too debased and corrupted for any spiritual incentive—Illustrations of the received doctrines of immortality, and its practical revelation—Death of Jonathan's young son—Sentence on Josiah—Stoning of Naboth—Miraculous translation of Elijah—Probable effects of this miracle on the righteous, and the sinful—Its consolation now—The word of God to be our guide by illustration as well as precept—No precept without illustration—Historical books add to the evidence of the *Jewish* belief in immortality.

THE books of the Proverbs and Ecclesiastes bear the same witness to the Mosaic revelation of immortality as the psalms already quoted. Solomon was, indeed, inspired individually with unusual wisdom; but that wisdom did not reveal to him *new* things concerning the law already given, but only enabled him to understand yet more fully its spiritual as well as temporal meaning. The gift of understanding vouchsafed to him, was very different from the inspirations of the prophets. Solomon asked for wisdom to govern a mighty kingdom, and that was granted him; but the records he has left behind him for the benefit of his fellow-creatures in future ages, are but the transcript of a mind and heart in all respects like those of his fellows, save that his wisdom gave him greater facility of thought and adaptation. Even his understanding, a gift of God direct as it was, could not, like the prophets', penetrate through the hidden things or disclose the future. His writings are simply human experiences, having for their groundwork the religion of his forefathers. He was a Hebrew himself, and the faith he followed was that of the Law given through Moses. All he taught, then, must have been revealed in that Law. He tells us nothing but what his father had written before him. He does not *reveal*, but simply *confirm*—is but another witness to the fact, that the Jewish religion must have taught and reiterated immortality as the "path of life" promised to the righteous, or neither David nor Solomon, nor the other psalmists, could have alluded to it as they do.

I was once present at a very beautiful lecture on the book of Ecclesiastes; given by a pious Christian divine,[*] and was much struck by his emphatic declaration that, if sceptics would but turn to that book, they must find how false and utterly without foundation was this charge against the Jews of their having no belief in immortality; that, if we had but that one book, it would be sufficient to prove how well grounded was our hope in that divine revelation. And this was the opinion of a Christian, dearest Annie; and is it not, therefore, a disgrace upon ourselves, when, either in sentiment or conduct, we seem

---

[*] The late Rev. Robert Anderson, of Trinity Chapel, Brighton.

to deny that it is the essence of our creed, and thus give a triumph to the scoffer, which it requires both time and labour to remove?

The constant reference to the "spirit" in Ecclesiastes proves at once Solomon's firm belief in the mingled nature of man, though many may say, and with apparent justice, that it is more a querulous complaint of the vanity of this life, than a triumphant assurance of a better. But to account for this, we must take the character of the king into consideration. It was, unhappily, only in his very early youth, that his heart was so right with God as to inspire his prayer for wisdom and to call down from a gracious Father the gifts of prosperity, such as no king of Israel ever enjoyed before or after him. But these gifts did not prove the blessings which they were intended to be. As is unhappily too often the case, they estranged the heart from the purer pleasures of his youth, and made him believe that happiness was only to be found in a succession of exciting earthly pleasures. Sensuality, and all the enervating luxuries of exhaustless wealth, were his sole pursuits, weakening his mental enjoyments, till even the joys of wisdom appeared to be as vain and profitless as the mere passing pleasures of the world.

When old age and its calmer mood came upon him, and, wearied and dispirited, he looked back on the scenes which had so engrossed him, but which had left only a sting behind, was it a marvel that his writings should bear the impress of such thoughts? and that it was easier for him to believe life to be all vanity and vexation of spirit, than to realise that spiritual peace and joy which his father had experienced? Yet David's life was, with very few intervals, one of trial and suffering, the very name of which Solomon knew not. If we could see the two outward lives placed before us, without their *inward* experiences, there are few who would hesitate in declaring that Solomon's career must have been the happier; and yet what a contrary evidence do their respective writings leave,—David, full of spiritual hope, and faith, and love, seeing the light of heaven so clearly through the dark clouds of adversity and trial, that he could yet rejoice, and find pleasures and lovely things for which to bless God, even upon earth; and Solomon, whose career had been one of unalloyed prosperity, beholding but vanity and vexation *below*, and, compared with David's, but a faint gleam of that heaven which awaited him above! But still, that he *did* behold it all, through the doubt and gloom beclouding his whole being, when he looked back on his profitless career, is in itself a weighty proof of immortality being indeed the essence of his creed.

These remarks allude solely to Ecclesiastes. The book of Proverbs (which we shall consider by-and-by) is written in a different spirit, and more as a book of public instruction, than as a vehicle for individual thoughts. Both books, however, agree in distinctly teaching that righteousness leads to *life* and wickedness to death; that though "all go to one place; all are of the dust, and all turn to dust again;" and "who knoweth the spirit of man that goeth upward, and the breath of the beast that goeth downward to the earth?" yet that the Lord will "judge between the righteous and the wicked;" that "whoso keepeth the commandment shall feel no evil thing; and a wise man's heart discerneth both time and judgment. Because to every man there is a time and judgment, the misery of man is great upon him; for he knoweth not *that* which shall be, and who can tell him *when* it shall be?" words which appear to me

to signify that man cannot be happy while doubtful as
to the nature of his employments in the *time* allowed
him on earth, and the period *when judgment* shall be
pronounced, and *what* it will be. This is exactly the
sentiment of a man who had tried earthly pleasures,
and, finding them insufficient for his happiness, imagines
there must be some preventing cause; and, not choosing
to consider that the cause lies in himself, charges, if not
exactly Providence, yet, at least, the order of things, as
acting against him, and preventing the perfect enjoyment of life which, if he could have had the government of his own affairs, he would have assured to himself. "There is no man that hath power over the *spirit* to
retain the spirit [if he had had no revelation of a separate
existence of the spirit, what could these words mean?];
neither hath he power in the day of death; and there is
no discharge in that war; neither shall wickedness deliver those that are given to it." But he tells us repeatedly that "*righteousness* delivereth from death." Consequently we know that both allude to some state of
existence beyond this. "Because sentence against an
evil work is not executed speedily, therefore the heart
of the sons of men is fully set in them to do evil."
"Though a sinner do evil a hundred times, and his
days be prolonged, yet surely I know that it shall be
well with them that fear God, who fear before him;
but it shall not be well with the wicked." This clearly
alludes to the judgment after death, and to the folly of
supposing that, because sentence against an evil work is
not executed speedily, it is forgotten and passed over.
In this life, the next verse tells us, "there are often
just men who suffer as if they had done the work of
the wicked, and the wicked as happy as if they had
done the work of the righteous;" therefore, to hope for

judgment on earth is vanity, and so he commended mirth, as if life might consist of eating and drinking jollily; but this was not sufficient to satisfy him; and so he applied his heart to wisdom, to see the business done on the earth, and try to reconcile the ways and works of God (for such is evidently the meaning of chap. viii. 17); but he could not succeed; for his heart and time had been too long devoted to worldly pleasures, to obtain at once, in his old age when weariness had over-taken him with doubt and gloom, the pure heart, en-lightened eyes, and spiritualised mind which had so enabled his father David to understand and proclaim the ways and works of a loving and compassionating God. He was compelled to remain satisfied with the belief that "the righteous and the wise and their work are in the hand of God."

The remainder of the ninth chapter may appear to favour the opinion of sceptics, that Solomon rather en-couraged the thoughtless and irregular pleasures of this life, than those that lead to the next. But to me it is only the return of the doubting and weary spirit, which chose to refer every thing to time and chance, instead of man's free will and the Lord's judgment, and so endeavoured (vainly, indeed) to lessen the stings of his own conscience by lessening individual responsibility; but this, in a Hebrew and a believer in God's Law, could not last long; and in the eleventh chapter we again find him referring to the works of God, as indeed inscrutable, but nevertheless demanding our adoration, bidding us "in the morning to sow the seed, and in the evening not to withhold the hand, for we know not which shall prosper, or whether both may not be good;" and in the twelfth chapter, after that sublime address, "Remember thy Creator in the days of thy youth," etc., and the exquisitely beautiful description of the dissolution of the human frame which follows, the believer in immortality bursts forth into the brief but emphatic exclamation of the heart's conviction, "Then shall the dust return to the earth as it was, AND THE SPIRIT SHALL RETURN UNTO GOD WHO GAVE IT."

Here there is neither doubt, supposition, nor suggestion. It is perfect *conviction*, triumphing over all the gloom and weariness that tinged his previous meditations, completing a most sublime picture *of the frame's* dissolution with the yet sublimer declaration of the spirit's immortality; and in the few words, "shall return unto God who gave it," expressing felicity perfect as the heart can conceive, removing at once all thought of death as annihilation, and teaching that however vain and weary life on earth might be, even to excite the wish to cast it from us and so be at rest, there was *no* rest even after death, save for those whose pleasures and pursuits in this life fitted them for the spirit's rest in heaven with its God. " Let us hear the conclusion of the whole matter," he continues, in the thirteenth verse of the same chapter, " FEAR GOD AND KEEP HIS COMMANDMENTS; FOR THIS IS THE WHOLE DUTY OF MAN. For God shall bring every work into judgment, with every secret thing, whether it be good or whether it be evil."

And this is the concluding sentiment of a man, who had been endeavouring to convince himself that life is all vanity and vexation of spirit, who had tried not only every earthly pleasure and sensual indulgence, but even the vast resources and deathless enjoyment of wisdom; but he had turned from the path of light, and so wisdom herself had become dark, and could give him no rest nor pleasure. And as, in his old age, he looked back on existence wasted, talents misapplied, inasmuch as they had lured him from the study which is above all others, "that he knoweth and understandeth ME, that I am the Lord who exercise loving-kindness, judgment, and righteousness on the earth; and that in these things I delight, saith the Lord." The thought pressed upon him, thus to fear God and keep His commandments, that is, to keep Him always before him, was, indeed, not only the whole duty, but the whole safety of man. The very assurance, "for God will bring every work to judgment," marks and confirms his belief in immortality, and, as the conclusion of his exhortations and meditations, removes every previous impression which this same book may have given. All men are liable to intervals of such gloom and doubt, so that their very impressions of the present life are changed: how much more those of that future, which they can only behold through faith and an earnest love of God! And none more so than those who, like Solomon, have tried all worldly pleasures and found them all wanting; but the nearer he approached the end of this existence, the clearer shone forth the belief, which as a Hebrew could never have been entirely dead within him, of that world in which the spirit will move and act when dust has returned to dust, and of those duties, so simple, that the child and the lowliest-minded could understand and observe them, and so exalted, that the sage and the sovereign, the loftiest intellect and the proudest station, would yet feel elevated in their performance, and every mental faculty be expanded in their contemplation.

The very fact of Solomon's reiterated complaint, that all he had tried was vanity, instead of fostering gloomy thoughts of this life, ought to be as convincing as if said in direct words, of the existence of a better. There is no allusion in these complaints, to the study of God's ways and works, through his word; because Solomon knew that in that study alone there was no vanity nor vexation; for it would neither fail in itself nor lead us wrong. It was mere earthly pleasure and speculative wisdom, that had proved so utterly vain; and that they had done so is positive PROOF of a higher and purer existence. God who, in the hearing of a whole people, had proclaimed Himself to be Love, would never have stored the hearts of His children with capabilities and affections, which were always to yearn for that which they found not, and be unsatisfied with what they had. If this life were all, it would have contained in itself the full completion of happiness for those who deserved it. Solomon was blessed with prosperity above all others. If death were the cessation of existence, why could he not enjoy, without a single alloy, the pleasures of this life? What need was there to think of God? There was no *present* evidence that his departure from His service had excited the Eternal's displeasure; for his prosperity continued uninterruptedly, nay increasing as life advanced. In considering his life and character, we could almost believe that God blessed him with every earthly blessing, and permitted their misuse to make manifest by positive example, as well as by the precepts of His law, how insufficient was even the most unclouded prosperity of itself to create happiness; and to prove that, as it was so, THERE MUST BE some higher and purer state of existence, in which the vast capabilities for happiness and love, with which He stored the human heart, shall be satisfied and filled. To the denier of revelation the book of Ecclesiastes must indeed be fraught with gloom alone. To the believer in the God revealed through Moses, it is in itself unanswerable evidence of the spirit's immortality.

Ecclesiastes being full of querulous reminiscences of faded pleasure, we seldom find a reference to the righteous, except that they, too, share the common fate of trial and death; but in Proverbs we have repeated references to them, as blessed far above the wicked, not in this life, but in a better. Ecclesiastes, as I have said before, appears more the transcript of individual thoughts from individual experiences, and so is tinged with the gloom and weariness of the writer. Proverbs seems more intended for the use of a community. It does not bear any individual tinge or personal reference, but enforces certain moral and religious truths, social and domestic duties—in short, pithy sentences, likely to fix themselves on the mind. More lengthy dissertations impress for the time, but are frequently forgotten very shortly afterwards. The *commentary* of a proverb is *experience*, and so the text remains, very often reminding man of an individual or social duty, for which a longer address would fail.

In reading the Proverbs of Solomon, we cannot fail to be struck by the constant allusions to "life" and "death," which are utterly meaningless, unless they refer to a futurity of which this life is but the threshold. "She who forsaketh the guide of her youth, and forgetteth the command of God, her house inclineth unto death, and her paths unto the *dead*. None that go unto her return again, neither take they hold of the PATHS OF LIFE." (ii. 19.) "For the commandment is a lamp, and the Law is light, and the reproofs of instruction are the WAY OF LIFE." (vi. 23.) "For whoso findeth me [the wisdom of the Lord, of which the preceding verses, from the eleventh to the thirty-fourth of the eighth chapter, give a most sublime description] FINDETH LIFE, and shall obtain favour of the Lord. But he that sinneth against me wrongeth *his own soul: all they that hate me love death.*" (viii. 35, 36.) Now, the wisdom here alluded to *cannot* be attained in its fulness by the children of earth; and, therefore, unless there be a life where the wisdom sought and cultivated here, can be perfected, Solomon's words are without meaning. Death is the fate of all, whether they seek wisdom or despise it. Nay, but too often it comes the earlier to those who have so pursued wisdom from pure love, as to forget the failing strength and suffering frame until too late, and the grave receives them, ere one-quarter of their race is run: while those who scorn such pure intellectual tastes, who think only of amassing wealth, or the petty ambition of vying with others in means or station, who look on the genius and the student as poor idle visionaries who are fit for nothing and but little removed from fools or madmen, live on in health and luxury, often beyond the time marked as man's allotted age. Where, then, is Solomon's wisdom in the above-quoted verses? Judge them as referring to physical life and death, and it is falsehood or folly; to the life and death which is eternal, and it is fraught with sublimity and truth.

"Treasures of wickedness profit nothing]we find in chap. x. 2, 3,] but RIGHTEOUSNESS DELIVERETH FROM DEATH. The Lord will not suffer the *soul of the righteous* to famish; but He casteth away the substance of the wicked." "*The fruit of the righteous is a tree of life;* and he that winneth souls is wise." (xi. 30.) "The merciful man doeth good to *his own soul;* but he that is cruel troubleth his own flesh." "The wicked worketh a deceitful work; but to him that *soweth righteousness shall be a sure reward.* As righteousness tendeth to

30

life, so he that pursueth evil pursueth it to his own death." (xi. 17–19.) "In the way of righteousness is LIFE; and in the pathway thereof there is no death." (xii. 28.) "The law of the wise is a fountain of life, to depart from the snares of death." (xiii. 14.) "The fear of the Lord is a fountain of life, to depart from the snares of death." (xiv. 27.) "The way of life is ABOVE to the wise, that he may depart from the *grave* beneath." (xv. 24.) "He that keepeth the commandment *preserveth his own soul*, but he that despiseth his ways shall die. The fear of the Lord tendeth to life, and he that hath it shall abide satisfied: he shall not be visited with [lasting] evil." (xix. 16–23.)

I preferred transcribing all these impressive verses, dearest Annie, to pausing to comment upon them. They bear so emphatically, so unanswerably, upon the subject we are considering, that it appears to me utterly impossible for any one to read the book whence they are extracted, and yet deny to us a revelation and belief in immortality—to us, I mean, as a *people;* for it is idle to assert that the knowledge was confined only to a few favoured individuals, when the writings of those individuals were open and known to the whole people of Israel.

Not one of the verses I have quoted will bear upon even physical life and death, without doing such violence to the daily experiences of man, as to be entirely rejected and disbelieved: whereas, regarded as referring to the future reward and punishment of the spirit, they are distinct, comprehensible, and comforting beyond measure, the more so from their perfect agreement, in word and style, with the expressions already used by Moses, which can only relate to a life and death hereafter, and with the prophecy of Ezekiel already so often quoted as relating to the same subject. The very fact of the familiar manner in which Solomon alludes to it, marks it a received popular truth, far more than if he had said, in direct words, "Such and such things are: *therefore*, choose righteousness, and depart from evil." Thus written, we might imagine they were imparted for the first time to the people; but the words of Moses, David, Solomon, and the Prophets, are so based upon a previous revelation and acknowledgment that, if we deny that they allude to a future state, we shall endeavour in vain to understand them, and must condemn the Bible as the word of falsehood, not of truth. Examine well the verses I have transcribed, and I am convinced that you will agree with me as to their immortal meaning.

The fearful state of Palestine during the continuance of monarchy prevented all clearer *theoretic* reference to this important subject. The people were in no state to be restrained from following their evil passions, by any thing so pure and spiritual as the incentive of immortality. Yet even in the historical books, we find no less than four *practical* illustrations of its truth, which must have struck the people with awe and belief, even in their iniquitous career. The first was the death of Abijah, Jeroboäm's son, who, we are expressly told, was to die young, and receive decent burial; because in him alone there was found some good thing toward the Lord God of Israel (see 1 Kings xiv. 13), in the house of Jeroboäm. Jeroboäm's wife herself sought the prophet, whose answer was, no doubt, afterwards heard by all the people; because it was connected with judgment on national sin: "and all the people mourned the child, according to the word of the prophet." This one simply recorded incident is in itself sufficient to overthrow the dogmas of materialists and unbelievers. If this life were all, where would be either the justice or the mercy of God, in sentencing the only righteous one of an evil house to an early death? The being merely removed from the evil threatened on his house, would be but a negative kind of recompense for that piety which had attracted the notice of his God, and is completely opposed to the proclaimed attributes of the Creator. If Moses's words, "Choose life, that thou and thy seed may live," and Ezekiel's, "When I say to the righteous he shall surely live, "David's "Thou hast delivered my soul from death, that I may walk before God in the land of the living," and Solomon's "Righteousness delivereth from death,"—if all these allude but to the physical life and death (so to speak) allotted to man, the death of Abijah so absolutely contradicts them all, that if the people of Israel had not had an assured hope in a future existence which was laid up with God for the righteous, it was enough to have excited them to revolt and rebellion, instead of awing them to submission. There was no need of death to have removed him from the evil visited on his father. The Eternal had equal power to guard and exalt him in life, and, according to his glorious attributes, and *would* have done so, had there been no purer happiness to be bestowed. But to the Hebrews, believers (even in their most degraded state) in immortality, the death of the only righteous in Jeroboäm's house confirmed the glorious truth which the death of Abel had first revealed, confirmed the words of David, that "precious in the eyes of the Lord is the death of His saints," and practically illustrated the words afterwards spoken by the Prophets, that "the righteous is taken away from the evil to come, and shall enter into peace;" "and for those who feared the Lord, and spoke of Him often one to another, a book of remembrance was written," marking them as the jewels of His crown.

Oh, when we are weeping over the cold remains of a beloved one, recalled in the first bloom of youth, dearest Annie, the early death of Abijah ought to satisfy us as to the wherefore they should go and we remain, and give us hope in the midst of tears.

And still more powerfully, if possible, is the Hebrew realisation of the revelation of immortality illustrated, in the only reward vouchsafed to Josiah for his goodness and pious efforts in the service of God. If you refer to the twenty-second and twenty-third chapters of the second book of Kings, and the thirty-fourth and thirty-fifth of the second book of Chronicles, you will find the whole history of this excellent young king, whose heart was perfect towards his God, and in whom, despite the fearful contagion of crime, no evil could be found. When he sent to the prophetess Huldah, to enquire concerning the book of the Law which had been found, and whose awful denunciation on the disobedient had so appalled him, her sentence of *mercy* for his individual righteousness was couched in words which, unless immortality had been the very essence of the Jewish faith, and as such inseparably entwined with the idea of death, would have been both meaningless, and contradictory of all Moses's promises of life as reward, if that life had indeed been merely *physical* and ceasing with earthly existence. "But to the king of Judah, who sent you to enquire of the Lord, thus shall ye say to him, Thus saith the Lord God of Israel, as touching the words which thou hast heard, *Because thy heart was tender, and thou hast humbled thyself before the Lord,* when thou heardest what I spoke against this place, ... I also have heard thee, saith the Lord. *Behold now I will gather thee to thy fathers*, and thou shalt be gathered to the grave in peace, and thy eyes shall not behold the evil which I will bring upon this place."

What but a received and realised belief in immortality, as a revelation from God himself, could have made Josiah regard this sentence as one of mercy and favour especially granted him, for his zeal, obedience, and humility? That he did consider it in this light, we know, by its being an increased incentive for him to continue in the path of righteousness, though he knew no effort of his could avert the long-doomed chastisement of his sinful people. He died, in exact accordance with the words of the prophetess, when only thirty, in the prime of youth and hope; and is not this, then, a convincing proof that the people of Israel then, equally with us now, regarded the words of Moses so often quoted, as alluding to a life and death beyond this world? that the belief was so inseparable from them, that it did not even need the reiterated words of the law to teach it? for we know that Josiah had never seen or read the Law, till it was discovered in cleansing out the neglected temple? Yet so powerful was the incentive of the promised reward to himself (not an early death, as sceptics may read it, but an early translation into peace and joy), that he never ceased his efforts for public and private reform. It would be folly indeed to imagine, that he looked forward to, and was promised by, the God who so loveth righteousness, the mere negative recompense of not seeing the evils about to befall his kingdom. To fulfil the words of His servant Moses, and retain His attribute of immutable truth, if the life there promised were only physical, and length of days and prosperity on earth the only reward for the righteous, Josiah should have been preserved to the farthest limit of mortality, and enjoyed nothing but prosperity and rest, instead of constant labour in the cause of God, and an early death. All the arguments I have brought forward in the case of Abijah, the perfect agreement of his early removal with the death of Abel, the Law and the Prophets, will bear with equal, if not with still more thrilling emphasis on the fate of Josiah. Abijah had only innate goodness to bring forward. Josiah had the addition of an earnest and faithful service, demanding (so to speak) still more at the hand of Him who through Moses *promised* reward, ay, and the reward of LIFE, to those who loved and sought Him and obeyed His ordinances. It would be useless to reiterate these arguments; but I cannot tell you, dearest Annie, the inexpressible consolation of these scriptural facts, the *practical* illustrations, as it were, of the words of Moses and the Prophets. There cannot be a doubt as to early death being far more often a *reward* than a chastisement; and to be such, there must be a future existence, and an undying soul.

The stoning of the righteous Naboth is the third incident confirming our immortality, which the historical books reveal. Here, again, unless we believe the reward of the righteous is to come, we must deny alike the attributes of our God, and the words of Moses. Naboth was evidently one of the seven thousand who, in the midst of national sin, remained faithful to his God; and therefore, if this earth were all, he ought to have been blessed with honours and riches, and long life over and above all his fellows. Instead of which, we find his lawful possessions coveted by the rapacious king; and by the diabolical arts of the queen he is falsely accused of blasphemy, brought out and stoned. Now, is there one believer in that God of infinite mercy, justice, and truth, whom the Bible reveals, who can read this incident and yet need direct words to teach him immor-

tality? Is there one Hebrew who, with this record
before him, can declare that the rewards and punishments taught by Moses are temporal only?—one of the
stranger faiths who can still refuse to the people of Israel
the belief in a futurity of bliss for the righteous, and
woe for the wicked, when their Bible narrates such a fearful triumph of the wicked over the righteous upon earth?
How could even the few righteous have continued steady
and faithful in seeking the path of life, with the earthly
fate of Naboth before them, contradicting all the promises
of their Lawgiver, if they had not known, from ages past,
that the "life" promised the righteous was not of earth,
and that though the wicked may triumph, their doom is
to be cut off for ever? If immortality had not been
universally known (though the masses were too wrapt in
sin to act upon the glorious knowledge), we may safely assert, that the death of Naboth would have been averted,
lest the efforts of the righteous, dispirited from such a
permitted termination to the good, should entirely cease;
but it was *not* averted, because it removed the righteous
victim from the evil of earth to a heaven of glory, confirmed immortality to the believer, and by the denunciations of God through His prophet on Ahab and Jezebel.
taught the wicked that the crime was noted for awful
chastisement, and bade them tremble, even while iniquity still held them by a chain.

The fourth confirmation of a future life, is the miraculous translation of the prophet Elijah, which has always
appeared to me ordained, not *only* as the reward of a
faithful prophet, because there were many equally righteous, and that one alone should be taken to heaven without the pang of mortal dissolution would seem like injustice towards others; but that his ascent should be a
palpable evidence of that heaven awaiting the righteous

after their work on earth was done, to arrest by a miracle the attention of the people, to remove all doubt with which a career of sin and all the mere animal pleasures might have surrounded death, to prove unanswerably that this life was but the threshold of another, and that it could not possibly end in annihilation: else wherefore had not all the righteous of previous ages been translated equally with Elijah? He was not the only one, by a great many, whose righteousness demanded "life;" and we know that the God whose justice is as infinite as His mercy, would never have thus shown favour to one alone, and condemned the rest of His faithful to annihilation. The translation of Elijah, in the midst of Israel's most terrible iniquity, has always appeared to me one of the most striking, most convincing, and most consoling proofs of a beneficent and most gracious Providence that the Bible gives.

A theoretic revelation of immortality would have been as utterly unheeded by the people, as were all the spiritual ordinances of the Law. They were in no condition for the reception of any thing so pure, if presented to them as a *new* truth, the acceptation of which was necessary for their salvation. It was too opposed to the present overflow of animal indulgences and earthly desires to have urged them to desert their evil course for the path of life; and God, in His mercy, instead of reiterating through chosen servants the rewards that the people were rejecting, performed a miracle so stupendous, so impossible to any but Himself, that even the most heedless and sinful must for the time have been startled into conviction of another and purer state of existence; and that, however they might drown the voice of the solemn truth, there must come a day when before the throne of God their souls, whether for good or for evil,

would stand in judgment.   For the righteous especially,
the translation of Elijah must have been of inexpressible consolation.   In periods of national sin and its consequent misery, not only to the sinning, but, from their
social nature, too often also to the good, our human nature not unfrequently so depresses and silences the spiritual, that comfort even from the righteous has departed,
and we cannot *realise* that which yet from our very heart
we *believe*.   This world, and its petty cares and exhaust-
ing struggles seem to chain the spirit to the earth, when
it most longs to spring on high.   Sin and sorrow seem
man's lot alone.   We forget that our souls are the breath
of God, and therefore mark us a creation "a little lower
than the angels," however man's sins may have defaced
the immortal likeness; and we find ourselves involun-
tarily believing, that we are mere insects in the sight of
God, over whom He is too mighty and too holy to hold
guard.   The most sincerely pious, the most earnest
strivers after good, have all had to contend with such
painful intervals, and more especially when all around
them is gloom and crime, and the voice of God is heard
but in denunciation upon sin.   To such, then, how thrice
blessed must have been the ascent of Elijah!   It must
have recalled their fainting faith—taught them, however
dark and sad their earthly career, even as was Elijah's
own, it was but temporary trial to end in an eternity of
joy.   The heaven which earth's sins had so obscured
was revealed in transcendent glory—immortality as
thrillingly proclaimed as if an angel's voice had spoken.
None other, indeed, could escape death; but their souls
were deathless, and their dwelling was above.

Do not regard this rendering of the translation of
Elijah as the mere dream of an enthusiast, dearest Annie.
The word of God is granted us to be our guide, not

merely by precept, but by example—not only by revelation in direct words, but by analogy. We are to look upon all it records as instruction, and *search* for its divine lessons, not be content with merely those which lie upon the surface. We must remember the Old Testament is OURS. That of the glorious truths it reveals, and the precepts it bestows, no one can deprive us, unless we disregard them ourselves, and, by indifference and neglect, permit others to think we have neither right nor interest in them. We, indeed, value and stand up for the Pentateuch as a Law and Revelation vouchsafed to us alone; but this is only a portion of our inheritance. If we rest satisfied with the Books of Moses, we deprive ourselves of a rich mine of spiritual wealth, instruction, and consolation, which, when thus neglected by its native guardians, naturally becomes the property of aliens, and by them is but too often and too strongly turned against ourselves. Again and again, the truth forces itself upon me, that as a nation we do not study our Bibles sufficiently, and it is proved by the very fact, that, while the Sabbath portions from the Law and Prophets are repeatedly translated and offered to the Jewish public, there is actually no such thing as the translation of the *whole* Bible* by a Jew. We know the Psalms, because they are almost all contained in our Prayers. We may know one or two chapters or occasional verses of the Proverbs, from the truths they teach in a short sentence, or the experiences with which they sympathise. We know those portions of the Prophets that teach our restoration and captivity; but those that bear on our moral guidance and spiritual consolation are carelessly passed

---

* Meaning in English; but this defect has been remedied since the author's demise.—L.

by. If the Historical Books are read, it is merely as a history of an antiquated past—not as *practical* illustrations of the Law, and confirmation of the after prophets. We must hope that this mistaken neglect of any part of the Word of Life is passing away, now that there is indeed a spiritual awakening amongst us. The more we study, the more we shall find the fulness of instruction which the Sacred Volume gives; that where there is no *precept*, there is still illustration; and that even the Historical Books themselves, apparently so confined to earthly deeds alone, will yet bear witness to and confirm the holy truth with which (however denied us) our Sacred Volume teems—the knowledge of, and received belief in immortality!

LETTER XXVI.

FROM THE SAME TO THE SAME.

Subject continued—Testimony of the prophets to immortality and resurrection still more clear and powerful than the previous writers, and why—State of the people—Provision for a still more awful temporal future—Mission of the prophets—Verses apparently alluding to temporal restoration, equally applicable to immortality—Meaning of the expression " days of heaven on the earth"—Doctrine of resurrection of the body does not contradict the immortality of the soul ; reconciliation of the two—Ideas as to the repeopling of Judea—The effect of our restoration ; erroneous suppositions thereon refuted—Extracts from Isaiah proving immortality ; magnificent imagery of the fourteenth chapter—Notice of the thirty-third—First allusion to a specified punishment after death, consoling evidence of the destiny of the righteous, and union of the two doctrines, resurrection and immortality—Notice of the forty-ninth chapter, fourth verse; of the forty-fifth of the fifty-seventh; abounds in direct allusions to our immortality, and the Hebrews' belief in it—Its deep consolation —Its explanation and commentary on the words of Moses—The fourth verse of the sixty-fourth chapter; its powerful testimony of a future state—Individual belief in immortality not enough; should be proved the heritage of Israel from the beginning.

WE now come to the Prophets, dearest Annie, and in them we shall find the doctrines both of the resurrection of the dead and of our soul's immortality, still more distinctly revealed than they have been yet. The awful time was nearing, when the prescience of the Eternal knew, that for the continued iniquities of His people His countenance would be turned from them, the direct interference of His Providence in visible judgments be withdrawn, His presence from the Holy of Holies, where

31

the high-priest had once been so favoured as to hold communion and receive reply, depart, the visible glory vanish, the very inspiration of His will to prophets and holy men in their captivity cease, and the Law be read with such painful restrictions, that its *spiritual* meaning might succumb before the care to observe the ceremonial. Suffering and toil, and contempt and wrath, were gathering round, in which the spiritual part of our mingled nature might be entirely lost. The free will of men had chosen evil, and brought this chastisement upon them. The prescience of the Eternal beheld it; and, while His justice might not withhold the chastisement, His mercy provided consolation. Communion direct with Himself, as had been the case during the continuance of His temple, was indeed at an end; but He inspired His prophets to write those immortal truths, which would lead the spirit up to Him by belief and obedience, even in captivity and woe. Earth was darkened; for the one temple was levelled with the ground, but heaven was brought still nearer. The body might toil and suffer through its allotted space; but the soul beheld its destiny, and could calmly endure. Flame and the rack, the sword and famine, might destroy the clayey shell; but the dying Hebrew knew his soul was deathless, beheld but heaven and rejoiced. While in his own land and under the direct government of God, while judgments and miracles were visible to manifest His Providence to the nation at large, while the conviction of immortality was so completely the sustaining essence of the Law, that to divide it from the intent of its ordinances was impossible: there was little need of words referring to it; but, when all these blessings ceased, and a wide barrier separated the Hebrew from his justly offended God, there was absolute need of direct words to bring the solemn and spiritual truth home to the heart to be its guide and consoler; and, *therefore,* God's mercy inspired the prophets to teach it more clearly and distinctly than the Law.

This is the simple reason of a fact which our opponents so often turn against us. They say, that the prophets were more spiritual than the Law; because they beheld and referred to the advent of Jesus, and to the religion he would teach. As a Hebrew, of course, I feel that this is a mistaken notion, and that none of our prophecies referred to, or were fulfilled in, Jesus and his new religion; and, therefore, I am anxious to provide you with a solid foundation in your own faith, for what may, at a first sight, appear plausible in another. I have already dilated at such length on the real mission of the prophets, that it needs no farther repetition, save to assert that, as they were inspired to teach the people greater spirituality, than their gross abuse, or rather disregard, of their Law had previously allowed them to attain, immortality naturally formed a part of their revealings as an incentive to a righteous career, when all, even partial, prosperity on earth would be denied them.

Isaiah, Ezekiel, Daniel, and Malachi, are those prophets in whom we find the clearest allusions to a future existence. The others contain many verses and references which can only bear upon the subject, but in less precise words. Many verses that are generally supposed to allude *only* to our restoration to Jerusalem, *I* myself believe refer with equal force to those words in which the soul will move and act meanwhile. The reward promised by Moses for perfect obedience to the law, was "that the days of the people in the promised land should be *as the days of heaven upon the earth.*" Now, this expression is positive confirmation that there is a heaven (so to speak), where time is so perfected in happiness, that for earth to receive the same is the greatest reward that could be promised to the children of men. If this heaven were nought to them, which, were physical death the end of our existence, must be the case: how could they have even comprehended the nature of this reward, and so received it as an incentive to righteousness? It would be much about the same as showing a beautiful picture to a brute beast, and desiring him to admire it, when it should be his. The determined sinfulness of our ancestors always prevented the realisation of this glorious promise; but we *know* that in our restoration it will be fulfilled, and therefore there is neither impiety nor contradiction in the supposition, that our souls will appear in judgment when freed from this life, and yet rejoin the body, at the resurrection of the dead for everlasting life, in that land which will be again an Eden, and where sin, and disease, and death will be so utterly unknown, that their days will indeed be as the days of heaven upon earth; for from heaven have the pure and pardoned spirits come, at the word of their God, to revive the body they have left.

But this is a subject demanding such deep thought and metaphysical disquisition, dearest Annie, that I must not, in justice to either you or myself, enter upon it now. I only want you clearly to understand, for the present, when we are entering a field where the doctrine of the resurrection of the body and the immortality of the soul are *both* brought forward, that the one *does not* contradict the other, as some unhappy sceptics choose to assert. With God both can be. In reflecting on such a subject, try and remember the contents of my ninth letter, that in this life we are no more capable of understanding the wisdom and the power, the works and intentions of the Eternal, than an unborn babe, the knowledge and discoveries of a natural philosopher. Yet that unborn babe has within himself the necessary capability, and, if spared to maturity, may attain the same vast amount of knowledge: and equally so have our *immortal souls* the *capabilities* to understand the ways and works of the Lord, and, in the gradations of that future laid up with Him, *may* attain to it, though on earth it is as much shut from them as the earth itself to the unborn child.

Feeling this, as we must do if we reflect at all, the speculative imaginings which will assail us, as to the destiny of the soul while the body lies in corruption waiting resurrection, unless directed by the revelation of the Holy Scriptures, must lead us into a wide sea of doubt and fancy, which will not only deprive us of rest and comfort, but lure us from our God.

But if we search the Scriptures, we shall know that our souls are deathless; that to hope (as the wearied are sometimes tempted to do) for their non-existence, is contradicted by the whole evidence of past and present life. That for every work done on earth, with every secret thing, God will bring it into judgment, whether it be good, or whether it be evil, contradicts at once the idea that the souls are torpid, or non-existent, till the great day of universal resurrection. They have their work to do until that day, in the various gradations of spiritual existence, and according to the judgment pronounced on their life on earth. And this is sufficient to guide and comfort us while below. The revival of corruption, the mysterious reunion of soul and body, it is our duty to *believe*, but neither to argue nor speculate upon. With God all things are not only possible, but founded upon a wisdom and love, which here we vainly endeavour to conceive, but which may perfectly satisfy us, that there will be neither *degradation* nor farther trial to the soul in its reunion with the body.

The resurrection will not be, the Bible tells us, till sin and death are utterly destroyed from off the earth; and therefore, we have *scriptural* authority for the hope and belief, that the revival of the body will form a tabernacle for the soul, pure as the soul itself, and, instead of the spirit sharing and suffering the infirmities of the body, as now, the body will share the purity and perfection of the soul.

That this is merely an individual supposition, I willingly acknowledge; for I have never met with it in any Jewish or Christian writer; but it is founded on a long, earnest, and prayerful study of those portions of all the Prophets which refer to our restoration to our own land. I am aware that many amongst us, and even amongst Christians, imagine that the repeopling of Judea will be achieved by political interference, that it will be accomplished naturally (so to speak); and occasional efforts have been made, and pamphlets have been written, to manifest the wisdom of a co-operation of certain nations, or promulgation of certain statutes, compelling or holding out rewards and privileges for the Jews to return to Judea; but to my feelings these efforts are utterly useless. It is impossible to read the Prophets with any attention, and not perceive that our return will be attended by miracles yet more stupendous than those which marked our egress from Egypt,—by a regeneration of the heart, and annihilation of all inclination to sin, which, in the present state of man, is impossible,— and by the resurrection of the dead, which will not be till the end of days, " when the sun shall not give light by day, nor the moon by night, but the Lord shall be thy everlasting light, and thy God thy Glory."

Our promised restoration, then, is a *confirmation*, instead of a denial, of our soul's immortality; for every reference to it marks the triumph of the *spiritual* over the merely *corporeal;* and this in itself is proof of our *mingled* nature, and of the continued existence of the spirit, however the body may lie in corruption. For the Lord to be our everlasting light and God our glory, our life in Judea *must* be the life of the *spirit*, however the body may have arisen and shared its purity. The Prophets give us no foundation whatever for the received idea, that the Jews look to a temporal deliverer and mere earthly glories, in the submission of their enemies, and ascendency over the nations as the sole enjoyment of their restoration; but they speak emphatically of Peace, peace eternal and spiritual, peace springing from the fruition of that thrice-glorious prophecy, "They shall not say one to another, Know ye the Lord; for they shall all know Him, from the least to the greatest of them;" a Peace, springing from that blessed, blessed unity of heart and spirit, which will lead *all* nations to worship in the mount of the Lord, and acknowledge Israel as indeed His first-born, whose glory it is to be His priests and people; a Peace which, from the cessation of individual and general sin, will rest, brooding like the dove over every human heart; a Peace, which will turn the swords into ploughshares, the spears into pruning-hooks; for the vain strivings of mere earthly ambition, the heart-burnings of imagined national wrongs, will have ceased for ever; a Peace which will tame even the wild beasts of the forest, and permit even a little child to lead them; a Peace which is of God, and marks the days of heaven on the earth; for "*the whole earth* shall be full of the knowledge of the Lord, as the waters cover the sea;" a PEACE, which is the offspring of innocence and joy, of a love that knows no death, and a faith that knows no doubt. Such and such alone is the promise attendant on our restoration; and shall we call this *temporal greatness* and human subjection of the nations? Dearest Annie, banish the mistaken thought. It has no foundation in our Scriptures; therefore it is wrong, and has no part in Judaism.

But I must not dilate on this subject, connected as it is with our argument of the undying nature and ordained superiority of the soul over the body in the latter days. I must try and confine myself to the testimony of the prophets, to our continued existence after *individual* death, not to national restoration. The subjects are indeed so united, that it is difficult to divide them. The first allusion to a decided existence after physical death, is the magnificent poem contained in the fourteenth chapter of Isaiah. That it is more a figurative illustration of what will be Israel's triumph over her insulting foes, than a direct reference to individual immortality, I grant; but even as a figure it is *most* important, proving, as it does, how completely the minds of the Hebrews must have been imbued with the subject, or it would never have so formed the groundwork of their literature. "*The grave from beneath is moved for thee to meet thee at thy coming,*" the prophet says, addressing Babylon under the figure of a mighty king; "*it stirreth up the dead for thee, even all the chief ones of the earth:* it has raised up from their thrones all the kings of the nations. All they shall speak and say unto thee, Art thou also become weak as we? Art thou become like unto us? Thy pomp is brought down to the grave, and the noise of thy viols: the worm is spread

under thee, and the worms cover thee. How art thou
fallen from heaven, O Lucifer, son of the morning!
How art thou cast down to the ground, thou who didst
weaken the nations! For thou hast said in thy heart, I
will ascend into heaven, I will exalt my throne above
the stars of God; . . . I will ascend above the heights
of the clouds; I will be like the Most High. Yet thou
shalt be brought down to the grave, to the sides of the
pit. They that see thee shall narrowly look upon thee,
and consider thee, saying, Is this the man that made
the earth to tremble, that did shake kingdoms? that
made the world as a wilderness, and destroyed the city
thereof? that opened not the house of his prisoners?"
Can any picture be more sublime than this?—the fate
of the mighty tyrant who thought to make his seat with
the Most High, and who had such power in the world—
the satirical astonishment of the dead, that he should
become one of them, and the worm be under and above
him? And then, lest it might be thought that the prophet alluded merely to the dead as *inmates of the grave*,
the eighteenth and nineteenth verses mark the distinction between their fate and that of the proud sinner,
whose earthly end was the same: "All the kings of the
nations, even all of them, *lie in glory*, every one in his
own house [figurative of the houses appointed in the
land of the living]. But thou art cast out of the grave
like an abominable branch, as the remnant of those that
are slain, thrust through with a sword, that go down to
the stones of the pit, as a carcase trodden under foot."
Now *all* who die become carcases and are down in the
grave, so that the distinction here made cannot possibly
have to do with the mere differences of burial. We
have already heard the *dead* chief ones of the earth
allude to their being weak, and having the worm as

their companion ; therefore, unless it alludes to something beyond the body, they cannot be said to *"lie in
glory."*

We have seen them *all together* rising to meet the
king of Babylon ; therefore it is not the body which
resteth "each in his own house." Nor would the mere
superiority of the pomp and place of burial be sufficient
to mark the difference between them. If death were
indeed annihilation, what could possibly signify the
honours or the disgrace of interment, either to those
that were gone or those who bemoaned them, I mean as
reward or punishment? To attach such a meaning to
this beautiful passage, changes it at once from the sublimest truth into incomprehensible mockery. Were
there not the eighteenth and nineteenth verses, we
might indeed suppose it a *mere* poetic imagining concerning the *dead* animated in their graves, with astonishment at their new guest; but the eighteenth and
nineteenth verses illustrate the *life* and *good*, *death* and
evil, set forth by Moses, and commented on by Ezekiel.

The nineteenth verse of the twenty-sixth chapter so
clearly reveals the resurrection of the dead, that it needs
neither commentary nor transcription—more especially
as it is more to immortality, as the groundwork of our
faith, than to the resurrection, that I am anxious to
draw your attention. The thirty-third chapter is, however, one which contains in itself such convincing evidence of our argument, that it demands notice. The
first twelve verses describe the fate of the enemies of the
Lord, the waiting of His faithful servants upon Him, the
information that the "Lord dwelleth on high," and that
Zion shall be filled with righteousness and judgment;
and wisdom and knowledge shall be its stable strength,
and the fear of the Lord its treasure; but that, for the

despising of the covenant, suffering and desolation cause the earth to mourn and languish, Lebanon to be ashamed and hewn down, Sharon to be like a wilderness, and Bashan and Carmel to shake off their fruits; those that are far off shall hear what the Lord hath done, and those that are near shall acknowledge His might. And then follows a description so vivid of what can only be realised in a future life, that it seems scarcely possible for even the greatest sceptic to read it in any other sense.

"The *sinners* in Zion are afraid, fearfulness hath surprised the *hypocrites*. Who among us shall dwell with the devouring fire?" they ask one of another; "who amongst us shall dwell with everlasting burnings?" This is remarkable as almost the first and only part of the Bible in which *punishment* after death is clearly specified as having entered into the imaginings of sinners, accompanied of course with terror. The Eternal's own sentence is excision, our sages' meaning of which we will examine hereafter.

The fifteenth verse returns to the consideration of what constitutes righteousness, and the destiny of the righteous. "He that walketh righteously and speaketh uprightly, he that despiseth the gain of oppressions, that shaketh his hand from holding of bribes, that stoppeth his ear from hearing of blood, and shutteth his eyes from seeing evil: *he shall dwell on high*, his place of defence shall be the munitions of rocks, his bread shall be given him, his water shall be sure." Now, we have already been told that the Lord dwelleth on high; consequently, we must feel that the "on high," where the righteous is to dwell, is with the Lord, and that can only be in the world to come. The Eastern hyperbole which concludes the verse, confirms its truth by its perfect agreement

with other passages. God Himself is termed the *Rock*
of our salvation, Abraham as the rock whence we were
hewn; and therefore, that our defence shall be the munitions, or stronghold, of the rocks, simply means that our
guardian and protector is the Lord, who laid the rocks
on their foundations. The bread we shall receive, and
the waters that are sure, are the same as those held out
to us in the fifty-fifth chapter: "Ho, every one that
thirsteth, come ye to the waters, and he that hath no
money, come ye, buy and eat; yea, buy wine and milk
without money and without price. Wherefore do ye
spend money on that which is not bread, and your labour
on that which satisfieth not? *Hearken diligently unto
me, and eat ye that which is good, and let your soul delight itself in fatness.*"

In the seventeenth verse, as is constantly the case
with the literature of the Bible, the pronoun changes
from the third to the second person. Still addressing the
righteous, Isaiah says, "Thy eyes shall see the king in
his beauty, they shall behold the land that is very far
off." The king here referred to is evidently the Lord;
for in the twentieth verse we read, "The Lord is our
judge, the Lord is our lawgiver, the Lord is our KING:
He will save us." No man in life can see that Holy
King, or behold with his mortal sight " the land that is
very far off;" but in heaven we shall see "as though in
the light of the Lord, ' and behold Jerusalem and Zion
indeed, as the prophet describes. In the eighteenth and
nineteenth verses he refers to the lingering feelings of
human terror clinging round the released soul, to the
wondering gaze for the usual officers of the land, and for
the pious people in whose possession it lies. But they
were no more visible; and in the twentieth verse we
find a beautiful picture of our holy land, as the right-

eous soul shall see it, from that pure dwelling where it
awaits the great and glorious day of the Lord. "Look
upon Zion, the city of our solemnities: thy eyes shall
see Jerusalem, a quiet habitation, a tabernacle that shall
not be taken down, not one of the stakes be removed,
neither shall any of the cords thereof be broken. But
there the glorious Lord will be unto us a place of broad
rivers and streams, wherein shall go no galley with
oars, neither shall gallant ship pass thereby. The Lord
is our judge, the Lord is our lawgiver, the Lord is our
king: He will save us. Thy tacklings are loosed; they
could not well spread the sail: then is the prey of a
great spoil divided; the lame take the prey. And the
inhabitant shall not say, I am sick; the people that
dwell therein shall be forgiven their iniquity."

The wording, and, in fact, the whole imagery, of this
glorious passage, proves that it is not *in* Jerusalem we
are first to see these things. They refer, indeed, to our
restoration, and to the blessings *then* awaiting us; but
it is part of the reward of the righteous when "dwelling on high," to look on earth with the eyes of the Lord,
in "whose light," as we have been expressly told, "we
shall see light." To look on "the land which is very far
off" cannot possibly allude to any position on earth; for,
though we may hear of and take an interest in lands
that are very far off, we cannot by any effort of art or
nature *see* them. But from above, and with the spiritualised vision of the soul, we may indeed behold them.
We shall look through ages, for to the immortal time is
unknown, and behold that favoured land as God has promised, where He will be to us all we need, and where
neither disease, nor sin, nor death can enter. The figurative term applied to the Eternal, "a place of broad
rivers and streams," is nothing new in the Eastern idiom.

"For my people have committed two evils," we find the Lord saying through His prophet Jeremiah; "they have forsaken me, the *fountain of living waters*, and have hewed them out cisterns, broken cisterns, that will hold no water." And numbers of similar passages might be extracted, to prove the referring to our God by the same reviving image. The imagery of the prophets, to obtain its way to the hearts and understandings of the people, was always founded on that which was most reviving and strengthening to human nature in a burning clime. A *refuge* from the storm—a *shadow* from the heat—a *rock* of strength—a *place of broad rivers and streams*—a *fountain of living waters*—all are Eastern figures permitted to be applied to the Eternal, to appeal to the hearts of the weary, and peculiarly applicable to the land of Judah, where drought and heat were the greatest affliction, shadow and water the greatest blessing, that could befall.

The prophecy we have been considering is a remarkable confirmation of that perfect agreement between the individual immortality of the soul and its immortal transit after death into a state of consciousness and work, according as it has prepared itself in this life, with the doctrine of the resurrection of the body, and our restoration to Palestine, which I brought forward in the first part of this letter. The prophecy *cannot* relate to any position in this life, nor *solely* to our restoration. The five concluding verses certainly describe Zion as she will be at that glorious time; but whom is the prophet desiring to "look upon Zion"? Undoubtedly, not a mortal inhabitant of the earth; for no mortal vision could embrace it. He addresses that soul of the righteous which he has already said shall "dwell on high and behold the king in his beauty," and desires him, as a part of his reward, to behold the city of his love, even as the tender mercy of his God has ordained it shall be restored, and where, at the resurrection of the body, he too shall move and act, bringing with him that perfection and purity which he has attained in heaven.

The next evidence (chapters xlix., l.) which Isaiah brings forward in confirmation of the Jewish belief in immortality, is his own experience. "I have laboured in vain," he says, in a moment of despondency, "I have spent my strength for nought, and in vain; YET SURELY MY JUDGMENT IS WITH THE LORD, AND MY WORK IS WITH MY GOD." Now, what comfort could this belief have brought, if death were annihilation? No man, unless the faith were strong within him, that his judgment and work, being with God, would bring sure peace and hope of reward, could have burst forth into such a rejoicing exclamation in the midst of human sorrow and disappointment. It is, indeed, but a single drop in the multitude of evidences which the Bible gives of Israel's belief in immortality; but it is important, as showing how completely the prophet's heart and mind were infused with it, as the natural and consoling accompaniment of his faith.

In a previous chapter also (the forty-fifth), we find abundant evidence of this truth. "Israel shall be saved in the *Lord with an everlasting salvation.*" "I am a just God and a Saviour, there is none beside me." "Look unto me and be ye saved, all the ends of the earth." "In the Lord shall all the seed of Israel be justified, and shall glory." Now, if we deny another and purer state of existence, these words are not merely incomprehensible, but utterly false. What had been the fate of Israel since the days of the prophet, and while he lived? Is there any evidence of their being saved on earth? What is the meaning of the term "saved in the Lord with an *everlasting* salvation"? Had we no other words but these, we have enough to prove the emphatic truth of immortality being the revealed, acknowledged, and treasured heritage of the Hebrews from the very beginning. The very prophecies are so based on it as an already received and believed truth, that, if it be denied, cr Palestine imagined to be the sole heritage of the Israelites, they fall to the ground as mocking fallacies, wanting both foundation and support. How could the mass understand such promises, if the fact of their being immortal beings had only then been revealed? How any man who calls himself either Christian or Jew can declare that in the Old Testament there is no evidence of immortality, passes my comprehension. The whole fabric falls at once, if you withdraw that only sustaining thread. There is neither God nor Bible to the deniers of immortality, as known unto the Jews. Their whole religion, Law and Prophets (nay, the very God their Scriptures reveal), are confirmed or denied by the simple fact of their believing or denying immortality,—it may be, not told in direct words, though we have them also, but as the basis, the vital essence, on which the whole is founded and has life.

The fifty-seventh chapter abounds in direct references to a future and more spiritual existence. Refer to the chapter, dearest Annie, and you will see the first and second verses distinctly describe not only the blessed death of the righteous, but the wherefore they are called. "The righteous perisheth, and no man taketh it [the lesson of his death] to heart; and merciful men are taken away, none considering the righteous is taken away from the evil. *He shall enter into peace;* they shall rest in their beds [or appointed homes], each one walking in his uprightness." The being merely removed from evil, it is clear, then, is *not* the only reward of the righteous. What would be the use of walking in his uprightness, if death were the common doom of all? Besides, why that great distinction between the subject of the first and second verse, and that of the ten verses following? If this life were indeed all, we should say that the "children of transgression, the seed of falsehood," were the happier; because they followed their inclinations without rebuke or hindrance, and appeared so to prosper, that "the very greatness of their way became a weariness to them;" but still they would not say, "There is no hope [left on earth], we will therefore seek the Lord." They "found the life of their hand," a powerful expression, denoting that they lived merely for the present, following the chances and flitting pleasures of the day, without a thought of the Eternal or of His dwelling. "Of whom hast thou been afraid or feared, that thou hast lied, and hast not remembered me, nor laid it [the recollection of me] to thy heart? have I not held my peace even of old?" evidently meaning that God would not interfere to manifest His judgments to the disobedient. He had already instructed them in those things that were acceptable to Him or not, and so left them to their own free will to spring up like grass and outwardly flourish; for had they consulted His word, they would have known, that the *wicked* who did so remained undisturbed in this life, to perish for ever. "Therefore He held His peace at them, even as He did at the sinners of old: yet still they feared Him not." "I will declare thy righteousness and thy works, for they shall not profit thee:" words how convincing that without love of, and obedience to the Lord—without, in a word, *religion*—even those acts and works which *appear* righteousness shall not profit us in our judgment before Him. "When thou criest, let thy companions deliver thee; but the wind shall carry them all away, vanity shall take them; but *those that put their trust in me* shall possess the land [of the living], and inherit my holy mountain [or the eternity to which the fifteenth verse alludes, and which has been noticed before in the thirty-third chapter, where the righteous soul is also promised to "dwell on high"]; and shall say [the righteous shall say to the wicked], Cast ye up, cast ye up, prepare the way, take up the stumbling-block out of the way of my people. For thus SAITH THE HIGH AND HOLY ONE WHO INHABITETH ETERNITY, WHOSE NAME IS HOLY, I DWELL WITH THE HIGH AND HOLY;" for such, to me, is the more correct rendering of the words. The particle* ב can be translated *with*, or *in*, or *at*, etc., any thing signifying connection, the joining of one with another; and as we have already read that God declares He "inhabiteth eternity," we know it cannot be circumscribed to any particular place; but that He who inhabiteth eternity saith, "I DWELL WITH THE HIGH AND HOLY [and] WITH HIM ALSO THAT IS OF A CONTRITE AND HUMBLE SPIRIT, TO REVIVE THE SPIRIT OF THE HUMBLE, AND TO REVIVE THE HEART OF THE CONTRITE ONES. For I will not contend for ever, neither will I be always wroth; for the SPIRIT would fail before me, and the SOULS that I have made."

Can any one assert that these exquisite verses allude to life on earth? Do they not fill the whole heart with their spiritual consolation, and the immensity of the Eternal's love towards those who *trust* in Him, and,

---

* There is no such particle here in the Hebrew; and the mistake of the author is doubtless owing to not inspecting the text, but depending on memory.—L.

from that trust, seek to love and serve Him? Many, perhaps, might say that the terms, " He shall enter into peace," and "rest in their beds," were of equivocal meaning, and might refer simply to the ending of trouble, from the cessation of existence. But the charge of the equivocal nature of the sentence is entirely disproved, not only by the fifteenth and sixteenth verses we have quoted at length, but by two assertions in the same chapter, " each one walking in his uprightness," and "There is *no peace,* saith my God, to the wicked;" but if the peace mentioned in the second verse, as the award of the righteous, be the mere peace of annihilation, the wicked would share it equally with the upright, and the death of the righteous be in no way superior. But "each one walking in his uprightness" is emphatically added, to prove that the peace and rest promised him is no negative species of reward, it is that blessing for which, more than any other, we yearn amid the stormy billows from which the earthly lives of the *righteous* are *never* exempt. The young, the active, the ardent and aspiring, may indeed feel that such a promise of peace and rest is but a small incentive to a righteous life; but let them wait a few very brief years, and the fulness of the bliss will be disclosed. Nor have we *only* that promise. The first and second verses do not stand alone, but are closely connected with the whole after-chapter, and especially with the fifteenth and sixteenth verses. Lest the sublime description contained in these brief words, "Thus saith the high and exalted One, who inhabiteth eternity, whose name is Holy, I dwell with the high and holy," should terrify us from seeking after righteousness as impossible so to be attained, as to allow us to join that high and holy choir who with their God inhabit eternity, we are told that "He dwelleth with *him also* that is of a contrite and humble spirit. That He will not be *always* wroth; for the spirit would fail before Him, and the souls which He hath made." You cannot read these verses too often, dearest Annie; for the more you do so, the more you must feel that the promise contained in them is our immortality, and clothed in such words of comfort, that it would be absolutely sin in us to hold back from accepting it on the plea of our unworthiness. If it did not relate to a future life, why should God say, "I will not contend *for ever*, nor will I be *always wroth*, for the *spirit* would fail before me, and the *souls* which I have made"? How can we dwell with Him who inhabiteth *eternity*, if the brief space of mortal life be the sole sphere allotted us? And again, to refer to the first verse, it not only relates to a future life in itself, but unanswerably confirms the words of Moses, so often quoted, "See, I have set before thee LIFE and GOOD, DEATH and EVIL," as bringing before us life eternal. If they mean mere temporal blessing, Isaiah's words are a contradiction; and if Isaiah's assertion that the righteous are taken from the evil, and shall enter into rest and peace, is believed to be a mere non-existence in the grave, the promise of the law is false, and has no meaning. The term "righteous," of course, signifies those who have chosen the GOOD in preference to the evil, and to whom therefore, by the law, LIFE is promised. Why then should the righteous be taken away to escape the coming evil? If his only sphere of happiness were this little earth, it was equally in the Eternal's power (and from His attributes we must believe it would have been so) to make the path of life smooth, and so fraught with joy as to have not even a dread of evil, and instead of being "taken away," which evidently means removed from sorrow, *before* the usual age allotted to man, his life would have been prolonged to the farthest limit, and full of health and joy to the very end. The words of Isaiah, then, are not only full of consolation and hope in their own absolute assertion of our immortality, but as explanatory, confirmative of, and a commentary upon the words of Moses, which we have already considered at so much length.

The conclusion of this very important chapter relates equally to the distinction between the righteous and the wicked, which can only be visible in a future existence; but as it does not bear so exactly on the subject we are considering, I shall leave you to study it by yourself. Only remember, dearest Annie, that the extreme comfort not of its lesson only, but of the preceding verses, consists in the fact, that it does not address the righteous and holy alone, but the humble, the lowly, and the contrite, those who may have gone on frowardly in the ways of their own heart, but repented in time, and so returned unto their God, with the assurance that He would neither contend nor be wroth for ever, but in His infinite mercy heal and restore comfort, not merely to the sinning ones, but to His mourners, promising peace to them, in contradiction to the confirmed wicked " to whom there is no peace, saith my God."

The last testimony borne by Isaiah to his faith in our immortality, is that glorious promise in the fourth verse of the sixty-fourth chapter, "For since the beginning of the world men have not heard, nor perceived by the ear, neither hath the eye seen, O God, beside thee, what he [thou hast] hath prepared for him that waiteth for him [thee]." Nothing can be a more sublime reference to a truth which while on earth we may only *believe*, and of which we can have no *visible* evidence, than these emphatic negatives. They give full space to the imagination

and affections, permit us to think on the promised future
as bliss, as ineffable as can be comprised in the revelations of the Eternal's fathomless love and untiring compassion. "From everlasting to everlasting," we are told,
is His long-suffering and forbearance; "as high as the
heaven above the earth," so immeasurable is His mercy
towards us; "as far as the East is from the West, so far
hath He removed our transgressions from us;" that His
dwelling is eternity, not merely "with the high and holy,
but with the contrite and humble;" that "the death of
His saints is precious in His sight," but that "in the
death of the sinner He hath *no* pleasure;" "*therefore,*
turn yourselves, and live ye;" that with Him "is the
fountain of light, and in His light we shall see light;"
that "He is the fountain of *living* waters," and therefore with Him there is no death; that with Him "is the
fulness of joy, and at His right hand everlasting pleasures." I might fill pages with similar passages; but
the above are sufficient to explain what I mean by asserting that Isaiah's *negatives* confirm, and give yet more
scope to the glorious expectations which previous *affirmative* passages had so thrillingly revealed. It is from
this chapter, this verse of *our* prophet, himself a Jew,
and speaking to the Jewish people ages before the
preaching of St. Paul, that the verse in Corinthians,
"Eye hath not seen, nor ear heard, neither have entered
into the heart of man the things which God hath prepared for them that love Him" (on which the Christians
lay so much stress, as proving how clearly to them immortality was revealed) is taken. Is it not then indeed
a disgrace to us, when by our lukewarmness, or indifference, we permit them to believe that they really are
right, and that we have no hope of heaven save through
them, when our own Bible not only promises all we need
on earth and hope in heaven for us as Jews, but is the

sole foundation and origin of all the sublime moral truths and immortal revealings, which the apostles, themselves Jews, preached to a darkened world? That Christianity taught immortality to the gentiles is indeed true; and we can well understand the feelings of intense gratitude with which such a revelation must be regarded. But all we uphold is simply, that to the Jews the revelation had been vouchsafed, not only in their law but from the very first of the creation; that neither their laws, nor their history, nor their Prophets, are comprehensible if we deny them the knowledge of existence after death; and that not only was this knowledge the very essence of *their* faith, but emanated from them over the whole world, as fulfilment of part of the promise made to Abraham, that "in his seed all the nations of the earth should be blessed." It is not enough that we *believe* in our immortality, dearest Annie. Living as a mere handful amongst those who assert that all our knowledge on this subject came from our intercourse with them, we must *know* and be ready, if called upon, to point out those passages in our own Scriptures from which all *their* quoted verses came. We must be able to show them the Divine foundation for our hope, and look for it, not merely to refute them, but to satisfy *our own hearts*, which cannot rest with the mere intuitive belief. We bear within ourselves the evidence that the soul is DEATHLESS; but that very instinct will lead us to misery and perchance apostasy, if we do not satisfy ourselves with the conviction not merely of faith, but of reason. Our own Scriptures abound with more than sufficient for both these in general opposing elements; and therefore am I so anxious, even at the risk of seeming tediousness, to bring before you the facts and verses which either directly, or by analogy, will bear upon the subject.

LETTER XXVII.

FROM THE SAME TO THE SAME.

Subject continued—Character and position of Jeremiah less spiritual
than Isaiah and Ezekiel, and why—His evidence equally important—Extracts from his book, seventeenth chapter; agreement with
David, chapter twenty-second, verse ten; the dead less to be lamented
than the living—Commentary on the deaths of Abijah, of Josiah,
and the words of Isaiah—Powerful evidence of immortality in the
twenty-second and twenty-third verses of the twenty-third chapter,
proved by the very ubiquity of the Eternal—Notice of the twenty-
third and twenty-fourth verses of the ninth chapter; incomprehensible to all except believers in immortality—Beautiful prophecy
of the thirty-first chapter, equally prophetic of our *immortal* as
our future *temporal* destiny; witnessed by the whole history of
persecuted Israel—Jeremiah could only have been written by a believer, and comprehended by believers, in immortality—Ezekiel,
third, eighteenth, and thirty-third chapters; notices thereon—Life
and death applied to the soul, not to the body; how proved—Ancient Hebrews rejected the idea of annihilation—Law and prophets
incomprehensible to materialists.

WE shall not find in the prophet Jeremiah either as
numerous or as direct allusions to our immortality, as in
Isaiah; but still we shall perceive much to *confirm* our
reiterated argument, strengthen individual hope, and nationally provide an incentive for us to retain unchanged
our faithfulness and constancy as children of Israel.
Jeremiah, though he abounds in most beautiful and consoling passages, still, as a whole, cannot be considered
such a spiritual prophet as Isaiah, and the fact is easily
accounted for. He was living in the very midst of, not
only national iniquity, for that was Isaiah's destiny also,

but of national misery. His character appears to have
been of still more human mould, if I may be allowed
the expression, than either Ezekiel's or Isaiah's. In both
of these the spiritual rose above the human. Their gift
of inspiration so pervades their writings, that we constantly lose sight of the mortal writer, and read only the
messenger of God; but in Jeremiah we are feeling with
the suffering man throughout. We read his utter repugnance to his fearful mission, the plainings of human
weakness, seeing more the utter misery of earth than
the future peace above. There was no distinction to
mark the righteous; and yet he knew from his own inward experience, that there were some still striving to
love and serve the Lord. He was himself persecuted
and torn on all sides by contending factions; the spirit
within urged him to the utterance of the Eternal's will,
while that very utterance increased his human sufferings,
not from individual feeling, but from the enmity it produced against him. His character was evidently of the
gentlest and most yielding kind, and his position inward
and outward the most painful that could assail even men
of sterner mould. The blackness covering the earth had
equally enrobed the heavens; and when we remember
that the prophets, though *inspired*, were still human as
ourselves, can we wonder that his book should be impressed more with earthly suffering than heavenly hope?
There seemed no breathing-space for the exhausted spirit,
save in the direct inspirings of the Lord, and even they
could bring no individual peace; for the denunciations
he was called upon to pronounce were fearfully at war
with his own gentle nature.

We should remember these facts, when we turn from
his book as more harrowing than comforting, more a relation of earth, than a witness of heaven. It is not when

in the very midst of trial, that we can realise to the full,
or bear witness to, the faith that is still within us. It is
afterwards that we know God has never forsaken us, and
our own experiences comfort ourselves and others. The
trials, too, that can only come from God, we can endure,
and thence derive inexpressible consolation even in the
midst of pain; but those which seem all of and•from
man crush us to earth, as if we could not rise again.

This was constantly Jeremiah's case, and therefore not
only does it account for his being less spiritual than
Isaiah, but renders his testimony to our future judgment
and to our immortal destiny (for he does bear witness to
both these) yet more valuable. I will transcribe some
of the verses that are incomprehensible, unless they bear
upon the judgment and life hereafter. In the seventeenth chapter, from the fifth to the ninth verse, we have
a description of the differing fates of the wicked and the
righteous, agreeing not only in sense, but in actual words,
with the previous testimony of David to the same truth
in the first Psalm. The ninth verse continues, "The
heart is deceitful above all things and desperately wicked;
who can know it? I, the Lord, *search the heart*, I try
the reins even *to give every man according to his ways,
and according to the fruit of his doings.*" (See also xxxii.
18, 19.) Now we know this will not be on earth, because
Malachi tells us that it will not be till the Lord maketh
up His jewels, according to the testimony of the book of
remembrance written before Him, that we shall "discern
between the righteous and the wicked, between him that
serveth God and him that serveth Him not." In xxii.
10, we find, "*Weep not for the dead, neither bemoan him;
but weep sore for him that goeth away; for he shall return no more, nor see his native country.*" But unless
the destiny of the dead be superior happiness, we must

equally bemoan them, as well as the exile, nay, still more;
for the exile may learn tidings of his country, may hope,
in spite of sorrowful reality, to behold it once again, may
find some enjoyment that would bid us cease to weep for
him; but if the dead have ceased to exist, they, still less
than the exile, "shall return no more, nor see their native country." Brief as the verse is, it is a powerful
witness as to the immortal hope with which the Hebrews
regarded death, and confirms the lesson taught them
years before in the death of Abijah—that death to the
good is more profitable than life.

"Am I a God at hand, saith the Lord, and not a God
afar off? can any one hide himself in secret places that
I shall not see him, saith the Lord? do not I fill heaven
and earth?" (xxiii. 23, 24.) If existence ended with
our residence on this little world, a mere atom in the vast
work of creation, what need was there either for this
knowledge or for that contained in chap. ix. 23, 24?
What would be either the use or warning of knowing
that the spirit of the Lord filled heaven as well as earth,
if we were never to know more of that heaven than its
name? And if death were annihilation, how easily could
we hide ourselves from the Lord, by self-destruction at
any moment! What is that withholds the hand of the
intending suicide? What has made man endure the
most terrible and unmitigated sufferings, rather than by
his own hand extinguish life? what but the unspoken,
but ever-active instinct that, though he may close *this*
life, he *cannot* annihilate existence? that, though his
eyes may see no more the light of day, God will still behold him? He cannot even in death hide himself from
Him; and this undying instinct is confirmed by the
words of the Lord Himself through Jeremiah. David
had already said, "Whither shall I go from thy spirit,

or whither shall I flee from thy presence? If I ascend *up into heaven, Thou art there.* If I make my bed in the grave, *behold Thou art there.* If I take the wings of the morning and dwell in the uttermost parts of the sea, even there shall thy hand lead me, and thy right hand shall hold me," with other passages applied to the ubiquity of the Eternal equally striking. And are not God's own words, "Can any one hide himself in secret places, that I shall not see him? do I not fill heaven and earth?" a direct and thrilling confirmation? And could these have been written by Hebrews, and received as God's inspiration by Hebrews, if belief in a future state, in the impossibility of annihilating existence, in the deathless nature of the spirit, had been things unknown, either to the individual writers or the mass whom they addressed? The same argument applies to the twenty-third and twenty-fourth verses of the ninth chapter. Why should so much stress be laid on "understanding and knowing the Lord that He exerciseth loving-kindness, judgment, and righteousness in the earth, and delighteth in these things," if life on earth were all? surely we should not be blamed if we preferred the wisdom which would guide us comfortably through our stated dwelling here, the might which would give us temporal dominion, the riches which would provide us with all sorts of luxuries and ease and influence. These things at least we might hope to understand, and make use of; but to that knowledge which we are told surpasses all other, our mere earthly nature never can perfectly attain; even the most righteous, the most spiritual are bounded in their yearning aspirations, their thirst for heavenly food; since the miseries, and evils, and sufferings of earth choke up and deaden the wisdom of God's word. They are constantly striving to realise faith, that He is indeed a God delighting in loving-kindness, judgment, and righteousness, and would do so, if the affairs of earth did not always seem to contradict these attributes. They are for ever lost in mists of darkness, and must cease to exist without either profit or comfort. But that this knowledge is placed by God Himself above all other, is in itself evidence of our spirits' immortality. He would never incite us to a study that we must die without perfectly attaining, unless He knew that there was a future existence laid up with Him, where "in His light we should see light," and all that was simple *faith* here would be the fulness of reality there. Except to firm believers in immortality, the twenty-third and twenty-fourth verses of the ninth chapter of Jeremiah must have been utterly unmeaning; and therefore that they *are* there, that it is God Himself proclaiming their consoling and glorious truths, ought to be all-sufficient to convince us, that the revelation was not merely known to the people of Israel, fallen as they were, but was *inseparable* from the religion of their God.

The same arguments equally apply to verses like these, with which all the prophets abound:—"The Lord hath appeared of old unto me, saying, Yea, I have loved thee with an *everlasting* love." To beings of a day, born to suffer a brief while and cease to exist, these words would be so devoid of meaning as almost to seem like mockery. The Almighty God could not so regard us, if He had doomed us to perish off the earth, as if we had never been. He could not love us with an *everlasting* love, if He had not planted a spirit within us, the emanation from Himself, which could understand and receive that deathless love; nor would He hold forth that love as an incentive for us to become righteous, if this earth were

all; for in the toil and trouble of this life, be it adversity
or prosperity, how seldom can we trace or distinguish
this promised everlasting love, save in the low still whisper *within* which, if we deny our immortal nature, is as
incomprehensible as the promise itself.   Such words, we
may be assured, would never be used to the mere creatures of a day, nor to men to whom the revelation of immortality was unknown.

The beautiful prophecy contained in the thirty-first
chapter, and which is generally supposed only to relate
to our temporal restoration, is to me quite as convincing
of our continued existence in a happier world, as any of
the more directly alluding passages : verses 31, 32, 33,
and 34 of course relate *only* to that thrice-glorious day
when, restored to our own land, we shall all, Jew and
gentile, know the Lord, and never turn from His covenant more; verses 35, 36, and 37 contain promises still
more sublime.   "Thus saith the Lord, who giveth the
sun for a light by day, and the ordinances of the moon
and stars for light by night; who divideth the sea when
the waves thereof roar, whose name is the Lord of Hosts,
If those ordinances depart from before me, saith the Lord,
then the seed of Israel also shall cease from being a
nation before me for ever.   Thus saith the Lord, *If* the
heavens above can be measured, and the foundations of
the earth searched out beneath, I will also cast off all
the seed of Israel for all that they have done, saith the
Lord."   And in the preceding chapter (verses 10, 11),
we find, "Therefore fear thou not, O my servant Jacob,
saith the Lord, neither be dismayed, O Israel; for, lo, I
will save thee from afar and thy seed from the land of their
captivity, and Jacob shall return, and shall be in rest and
in quiet, and none shall make him afraid.   For I am with
thee, saith the Lord, to save thee though I make a full

end of the nations whither I have scattered thee, yet will I not make a full end of thee; but I will correct thee in measure, and not leave thee wholly unpunished."

Now, dearest Annie, I have no doubt that, on the first reading, you will wonder what these verses can have to do with the promise of immortality. Simply, that *unless we* are immortal beings, and unless all Israel knew that they were such, the promises are, if not without meaning, utterly false, and impossible to be fulfilled. How has Israel been benefited by being that chosen seed of the Eternal, which is to endure until the work of creation can be searched out and understood, in other words, for ever, if physical death be the cessation of his existence? How can he be said to be in rest and quiet, to be corrected only *in measure*, and not made a full end of, when we glance back on the history of Israel from their first dispersion until this very present time, and read of misery, and blood, and torture, not of the frame alone, but of the heart, and of wholesale massacres and sufferings, at which even the flesh creeps, and every nerve tingles? Israel, indeed, still exists; but the millions on millions who have endured every possible and impossible suffering, and perished miserably *only* for being of this chosen seed, if death be annihilation, what is their reward for constancy to a persecuted faith and a Father's promises? Are not they made a full end of? cast off for all that, not they, but their ancestors have done; ceased for ever from being one of the chosen people; and is not all this in direct contradiction to the words of a God of truth? What good, temporal or spiritual, is it to remain Jews, if death brings the same "full end" to them as to all men? What is it that has so inspired Israel with the spirit of martyrdom, that men, women, and children have all chosen

the most cruel deaths—have endured the greatest indig-
nities to which human nature can be exposed—resigned
all affections, honours, luxuries, even life itself on earth
—what is it that has done this—what can have done
it, if the firm belief, almost the realisation, of their
spirits' immortality were not the very essence of their
faith and being? How could these gracious promises
have brought the comfort, the strength, which we know
they have done from the time of their bestowal, and
do still: unless Israel had, individually and nationally,
a perfect knowledge of his undying existence when this
life is closed? Without it nothing could have saved
him from complete amalgamation with the nations
amongst whom we have been scattered,—nothing but
an unchangeable hope and trust that individually each
would reap the fruit of his doings, sown in misery and
agony below, with Him who had said He would correct
in measure, "BUT NOT cast off entirely," though nationally their position was the lowest and most fearful trial
for their fathers' sins.

Dearest Annie, had we but these verses, we would
have enough to convince us of our destined immortality,
of our learning *after death* the full value of our heritage
as the seed of Abraham, and of our constancy to that
faith which God Himself, for Abraham's sake, bestowed.
If we would but engrave the verses I have quoted on
our hearts and minds, would but remember that they
are spoken by a God of Truth, "in whom there is no
variableness nor shadow of turning," whose words, once
spoken, are for everlasting: they would alike explain,
and receive confirmation from, the history of our people,
from the building of Jerusalem in the Past, to our restoration in the far Future. If the millions and millions
that have perished in these eighteen centuries of trial

and persecution are not, indeed, entirely "cast off for all that they have done," if they are only corrected in measure, and not made a full end of, which from God's own words we dare not for an instant suppose without the sin of doubting Him: we know they *must exist still;* and to exist still, there must be a portion of our nature that cannot die—there must be a world where that deathless essence moves and acts, and that world must be of a purer, happier, higher nature than this; for it is only by the exercise of our highest, purest, and most spiritual capabilities while on earth, that it can be even faintly imagined.

There are very many other verses and passages in Jeremiah, both in his Prophecy and his Lamentations, that could only be written by one who firmly believed in the immortality of the soul himself, and who felt assured that those whom he addressed believed in it also; but as to transcribe and comment upon them would only be a repetition of already reiterated arguments, I prefer leaving them to your own private consideration, convinced that, your mind once awakened, you will need but little more assistance to trace this glorious doctrine as clearly gleaming up through the whole Hebrew Scriptures as if written in direct words.

Ezekiel, too, having dilated upon him so fully in my fifteenth letter, I shall pass with very little notice. I have already told you that the life and death to which he refers in the eighteenth and thirty-third chapters, *can only mean* the life and death of *the soul,* as no effort whatever of the naturally righteous, no repentance, however earnest, of the wicked, can avert the death of the body, the physical cessation of existence. The third chapter, from the eighteenth to the twenty-second verse, the whole of the eighteenth chapter, the thirty-third chapter to the twenty-first verse, are all emphatic reiterations of the same subject, and *cannot* be twisted to mean anything else but the judgment of the soul apart from the body,—reiterated too at a time when all men seemed to share the same fate of sorrow and persecution, without the least manifest distinction between the righteous and the wicked, when all incentive to the worthy on earth seemed at an end, in order that not only might the individually righteous go on humbly rejoicing, and the individually wicked tremble, though judgment appeared delayed; and to tell us that the priests and guardians of Israel were guilty or not guilty in the sight of their God, according as they warned the people of their trespasses, or left them to their own devices. " So thou, O son of man, I have set thee a watchman unto the house of Israel; therefore thou shalt hear the word at my mouth, and warn them from me. When I say unto the wicked, O wicked man, thou shalt surely die: if thou dost not speak to warn the wicked from his way, that wicked man shall die in his iniquity; *but his blood will I require at thy hand.* Nevertheless, if thou warn the wicked of his way to turn from it, if he do not turn from his way: he shall die in his iniquity; *but thou hast delivered thy soul.*" Now, what can this mean, if death were the entire cessation of existence to all men? The righteous, and the wicked, and the watchman, whether he warned them or not, all must share the same fate. And again, why should God say, "As I live, I have no pleasure in the *death of the wicked:*" if death were annihilation, and no judgment beyond? We might rather suppose that the holy and righteous God would rejoice that His beautiful creation was encumbered no longer by sinners: nay, we know from His attributes, that so it would have been,

were there not a judgment beyond, and that judgment
for the wicked dying in his iniquity such, as the everlasting love, the infinite mercy of the Eternal, so revolted
from, that as a father He besought the very sinners to
repent—"Turn ye, turn ye from your evil ways, for why
will ye die, O house of Israel?" Neither these words,
nor those of verses 17, 18, 19, and 20,—"Yet the children of Israel say, The way of the Lord is not equal;
but as for them, their way is not equal. When the
righteous turneth from his righteousness and committeth
iniquity, *he shall even die thereby.* But if the wicked
turn from his wickedness, and do that which is lawful
and right, *he shall live thereby.* Yet ye say, the ways
of the Lord are not equal. O house of Israel, I will
judge you, every one after his ways,"—would ever have
been addressed to a people to whom *immortality had
still to be revealed.* Their objections "the ways of God
are not equal," meaning that on earth the ways of the
Eternal are so plunged in darkness, that we cannot discover who are objects of His favour and who are not,
are not peculiar to the Hebrews, but are raised in every
age and by the voice of every people, under whatever religious denomination they may be classed. God, through
His prophet, reproved this want of faith and unfounded
complaint; but unless the doctrine of immortality had
been revealed and received long before, His words would
have been without meaning and without power; for the
whole aspect of this world would have denied them.
You will wonder, perhaps, why I so constantly refer to
the idea of annihilation, as its impossibility is so self-
evident that it scarcely needs refutation. I refer to it
only to prove that the *ancient Hebrews* rejected it equally
with ourselves; that the Law and the Prophets unite in
bearing witness to the assertion that to the people of

God their immortal heritage was known from the very beginning; that to materialists, to those who believed physical death the end of existence, the Law and the Prophets would have been utterly devoid of meaning, and, to have reached the understanding so as to guide the people, must not only have been couched in very different language, but incited them to righteousness by very different rewards. Remember, dearest Annie, I do not only want to satisfy you individually as to the important fact of our immortality being preached throughout the Bible, but thoroughly to convince you that, as the very essence of our religion, it was known to, acted upon, and held forth as an incentive to the children of earth, from the death of Abel downwards—concentrated in the hearts of the righteous of the descendants of Shem and, emanating from them, and for their sakes, on those to whom the Law was given.

LETTER XXVIII.

FROM THE SAME TO THE SAME.

Subject continued—Of Ezekiel's testimony to our resurrection and restoration—Daniel, a mysterious prophet—Powerful witness to the
Hebrew's belief in immortality—Notice of his twelfth chapter, connection of immortality and resurrection—Minor prophets, written
for believers in a future state, infused by the doctrine of immortality
—Extracts, Amos, verse five—Micah vii. agrees with the thirty-first
chapter of Jeremiah, and contains the same truths—Extracts from
Habakkuk; power by faith to win salvation—Immortality revealed
in the necessity of faith; its merciful ordainment—Charge that faith
forms no part of Judaism, refuted—Its position, necessity, and rejection of all worship without it—Malachi confirms all the previous prophecies, and illustrates the law—Extract therefrom—Needs no comment—Fallacy of the charge against Judaism that it neither taught
nor believed in immortality—How we should prove it—Malachi
impossible to be turned into the sense of the materialist—Testimony
of the last prophet doubly important.

THE thirty-seventh chapter of Ezekiel is such an emphatic and thrilling description of the power of God to
restore the corrupt to life, and the resurrection of the
dead, that it needs no comment here, especially as it is
a subject distinct from immortality, and seldom or never
denied, as an article of the Jewish creed. The eight
concluding chapters of this same sublime prophet so
powerfully delineate our Holy Land, as it will be after
the resurrection and Israel's restoration, agreeing so
forcibly with the ordinances of the Law, and all the
promises of God, that to suppose the faith of the children of Israel will ever merge into another, appears

34

actually impossible to any one, who reads these chapters even without any other prophecy.

In Daniel, mysteriously incomprehensible as he generally is, we find exactly the same reference to our immortality and resurrection, and in the same imagry, though, if possible, still more forcibly and clearly (see chap. xii. 1–3): "At that time shall Michael stand up, the great prince who standeth for the children of thy people; and there shall be a time of trouble, such as never was, since there was a nation, even to that same time." This of course alludes to the end of the days before the tremendous revolution of earth and heaven, which the Scriptures tell us is to herald the restoration of Israel. "And at that time thy people shall be delivered, EVERY ONE THAT SHALL BE FOUND WRITTEN IN THE BOOK. And many of them that sleep in the dust shall awake, some TO EVERLASTING LIFE, and some to shame and everlasting contempt. And they that are wise shall shine as the brightness of the firmament, and they that turn many to righteousness, as the stars for ever and ever." (Dan. xii. 1–3.)

I have already given you my ideas on the perfect compatibility and connection of the two doctrines of Immortality and Resurrection, dearest Annie; and these verses forcibly confirm them. The bodies must indeed awake; for they have slept in death; but the souls which must rejoin them to fit them for everlasting life have never ceased to exist. Observe, too, the same figure is used by Daniel as Moses, David and Isaiah had used before, and Malachi after him, "The book of remembrance written before the Lord for those that feared Him, and thought often on His name." Do not heed the remarks of scorners, as to the impossibility of the literal words. In addressing man, that language and those figures were used which his senses could most clearly understand. In a higher state of existence there will be higher images found.

The words are so clear in themselves, that they need no comment. They do not contain a *mere allusion*, like many verses in the previous prophets, but *direct* intelligence, which cannot possibly be turned into any other meaning than the resurrection of the dead and consequent immortality of the soul, and the wide distinction which shall be made between the righteous and the wicked. "They that are wise," we know from the verses of Jeremiah which I have so often quoted, signifies the acquirers of that knowledge which God Himself has pronounced to be superior to every other, the knowledge of Himself—not the wisdom of either the learning, the ambition, or the wealth of this world; and "those that turn many to righteousness, as the stars for ever and ever" ought to urge us on, by example yet more than precept, to evince the superiority of the strivings after righteousness over every other thought and pursuit,— ought to rebuke that mock humility, which would bid us shrink from usefulness and good on the vain plea of unworthiness,—and to incite us by earnest individual endeavour "to do justly, to love mercy, and to walk humbly with our God," and, by the effects on domestic and social happiness thence proceeding, to lead others in the same safe and peaceful paths. With such words before us, distinguishing "those that turn many to righteousness" as destined for a glorious place in heaven, who can hold back, and pass through life without one thought, one hope, one effort for the benefit of his fellow-creatures?

"Many shall be purified, and made white, and tried, but the wicked will do wickedly, and none [therefore] of the wicked can understand; but the wise shall understand." This alludes to the same "end of days" as the previous verses, and marks very powerfully the distinction between those who, inclined to evil, yet resist it, and seek the good, and those who determinedly pursue wickedness, and so turn from them the grace of God "that their eyes are blinded and their ears heavy," so that they cannot understand His ways, and are left in His wrath to their own darkness; but the "wise shall understand," because they have "made the Lord their study, and know in what things are His delight."

Though in the minor prophets there may be but few verses which will bear in direct words on our immortality; yet it is as impossible to divide the doctrine from them as the soul or animating principle from ourselves. They could not have been written by men who were *not* believers in immortality, nor understood by a multitude to whom that truth had still to be revealed. The very moral and spiritual religion which they preached to vivify the Law and, removing mere formal observance, to restore it to its intended purity, proved *their* perfect acquaintance with a higher state of existence, and the multitude's acknowledgment of it as the individual essence of their religion. What would have been either the use or benefit of so cultivating the higher and purer qualities, as by so doing to approach nearer and nearer the likeness of God, if we were to share the common fate of all men, wicked as well as righteous, and die without once knowing the end and aim of their spiritual aspirations, the idea and love of our Maker still unsatisfied and unfilled? Why cultivate love, and reverence, and piety, in preference to earthly power, and wealth, and fame, if this little earth were our only destined sphere? But the question has been asked too often to need reiteration. I am only anxious that you should feel as strongly as I do, that every moral and spiritual precept of the prophets, presupposes immortality as the groundwork of their faith, and that they are without such supposition actually incomprehensible.

"For thus saith the Lord unto the house of Israel, SEEK YE ME, AND YE SHALL LIVE." "Seek ye the Lord, AND YE SHALL LIVE." "Seek Him that maketh the seven stars and Orion, and *turneth the shadow of death* UNTO THE MORNING, and maketh the day dark with night," etc. "*Seek good and not evil,* THAT YE MAY LIVE." (Amos v.)

The remarks already made wherein life and death are thus used, will equally apply to the above verses. I have only transcribed them as increasing the weight of evidence. And in the same way the words of Micah vii., "Who is a God like *unto* thee that pardoneth iniquity, and passeth by the *transgression of the remnant of his heritage?* He retaineth not his anger for ever, because he delighteth in mercy. He will turn again. He will have compassion upon us. He will subdue our iniquity, yea, Thou wilt cast all their sins into the depths of the sea. Thou wilt perform the truth to Jacob, and the mercy to Abraham, which Thou hadst sworn unto our fathers from the days of old," allude as strongly to immortality, and are as incomprehensible if we deny it, as the promises of the thirty-first chapter of Jeremiah already brought forward. By the words "the remnant of His heritage" it is unanswerably clear, that it is Israel in his miserable captivity, whom the prophet addresses; but what comfort, what truth, could there be in these promises, if there were no other state of existence? In every land, in every age, we have been and are subject to the most awful persecution and misery,

if not by actual violence, by contempt and abasement,
and being socially and politically denied our privileges
of men and citizens. We know and acknowledge these
things as the effect of our fathers' sins, in their determined departure from their law and their God; but unless there had been a clear revelation of another world,
where these temporary ills and sufferings cannot enter,
the promise of Micah was utterly false, and must have
been indignantly rejected by the mass, as impossible to
be fulfilled. How could our iniquity be pardoned? How
could the transgression of the *remnant* of His heritage
be passed over, if physical death entirely closed the
scene? How could He be declared not to retain His
anger for ever, but delight in mercy, and have compassion upon us, if a few brief troubled years of misery,
and but too often a death of horror, were the *sole* portion of the wretched Jews? How could the truth (or
promise) be performed unto (the seed of) Jacob, and the
mercy to (the seed of) Abraham, as sworn unto our
fathers in the days of old, if the countless millions who
have perished by persecution, the unborn thousands who
will yet die in their captivity, have no existence beyond
this earth, no individuality in heaven? It is useless to
follow the argument farther. If we believe in God and
in His word, the history of the Jews from their dispersion to the present time, in every age, and clime, and
people, is evidence trumpet-tongued of revealed and destined immortality.

"Art thou not from everlasting, O Lord my God, my
Holy One? WE SHALL NOT DIE" Habakkuk says in the
twelfth verse of his first chapter, following it with an
humble inquiry as to why "He who is of purer eyes than
to behold iniquity" should so bear with the treacherous
and wicked, as to permit them to go on their way

rejoicing and triumphing over the righteous; the subject does not conclude with the chapter, as the division
might lead us to suppose. The second continues it, by
the prophet declaring he will stand on the watch-tower
and look for the reply, but it was not to come distinctly.
God said, "Write the vision and make it plain upon the
tables, that he may run that readeth it. For the vision
is yet for an appointed time, but at the end it shall
speak and not lie. Though it tarry *wait* for it, because
it will surely come, it will not tarry." This alludes to
the inspirings of the prophetic spirit within him reproving the impatience which would see the end at once.
The next verse answers his inquiries directly. "The
soul which is lifted up [to inquire more than God
chooses to reveal] is not upright within him; BUT THE
JUST SHALL LIVE BY HIS FAITH." In these few words
we have one of the sublimest references to our immortal
destiny which the prophets contain. What could be the
use of faith, if we were only created for a life which is,
as it were, revealed to mortal sight? There is no virtue
so scoffed at, and so little understood, as that which God
Himself declares will win us LIFE! And it is because it
is of Him, that it leads to Him, and therefore seemingly
is of no possible use in a mere worldly career, that it *is*
so scorned. The very fact of its being deemed romance,
and folly, and superstition by men whose only aim is to
amass wealth, and who live up to all the goods and plea
sures and luxuries of earth, whose minds are so nar-
rowed that they can see nothing beyond their individual
interests, and so declare they will believe nothing but
what can be proved, nothing but what they can understand,—this very fact is proof of its spiritual and deathless nature, incompatible with the mere animal or earthly
part of our existence. Created as we are with capa

bilities, feelings, impulses, aspirations for ever looking
beyond, utterly distinct from, the wants of the animal,
there would and must be constant suffering without
faith; and were there no other existence, we may be
sure a merciful God would have created us differently.
He would never have endowed us with faculties doomed
to die imperfect. He would never have promised that
the just shall LIVE by his faith, if there were not some
other existence where that faith would be swallowed up
in reality, and our vain yearnings all be filled. He
would never have given this solemn promise, if there
were nought beyond the present scene; for it would be
demanding a most difficult virtue from His children,
which would neither profit nor save them, and could
only excite thoughts, and hopes, and feelings never to be
fulfilled. And not only are these blessed words evidence
unanswerable of a revealed and destined immortality, but
contain in themselves the most intrinsic evidence of their
divinity. None but the universal Father would have
made the sole condition of His children's salvation a
virtue *attainable by all*, from the lowest to the highest,
the poorest to the wealthiest, the most deficient in intellect to the wisest, the youngest child to the greatest
sage. None but the Eternal, to whom all creation and
all time are revealed, would have demanded a virtue
utterly distinct from the things of sense and sight, the
use of which could only be known to Him and with Him.
Had wisdom, power, and riches been made the condition
of LIFE, how few could have attained to it; but *faith* is
in the power of all, though not all may choose to encourage and use it. And because it *is* in the power of
all, because it is absolutely necessary not only for our
happiness as individuals, but for our obedience and loving service, as children and subjects of our God, because

without it neither reason, nor riches, nor might could enable us to understand, and to endure calmly the evil, and sin, and sufferings in ourselves and around us, because without it, even God Himself must be denied or doubted: *therefore*, it is made the condition of our salvation and acceptance; and O, how thankful should we be that so it is! How often are there conditions and circumstances in life, when we can do nothing but *believe*, when we can realise nothing but faith, when prayer itself seems to have lost its comfort, when the spirit is so crushed under the burden of the clay that the very sense of God's love is darkened, when all that had seemed beautiful and good is changed into deformity and evil, when our very wisdom and reason seem leagued against us, and tell us all is vanity and vexation. Still, still, if we can but *believe* that all will be clear again, that our Father has not forsaken us, though the comfort of resting on Him seems to have departed, if we can but feel "Yea, though he slay me, yet will I trust in Him:" we are safe—safe, though every outward service is denied us, safe, however man may deem us wanting, safe, not only for eternal life, but for returning temporal joy.

And yet, dearest Annie, there are those who declare the Jews have no faith; that faith forms no part of Judaism; ay, even amongst ourselves I have heard this charge, and every pulse has throbbed with the vain wish to prove to them their great, their fearful error. Habakkuk does but reiterate that which the Hebrews had known from the time that "Abraham *believed* in the Lord, and his faith was accounted to him as righteousness," and Moses was rebuked when he struck the rock, "because ye believed me not," through all the varied phases of their history—rebellion, and doubt, and insubordination which had obtained yet more powerful domi-

nion in the time of the prophets than before; and even
they, holy and righteous men, were led to demand how
it was the wicked should so triumph and that He, who
was of purer eyes than to behold iniquity, could yet
bear with them, forgetting in the triumphs around them
the words of their prophet-king, "That when the wicked
flourish, it is that they shall be destroyed for ever." And
God, therefore, in His mercy, declares that the vision, or
His judgment between the righteous and the wicked,
"shall yet speak and not lie;" that though it tarry, man
was calmly to wait for it; for "the soul which is lifted
up to inquire more than it is right or needful for man
in this world to know, is not upright within him;" but
the just, however tried and sad his life on earth, is
secure of LIFE IN HEAVEN through his FAITH.

.And this is all repeated, in different words perhaps,
but exactly the same sense, in the last of the prophets,
Malachi.   Though containing only four chapters, it is to
me one of the most important of the prophetic books.
As, however, my present task is only to bring together
all the scriptural evidence of the revelation of immortality, I cannot enter upon it as it deserves.   The 13th,
14th, and 15th verses of the third chapter reiterate the
people's complaint, that it is vain to serve God, and what
profit is it to keep his ordinances, and walk mournfully
before Him?   "The proud are happy, they that work
wickedness are set up, yea, that tempt God are delivered."   And are not these the unspoken, perhaps, but
the constant thoughts of the many in the present day?
ay, coming sometimes even to those whose hearts are
right with God?   And what is God's reply?   Words
which we have quoted so many times in the course of
our correspondence, that it would seem almost needless
to transcribe them here, were .they not needed as the

last precious link in the chain of evidence as to the Hebrew's knowledge of his immortality, which the Bible gives: "Then they that feared the Lord spoke often one to another, and the Lord hearkened and heard it, and a book of remembrance was written before Him for them that feared the Lord and thought upon His name; and they shall be mine, saith the Lord, on that day when I make up my jewels, and I will spare them, as a man spareth his own son that serveth him. THEN SHALL YE RETURN AND DISCERN between the righteous and the wicked, between him that serveth God and him that serveth Him not. For behold, the day cometh that shall burn as an oven; and all the proud, yea, and all that do wickedly, shall be stubble, and the day that cometh shall burn them up, saith the Lord of Hosts, and it shall leave them neither root nor branch; but unto you that fear my name shall the sun of righteousness arise, with healing in his wings. And ye shall go forth and grow as calves in the stall, and ye shall tread down the wicked; for they shall be as ashes under the soles of your feet on the day that I do this, saith the Lord of Hosts."

With verses like these, is it possible that either Jew or Christian can need more to prove to him the solemn truth that immortality *was revealed* to the Hebrews as a people ages before the Christian era, and that it is addressed *to* the Jews? that the promises are made to no *new* creed, but to the followers of the Mosaic Law? And that to keep faithful to that Law, as far as their captivity would permit, was *the* proof of their righteousness before God, is revealed in the next verse:—"REMEMBER YE THE LAW OF MOSES MY SERVANT, WHICH I COMMANDED UNTO HIM IN HOREB FOR ALL ISRAEL, THE STATUTES AND JUDGMENTS." How, then, can we, dare we, by indifference and silence, by living as if we had no thought or hope beyond this earth, give a colouring to the mistaken idea that all our knowledge of and belief in immortality is derived, unconsciously to ourselves, from our intercourse with Christians? that it forms, and formed, no part of the Jewish faith? How can Jew or Christian read the Old Testament and yet believe this? And, still more remarkable—how is it that no Jew has ever yet, frequently and variously as this charge has been made, turned to his Bible and replied, his immortal hope is there? It is *not* enough to assert we believe in it, that all our ancient fathers make it the groundwork of their writings: we must *prove* it ours from that one Book, which both religions believe divine.

The verses I have transcribed need no comment, dearest Annie. No effort of the unbeliever can twist them into any other meaning than that future state, where ALONE the distinction between the righteous and the wicked can be discerned. They may cavil and scepticise on the term "Book of Remembrance;" but their remarks are of small importance to the believer, who knows that all such human terms are merely used by the infinite compassion of the Eternal, to reach the limited comprehensions of the *human* beings whom He addresses; and that to appeal to them in the imagery of heaven would be as perfectly useless and incomprehensible to them as to speak in the finest poetry to a new-born babe. The meaning is, simply, that not a thought, or word, or feeling which aspires to the fear and love of God, passes unnoticed by Him; that, although the righteous may seem forgotten on earth and the wicked to triumph unrebuked, although those that seek to love and serve Him are tried by every kind of suffering, and those that care not for Him are prosperous and happy, for the former (the righteous) every sigh and tear of uncomplaining pain, every word and action tending to God's glory, are nevertheless registered with Him, to mark them as His when physical death has closed this outward scene; while as to the wicked, they flourish to be consumed, root and branch, from before the Lord. This is the meaning of Malachi's words, agreeing alike in imagery and sense with all the prophets who wrote before him, and still more clearly given, to console and strengthen us in the path of right when the prophetic spirit had utterly departed from us, and Israel for continued iniquity was left to his own devices and doomed to drain the cup of fury proffered by all the nations. The distinction between the righteous and the wicked could be made even less visibly then, than when God still spoke to Israel through His prophets; and therefore, lest they should despair, His mercy inspired His last prophet to write such a promise as could not be mistaken or twisted into any other sense. This is the inexpressible comfort of Malachi, the intrinsic evidence of its divinity and truth.

35

LETTER XXIX.

FROM THE SAME TO THE SAME.

Subject continued—Evidence of the book of Job—Supposition as to
its identity and authorship—Its intent—Imbued with a belief in immortality—The belief referred to in divers terms by Elihu; agrees
with the testimony of both Law and Prophets—The multitudes familiar
with the subject—The *truth witnessed* by the writings of our sages;
the thousands of our martyrs—Not received from Christians—Hebrew literature entirely distinct from Christians'—Immortality
proven by constancy in persecution, from the martyr-mother downward—The basis and essence of all our writings.

WITH the prophecy of Malachi, dearest Annie, we concluded the chain of evidence which the Bible gives us
as to the Hebrew's right both to revealed and destined
immortality. Your remarks, as I have proceeded, have
given me real comfort; for when the heart and mind are
full of a subject, it often happens that we fail to bring it
as clearly and consolingly before the affections and understanding of another as it is to our own.

You are surprised that I have not brought forward
the Book of Job as additional evidence, as it appears to
you that in Elihu's address there are some verses that
bear very strongly on the subject. There are; but I did
not mention them till we had fully examined the more
important references to the subject. The Book of Job
has given rise to more speculation than any other in
the Holy Scriptures; some even going so far as to declare Job to be merely an imaginary character, and his
whole life a moral tale written by Moses to convey

certain truths to the people more engagingly than as mere axioms. But that there *was* such a character as Job, and that he was pre-eminent for his piety and righteousness, we know to be an undoubted truth, from the fact of God Himself referring to him through His prophet Ezekiel, no less than twice in the fourteenth chapter. "Though these three men, Noäh, Daniel, and Job, were in it, they should but deliver their own souls through their righteousness, saith the Lord God" (fourteenth and twentieth verses). That he lived before the Law was given, we may infer from the mode of life described being patriarchal, and having no reference whatever to the ordinances of the Law. It is possible that the narrative is enlarged, and the conversations made fuller and more in regular order, than took place in reality, for the purpose of illustrating the solemn truth, that man may not question the ways of his Maker; that it is enough for him to know that God is wise, and merciful, and good; that to suppose trial sent from Heaven proves some sin and iniquity in the appointed sufferer, is as wrong as for that sufferer to imagine that his endeavours after righteousness ought to have exempted him from trial; that the Eternal's dealings with man are as inscrutable as His work of creation; and that till man can penetrate the latter, he may not hope without impiety to explain the former. Such has always appeared to me the real meaning of this sublime book. Its elevated style seems to mark Moses as its author, and most probably during his sojourn with his father-in-law Jethro, in Midian. It is completely distinct from the style and language of either the Historical Books or Prophets; but that its author was inspired, as all the other writers of the Sacred Scriptures, there can be no doubt, or it would not have stood the test of ages.

Whoever compiled it believed in a revealed immortality himself, and taught it to others. Read over the thirty-third chapter attentively, especially from the twelfth to the thirty-first verse, and you will find the infinite mercy of God to save man through trial and probation from eternal death most clearly revealed. God speaketh once and twice, sometimes through outward circumstances of life, sometimes in the visions of the night, when deep sleep falleth upon men, but still man perceiveth it not. Then He openeth their ears, that He may withdraw man from his proud and evil purpose, and so save his *soul* from the grave, his life from a violent end. He chasteneth him with such strong pain through the multitude of his bones, that his life abhorreth bread and dainty meat; his flesh is consumed away that it cannot be seen; and his bones, which were not seen, stick out. Death is near, both physically and spiritually; but if then there be found a messenger, or interpreter, or angel with God, pointing out to Him some uprightness in the sufferer, God will be gracious unto him, and, delivering his *soul* from going down into the pit, declare He hath found a ransom for him; his flesh shall be fresher than a child's, he shall return unto the days of his youth. He will pray unto God, and He will be favourable unto him; and he [the purified] shall see His [God's] face with joy, for He [God] will render unto man his righteousness, imperfect as it may be, still it has been remembered, and so saved his soul, for such must be the real meaning of verses 24, 25, and 26. It is no return to mere physical life and health; for the flesh of a child and days of youth cannot return to middle age without a miraculous intervention, which, even in Bible times, was never the case; and we know that it *is* middle or old age, from the expression, " he

shall *return* unto the days of his youth." Man cannot
see the face of his God, nor trace on earth the reward
for his righteousness; therefore these verses can only
mean that, purified by suffering, his *soul* has put on its
angelic nature, and is saved from that darkness to which
a continuance in iniquity must have consigned it. Nor
will suffering be *always* needed to produce this blessed
effect. "God looketh down on man," verse 27 continues,
"and if any say, I have sinned and perverted the right,
and it profiteth me not: He will deliver his soul from
going into the pit, and his life shall see the light." How
exactly these consoling verses agree with the thirty-
second Psalm, "I said I would *confess my transgressions*
unto the Lord, and thou forgavest the iniquity of my
sin;" and with the spirit of all the Prophets, and the
words of Ezekiel, "When the wicked man turneth from
his wickedness, and doth that which is lawful and right,
he shall save his soul alive;" and how utterly devoid of
meaning, unless applied to that world, where alone our
life can see the light. "Lo, all these judgments God
worketh oftentimes with man, that He may bring his
soul from the grave, to be *enlightened with the light of
the living.*" And in the thirty-fourth chapter Elihu reproves Job for thinking, "that it profiteth a man nothing
that he should delight himself in God. Hearken unto
me," he continues, "ye men of understanding, far be such
wickedness from God, and iniquity from the Almighty.
For the work of man shall He render unto him, and
cause every man to find according to his ways. Yea,
surely God will not do wickedly, nor the Almighty pervert judgment. Who hath given them a charge over the
earth, or who hath disposal the whole world? If He
set his heart on man, He *gathereth to Himself his spirit
and his breath*, [though] all *flesh* may perish together,

35*

and man turn again unto dust." This agrees exactly with the words of the Prophets on the same solemn subject; and the arguments I brought forward when examining them, that the very promise of rendering unto every man according to his ways, presupposes a revelation and belief in another and purer state of existence, bear equally upon Job. "There is no darkness nor shadow of death where the workers of iniquity may hide themselves" (v. 22), is another such perfect agreement with the words of Jeremiah (xxiii. 24), "Can any one hide himself in secret places, that I shall not see him? saith the Lord: do I not fill heaven and earth?" on which I wrote so fully, that it would not need a separate notice, did it not so *exactly confirm* my argument, that death *cannot be annihilation,* or we could *easily* hide ourselves from God.

We find in Job, then, both strong and conclusive additions to the chain of evidence proving immortality which *our* Scriptures give. That its author was a Hebrew, and the book received and read by Hebrews, no one can deny; and, therefore, if we grant that it does refer to immortality, we must also grant that the revelation was already known and believed in, or the references to it would have received neither attention nor belief.

Diverse as are the respective characteristics of the writers on this subject, widely distinct as are their individual positions, separate as are the periods of their existence, all use the same imagery—all refer to the same pre-revealed and self-confirming truth. In addressing the multitudes, if they had been utterly ignorant of the subject, the inspired servants of God would have either *not* alluded to it at all, or spoken it in direct terms, as the apostles of Jesus did to the heathen nations. But the Hebrew multitudes, how ver sunk in sin and misery, however they might long for temporal relief, and be guided in their age of darkness more by the hope of temporal reward and the fear of temporal chastisement, yet knew their souls were deathless, that they *could not* hide themselves from the searching eye of God, even by falling on the swords of their enemies, or being consumed on their own fires. We cannot read the Bible without feeling this; we cannot be followers of God's Holy Law and believe in His proclaimed attributes without, from our very souls, believing it.

Once convinced that our Bible is the foundation and the support of this belief, that it bears in itself undeniable witness of the glorious revelation being the heritage of Israel from the very beginning, and so was universally known to the seed of Abraham long ages before the Christian era, little more is needed. The truth is evidenced not merely by the writings of our sages, but by the thousand and thousand martyrs who, ranking amid the very lowest and most ignorant of the Jewish multitude, had yet so firm a faith in the reward awaiting those who remained true to the God of their fathers, so deep a horror of the punishment of apostasy, that it was comparatively easy to die themselves by the most cruel tortures, and see their wives and children die, than embrace the faith of the stranger. There was *then* no peaceful and friendly blending of Hebrew and Christian, as there is now; and if there had been, the Roman Church of the middle ages kept its doctrines of religion somewhat too closely the portion of the priests, for the Jews to have learned any ideas of immortality through them. I am aware that it is said repeatedly, that the Jews of England cannot feel as the Jews of former times; because they must have imbibed, from association with Christia .. so many of their religious ideas. This is an assertion made by those who can know nothing of Jewish literature, and very little of Jewish history. The writings of our sages, various as they are, mostly bear date when the intermixture of Jew and Christian was utterly unknown; when there were no printed books and few manuscripts; and when, in fact, the Christian religion held sway over a very small portion of the globe, and its doctrines had neither been clearly defined, nor settled within themselves, as is proved from the multiplicity of schisms in the early churches. Our writings bear also intrinsic evidence of their perfectly Jewish origin, from their containing many exclusive and rigid, and also speculative theories, entirely opposed to the Christian creed. The only books which contain English translations of the writings of our sages with which I am acquainted, are the "Conciliator" of Menasseh Ben Israel, which contains the views of very many of our authors; the Hebrew Review, in which we find long and most interesting quotations from Maimonides, Joseph Albo, Jacob ben Asher ben Jehiel, Nachmanides, portions of the Talmud and Mishnah, with comments on the latter by Naphtali Hertz Wesseley; and a compilation from our earliest sages in four sermons, by Rabbi Abram Belais, in all of which the doctrine of the soul's immortality is so completely the groundwork, that to deny the belief to the Jews as a people, is one of the most unfounded and mistaken assertions ever made. It cannot be seriously entertained by any one, whatever his creed may be, who is at all acquainted with our literature; but as that literature is, for the most part, Hebrew, and entirely unattainable to the mass of either Jews or Christians, it becomes a positive duty to know and give our reason and foundation for this belief. It is not enough either for our own satisfaction, or the information of honest enquirers of another creed, merely to believe, and assert that belief. We must point to the Book which both parties believe divine, and establish that the foundation of all we believe is *there;* that from thence all the writings of our sages spring; and that the whole history of persecution evinces that immortal hope which, as the heritage of Israel from ages past, *alone* created martyrs. Unless it had been as clearly known and revealed to us as we are told it is to Christians, what could have sustained us in the mental and bodily sufferings of the countless victims of hate and persecution? What could have upheld us at the stake, or bade us endure famine, torture, heart-crushing agony in seeing beloved ones droop, and suffer, and die, without the power of saving them, when one word of retractation would have given us life, and honour, and temporal peace? Every religion has had its martyrs, but none like the Jews. None have been such marked victims of every clime and every age; liable even now, in this era of freedom and enlightenment, to crushing degradation, physical torture, we need a spirit of endurance far more than any other race on the face of the globe. And if we had no immortal hope, what could be our sustainer? Dearest Annie, were there no evidence but this, were our Bible and its commentators mute as to the revelation of this doctrine, we should still have enough, more than enough, in the history of our martyrs, to prove how completely it was the indivisible essence and vital breath of our creed. The martyr-mother in the time of Antiochus, by her addresses to each of her tortured sons, marks in what manner this consoling and strengthening belief actuated the Israelites in their various ages of martyrdom. No one who reads this remarkable chapter in the Apocrypha,* and remembers that it lays bare the heart and mind of an Israelitish mother, taken indiscriminately from the people (not one of either higher rank or talent than her fellows), and living several centuries before the Christian era, but must allow that the firm hope and consolation of immortality must have been known and clearly defined to Israel; must have been indivisible from their creed; must have been revealed as divine, or in such a moment it must utterly have failed. No merely human imaginings could, in such a trial, have had either power or strength.

I wish I could have given you some extracts from the authorities I have quoted, in support of my own arguments; but the doctrine so completely *imbues* their writings, that it would be difficult to quote them without transcribing whole pages. I am wrong to say my *own* arguments; as they are arguments founded mainly on the opinions of all orthodox Jewish commentators on the word of God, only so far simplified as to be divided from the metaphysical speculations and researches in which our sages so delighted to indulge. But the immortality of the soul is never made a matter of either metaphysics or speculation; it is the one simple divine truth, indivisible from the belief in the existence of a God of justice and love, on which every other doctrine and ordinance of religion, and metaphysical and speculative enquiry, is founded. Deny them this truth, and the ancient sages of Israel could not have written a single line. Instead of which, it shines up from their mighty tomes in such clear and lucid light, that the Christian enquirer has

---

* Apocrypha, 2 Maccabees, chap. viii. The subject has been already so enlarged upon in the "Women of Israel," that it would be plagiarism in the author to do more than merely notice it here.

but to seek them, to perceive how little was its revelation through Jesus needed to us, the first-born of the
Lord. To the heathen nations, indeed, it was, and God
in His infinite mercy permitted a religion grafted on
Judaism, and the very apostles of which were all Jews,
to carry it abroad, that even in our dispersion, and captivity, and banishment from our God, in the seed of
Abraham, and from the revelation *first* made to them "all
the nations of the earth shall be blessed."

LETTER XXX.

FROM THE SAME TO THE SAME.

Subject concluded—Mendelssohn's Phaedon incomplete—Supposition
as to the wherefore the destiny of soul should be so veiled—No necessity for faith were it revealed—Word of God enough—Impossibility for the finite to understand the infinite—Death no chastisement were the soul's destiny revealed—Instinct, the incentive to
procure the good and depart from evil, not enough for immortal
beings—Death of the soul—Opinions concerning excision—Should
be guided by Scripture, not speculation—Opinion of Maimonides—
Excision not annihilation—No cessation of existence—Suppositions
of futurity allowable, if based on God's word—Ideas on celestial
beings—Whence founded—Gradations of rank in the hosts of heaven—Individual suppositions; general Jewish ideas of Satan, hell,
and evil angels; whence founded—Reconciliation of the discoveries
of the astronomers with the scriptural revelation of immortality:
neither necessity nor basis for doubt—Idea of a previous existence
neither biblically nor internally proved; of a better and purer,
proved by both—Impossibility to flee from God—Imperative necessity to cultivate the spiritual; belief in immortality cannot be attained without effort; its vast importance in this life, and unspeakable consolation.

My last communication was shorter than usual, dearest
Annie; because I rather wished you to bring forward
yourself the farther questions to which our lengthened
examination of this important subject may have given
rise, than start them myself. Correctly, as I perceive
by your letter, I have surmised them.

I did not add Mendelssohn's Phaedon to my list of
authorities as to the Jewish opinion of the immortality
of the soul, because, bold as the declaration may seem,
the work disappointed me. As the supposed opinions

of a heathen philosopher, reasoning from analogy, from acute perception, from the extraordinary power of a mind unusually gifted, but unenlightened by revelation, the work is perfect. We feel that reason alone is sufficient for conviction, that the soul cannot be annihilated, and must have a separate existence. As the work of a Jewish believer, to whom the Holy Scriptures in their original tongues and all their commentators were open, it is incomplete and disappointing. He could not, indeed, have put into the mouth of Socrates, allusions to a Divine revelation; he could not have infused the spirit of a heathen with the spirit of a Jew; but when the Phaedon was accomplished, when he had concluded his imaginary conversation, which proved so clearly, that even to the unenlightened by religion the soul's immortality was a realised and accepted fact, he should have added a chapter with the views of the Jew, and proved that, though reason was the guide of the heathen, FAITH was enough for the Hebrew, and that God's revealed attributes taught him in a few brief words, what the heathen needed argument on argument to prove. Had he done this, he would indeed have left us a debt no after-ages could repay; he would have provided strength and consolation for the young and weak amongst his own, and checked at once the charge of immortality not being a part of Judaism. His book, whose widely spread popularity has brought such honour to his name, would have evinced not merely the sound reasoning of the philosopher, but the pure faith of a Scriptural Jew, and done more for the honour and glory of his holy religion than any modern Hebrew had accomplished. These are merely individual opinions, my dearest Annie, and I am very bold, perhaps, to put them forward; but the feeling of disappointment with which I laid down the book was absolutely painful. There was no evidence of the Hebrew within its pages; the follower of any creed might have compiled it. It could not teach the Christian the immortal hope and spiritualised faith of the Jew; and therefore, though it may bid us venerate the genius of the philosopher, we cannot quote or lean upon it as a witness of the faith of a believer.

Why should a doctrine of such vast importance be always bounded by mere conjecture?—you ask me, dearest Annie. You do not mean conjecture as to the truth of our immortality, since that could not be clearer, but as to the nature of the soul, and its destiny hereafter, both as to reward and punishment. You must remember, that our mingled human and spiritual nature, while on earth, will not allow the perfect comprehension of spiritual things; that we are in a *preparatory* state of existence, while in this body and on the earth; that even were the precise nature of the soul and the glory and bliss of heaven more clearly revealed, we should either no more understand them, than an infant the pleasures of a virtuous and perfected manhood, or it would entirely unfit us for those duties which we are commanded to attend to here, and (stronger reason than either) there would be no exercise for that virtue— FAITH, the encouragement or non-encouragement of which marks the heart right or wrong with God. I have endeavoured throughout our correspondence to prove to you the absolute necessity of faith for our acceptance before God, that throughout our Scriptures it is made almost the sole condition of our salvation, because if we have faith, obedience and love follow instinctively, and God will be served and loved, because we believe He is the being He has proclaimed Himself. We *believe* that our souls are an emanation from Him, and therefore deathless; we believe that He has laid up with Him, for those that love Him, fulness of joy and life everlasting. If all were revealed, where would be the excuse of this saving virtue? Man may laugh it to scorn, may suppose it fit only for women and children, may declare he will believe nothing without proof; but as long as we have the word of God to tell us that faith *is* righteousness and *life*, we deserve to forfeit His blessing if we renounce it because the multitude may do so, and by baleful example invite us to follow. There is, perhaps, to the generality of mankind, no virtue more difficult to attain, more especially in this fearfully utilitarian age; but its very difficulty marks its union with the spiritual part of our nature and its absolute necessity, if we wish to make any advance beyond this earth, and its confusing interests and worldly thoughts. We bear within ourselves, if we would listen to its "still small voice," evidence of a higher and purer destiny than life on earth; we have God's word to tell us our souls were created in His image, and must, therefore, be like Himself immortal, to reveal an existence beyond the grave, and to assure us, that *there* the distinction between the righteous and the wicked will be discerned; and what more do we need? If we believe God is truth, we are as assured of our immortality, as though it were based on palpable and visible certainty. It is often argued, that no one has returned to tell us what follows death; but it is God's mercy that withholds this return, for our human nature could not bear the visible presence of a spirit, merely to read of which will cause the flesh to creep and the blood to curdle; and even if we could, is it possible that we should believe the word of a fellow-creature more than the word of God? On almost every subject, while on earth, our thoughts are pounced, be-

cause, while in a finite body, we cannot hope to understand the infinite. We know enough for our guidance,
while in this state of existence; and FAITH will or ought
to be sufficient to convince us, that our future destiny
will so be ordered by a God of love as to satisfy every
high, and pure, and ennobling aspiration, the faint whisperings of which we have felt even on earth, to permit
us the indulgence of the highest feelings, perfected virtue,
adoration, unshadowed love, and active service which
real love ever prompts, without one of those imperfections and painful alloys to which, in this life, even the
purest emotions are subject. That in His presence is
the fulness of joy, and at His right hand everlasting
pleasure; that with Him is the fountain of life, and in
His light we shall see light; that He hath declared
through His prophet, that eye hath not seen, neither
hath the ear heard, what He hath prepared for those
that love Him, are sufficient, if we believe the Bible, for
us to imagine the destiny of the righteous.

Were more revealed, were certainty the portion of
the children of the earth, as to the glories of heaven:
there would not only be no need for faith (and without
which no service is acceptable), but death would not
be, as it is intended, the chastisement to which all men
are liable, from the universal liability to evil. As all
men, however righteous in the main, however desirous
of walking in the paths of righteousness, have still
faults and imperfections, and are never perfectly holy in
the sight of the holy God, as none can be so justified
before Him, as to have no need of either purification or
chastisement, to render their hearts more perfect: death
comes to all indiscriminately, either by the suffering
of disease, to purify the departing; or by the anguish
of bereavement to impress on man, that this world is

not all, and so startle him with a consciousness of God and religion, which, without such trial, might never have been his. We are to live by faith, we are told. If, however, the reward of the good and the punishment of the wicked were clearly visible, where would be the incentive to choose the good and eschew the evil, save instinct alone? We require no instruction not to meddle with fire, because its ill effects are palpable and known. We cannot possibly take any credit to ourselves for not touching it, because the mischief we should do ourselves is so very evident. Now, if we could *be quite sure* that by pursuing evil instead of good, we were exposing our immortal souls to the same suffering through endless eternity, as we do our bodies when in contact with a destructive element: not all the temptations and allurements of sin would have more effect upon us, than the inviting blaze on a frosty day, when we make use of its warmth, but would not think of throwing ourselves into it. In the same manner, the delight of reciprocal affection is (as it were) so palpable, so love-rewarding, that there is not the least credit attached to us for indulging in it. Its effects produce such happiness, that we care not for any intervening obstacle or trial, so we can attain it at last: we are *certain* of what we seek, and therefore we seek it instinctively. So would it be were the bliss after death clearly revealed. The same mere instinct would lead us to strive for good, as to avoid suffering. But instinct is a mere animal guide: immortal beings demanded something more, both as to the greater difficulty of obedience and belief in a Father's word. Earth is indeed fraught with temptation. The path of evil is infinitely easier to tread than the path of good, and brings with it much more palpable joys and pleasures, and all the triumph of success.

And this is all permitted as a trial of that virtue—faith, the childlike reliance on a Father's word, which is more acceptable than any other.   Even in the common intercourse of man with man, what insult is greater than doubting or denying an alleged truth? and can we not imagine that to doubt God's word is so sinning against His holiness and truth as to deprive us of the good, in which, because He has merely *said* but not *proved* it, we disbelieve?

With regard to that "death of the soul" to which I have so often told you that I believe Moses and almost all the sacred and prophetic writers refer, and called by the Jewish writers excision, our opinion must be still more bounded than concerning the destiny of the righteous.   All the Rabbinical writers, however they may differ as to the *precise* nature of this punishment, agree as to its infliction being in the hands of God alone, and utterly distinct from the practical jurisprudence of the Hebrews.   Their opinions are, as was unavoidable, much too speculative for instruction or guidance.   Some, founded on the supposition that a long life on earth is *always* a sign of favour in the sight of God, imagine that sudden and early death is meant by the term, "the soul shall be cut off;" but this appears to me to be too contradictory to the spirit of the Scriptures which, in the death of Jeroboam's young son, *because* of the good found in him; in the death of Josiah, *because* his heart was tender, and he humbled himself before God; in the expression of David, "*precious* in the sight of the Lord is the *death* of his saints;" in the words of Isaiah, "the righteous is taken from the evil to come;" and also of Ezekiel, "I have *no pleasure* in the *death* of the wicked, but rather that he should turn from his wickedness and *live*," seems to teach us, that early death rather evinces favour than displeasure in the sight of God, and that the wicked are often spared longer than the truly righteous, that they may "repent and live." Of course, on this subject there can be no certain opinion; our only safety lies in reasoning on the words of Scripture, not in our own speculations. According to them the close of physical existence in youth or age can never mean the punishment of excision. The sinner may be violently removed in his early youth by accident or disease; because through the prayers and efforts of righteous relations, and the mercy of His God, he may be thus removed from a continuance in iniquity, which would doom him to an eternity of woe. The righteous may be removed in his first youth or engaging childhood; because he may not need the purifying trials and sufferings of earth, or is taken, because some good thing is found in him, "from the evil to come." The sinner may live to the full age of mortality, either to give him time to turn from his iniquity that he may live; or because his sins have so turned God from him, "that he flourished like grass to be destroyed for ever." The righteous servant of God may live the full length of days on earth tried by adversity and sorrow; because God has seen that probation was needed to perfect the seeds of virtue, and by trial on earth he would be prepared to shine as the stars of heaven for evermore; or that he might do his Father's work on earth, by teaching man the blessing, and hope, and strength of a religious life and unchanging trust in God. No man, therefore, can attempt to pronounce judgment on the ways of God, as marked in the varied close of physical existence, nor imagine for a single moment, that an early death presupposes some iniquity for which "the soul should be cut off."

My own opinion as to the meaning of excision is that of Maimonides, "Death in this world, and perdition in the life to come; that the soul, a distinct essence from the body, shall not participate in the existence of the future world, but shall be cut off from life eternal;" and that the sins which demand this fearful sentence lie between man and his Maker, through an uninter-- rupted course of seeming worldly prosperity; that it does not relate to those social sins which receive the judgment of the state, but which circumstances very often, more than actual perversion of character, impel. The sin which is *punished on earth* may be redeemed by penitence in heaven; but the death of the soul is threatened against those who live entirely without God (if, indeed, there can be such), and who, though seem- ingly harmless before man, may be cast off for their iniquities in the sight of God.

By the death of the soul, however, we must not ima- gine that annihilation follows physical death, and there- fore that the threatened chastisement on the irredeem- ably wicked is of a negative, not a positive nature. The Bible gives us reason to believe, that *judgment will be pronounced* on the souls of *all men*, the righteous and the wicked, and that it will be *only* after death, and in a future state, that the distinction will be discerned be- tween them. It follows, then, undeniably, that there *is no cessation of existence* in the soul of the sinner,* any more than in that of the righteous, that both *must* appear before God, there to receive individual sentence, and that the life or death there pronounced will be

---

* The Rabbins say, that as God gives strength to the righteous to bear their felicity, so He imparts the same to the wicked to endure their punishment.—L.

positive in its *bliss,* or *suffering,* not merely negative, as a cessation of existence would be. The words, life and death, are used in addressing humanity, because in our present existence they are fraught with deepest meaning; but we know not how much fuller and more extended may be their signification when the soul is free; how ineffable may be the bliss of the one, how intense the suffering of the other. The death of this life is not an *end,* but a *change* (and for the proof of this in a *natural* point of view, dearest Annie, Mendelssohn's Phaedon will be as valuable, as in a theological sense it is incomplete). The death of the soul, therefore, we cannot suppose an *end,* but also a *change;* and that change may be, not merely a deprivation of the life of the righteous, and a descent into an inferior and darkened sphere, but from that very deprivation may spring a sense of suffering impossible to be imagined, till the bliss of which we are deprived is fully realised, as it may be ere final sentence is pronounced.

On this subject, it is better that the mind should not linger too long, only so long, indeed, as to permit us to obtain through God's holy word such ideas of futurity, as will urge us to remain constant and firm in our endeavours to tread the path of piety and right, and to .eep aloof from even the appearance of evil, however tempted by the multitude to follow, or however easy the path may seem. The knowledge that after death the distinction between the righteous and the wicked will be made evident, cannot and ought not to puff up our hearts with uncharitableness towards our fellow-creatures. Those whom our finite judgment may condemn may have some redeeming virtue before God, and we have no right, therefore, even to think of death-consigning in our brother. The extreme of punishment

after death is threatened, that we may have the incentive
to flee from that, as well as, through the hope of acceptance, to pursue the good; but the repugnance with which
our merciful Father beholds it as the portion of any one
of His children, is forcibly evident in the reiterated
injunctions of His word, "to choose the good and not
the evil; to confess our sins and repent and amend;
that iniquity should not be our ruin; that He has *no
pleasure* in the death of the sinner; that if the watchman whom He has appointed to warn the people of their
errors should fail, *he* has trespassed, and not the actual
sinner." Verses innumerable may be quoted breathing
this same loving and forbearing spirit, and teaching,
that the idea of suffering after death is not more repug-
nant to our notions of an ever-loving long-suffering God,
than to have occasion to inflict it is to Him, however
His attribute of justice may demand it. We cannot
read His word without feeling this to our heart's core.

You ask me, if I imagine that all the righteous receive the same kind and measure of reward, and all
those who do wrong, the same chastisement; that it
appears to you, there are so many gradations in good
and evil in this life; that some are so purely spiritual as
to realise pious thoughts and feelings with scarce an
effort, and others are so completely animal in their nature, as, though they do no actual wrong, to find it impossible to conceive any thing intellectual or spiritual;
that many are moral without being religious; that some
do some things that are actually wrong and yet, in the
main, are charitable and good; that some are fearfully
tried, and others pass through life without one tribula-
tion: that you think of these things till you become puz-
zled and uncomfortable. So did I once, dearest Annie;
but a consideration of the *attributes* of God brought

me peace. My opinions on this subject, of course, can
be only individual; therefore, do not adopt them as any
thing more than a supposition founded on the love, and
truth, and justice of the Lord.

I do not believe, that the reward of all souls is the
same, or that at the moment of their release from this
body they attain the supreme of felicity, except in comparison with that which they have left. I believe, that
there are gradations of angels, or purer beings; and that
we enter that rank amongst them *after death*, for which
our conduct in our sojourn here has most fitted us. That
the lowest rank of these beings is so infinitely higher and
happier than man, that even to become one of them
may be alluded to in the words "fulness of joy," and
that for each stage there are capabilities, aspirations,
active service, leading us higher and higher yet, till
the supreme of felicity is attained. There may be two
human beings, created with the same spiritual, gentle,
holy dispositions, seeking but the good. The one may
know nothing but suffering on earth, from social and
domestic position; the other's lot may be all joy. Now,
I believe, that the soul of the former will be translated
to a higher grade of spiritual beings than the latter,
though to both will be given the "fulness of joy;" that,
where life has been all mystery and sorrow, the soul
will join those spirits to whom the *ways*, as well as the
works of the Eternal are revealed, while to those who
have had no such trial, whose existence has been all joy
and peace, save the few petty trials which every life
must bring, though it attain felicity which, compared
with the purest joy on earth is too perfect for this world
to conceive, is still in a lower rank of angels, to the soul
which has been so tried in life, and must work through
the varied plans of spiritual existence, to reach that rank

to which the tried and purified spirit had sprung at
once. This idea is founded alike on the attributes of
God and on the fact, that the Scriptures give us undoubtedly to understand that heaven, or space, is peopled
with a variety of angels, archangels, ministers, spirits,
hosts of heaven; "angels that excel in strength, and do
His commandments, hearkening to the voice of His
word;" "ministers that do His pleasure;" "seraphim,"
who are entrusted by the Lord to "touch the lips and
heart of Isaiah," to speak unto the people; "Michael the
prince of the angels" who talked with Daniel; and very
many times the Eternal is mentioned as seen in a vision
by His prophets, with the host of heaven on either side of
His throne, from which issued spirits flying hither and
thither to execute His will; Cherubim, to whom Ezekiel
refers in such mysterious yet magnificent imagery, in his
first and tenth chapter,—all uniting to give us the most
sublime ideas of the inhabitants of heaven, that the
mind while in this body can conceive. To have entered
more minutely on a theme so purely spiritual, that some
of the lower natures of man cannot even conceive it,
would have been useless, while still earth as well as
spirit. The Bible just gives us sufficient information to
permit the calm acquiescence of faith, that such things
are, impossible as it is for us to comprehend them.
And that there are varied grades and offices in the host
of heaven authorises the supposition, that the soul joins
that rank after death for which it is best prepared.

For those mere animal natures, to whom all thought
of the unseen and spiritual seems entirely unattainable,
and who may yet have done their social and domestic
duties, and obeyed the laws of the state, because either
naturally inclined to follow right, or because they have
had no temptation to do wrong, I believe there are pre-

paratory worlds where the soul will learn its spiritual des-
tiny, and become gradually fitted for its angelic existence. That death will bring it, as the souls of all men, before the judgment seat of God, there to receive sentence,
which though distinct from that of the wilful and confirmed sinner, will yet cause suffering in the glance back
on wasted life (for the *power* to cultivate the spiritual
and intellectual, in preference to the mere animal, rests
with *all* men), and the preparatory state, in which the
soul must work to win its spiritual companionship,
though higher and still joy compared to life on earth, is
yet fraught with the vain regret for the rank it *might*
have gained, had it not lost its time on earth and the
yearning aspiration to obtain it.

Remember, dearest Annie, these are merely the suppositions of a being weak, finite, blinded as yourself,
founded, indeed, on an earnest and prayerful study of
God's proclaimed attributes and revealed Word.   Our
ancient fathers had also a belief in the variety and gradations of the hosts of heaven; but for the above advanced opinions I alone am responsible.   I have brought
them forward, simply in answer to those perplexing
doubts and questions which had naturally risen in your
mind; but I do not tell you to adopt them, if your faith,
or reason, in any way revolts from them.   All men picture heaven according to their own imaginings.   If these
imaginings owe their origin to the study of God's word,
they cannot go far wrong; at least as concerns their
soul's health, and their desire to win life in heaven, by
the tenor of their life on earth.   Of one truth we may
be quite sure, that the more intellectual and purely spiritual we become in this life, the higher and purer felicity we shall attain in the next.

I am quite aware that all this is contrary to the

Christian doctrine of heaven and hell, Jesus and Satan. That there may be certain portions of our theological works in which the Jewish doctors of the early ages wrote such an idea as Milton has embodied in his "Paradise Lost," with the exception of the intervention of Jesus, as some Christians assert, I cannot deny; for I am not acquainted with the deep Jewish works in question. But even if they did, their opinions can no more be adopted as articles of belief than the poem of Milton; for the New Testament gives no more foundation for the latter, than the Old for the former. In fact, *Scriptural* Judaism must deny the supremacy of Satan and existence of hell as believed in by Christians; for nowhere do we find either words or thoughts capable of such construction. Wherever the Hebrew word translated *hell* is used, it means, and ought to be written, either *pit* or *grave*, words to which we attach a very different signification. Satan is the Hebrew word for *adversary*, and means an angel, spirit, or messenger of God, employed to try men by such painful afflictions as befell Job—the spirit walking up and down the earth, and going to and fro in it by the Eternal's permission, to try the strength of man's faith and virtue. This is evident, both from Job i. and ii. and Zech. iii. 1, 2; and by comparing the twenty-fourth chapter of second of Samuel, first verse, with the twenty-first of first Chronicles, first verse, the *only* parts of the Hebrew Scriptures in which Satan is mentioned. To enter on the subject as I should like, would lead us too far at present; therefore I must leave these quoted chapters to your own consideration, only begging you to remember that, were the Satan of our Bible the Satan of Milton, he certainly neither would nor could have appeared with the sons of God before the Eternal's throne, and be permitted by Him to his mission. Wherever "evil angels" are mentioned (and I rather think it is but once, in Psalm lxxviii. 49), it simply signifies *messengers of evil* to a sinful people, *not* evil spirits opposed to God. The great necessity for youthful Hebrews to be clear on these opposing points occasions my mentioning them, not to condemn or falsify the belief of another, but merely to clearly understand our own.

Your next doubt I am not at all surprised at, dearest Annie, though I trust easily to remove it; that the vast discoveries of astronomers, the marvellous systems of stars and planets, compared with which our earth is but a particle, appear to contradict our ideas of heaven; that it seems impious in the beings of such a small and, compared with other systems, insignificant world, to expect so much at the hand of God. It might, indeed, be so, if we had not the Revelation of God's will to guide us through this life, and promise the attainment of another. All those mighty worlds, those revolving systems, which are to us but the stars and planets of the night, have been created, and may be still creating by the Lord. All are under His guidance and control, equally with our earth, and their inhabitants, of whatever nature they may be, equally responsible to Him. It has been said, they may be worlds in which our souls must move and act before supreme felicity can be attained; and if they are, they do not deny the promises of the Bible. We must be with God, wherever our future destiny be cast: we cannot hide ourselves from Him; for He filleth heaven—a word signifying every system which shines in the expanse, like stars; and from the high and pure aspirations which alone can lift us from earth, from the evidence of love, of intellect, in the creative genius of the sculptor, artist, musician, and poet, in the contemplative discoveries of the philosopher and divine, the more palpable researches of the astronomer and student of nature under all its forms, a mighty evidence, not alone in what is realised, but in what is seen in the dim distance impossible to be grasped on earth, yet still attainable,—we *know* that it is to a higher and purer state of existence we are destined; and what does it matter *where* that destiny is? It will be with God and the fulness of joy, for He has promised it; and if our souls need higher instruction in those preparatory worlds, an instruction more suited for their more perfected faculties than the instruction intended for us while on earth, another revelation will be given. Wherever and whatever we are, we are His; for those vast systems are His creation, equally with His heaven and our earth; and therefore wherever we are, we shall be with Him still, for we cannot flee from His presence, either in heaven or the grave.

There is no contradiction then in the discoveries of astronomers and the promises of our Bible. Were the destiny of the soul more clearly defined, there might be; but there is none now. God promises to the righteous joy and peace, incomprehensible in its perfection to human sense; and therefore wherever they are, we *know* that such will be given them. He has said, He will judge every man according to His ways, and therefore we *know* sentence will be pronounced on every soul for its own actions in this life, to whatever other sphere it may be destined. Some have said, How do we know that we have not existed before, and that this world is not a to previous existence, the same as other worlds will be to this? It may be; but neither the Bible, nor *internal* evidence say that so it is; and therefore we have not the smallest foundation for the belief. Whereas, that we are ascending in the scale of being, that we are destined for something higher and better, and nearer God, we are told both by His revealed word and the internal voice of our own immortal souls.

Dearest Annie, cultivate, encourage, listen to, this internal voice, that it may attain such ascendency as to render it equally impossible to disbelieve in immortality as to disbelieve in God. I believe there are very few, if any who, were the question put, would deny a belief in a future existence: they cannot; for we find that they often believe in spite of themselves. But if we desire to be better, happier, wiser, this belief ought not to be merely tacitly held as an article of creed, which concerns us little here below, but should be so ever present, so intimately entwined with our being, that it can explain at once every seeming contradiction in the ways of God, as displayed in the affairs of men. It would throw a halo over the history of the PAST; teach us to bear calmly with the difficulties and seeming injustice of the PRESENT, and look to the FUTURE with so strong a faith, that hope would seem certainty, and bereavement itself lose its deepest anguish. It would not render us careless or indifferent to the aspect of this life, as some sensualists assert. It would urge us beyond every other incentive to remove misery and vice from our fellows, that the animal might be subdued, and the intellectual and spiritual obtain their intended superiority. But it is a subject only too often lost in the pressure of the world. We do not instil it sufficiently into the minds and hearts of our children, and so in manhood, though it may be believed, it fails to become their guide. We think it a subject connected only with suffering and death, that this world is, or ought to be, enough for our enjoyment, and more than enough to occupy our thoughts. But all this is false and mistaken reasoning. This world would be a chaos of darkness and misery, and injustice and wrath, without the belief in another: while with that belief its very clouds are illuminated by the light of heaven gleaming through, and every seeming contradiction is tending to the furtherance of that divine rule of love and justice, which we *know* we shall understand above.

But this pure and comforting faith cannot be obtained without effort and perseverance. It is not a gift of God depending on His grace alone; for He has endowed ALL His creatures, from the highest to the lowest, with the capability of attaining it. Our first endeavour must be to examine into the foundation of this belief, and, once convinced its origin is divine, we should not pause till we can so realise it, as to bring it to bear on every event of life, and no more separate it from our thoughts than we can the omnipresence and omnipotence of God. And this *can* be attained; and not only will its attainment bring comfort and strength unspeakable in itself, but actually advance that in which we believe. The more we cultivate the intellect and a healthy imagination: the more shall we realise the spiritual, and deaden the mere animal of our mingled nature. The more we give the soul or spirit ascendency while on earth, and so advance it more in the knowledge of our God and His unseen worlds: the better are we prepared for the higher and purer state of being which we know awaits us, and the higher shall we rank amidst those immortal hosts of heaven which surround His throne. We dare not hope to attain spiritual felicity in heaven, if we strive not for it on earth, or realise its blessedness, unless the awakened and ripened intellect has led the spirit to contemplate its own. Dearest Annie, I could write on this most important and most solemn subject, to us Hebrews especially, more and more, in the inexpressible longing to bring its peace, its joy, its comfort, home to you, whose early trials and eager heart need it so strongly; but hand and brain both fail. I can only reiterate, Seek, strive, pray for this precious blessing, a firm and ever active relief in this immortality, which God's holy word proclaims, and his grace will grant to the full.

LETTER XXXI.—CONCLUSION.

FROM THE SAME TO THE SAME.

Conclusion—Joyful anticipations of a reunion—State of modern Jews —All cannot be judged by those of England—Necessity of a Jewish press, no intellectual advancement without it—Much depends on individuals—Wrong to judge by outward appearances—The Eternal's rebuke to Elijah ought to guide and console us in all ages— Faith necessary even here—Conclusion.

September, 1846.

Joy, dearest Annie! we shall be together once again, never to part, I trust, till a happier home shall offer for you than your old friend can give. All through our correspondence, I have been hoping and striving to accomplish this end; for though you have carefully avoided referring to petty trials, I can feel they are many and painful, and from them, at least, my love may guard you. Come to me, then, my Annie—my lonely home will indeed be brightened by the presence and affection of one, who needs not the ties of blood to be felt, indeed, all my own. Congeniality of tastes, and

pursuits, and a warm sympathy, at least, with the natural enjoyments of the young, will, I trust, provide you
a companion as well as a friend. I have settled the
whole business with the family with whom you are residing; therefore do not allow any of the petty annoy-
a ces, as to what they will think and how you can tell
them, interfere with the pleasure which, if I judge you
by myself, I know the idea of our reunion will bring. I
would not write to you till all the preliminaries were
settled, and there was nothing to damp our mutual anticipations. How much we shall have to talk over!
How many little things, that in our correspondence on
serious topics we have been compelled to overlook!
Hoping to meet so soon, when conversation will be
much more satisfactory than the most explicit writing,
I shall not reply to your last most affectionate letter,
except to thank you warmly for the feelings it so elo-
quently expressed, and to assure you that, had your
earnest and thoughtful enquiries into our holy faith cost
me far more time and labour to answer than they have,
your fond and grateful acknowledgment of all the comfort and peace my answers have imparted, would have
made me feel that a blessing had attended every hour
devoted to you. But do not let affection for me, my
Annie, urge you to give me more than my due. To the
blessing of your Father in heaven, on my lowly efforts,
and to your own sweet disposition, which prompted you
to seek and listen to the counsels of more experienced
age, you owe the comfort and joy which, you tell me, you
can realise now more fully than you have ever yet done.
Many might have felt the same doubts, the same anxiety,
the same restlessness; but there are few who would so
banish secret pride and self-sufficiency, as either to feel
or acknowledge themselves convinced. There are but

too often dispositions which would rather bring argument against argument for neither use nor pleasure, save to evince their own wisdom and seek to overthrow the calm belief of another, and substitute the shallow theories of their own unbelief in their stead, thus strengthening their own prejudices even while they deny the existence of prejudice altogether as actuating themselves.

I am grateful, indeed, that you were not one of them; for they can neither know happiness nor safety. Your mind only needed a guiding thread to realise to the full all the blessings of a firm religious hope, all the depth, and consolation, and spirituality of our holy faith, in contradistinction to the formality, imperfection, and want of spirituality with which it is so often charged.

You will mingle now more with your own people than you have done yet. You will, I trust, worship God in His house, with the congregation and in the language of His people. But though you will find many families in whom spiritual Judaism has found a resting-place, many eager and earnest to forward the cause of God by increased spirituality in themselves, and a careful nationally religious education of their children, you must not hope to find scriptural Judaism yet the prevailing feeling. It is advancing. If we compare the thoughts and sentiments on the religion of the Hebrews in almost all countries of the present day with those of fifty years back, we shall find there has been, indeed, a mighty movement; though, as merely looking on the present, we may feel the movement is so small as to be almost invisible, and we sometimes are led to despond more than to hope. We may watch too, with dread, the too violent reforms, the too indiscriminative clipping away of old established, and so somewhat treasured forms; but better, far better, this agitation, than the stagnant waters of apathy and indifference, in which fifty years ago all Judaism was plunged. That the modern Jews scattered over the world cannot be judged by the progress of those in England, France, or America, is true. In Russia, Poland, Gibraltar, the northern coasts of Africa, the Holy Land itself (alas, that so it should be!) the Jewish population are generally composed of the most ignorant, debased, and superstitious. Every where, where ignorance, servility, and superstition abound, scriptural Judaism is utterly unknown. They retain all the fearful effects of mental and moral bondage and physical persecution. But no man with any honesty of feeling will judge of the spirit of a religion by such nominal followers.

A miracle retains them *Jews*, in their observance of certain distinguishing covenants and ordinances, even in the lands where the very fact of their being Jews debases them socially and physically, and so mentally and morally; but the true observer of human nature will look on the religious and moral bearing of the nations in which the people of God are thus debased, and acknowledge that they must be more than human, for the pure spirit of their faith to act upon them in such a situation.

What is Christianity in Russia? in Spain? in some parts of Germany, and many other lands? can we trace the pure spirit which is to regenerate mankind and bring them back to God? And why, then, should we demand more from Judaism? Divine as the religion is, its followers are human, and thus liable to all the human conditions of national position and individual imperfection. It is in free and enlightened nations, where the Jews are permitted a position like any other MAN, where they have peace and leisure to give the intellectual and spiritual their ordained ascendency, that the real spirit of their religion must be sought, and will be found.

That even amongst them there are nominal Jews, indifferent to any pursuit but interest, any pleasure but worldly aggrandisement, so careless of the restrictions of their religion as either to neglect, or most unwillingly to perform them, and that there are others still, the mere spiritless formalists of the age of bondage, must not disappoint you, dearest Annie, or lead you to imagine that the religion I have placed before you, as the Judaism of the Bible, is merely the religion of an individual, and not Judaism. The great drawback to *intellectual* Judaism, to knowing *what* our religion is, and on what principles it is founded, to its appealing to the heart and mind, has been the absence of a *Jewish press.* Merely to receive religion from the lessons of parents and teachers in our childhood—to read the Sabbath portions—could never be enough; and it is because we have never had a Jewish press, that we are so far behind our Christian brethren in spiritual and intellectual religion. This deficiency, within the last few years, has begun to be felt, and so we may earnestly hope, will gradually be supplied. If we once, as individuals, can *know* what is our religion, and what is incumbent on us each to feel and do: we shall each work in our own sphere, and so gradually but surely extend the spiritual and intellectual religion, which is the spirit of our faith, and which, though given to man in his earliest infancy, is yet adapted for his highest perfection, and supplies him with a guard from sin, and hope of joy, through all the varied phases of his existence, from the infancy of humanity to the state to which he was eventually and spiritually destined, " a little lower than the angels." Whilst the press is but just commencing, its deficiency more felt than

supplied, let us not trouble ourselves so much with the
religion of our brethren as with that of our own hearts.
Let us not be content with the Judaism which is *apparent in others;* but let us study and know what Judaism really is from the word of God, and seek to become
scripturally Hebrews—not such because our fathers
were. Let us not heed the tauntings of scoffers who,
alluding to the mere nominal Jew or frigid formalist,
demand if that be the religion of God which is to last
for ever, and shed its spirit over the whole world? Let
us be prepared to make manifest the Judaism of the
Bible, and point to God's word as the teacher and con-
tainer of the religion which will indeed last for ever, and
over which neither circumstances nor time can have any
power, though its human followers must be influenced by
both. If we would but look more into our Bibles than
around us—would but have the moral courage to break
from the trammels of custom, and stand forward as the
followers and upholders of the spirit of the *Prophets,* as
well as of the Law; would we but feel and declare that
the Judaism of the Bible is the religion of God, not the
Judaism of the world: how different would be the intellectual and spiritual aspect of the religion of the Jews.
And I feel that THIS WILL BE, dearest Annie, though
neither you nor I may behold it to any extent. It is
working now; and if we can but establish in every land
a vernacular Jewish press, it will work more and more.
The grammatical study and acquirement of our own
noble language, the Hebrew, which is *now* made part of
the education of every Hebrew child, will forward this
glorious end. The light is dawning over many lands,
but a faint, faint streak indeed, but enough to promise,
for God himself has said it, that it will "brighten more
and more into the perfect day," and permit "the Sun of

Righteousness" to rise and shine on all the nations, as the light of heaven on the earth. Ages may pass, indeed, ere this will be, but man has power of progression in himself, and WILL attain it.

I did not intend to write you so much, my dearest Annie; but on this subject my pen will run on in spite of me. Perhaps the above assertion (which in my own heart is positive belief), as the most comforting to earnest Hebrews, is the best with which I could conclude our lengthened correspondence. You will not quarrel with it at all events; and, when disappointed and doubting at the absence in some of all visibly spiritual Judaism, remember, that the very feeling in yourself is evidence of the invisibly working power, that many others are probably at the same moment experiencing the same emotions. Elijah complained that he alone was left to love and serve God; and the reply of the Omnipotent will bear on all ages, and in all climes:—"Behold, there are seven thousand who have not bowed the knee to Baäl, nor kissed him," meaning, had remained faithful to their God, though so invisibly, that even the prophet knew it not. However small the number of those whom we know and can depend on to give back our own thoughts on religion, it is *no* proof that we stand alone. In the sight of God there may be seven times seven thousand spiritual and faithful Jews forwarding the honour of their faith, and working in His service, though we know it not. The answer to Elijah ought to impress this solemn truth on our minds, and remove alike despondency and doubt. We are too apt to judge only by what we *see*, when, had we but faith, the mind would take a wider and truer grasp, and teach us to *believe* that, even as *we* feel, so may others, and as we labour, so do they.

And now, dearest Annie, though I will not say farewell to *you*, I will to our correspondence; and with the earnest hope and belief that personal intercourse will but deepen the mutual interest and affection which commenced in our childhood, and has inexpressibly increased during our examination of a subject so momentous, so entwined with our very being, as our Faith,

I remain

Your affectionate and true friend,

INEZ VILLENA.

THE END.

www.ingramcontent.com/pod-product-compliance
Lightning Source LLC
Chambersburg PA
CBHW030940110726
47900CB00004B/1064